T0234793

Lecture Notes in Computer Science　　　10563

Commenced Publication in 1973
Founding and Former Series Editors:
Gerhard Goos, Juris Hartmanis, and Jan van Leeuwen

Editorial Board

David Hutchison
  Lancaster University, Lancaster, UK
Takeo Kanade
  Carnegie Mellon University, Pittsburgh, PA, USA
Josef Kittler
  University of Surrey, Guildford, UK
Jon M. Kleinberg
  Cornell University, Ithaca, NY, USA
Friedemann Mattern
  ETH Zurich, Zurich, Switzerland
John C. Mitchell
  Stanford University, Stanford, CA, USA
Moni Naor
  Weizmann Institute of Science, Rehovot, Israel
C. Pandu Rangan
  Indian Institute of Technology, Madras, India
Bernhard Steffen
  TU Dortmund University, Dortmund, Germany
Demetri Terzopoulos
  University of California, Los Angeles, CA, USA
Doug Tygar
  University of California, Berkeley, CA, USA
Gerhard Weikum
  Max Planck Institute for Informatics, Saarbrücken, Germany

More information about this series at http://www.springer.com/series/7408

Yassine Ouhammou · Mirjana Ivanovic
Alberto Abelló · Ladjel Bellatreche (Eds.)

Model and Data Engineering

7th International Conference, MEDI 2017
Barcelona, Spain, October 4–6, 2017
Proceedings

 Springer

Editors
Yassine Ouhammou (iD)
ISAE-ENSMA
Chasseneuil
France

Mirjana Ivanovic
University of Novi Sad
Novi Sad
Serbia

Alberto Abelló (iD)
UPC-Barcelona Tech
Barcelona
Spain

Ladjel Bellatreche
ISAE-ENSMA
Chasseneuil
France

ISSN 0302-9743   ISSN 1611-3349   (electronic)
Lecture Notes in Computer Science
ISBN 978-3-319-66853-6   ISBN 978-3-319-66854-3   (eBook)
DOI 10.1007/978-3-319-66854-3

Library of Congress Control Number: 2017952849

LNCS Sublibrary: SL2 – Programming and Software Engineering

© Springer International Publishing AG 2017
This work is subject to copyright. All rights are reserved by the Publisher, whether the whole or part of the material is concerned, specifically the rights of translation, reprinting, reuse of illustrations, recitation, broadcasting, reproduction on microfilms or in any other physical way, and transmission or information storage and retrieval, electronic adaptation, computer software, or by similar or dissimilar methodology now known or hereafter developed.
The use of general descriptive names, registered names, trademarks, service marks, etc. in this publication does not imply, even in the absence of a specific statement, that such names are exempt from the relevant protective laws and regulations and therefore free for general use.
The publisher, the authors and the editors are safe to assume that the advice and information in this book are believed to be true and accurate at the date of publication. Neither the publisher nor the authors or the editors give a warranty, express or implied, with respect to the material contained herein or for any errors or omissions that may have been made. The publisher remains neutral with regard to jurisdictional claims in published maps and institutional affiliations.

Printed on acid-free paper

This Springer imprint is published by Springer Nature
The registered company is Springer International Publishing AG
The registered company address is: Gewerbestrasse 11, 6330 Cham, Switzerland

Preface

The 7th International Conference on Model and Data Engineering (MEDI 2017) took place in Barcelona during October 4–6, 2017. MEDI conferences present the latest research on models and data theory, development of advanced technologies related to models and data, as well as their advanced applications. MEDI 2017 followed the success of the six previous events. It focused on model engineering and data engineering.

These proceedings contain the technical papers selected for presentation at the conference. MEDI 2017 received 69 submissions from over 30 countries. Each paper was reviewed by at least three reviewers and the Program Committee accepted 20 long papers and 7 short papers. This selection led to an excellent scientific program since the scope of the papers covered all recent and relevant topics in the areas of advanced information systems, mining complex databases, ontology-based applications, model-driven engineering, formal modeling, and systems assessment.

In addition to the technical papers selected for presentation at the conference, these proceedings also contain the papers of two invited keynote speakers. Bernhard Rumpe from RWTH Aachen University, Germany gave a talk entitled "Advances in Model Language Engineering" centered towards model-driven engineering. The second talk, entitled "Schema Evolution and Gravitation to Rigidity: A Tale of Calmness in the Lives of Structured Data", was given by Panos Vassiliadis from the University of Ioannina, Greece. We would like to thank the keynote speakers for their contribution to the success of MEDI 2017.

MEDI 2017 would not have succeeded without the support and cooperation of the Program Committee members and also the external reviewers, who carefully reviewed and selected (210 reviews) the best contributions. We would like to thank all the authors who submitted the papers, the reviewers, the Program Committee members, and the Organization Committee members for their investment and involvement in the success of MEDI 2017.

The EasyChair system was used for the management of MEDI 2017 and it provided a very helpful framework for the submission, review, and volume preparation processes.

October 2017

Yassine Ouhammou
Mirjana Ivanovic
Alberto Abelló
Ladjel Bellatreche

Organization

General Co-chairs

Alberto Abelló   Universitat Politecnica de Catalunya, Spain
Ladjel Bellatreche   ISAE-ENSMA, France

Program Committee Co-chairs

Mirjana Ivanovic   University of Novi Sad, Serbia
Yassine Ouhammou   ISAE-ENSMA, France

Organizing Committee Members

Besim Bilalli   Universitat Politecnica de Catalunya, Spain
Petar Jovanovic   Universitat Politecnica de Catalunya, Spain
Sergi Nadal   Universitat Politecnica de Catalunya, Spain
Oscar Romero   Universitat Politecnica de Catalunya, Spain
Jovan Varga   Universitat Politecnica de Catalunya, Spain

Program Committee Members

El Hassan Abdelwahed   University of Cadi Ayyad, Morocco
Alberto Abello   Universitat Politecnica de Catalunya, Spain
Yamine Ait Ameur   IRIT/INPT-ENSEEIHT, France
Idir Ait Sadoune   LRI - CentraleSupélec, France
Shaukat Ali   Simula Research Laboratory, Norway
J.M. Almendros-Jimenez   Universidad de Almeria, Spain
Sabeur Aridhi   University of Lorraine, LORIA, France
Costin Badica   University of Craiova, Romania
Kamel Barkaoui   Cedric - CNAM, France
Ladjel Bellatreche   LIAS/ENSMA, France
Orlando Belo   University of Minho, Portugal
Sidi Mohamed Benslimane   University of Sidi Bel Abbes, Algeria
Jorge Bernardino   ISEC - Polytechnic Institute of Coimbra, Portugal
Alexander Borusan   TU Berlin, Germany
Omar Boussaid   ERIC Laboratory, France
Drazen Brdjanin   University of Banja Luka, Bosnia and Herzegovina
Francesco Buccafurri   University of Calabria, Italy
Javier Troya Castilla   Universidad de Sevilla, Spain
Damianos Chatziantoniou   Athens University, Greece
Federico Ciccozzi   Mälardalen University, Sweden
Antonio Corral   University of Almeria, Spain

Alain Crolotte	Teradata Corporation
Florian Daniel	Politecnico di Milano, Italy
Alex Delis	University of Athens, Greece
Georgios Evangelidis	University of Macedonia, Greece
Anastasios Gounaris	University of Thessaloniki, Greece
Emmanuel Grolleau	LIAS/ENSMA, France
Brahim Hamid	IRIT- University of Toulouse, France
Slimane Hammoudi	ESEO, France
Patrick Hung	University of Ontario, Canada
Luis Iribarne	University of Almería, Spain
Mirjana Ivanovic	University of Novi Sad, Serbia
Petar Jovanovic	Universitat Politècnica de Catalunya, Spain
Nadjet Kamel	University Ferhat Abbes, Algeria
Zoubida Kedad	University of Versailles, France
Selma Khouri	ESI, Algeria
Adamantios Koumpis	University of Passau, Germany
Regine Laleau	Creteil University, France
Yves Ledru	LIG/University of Grenoble, France
Carson Leung	University of Manitoba, Canada
Zhiming Liu	Southwest University, China
Ivan Luković	University of Novi Sad, Serbia
Sofian Maabout	LaBRI/University of Bordeaux, France
Yannis Manolopoulos	Aristotle University of Thessaloniki, Greece
Dominique Mery	LORIA/University of Lorraine, France
Tadeusz Morzy	Poznan University of Technology, Poland
Chokri Mraidha	CEA LIST, France
Yassine Ouhammou	LIAS/ENSMA, France
Jose I. Panach Navarrete	Universitat de València, Spain
Apostolos N. Papadopoulos	Aristotle University of Thessaloniki, Greece
Oscar Pastor Lopez	Universitat Politecnica de Valencia, Spain
Jaroslav Pokorný	Charles University, Czech Republic
Giuseppe Polese	University of Salerno, Italy
Elvinia Riccobene	University of Milan, Italy
Oscar Romero	Universitat Politècnica de Catalunya, Spain
Dimitris Sacharidis	TU Wien, Austria
Milos Savic	University of Novi Sad, Serbia
Klaus-Dieter Schewe	Software Competence Center Hagenberg, Austria
Timos Sellis	Swinburne University of Technology, Australia
Neeraj Singh	IRIT/INPT-ENSEEIHT, France
Spyros Sioutas	Ionian University, Greece
Riccardo Torlone	Roma Tre University, Italy
Ismail Toroslu	Middle East Technical University, Turkey
Farouk Toumani	Limos/Blaise Pascal University, France
Goce Trajcevski	Northwestern University, USA
Javier Tuya	University of Oviedo, Spain
Theodoros Tzouramanis	University of the Aegean, Greece

Michael Vassilakopoulos   University of Thessaly, Greece
Panos Vassiliadis   University of Ioannina, Greece
Edgar Weippl   SBA Research, Austria
Robert Wrembel   Poznan University of Technology, Poland

Additional Reviewers

Berkani, Nabila   Kougka, Georgia
Boden, Christoph   Mallios, Nikolaos
Caruccio, Loredana   Mammar, Amel
Cicchetti, Antonio   Mezni, Haithem
Criado, Javier   Moussaoui, Mohamed
Dudoladov, Sergey   Nadal, Sergi
Gajić, Dušan   Naskos, Athanasios
Gnaho, Christophe   Pazdor, Adam
Inoubli, Wissem   Tanbeer, Syed
Ivančević, Vladimir   Tzouramanis, Theodoros
Jiang, Fan   Vicente-Chicote, Cristina
Kefalas, Pavlos   Zhang, Man

Contents

Modeling Heterogeneity and Behavior

Model-Based Applications

Ontology-Based Applications

Keynotes

Advances in Modeling Language Engineering

Katrin Hölldobler, Alexander Roth, Bernhard Rumpe,
and Andreas Wortmann[✉]

Software Engineering, RWTH Aachen University, Aachen, Germany
http://www.se-rwth.de

Abstract. The increasing complexity of modern systems development demands for specific modeling languages capturing the various aspects to be tackled. However, engineering of comfortable modeling languages as well as their tooling is a challenging endeavor. Far too often, new languages are built from scratch. We shed light into the advances of modeling language engineering that facilitates reuse, modularity, compositionality and derivation of new languages based on language components. We discuss ways to design, combine, and derive modeling languages in all their relevant aspects. For each of these activities, we illustrate their application for the model-driven development of a data exploration tool. The tool itself uses a set of meta-information, namely the structural model to derive all necessary software components that help to gather, store, visualize and navigate the data.

> *The limits of my language*
> *mean the limits of my world*
>
> – Ludwig Wittgenstein

1 Motivation

The use of models to understand and shape the world is a very foundational technique that has already been used in ancient Greece and Egypt. Scientists model to understand the world and engineers model to design (parts of) the world. Although modeling has been employed for ages in virtually all disciplines it is fairly new that the form of models is made explicit in so-called modeling languages. Computer science has invented this approach to provide formality and a precise understanding of what is a well-formed model to the communication between humans and machines.

Programming languages in general, SQL [7], XML [2], and the Unified Modeling Language (UML) [22, 42, 43] in particular have been created to enable highly precise communication. Despite these efforts, it is clear that researchers and practitioners of many domains are dissatisfied by solving domain-specific problems with general purpose languages or unified languages that try to cover everything. The general aspiration of such languages create a conceptual gap between

© Springer International Publishing AG 2017
Y. Ouhammou et al. (Eds.): MEDI 2017, LNCS 10563, pp. 3–17, 2017.
DOI: 10.1007/978-3-319-66854-3_1

the problem domains and the solution domains that raises unintended complexities [18]. As a result, Domain-Specific Languages (DSLs) and Domain-Specific Modeling Languages (DSMLs) [48] were created to match domain specific needs. Due to the ongoing digitization of virtually every domain in our life, work, and society, the need for more specific languages raises. It is apparent, that we need to be able to accommodate new and changing domains with appropriate domain-specific languages – ideally on-the-fly. This raises three questions:

1. How to design new DSLs that fit specific purposes?
2. How to engineer a DSL from predefined components?
3. How to derive DSLs from other DSLs?

In this paper, we give an overview of the current state of the art on the design of DSLs, discuss the mechanisms enabling their composition, and describe how to derive new DSLs from predefined ones, such that we prevent restarting design of the language from scratch each time, but instead successfully engineer language from reusable components. These mechanisms to derive and compose languages are the core of what we today calls *software language engineering* (SLE) [32]: the discipline of engineering software languages, which are not only applied to computer science, but to any form of domain that deals with data, their representation in form of data structures, smart systems that need control, as well as with smart services that assist us in our daily life.

The rest of this paper is organized as follows: First, Sect. 2 presents current language definition techniques and sketches language creation by example. Afterwards, Sect. 3 introduces language composition techniques and illustrates their application, before Sect. 4 highlights language derivation techniques. Section 5 presents the case study of modeling a data explorer application leveraging software language engineering techniques. Ultimately, Sect. 6 concludes this paper.

2   Language Engineering

Model-driven engineering [18] lifts abstract models to primary development artifacts to facilitate software analysis, communication, documentation, and transformation. Automated analysis and transformation of models require that these adhere to contracts that analyses and transformations can rely upon (and be developed against). Such automation is feasible, where models conform to modeling languages. For many popular modeling languages, such as UML [22], AADL [16], or Matlab/Simulink [1], research and industry have produced useful analyses and transformations. These rely on making the constituents and concerns of languages machine processable. To this effect, the discipline of SLE investigates disciplined and systematic approaches to the design, implementation, testing, deployment, use, evolution, and recovery of modeling languages.

Similar to research in natural languages, SLE commonly defines languages as the set of sentences they can produce [3]. Operationalizing languages, however, requires more precise characterizations. To this effect, languages usually are defined in terms of their syntax (possible sentences) and semantics (meaning) [26], which can be concretized to requiring a concrete syntax (words), an abstract syntax (structure), static semantics (well-formedness), and dynamic semantics (behavior) for language definition [3]. The technical realizations of modeling languages often follow the latter distinction. As "software languages are software too" [15], their technical realizations are as diverse as other representatives of other software categories. This complicates comprehensibility, maintenance, evolution, testing, deployment, and reuse.

To shed light onto this diversity, this section presents different mechanisms to define modeling languages and highlights selected language development environments employing these mechanisms. Afterwards, we illustrate development of a language to represent a variant of UML class diagrams that will serve as running example for the subsequent sections.

2.1 Engineering Modeling Languages

Research has produced various means to develop solutions for representing the different concerns of modeling languages. Lately, two different language implementation techniques have been distinguished:

1. Internal modeling languages are realized as fluent APIs [17] in host programming languages whose method names resemble keywords of the language. Omitting syntactic sugar (such as dots and parentheses) as supported by modern programming languages (*cf.* Groovy, Scala) enables to create chains of method calls that resemble models. This method is suitable to language prototyping and yields the benefit of enabling to reuse the host language's tooling (such as parsers, editors, compilers, *etc.*). The expressiveness of the modeling language depends on the host programming language.
2. External modeling languages feature a stand-alone syntax that requires tooling to process its models into machine-processable representations. While this creates additional effort over internal languages, external languages can leverage a greater language definition flexibility. However, language-related tooling must be provided by the language engineer.

The majority of modeling language research focuses on external languages, which yield greater flexibility in language design. Consequently, research has produced more solutions to the definition of external languages, which is why we focus on their realization techniques in the following.

Engineering language syntaxes historically is related to the development and processing of (context-free) grammars [33], which are sets of derivation rules that at least enable describing the languages' abstract syntaxes. Many approaches to grammar-driven language engineering also support specifying a language's concrete syntax in the same grammar as well [21]; hence, enabling efficient language development and maintenance. Metamodels are another popular means to develop the abstract syntax of languages [48]. Here, classes and their relations structure the syntax of a language. While these do not support the integration of concrete syntax (and, hence, always require providing editors), they enable reifying references between model elements that are name-based in grammars, as first level references.

Concrete syntaxes are either textual [34,49], graphical [10], or projectional [48]. Textual and graphical languages both require parsing, whereas projectional syntaxes (*e.g.,* forms enabling editing the abstract syntax directly [47]) usually are bound to specific editors. In contrast, textual syntaxes enable to reuse established software engineering tooling, such as editors or version control systems.

Whether the well-formedness of models is subject of their syntax or their static semantics is subject to debate. Nonetheless, various techniques have been established to enforce the well-formedness of models with respect to properties that cannot be captured by grammars or metamodels (*e.g.,* preventing to class members of the same name). Popular approaches to well-formedness checking are programming language rules and Object Constraint Language (OCL) [40] constraints. Both require a model's internal representation and raise errors if these are not well-formed according to the individual rule. As OCL is a modeling language itself, this requires interpreting it or translating the constraints to programming language artifacts actually executing the models under development.

Executing models is a popular way to realize their dynamic semantics. This can have the form of interpretation [30] or transformation [6]. With the former, a software (the interpreter) processes the models and executes according to their description. This interpreter can be part of the models or a separate software. Transformations process models and translates these into other formalisms with established semantics, such as a programming language. Model-to-text (M2T) transformations [36] read models of a specific language and translate these to plain text (such as programming language code), whereas model-to-model (M2M) transformations [36] translate models from an input modeling language to an output modeling language. The former lends itself for ad-hoc transformation development using template engines or string concatenation (as the output language is not required), but lacks the structure and verifiability of M2M transformations.

Language workbenches [13] are software development environments supporting language engineering. Based on an, usually fixed, integration of language definition constituents, they facilitate creating languages and corresponding tooling. For instance, GEMOC Studio [5] employs ECore [44] metamodels for abstract syntax, OCL for static semantics, and Kermeta [30] for weaving interpretation capabilities into its languages. Concrete syntax can, *e.g.,* have the form of Xtext [14] grammars or Sirius [46] editors. The meta programming system (MPS) features projectional language engineering on top of a metamodel and combines this with well-formedness checking and execution through M2M transformations. The Neverlang language workbench [45] supports grammar-based language definition and focuses on combining these with language processing tools. It executes models via interpretation.

The next section illustrates engineering of a textual modeling language for class diagrams (CDs) with the MontiCore language workbench.

2.2 Language Engineering with MontiCore

MontiCore [34] is a language workbench for efficient development of compositional modeling languages. The concrete and abstract syntax of languages are defined as extended context-free grammars and it supports a Java-based well-formedness checking framework as well as model execution through M2M and M2T transformations. From the grammars, MontiCore generates parsers and abstract syntax classes. The parser enables processing textual, conforming models, into instances of the languages' abstract syntax classes. Java context conditions process these instances to check their well-formedness before M2M transformations [27] or template-based code generators [41]. MontiCore supports language inheritance, language embedding, and language aggregation [25] to reuse and combine languages with little effort.

Consider the excerpt of the MontiCore grammar depicted in Fig. 1, which describes the class diagram for analysis (CD4A) modeling language: After the keyword **grammar** and its name, the grammar extends existing types to reuse previously defined grammars (l. 1). Afterwards, a body of productions follows that characterize a variant of class diagrams. Each production is defined by a left-hand-side (*e.g.*, CDDefinition in l. 2) and a right-hand-side, which contains terminals (*e.g.*, "classdiagram" in l. 2) and non-terminals (*e.g.*, CDInterface in l. 3). Different operators (*e.g.*, * in l. 3, ? in l. 13, and + in l. 15) define the quantity or presence of a part on the right-hand-side. MontiCore also supports additional grammar constructs to extend the generated AST (*e.g.*, astimplements in l. 13).

```
01  grammar CD4Analysis extends Type {
02      CDDefinition = „classdiagram" Name "{"            MCG
03          (cDClasses:CDClass | CDInterface | CDEnum | CDAssociation)*
04      "}"
..
13      CDClass astimplements ASTCDType = Modifier? "class" Name
14          ( "extends"  superclass:ReferenceType )?
15          ( "implements" interfaces:(ReferenceType || ",") +)?
16          ( "{" (CDAttribute)* "}" | ";" );
17  }
```

Fig. 1. An excerpt of a MontiCore grammar for the CD4A language.

With this grammar, the CD4A model shown as an excerpt in Fig. 2 can be created. It describes a simplified banking system consisting of a package declaration (l. 1); an abstract **Account** class to describe different types of accounts (ll. 3–7); an interface to model employees (l. 17) and its implementation (ll. 18–20); and multiple associations (*e.g.*, l. 55). From this grammar, MontiCore produces a parser and an abstract syntax class for each production. The latter captures the production's right hand side by providing members capable of storing its content.

```
01 package banking;                                          CD4A
02 classdiagram BankingSystem {
03    abstract class Account {
04       long number;
05       int balance;
06       int overdraft;
07    }
...
17    interface Employee;
18    class Consultant implements Employee {
19       String name;
20    }
...
55    association [1] Account <-> [[name]] Consultant;
56 }
```

Fig. 2. An example of a CD4A model describing a lightweight banking system.

In addition, an infrastructure to check context conditions, which are predicates defined with respect to the abstract syntax to determine the language's consistency. For example, to restrict the modifiers of classes to abstract only (l. 13 in Fig. 1).

3   Composing Modeling Languages

Model-driven development is successful when initiated bottom-up [50], *i.e.,* developers employ modeling languages considered suitable for their challenges instead of using predefined, monolithic general-purpose modeling techniques. For their efficient development, evolution, validation, and maintenance, such languages should be retained as independent as possible. Ultimately, however, combining such languages mandates their efficient *composition* [3]. Considering, for instance, software of the smart and modular factories imagined with Industry 4.0, these demand integrating business processes, domain models, behavior models and failure models of the automation systems, assembly plan models, manipulator kinematics, *etc.* Integrating these modeling languages into a combined software requires operations for their composition.

Software engineering itself is another prime example of a domain leveraging language composition to facilitate development, evolution, and maintenance. To this effect, research and industry have produced languages for 1. modeling structure and behavior of the software under development, such as UML [22]; 2. describing database interaction, such as SQL [7] or HQL [29]; 3. describing software build processes, such as Maven's Project Object Models [37]; 4. describing configuration of product lines [4], such as feature diagrams [6]; 5. describing model changes in a structured fashion, such as delta modeling languages [24] 6. extending models with additional, external information (tagging languages [20]); 7. coordinating the use of different modeling languages, such as the BCOol language [35]; 8. transforming of models of other languages, such as ATL [31] or the FreeMarker [39] template language; and 9. describing the syntax and semantics of modeling languages, such as ECore [44], Kermeta [30], or MontiCore [34].

Consequently, structured reuse of language parts is crucial to enable efficient SLE. And while research on language integration has produced reuse concepts and related these to language definition concerns [3], the diversity of language realization techniques has spawned very different reuse mechanisms [11]. Generally, we distinguish *language integration*, which produces a new language, from existing languages, from *language coordination*, in which the sentences of two languages (*i.e.,* their models) are related to enable achieving a common goal.

For integrating languages, concepts such as merging of metamodels [9], inheriting and embedding of grammars [25], and importing of metamodel and grammar elements [12] have been conceived. These mechanisms enable a white-box integration to extend and refine existing abstract syntaxes to domain requirements, but rarely consider including integration of other language concerns. For instance, efficient creation of models of language produced through of merging, inheritance, or importing of parts of other languages requires creating or extending proper editors. Even when editors for the base languages exist, this requires handcrafting editing capabilities for the extensions. The same challenges arise for reusing language semantics. As these usually are realized through interpretation or transformation, the corresponding tools of extended languages must be extended also. Yet, there are only few approaches that support compositional semantics realizations, such as code generator composition mechanisms [41].

Coordination of modeling languages is less invasive but mandates means to reason over models of coordinated languages – either for their joint analysis or their joint execution. The former, for instance requires checking the validity of feature models or model transformations with respect to the referenced models. To prevent tying the referencing languages to abstract syntax internals of the referenced languages, abstraction mechanisms, such as the symbol tables of MontiCore [25] have been developed. Joint execution of model of different languages requires exposing and combining their execution mechanisms. Where languages originate from the same language workbench, this integration has been addressed (*e.g.,* by exposing the executable interfaces of model elements [8]). Truly heterogeneous, generalizable coordination has yet to be achieved.

In the next section, we sketch how applying language integration mechanisms to the CD language enables preparing it for code generation.

3.1   Extending and Refining a MontiCore Language

To enable describing software-related properties of domain models more precisely, we extend the CD4A language with additional language constructs such as constructors, methods, and visibility. To reuse the CD4A language, we refine it by removing modeling of method bodies from the modeling language. For the former, we employ MontiCore's language inheritance, for the latter, we introduce new well-formedness rules. An excerpt of the newly created CD4Code language is shown in Fig. 3. It extends the CD4A language (l. 1) and reuses the start production (l. 2). In addition, the CDClass production is extended with a CDClassBody production, which adds methods and constructors (l. 35).

```
01  grammar CD4Code extends CD4Analysis {
02    start CDDefinition;                              MCG
03
04    CDClass astimplements ASTCDType = Modifier? "class" Name
05      ( "extends"  superclass:ReferenceType )?
06      ( "implements" interfaces:(ReferenceType || ",") +)?
07      ( CDClassBody | ";" );
...
35    CDClassBody = "{" (CDAttribute | CDMethod | CDConstructor)* "}";
36    CDConstructor = ...;
37    CDMethod = ...;
38  }
```

Fig. 3. An excerpt of the CD4Code extension of CD4A.

4 Deriving Languages

Software engineering leverages modeling languages to mechanize working with models of other languages, such as transformation languages [28,31], delta modeling languages [24], or tagging languages [20]. Such languages have in common that these are either overly generic or are specifically tied to a *host language* (*i.e.*, the languages whose models are transformed or tagged). The former requires developers to learn completely new languages that are independent of a (possibly well-known) host language, while the latter raises the challenge of engineering and maintaining specific languages as well as their specific tooling (editors, analyses, transformations), which is hardly viable.

To address the latter, methods to develop new languages by deriving their syntaxes from related host languages have been developed. These methods rely on processing the host languages' (abstract) syntaxes and creating new (abstract) syntaxes from these. Where the host languages are defined through grammars, such derivation can produce derived concrete syntaxes. For metamodel-based language definition, this would require deriving editor (parts) instead. Automating creating well-formedness rules and behavior implementations of derived languages is more challenging as both may differ from the host languages completely. Where, for example, Statecharts describe state-based behavior, a transformation language derived from Statecharts describes how to translate Statechart models into something else. The behaviors of both languages are unrelated. The same holds for their well-formedness rules.

The next section applies language derivation to the CD4A language to create a domain-specific transformation language from it.

4.1 Deriving a Domain-Specific Transformation Language

In [28] derivation rules to derive a domain-specific transformation language (DSTL) form a given modeling language were presented. A DSTL is composed of a common base grammar that provides modeling language independent parts of the DSTL as well as a derived grammar for the modeling language dependent parts. The derived grammar is created according to the derivation rules presented. The derivation rules create the non-terminals for the different operators of the DSTL and the start symbol. The start symbol combines the non-terminals provided by the base and the derived grammar to form a transformation rule. This derivation process was applied to create the DSTL CDTrans that is suitable to describe transformations for class diagrams modeled using the modeling languages described in Sect. 2.2. Figure 4 demonstrates the derivation rules for the non-terminal **Attribute** of the CD4A grammar. The non-terminal of CD4A is depicted at the top, the derived non-terminals at the bottom.

```
01  Attribute =
02    Modifier? Type Name ("=" Value)?";";           MCG
03

01
02  interface Attribute;                  // rule 1    MCG
03
04  Attribute_Rep implements Attribute =  // rule 2
05    "[[" lhs:CDAttribute? ":-" rhs:CDAttribute? "]]";
06
07  Attribute_Neg implements Attribute =  // rule 3
08    "not" "[[" Attribute "]]";
09
10  Attribute_Pat implements Attribute =  // rule 4
11  /* transfered syntax of the attribute plus schema variables */ ;
12
13  TFRule =                              // rule 5
14    (Class | Attribute | CD | /*interface nonterminals*/ )*  Where?;
```

Fig. 4. Application of the derivation rules described in [28].

In [28] there are basically five derivation rules described. The first of which derives interface non-terminals for the non-terminals and keywords of the modeling language (**Attribute**, l. 2). The second rule derives non-terminals for the replacement of each model element (cf. **Attribute_Rep**, l. 4), while the third rule derives non-terminals to forbid model elements[1] (**Attribute_Neg**, l. 7). The forth rule derives the non-terminals to transfer the concrete syntax of the model elements to the DSTL (**Attribute_Pat**, l. 10) and allows to use schema variables (consisting of a name that starts with a $-sign), e.g., for names of modeling elements such as the attribute name. Finally, the start symbol that combines the interface non-terminals to an alternative and adds the option to specify an application constraint is created in the fifth derivation rule (**TFRule**, l. 13). For further explanation please refer to [28].

A transformation rule modeled using CDTrans is shown in Fig. 5. This transformation matches an arbitrary class (indicated by the schema variable $_) that has a public attribute (l. 2). The public visibility of the attribute is changed to private (l. 2) and public access methods are added (ll. 4–5). Please not that transformation rules modeled via CDTrans use an integrated notation of the left-hand side (LHS) and right-hand side (RHS) of a transformation rule. Thus, modification within the pattern are expressed directly at the pattern element affected by the modification (cf. Fig. 5, ll. 2, 4–5). The left part of the replacement operator ([[:-]]) (i.e., left of the :- is part of the pattern), while the

---

[1] This corresponds to negative application conditions [23].

```
01 | class $_ {
02 |    [[public  :- private]] $type $attrname;
03 |
04 |    [[ :-  public $type $get(); ]]
05 |    [[ :-  public void $type $attrname); ]]
06 | }
07 |
08 | where {
09 |    $get = "is"  +  capitalize($attrname);
10 |    $set = "set" +  capitalize($attrname);
11 | }
```
MTR

Fig. 5. A model transformation rule to encapsulates attributes by changing its visibility to private and adding public access methods.

part right of it replaces the left part or is added if the left part is left blank. Finally the where clause is used to calculate the values of the variables $get and $set used for the names of the added access methods. capitalize(...) is a built in function to capitalize a string value, *e.g.,* names.

5   Engineering a Data Explorer

To demonstrate the applicability of the presented concepts and methods, we present a use case for model-driven development of data-centric applications from structural models, *i.e.,* CD4A models (cf. Sect. 2.2). This demonstrates (a) the use of CD4A for generating executable data-centric applications, and (b) the use of domain-specific transformations for code generation. In general, a data-centric applications manages structured and consistent information by providing SCRUD (search, create, read, update, and delete) functionality [38] through a graphical user interface. The strength of data-centric applications is that the generated source code is aware of the managed data. For example, from the CD4A model in Fig. 2, the data-centric application shown in Fig. 6 is generated.

As only one kind of input models is used as input, adaptation and customization concerns are addressed by the code generator and in the generated code. An overview of different adaptation approaches for generated code is given in [19]. Where adapting the generated code is not feasible, code generator customization can be achieved by integrating transformation- and template-based code generation using the CD4Code language (cf. Sect. 3.1) as an intermediate representation of the object-oriented structure of the target code.

An overview of the code generation approach is shown in Fig. 7. After parsing the CD4A model, the resulting AST is transformed into a CD4Code AST, which is gradually transformed (cf. Sect. 4.1) until the CD4Code AST describes the object-oriented structure of a data-centric application. Since CD4Code does not contain target language specific source code, templates are attached to CD4A method and constructors to realize their bodies. In addition, default templates are added to describe the mapping of CD4Code language concepts to Java source code. Finally, the transformed CD4Code AST and the templates are passed to a template engine to generated Java source code.

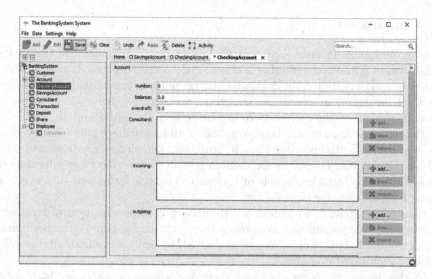

Fig. 6. Part of the data explorer generated from the CD4A model in Fig. 2.

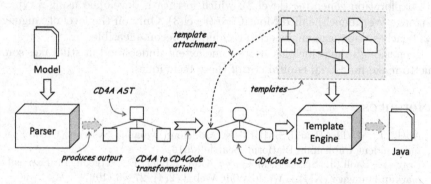

Fig. 7. An overview of the code generation activities that uses domain-specific transformations on the CD4Code AST and additional templates.

Adaptability and customizability of the code generation approach is achieved by employing transformations on the CD4Code AST and attaching templates to individual CD4Code AST nodes in the intermediate representation. This code generation approach shows the effective use of transformations to reduce complexity of template-based code generation by outsourcing computations on the AST to pattern matching, which is used in transformation-based approaches. It, furthermore, shows that transformations in code generation may enable reuse if the same intermediate representation is used.

6   Conclusion

Ludwig Wittgenstein once said that the limits of his language are the limits of his world. While programming languages are pretty expressive in describing structure and operations and data, and general-purpose modeling languages like the UML are good in specifying structure, architecture, behavior of software systems, these languages suffer from not being very domain oriented.

Today many domains are being digitalized and a lot more non-software people have to deal with encoding their information, knowledge, methods and procedures. Thus good languages for domain people to describe their information are needed. This includes models of various unforeseen forms and thus needs a strong field of language engineering.

Language engineering includes a systematic way of development of language components, integrating and composing them into larger languages, modifying and extending language components as desired, to easily accommodate the evolution of digitalized domains.

In this paper, we have discussed these techniques on three levels: a data exploration tool for a concrete data structure (level 1) is generated using a data exploration generator (level 2), which in turn is developed using a typical Language Workbench, called MontiCore (level 3). Only on the level of language workbenches, language engineering techniques become feasible.

Even though the principles are to some extent understood, it still takes some time to make industrial capital out of these techniques.

References

1. Abell, J.: MATLAB and SIMULINK. Modeling Dynamic Systems. CreateSpace Independent Publishing Platform, Seattle (2016)
2. Bray, T., Paoli, J., Sperberg-McQueen, C.M., Maler, E., Yergeau, F.: Extensible markup language (XML). World Wide Web J. 2(4), 27–66 (1997)
3. Clark, T., den Brand, M., Combemale, B., Rumpe, B.: Conceptual model of the globalization for domain-specific languages. In: Cheng, B.H.C., Combemale, B., France, R.B., Jézéquel, J.-M., Rumpe, B. (eds.) Globalizing Domain-Specific Languages. LNCS, vol. 9400, pp. 7–20. Springer, Cham (2015). doi:10.1007/978-3-319-26172-0_2
4. Clements, P., Northrop, L.: Software Product Lines. Addison-Wesley, Boston (2002)
5. Combemale, B., Deantoni, J., Barais, O., Blouin, A., Bousse, E., Brun, C., Degueule, T., Vojtisek, D.: A solution to the TTC'15 model execution case using the GEMOC studio. In: 8th Transformation Tool Contest. CEUR (2015)
6. Czarnecki, K.: Generative programming-principles and techniques of software engineering based on automated configuration and fragment-based component models. Ph.D. thesis, Technical University of Ilmenau (1998)
7. Date, C.J., Darwen, H.: A Guide to the SQL Standard, vol. 3. Addison-Wesley, New York (1987)
8. Deantoni, J.: Modeling the behavioral semantics of heterogeneous languages and their coordination. In: Architecture-Centric Virtual Integration (ACVI), pp. 12–18. IEEE (2016)

9. Degueule, T., Combemale, B., Blouin, A., Barais, O., Jézéquel, J.M.: Melange: a meta-language for modular and reusable development of DSLs. In: Proceedings of the 2015 ACM SIGPLAN International Conference on Software Language Engineering, pp. 25–36. ACM (2015)
10. Ellner, S., Taha, W.: The semantics of graphical languages. In: Proceedings of the 2007 ACM SIGPLAN Symposium on Partial Evaluation and Semantics-Based Program Manipulation, PEPM 2007, pp. 122–133. ACM, New York (2007)
11. Erdweg, S., Giarrusso, P.G., Rendel, T.: Language composition untangled. In: Proceedings of the Twelfth Workshop on Language Descriptions, Tools, and Applications, LDTA 2012. ACM, New York (2012)
12. Erdweg, S., Kats, L.C.L., Rendel, T., Kästner, C., Ostermann, K., Visser, E.: Library-based model-driven software development with SugarJ. In: Proceedings of the ACM International Conference Companion on Object Oriented Programming Systems Languages and Applications Companion, pp. 17–18. ACM (2011)
13. Erdweg, S., et al.: The state of the art in language workbenches. In: Erwig, M., Paige, R.F., Wyk, E. (eds.) SLE 2013. LNCS, vol. 8225, pp. 197–217. Springer, Cham (2013). doi:10.1007/978-3-319-02654-1_11
14. Eysholdt, M., Behrens, H.: Xtext: implement your language faster than the quick and dirty way. In: Proceedings of the ACM International Conference Companion on Object Oriented Programming Systems Languages and Applications Companion, SPLASH 2010, pp. 307–309. ACM, New York (2010)
15. Favre, J.-M., Gasevic, D., Lämmel, R., Pek, E.: Empirical language analysis in software linguistics. In: Malloy, B., Staab, S., Brand, M. (eds.) SLE 2010. LNCS, vol. 6563, pp. 316–326. Springer, Heidelberg (2010). doi:10.1007/978-3-642-19440-5_21
16. Feiler, P.H., Gluch, D.P.: Model-Based Engineering with AADL: An Introduction to the SAE Architecture Analysis and Design Language. Addison-Wesley, Boston (2012)
17. Fowler, M.: Domain-Specific Languages. Addison-Wesley Professional, Boston (2010)
18. France, R., Rumpe, B.: Model-driven development of complex software: a research roadmap. In: Future of Software Engineering (FOSE 2007), no. 2, pp. 37–54 (2007)
19. Greifenberg, T., et al.: Integration of handwritten and generated object-oriented code. In: Desfray, P., Filipe, J., Hammoudi, S., Pires, L.F. (eds.) MODEL-SWARD 2015. CCIS, vol. 580, pp. 112–132. Springer, Cham (2015). doi:10.1007/978-3-319-27869-8_7
20. Greifenberg, T., Look, M., Roidl, S., Rumpe, B.: Engineering tagging languages for DSLs. In: Conference on Model Driven Engineering Languages and Systems (MODELS 2015), pp. 34–43. ACM/IEEE (2015)
21. Grönniger, H., Krahn, H., Rumpe, B., Schindler, M., Völkel, S.: MontiCore: a framework for the development of textual domain specific languages. In: 30th International Conference on Software Engineering (ICSE 2008), Leipzig, Germany, 10–18 May 2008, Companion Volume, pp. 925–926 (2008)
22. Object Management Group: OMG Unified Modeling Language (OMG UML), Infrastructure Version 2.3, 03 May 2010
23. Habel, A., Heckel, R., Taentzer, G.: Graph grammars with negative application conditions. Fundam. Inform. **26**(3), 287–313 (1996)
24. Haber, A., Hölldobler, K., Kolassa, C., Look, M., Müller, K., Rumpe, B., Schaefer, I., Schulze, C.: Systematic synthesis of delta modeling languages. J. Softw. Tools Technol. Transf. (STTT) **17**(5), 601–626 (2015)

25. Haber, A., Look, M., Mir Seyed Nazari, P., Navarro Perez, A., Rumpe, B., Völkel, S., Wortmann, A.: Composition of heterogeneous modeling languages. In: Desfray, P., Filipe, J., Hammoudi, S., Pires, L.F. (eds.) MODELSWARD 2015. CCIS, vol. 580, pp. 45–66. Springer, Cham (2015). doi:10.1007/978-3-319-27869-8_3
26. Harel, D., Rumpe, B.: Meaningful modeling: what's the semantics of "semantics"? IEEE Comput. **37**(10), 64–72 (2004)
27. Hermerschmidt, L., Hölldobler, K., Rumpe, B., Wortmann, A.: Generating domain-specific transformation languages for component & connector architecture descriptions. In: Workshop on Model-Driven Engineering for Component-Based Software Systems (ModComp 2015). CEUR Workshop Proceedings, vol. 1463 (2015)
28. Hölldobler, K., Rumpe, B., Weisemöller, I.: Systematically deriving domain-specific transformation languages. In: Conference on Model Driven Engineering Languages and Systems (MODELS 2015), pp. 136–145. ACM/IEEE (2015)
29. Iverson, W.: Hibernate: A J2EE (TM) Developer's Guide. Addison-Wesley Professional, Boston (2004)
30. Jézéquel, J.-M., Barais, O., Fleurey, F.: Model driven language engineering with kermeta. In: Fernandes, J.M., Lämmel, R., Visser, J., Saraiva, J. (eds.) GTTSE 2009. LNCS, vol. 6491, pp. 201–221. Springer, Heidelberg (2011). doi:10.1007/978-3-642-18023-1_5
31. Jouault, F., Allilaire, F., Bézivin, J., Kurtev, I., Valduriez, P.: ATL: a QVT-like transformation language. In: Companion to the 21st ACM SIGPLAN Symposium on Object-Oriented Programming Systems, Languages, and Applications (2006)
32. Kleppe, A.: Software Language Engineering: Creating Domain-Specific Languages Using Metamodels. Addison-Wesley, Boston (2008)
33. Knuth, D.E.: Semantics of context-free languages. Theory Comput. Syst. **2**(2), 127–145 (1968)
34. Krahn, H., Rumpe, B., Völkel, S.: MontiCore: a framework for compositional development of domain specific languages. Int. J. Softw. Tools Technol. Transf. (STTT) **12**(5), 353–372 (2010)
35. Larsen, M.E.V., Deantoni, J., Combemale, B., Mallet, F.: A behavioral coordination operator language (BCOoL). In: 2015 ACM/IEEE 18th International Conference on Model Driven Engineering Languages and Systems (MODELS) (2015)
36. Mens, T., Van Gorp, P.: A taxonomy of model transformation. Electron. Notes Theor. Comput. Sci. **152**, 125–142 (2006)
37. Miller, F.P., Vandome, A.F., McBrewster, J.: Apache Maven (2010)
38. Mir Seyed Nazari, P., Roth, A., Rumpe, B.: Mixed generative and handcoded development of adaptable data-centric business applications. In: Domain-Specific Modeling Workshop (DSM 2015), pp. 43–44. ACM (2015)
39. Radjenovic, J., Milosavljevic, B., Surla, D.: Modelling and implementation of catalogue cards using freemarker. Program **43**(1), 62–76 (2009)
40. Richters, M., Gogolla, M.: On formalizing the UML object constraint language OCL. In: Ling, T.-W., Ram, S., Lee, M. (eds.) ER 1998. LNCS, vol. 1507, pp. 449–464. Springer, Heidelberg (1998). doi:10.1007/978-3-540-49524-6_35
41. Ringert, J.O., Roth, A., Rumpe, B., Wortmann, A.: Language and code generator composition for model-driven engineering of robotics component & connector systems. J. Softw. Eng. Robot. (JOSER) **6**(1), 33–57 (2015)
42. Rumpe, B.: Modeling with UML: Language, Concepts, Methods. Springer, Cham (2016). doi:10.1007/978-3-319-33933-7
43. Rumpe, B.: Agile Modeling with UML: Code Generation, Testing, Refactoring. Springer, Cham (2017). doi:10.1007/978-3-319-58862-9

44. Steinberg, D., Budinsky, F., Merks, E., Paternostro, M.: EMF: Eclipse Modeling Framework. Pearson Education, London (2008)
45. Vacchi, E., Cazzola, W.: Neverlang: a framework for feature-oriented language development. Comput. Lang. Syst. Struct. **43**, 1–40 (2015)
46. Viyović, V., Maksimović, M., Perisić, B.: Sirius: a rapid development of DSM graphical editor. In: 2014 18th International Conference on Intelligent Engineering Systems (INES), pp. 233–238. IEEE (2014)
47. Voelter, M., Solomatov, K.: Language modularization and composition with projectional language workbenches illustrated with MPS. In: Software Language Engineering, SLE, vol. 16, p. 3 (2010)
48. Völter, M., Benz, S., Dietrich, C., Engelmann, B., Helander, M., Kats, L.C.L., Visser, E., Wachsmuth, G.: DSL Engineering - Designing, Implementing and Using Domain-Specific Languages (2013). dslbook.org
49. Wachsmuth, G.H., Konat, G.D.P., Visser, E.: Language design with the spoofax language workbench. IEEE Softw. **31**(5), 35–43 (2014)
50. Whittle, J., Hutchinson, J., Rouncefield, M.: The state of practice in model-driven engineering. IEEE Softw. **31**(3), 79–85 (2014)

Schema Evolution and Gravitation to Rigidity: A Tale of Calmness in the Lives of Structured Data

Panos Vassiliadis[✉]

Department of Computer Science and Engineering,
University of Ioannina, Ioannina, Hellas
pvassil@cs.uoi.gr

Change is the essential process of all existence – Star Trek's Spock

Evolving dependency magnets, i.e., software modules upon which a large number of other modules depend, is always a hard task. As Robert C. Martin has nicely summarized it (see http://www.oodesign.com/design-principles.html), fundamental problems of bad design that hinder evolution include *immobility*, i.e., difficulty in reuse, *rigidity*, i.e., the tendency for software to be difficult to change and *fragility*, i.e., the tendency of the software to break in many places every time it is changed. In such cases, developers are reluctant to evolve the software to avoid facing the impact of change. How are these fundamentals related to schema evolution? We know that changes in the schema of a database affect a large (and not necessarily traced) number of surrounding applications, without explicit identification of the impact. These affected applications can then suffer from syntactic and semantic inconsistencies – with syntactic inconsistency leading to application crashes and semantic inconsistency leading to the retrieval of data other than the ones originally intended. Thus, the puzzle of gracefully facilitating the evolution of data-intensive information systems is evident, and the desideratum of coming up with engineering methods that allow us to design information systems with a view to minimizing the impact of evolution, a noble goal for the research community.

Several research paths towards this goal are being pursued. A first path involves works concerning an algebra of schema evolution operations, that can allow the description of the history of schema changes in a semantically rich sequence of operations [4,7]. Another path involves the management of the impact of changes [1,9]. A fairly novel path involves the identification of profiles and patterns in the usage of relational database access technologies in open source projects [5,6,10]. Moreover -and in particular, what interests us in the context of this talk- *as all engineering should be based on well-understood mechanics and laws, the research community has also tried to uncover mechanics and patterns that govern schema evolution.* Knowing the underlying mechanisms of schema evolution is fundamental in engineering solutions that gracefully handle it: without this knowledge we can easily stray in solutions that have no relationship to real-world problems. Although the body of work is rather small compared to the importance of the matter, one cannot ignore that access to schema histories was practically impossible before the proliferation of Free and Open Source Software (FOSS). Thus, apart from an original study in the early '90s [12], it was

© Springer International Publishing AG 2017
Y. Ouhammou et al. (Eds.): MEDI 2017, LNCS 10563, pp. 18–23, 2017.
DOI: 10.1007/978-3-319-66854-3_2

only in the late '00s that the problem gained a certain momentum that continues till today [2–4,8,11,19], basically due to the availability of FOSS projects that contain DDL files in their history.

Since our team in the University of Ioannina started working on this topic, in 2013, we have encountered several interesting patterns of schema evolution; these findings will constitute the main body of this keynote talk.

In [13,14], we have studied how the schema of a database evolves in terms of its size, growth and activity. Our findings indicate that *schemata grow over time in order to satisfy new requirements, albeit not in a continuous or linear fashion, but rather, with bursts of concentrated effort of growth and/or maintenance interrupting longer periods of calmness* (Fig. 1).

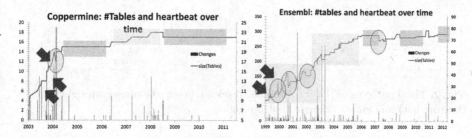

Fig. 1. Summary of [14] with schema growth over time (red continuous line) along with the heartbeat of changes (spikes) for two datasets. Overlayed darker green rectangles highlight the calmness periods, and lighter blue rectangles highlight smooth expansions. Arrows point at periods of abrupt expansion and circles highlight drops in size. (Color figure online)

A different, innovative research path that we have ignited in [17,18] was to study profiles and patterns of *tables*, rather than *schemata*. We have tried to correlate static properties of tables, like the point of birth, or their schema size at birth, with characteristics of activity, like the sum of changes the tables have undergone, or their survival (we like to refer to tables removed as "dead" and table that made it to the last known version of the history that we study as "survivors"). We came up with four patterns (Fig. 2).

1. The Γ *pattern* pattern (albeit with several exceptions) suggests that tables with large schemata tend to have long durations and avoid removal.
2. The *Comet pattern* suggests that the tables with most updates are frequently the ones with medium schema size.
3. The *Inverse Γ pattern*, the one with the fewest exceptions, states that tables with medium or small durations produce amounts of updates lower than expected, whereas tables with long duration expose all sorts of update behavior.
4. The *Empty Triangle pattern* indicates that the majority of removed tables have mostly short lives, which in turn, implies a low probability of deletion for old timers.

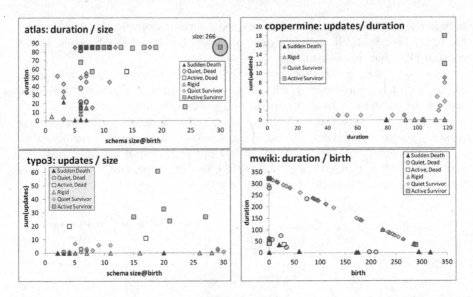

Fig. 2. The 4 patterns of [17,18]: Gamma (top left), inverse Gamma (top right), comet (bottom left) and empty triangle (bottom right).

In [16] we have studied how survivors differ from dead tables with respect to the combination of duration and activity profile. The resulting pattern was named *Electrolysis pattern* due to the intense antithesis in the lives of dead and survivor tables (Fig. 3):

1. Dead tables demonstrate short or medium lifetimes (much shorter than survivors), practically never at high durations. Moreover, with few exceptions, the less active dead tables are, the higher the chance to reach shorter durations.
2. Oppositely to dead tables, survivors are mostly located at medium or high durations. The more active survivors are, the stronger they are attracted towards high durations, with a significant such inclination for the few active ones that cluster in very high durations (which makes the antithesis with the dead ones quite intense).

If time permits, this talk will also cover recent results in topics like foreign key evolution [15] and evolution of Web Services [20].

A key message of this talk is that change is at much lower levels than one would expect. We encounter this observation again and again, in several of the aforementioned research explorations, and, we are quite confident to say that *the absence of evolution is clearly more evident that evolution itself*. This has to do both with survival and activity. In terms of survival, deletions of tables and attributes are much more infrequent than additions. Calmness in the growth of the schema is more frequent than schema growth; moreover, tables are rarely resized. In terms of activity, quiet tables with low rates of change are the majority; rigid tables outnumber the (really few) active ones, both in the survivor and,

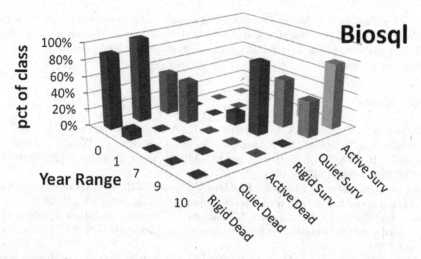

Fig. 3. The Electrolysis pattern [16]: the left axis denotes durations in years; the right axis denotes the level of activity (or, *LifeAndDeath* class) of tables (rigid have undergone zero change, active have an update rate of 10% or more, and quiet is the -majority of- all the rest; the vertical axis denotes the percentage of tables with respect to their activity class

in particular, in the dead class. Therefore, the presence of growth and occasional maintenance actions should not eventually overshadow the absence of restructuring and update that is a significant characteristic of the life of a schema in the long term.

We attribute this phenomenon to what we have named as *gravitation to rigidity*. Any change in the schema requires the maintenance of the surrounding applications. Especially in the case of deletions, renames or type updates, the result might be syntactic inconsistency (and therefore failure) of the application, which is a grave consequence, especially if different developers are involved. The plethora of concurring signs that point towards gravitation to rigidity is possibly the single most important discovery of this line of research and a clear sign of vulnerability in the way the relational model, queries and applications are entangled.

We kindly refer the interested researchers to our website http://www.cs. uoi.gr/~pvassil/projects/schemaBiographies/index.html that contains pointers to available data sets, the tools that we have built and material around our published work.

Acknowledgements. The results of our team in the University of Ioannina on the topic of studying and understanding the mechanics of schema evolution would have never been possible without the collaboration and dedication of many colleagues and students. The list of people who have contributed to this effort includes my colleague and long-time collaborator Apostolos Zarras, as well as several of my students who have worked on the topic, specifically Ioannis Skoulis, Fanis Giahos, Michael Kolozoff,

Athanasios Pappas, and Maria Zerva. Special mention also goes to my long-term collaborator George Papastefanatos and my PhD student Petros Manousis, with whom we have collaborated for long on the topic of managing schema evolution, from its engineering perspective.

References

1. Cleve, A., Brogneaux, A.-F., Hainaut, J.-L.: A conceptual approach to database applications evolution. In: Parsons, J., Saeki, M., Shoval, P., Woo, C., Wand, Y. (eds.) ER 2010. LNCS, vol. 6412, pp. 132–145. Springer, Heidelberg (2010). doi:10.1007/978-3-642-16373-9_10
2. Cleve, A., Gobert, M., Meurice, L., Maes, J., Weber, J.H.: Understanding database schema evolution: a case study. Sci. Comput. Program. **97**, 113–121 (2015)
3. Curino, C., Moon, H.J., Tanca, L., Zaniolo, C.: Schema evolution in Wikipedia: toward a web information system benchmark. In: Proceedings of ICEIS 2008. Citeseer (2008)
4. Curino, C., Moon, H.J., Deutsch, A., Zaniolo, C.: Automating the database schema evolution process. VLDB J. **22**(1), 73–98 (2013)
5. Decan, A., Goeminne, M., Mens, T.: On the interaction of relational database access technologies in open source Java projects. CoRR abs/1701.00416
6. Decan, A., Goeminne, M., Mens, T.: On the interaction of relational database access technologies in open source java projects. In: Post-proceedings of the 8th Seminar on Advanced Techniques and Tools for Software Evolution, Mons, Belgium, 6–8 July 2015, pp. 26–35 (2015)
7. Herrmann, K., Voigt, H., Behrend, A., Lehner, W.: CoDEL – a relationally complete language for database evolution. In: Morzy, T., Valduriez, P., Bellatreche, L. (eds.) ADBIS 2015. LNCS, vol. 9282, pp. 63–76. Springer, Cham (2015). doi:10.1007/978-3-319-23135-8_5
8. Lin, D.Y., Neamtiu, I.: Collateral evolution of applications and databases. In: Proceedings of the Joint International and Annual ERCIM Workshops on Principles of Software Evolution (IWPSE) and Software Evolution (Evol) Workshops, IWPSE-Evol 2009, pp. 31–40 (2009)
9. Manousis, P., Vassiliadis, P., Papastefanatos, G.: Automating the adaptation of evolving data-intensive ecosystems. In: Ng, W., Storey, V.C., Trujillo, J.C. (eds.) ER 2013. LNCS, vol. 8217, pp. 182–196. Springer, Heidelberg (2013). doi:10.1007/978-3-642-41924-9_17
10. Meurice, L., Nagy, C., Cleve, A.: Static analysis of dynamic database usage in Java systems. In: Nurcan, S., Soffer, P., Bajec, M., Eder, J. (eds.) CAiSE 2016. LNCS, vol. 9694, pp. 491–506. Springer, Cham (2016). doi:10.1007/978-3-319-39696-5_30
11. Qiu, D., Li, B., Su, Z.: An empirical analysis of the co-evolution of schema and code in database applications. In: Proceedings of the 2013 9th Joint Meeting on Foundations of Software Engineering, ESEC/FSE 2013, pp. 125–135 (2013)
12. Sjøberg, D.: Quantifying schema evolution. Inf. Softw. Technol. **35**(1), 35–44 (1993)
13. Skoulis, I., Vassiliadis, P., Zarras, A.: Open-source databases: within, outside, or beyond Lehman's laws of software evolution? In: Jarke, M., Mylopoulos, J., Quix, C., Rolland, C., Manolopoulos, Y., Mouratidis, H., Horkoff, J. (eds.) CAiSE 2014. LNCS, vol. 8484, pp. 379–393. Springer, Cham (2014). doi:10.1007/978-3-319-07881-6_26
14. Skoulis, I., Vassiliadis, P., Zarras, A.V.: Growing up with stability: how open-source relational databases evolve. Inf. Syst. **53**, 363–385 (2015)

15. Vassiliadis, P., Kolozoff, M.R., Zerva, M., Zarras, A.V.: Schema evolution and foreign keys: birth, eviction, change and absence. In: 36th International Conference on Conceptual Modeling (ER 2017), Valencia, Spain, 6–9 November 2017 (2017)
16. Vassiliadis, P., Zarras, A.V.: Survival in schema evolution: putting the lives of survivor and dead tables in counterpoint. In: Dubois, E., Pohl, K. (eds.) CAiSE 2017. LNCS, vol. 10253, pp. 333–347. Springer, Cham (2017). doi:10.1007/978-3-319-59536-8_21
17. Vassiliadis, P., Zarras, A.V., Skoulis, I.: How is life for a table in an evolving relational schema? Birth, death and everything in between. In: Johannesson, P., Lee, M.L., Liddle, S.W., Opdahl, A.L., López, Ó.P. (eds.) ER 2015. LNCS, vol. 9381, pp. 453–466. Springer, Cham (2015). doi:10.1007/978-3-319-25264-3_34
18. Vassiliadis, P., Zarras, A.V., Skoulis, I.: Gravitating to rigidity: patterns of schema evolution - and its absence - in the lives of tables. Inf. Syst. **63**, 24–46 (2017)
19. Wu, S., Neamtiu, I.: Schema evolution analysis for embedded databases. In: Proceedings of the 2011 IEEE 27th International Conference on Data Engineering Workshops, ICDEW 2011, pp. 151–156 (2011)
20. Zarras, A.V., Vassiliadis, P., Dinos, I.: Keep calm and wait for the spike! insights on the evolution of Amazon services. In: Nurcan, S., Soffer, P., Bajec, M., Eder, J. (eds.) CAiSE 2016. LNCS, vol. 9694, pp. 444–458. Springer, Cham (2016). doi:10.1007/978-3-319-39696-5_27

Domain Specific Languages

A Model-Driven Ecosystem for the Definition of Data Mining Domain-Specific Languages

Alfonso de la Vega[✉], Diego García-Saiz, Marta Zorrilla, and Pablo Sánchez

Dpto. Ingeniería Informática y Electrónica, Universidad de Cantabria,
Santander, Spain
{alfonso.delavega,diego.garcia,marta.zorrilla,p.sanchez}@unican.es

Abstract. Data mining techniques are making their entrance in nowadays companies, allowing business users to take informed decisions based on their available data. However, these business experts usually lack the knowledge to perform the analysis of the data by themselves, which makes it necessary to rely on experts in the field of data mining. In an attempt to solve this problem, we previously studied the definition of domain-specific languages, which allowed to specify data mining processes without requiring experience in the applied techniques. The specification was made through high-level language primitives, which referred only to familiar concepts and terms from the original domain of the data. Therefore, technical details about the mining processes were hidden to the final user. Although these languages present themselves as a promising solution, their development can become a challenging task, incurring in costly endeavours. This work describes a development ecosystem devised for the generation of these languages, starting from a generic perspective that can be specialized into the details of each domain.

Keywords: Model-driven software development · Domain-specific languages · Data mining

1 Introduction

Data mining techniques are nowadays having an ever-increasing popularity. One of the main reasons for this is the digitalization of more and more systems and services from our society, whose stored data are being used to make informed decisions. For instance, *Netflix* determines what media contents to produce based on the analysis of their users activity and ratings information [16].

Nevertheless, the requisites to work with this kind of techniques are very complex, ranging from statistics to algorithmic and data management concepts. These requisites make very difficult that average users, who are experts in their business field but not in analysis techniques, understand and carry out the analysis of their data directly, making necessary to hire or rely on external experts in the area. As an insight, there is a high-demand for *data-science* denoted professionals [14], which clearly surpasses current availability.

© Springer International Publishing AG 2017
Y. Ouhammou et al. (Eds.): MEDI 2017, LNCS 10563, pp. 27–41, 2017.
DOI: 10.1007/978-3-319-66854-3_3

In order to alleviate this problem, we explored the creation of domain specific languages (DSLs), with the objective of making them usable by business experts with limited or no knowledge in data mining. The complexity which analysis tasks like data transformation and data modeling contain gets hidden behind concepts and terms that belong to the concrete domain being analysed. Therefore, a business expert would be able to define a mining process by combining high-level language primitives with common terms they use daily.

In a previous work [17], we developed a DSL with these characteristics for the educational domain. This DSL allowed teachers to analyse the performance of a course, by studying the data stored in the e-learning infrastructure that hosted the course.

Although this case study demonstrated the creation of DSLs for non-experts in data mining had potential, it also showed that the associated cost of such a creation can be high. Nevertheless, during the development of the DSL, we noticed some of its elements could be reused in the definition of other similar DSLs, therefore reducing their development time, and hence, their cost.

The results of studying the previous discovery are described in this work. We present a framework that can be used to define data mining languages for non-experts in a more efficient way than to start from scratch each language. This efficiency is provided by the usage of a generic infrastructure, which is shared among the generated DSLs, and that can be specialized to incorporate the details and conditions of each domain.

To determine the benefits provided by the infrastructure, two languages were generated with it: (1) the initially developed educational DSL; and (2) a language for the analysis of diabetes disease clinical data. The infrastructure denoted high-reuse of language components that helped with reducing the overall development time.

After this introduction, the paper is organized as follows: Sect. 2 describes the field of data-mining for non-expert users through a literature review. In Sect. 3, we explain the motivations behind this work by describing a previous DSL development for the educational domain. The presented infrastructure for analysis DSLs definition is introduced in Sect. 4. Finally, Sect. 5 summarizes this work, remarking its main contributions and enumerating future directions.

2   Data Mining for Non-expert Users

This section justifies the promotion of DSLs for data mining through an analysis of the state of the art in the data mining for non-experts field.

As starting point of this research, we wanted to check the following hypothesis: data mining techniques, on their current state, are not adequate for users without a solid knowledge in them, which restricts their usage to experts in the area. If non-expert users want to apply these analysis techniques, their complexity has to be tackled or hidden beneath an understandable interface.

The correctness of this hypothesis was verified by performing a systematic literature review, following the guidelines of Kitchenham and Charters [9] and

Jalali and Wohlin [7]. The objective of this review was to find works whose aim is to make data mining techniques easier to apply by non-expert users. These works are often framed into the concept of *data mining democratisation* [1].

The results of this review, which involved the analysis of more than 500 articles and tools, are in the process of being published. The protocol that guided the review process can be consulted in an external website[1]. Through this review, we discovered several tools and publications which were classified into four groups, according to their characteristics. These four groups, with a representative work of each one of them, are introduced in the following.

Ad-Hoc Solutions. This group comprises data mining applications that are specifically crafted to solve a concrete problem in a fixed domain. For instance, authors of [8] present a tool for the study of time-series data from haemodialysis treatments. In these case studies, the problem which data mining techniques have to solve is well-known from the beginning, and therefore algorithms are selected and optimized around this precise problem. The devised data mining processes are then integrated into an application, which allows final users to apply the processes by means of an intuitive interface.

The problem these applications present comes from the associated cost of developing such a specialized solution from scratch. Moreover, tools developed this way tend to not be easily transferable to other domains or problems.

Workflow-Based Applications. Currently, there are several free and commercial applications that allow to quickly specify a data mining process by the definition of a workflow through a graphical interface. A workflow is a collection of interconnected building blocks, where each block implements a task or step in the data mining process such as loading or filtering data, or executing an algorithm. Weka [6] or KNIME [3] are good examples of these applications.

Although workflows reduce the required time to define a data mining process, they are not oriented for non-expert users. Each building block has to be selected and configured for its precise task, and then the blocks have to be interconnected to achieve the desired results. The parametrization of each block and the orchestration of the workflow are not yet simple enough tasks to be carried out by non-expert users.

Approaches to Develop Non-expert-Oriented Applications. This category contains development methodologies or architectures, whose aim is to ensure that the resulting data mining applications created by following them can be used by non-expert users.

Authors of [18] presented a services-based solution. Each service offers a data mining process, whose configuration was either predefined for each case or automatically obtained [2]. Then, web-based applications for final users are developed, which allow to employ the defined services in a friendly way.

---

[1] http://personales.unican.es/delavegaa/files/medi/reviewProtocol.pdf.

The usage of these methodologies still makes necessary the presence of experts, at least in the development stage. Nevertheless, they tend to benefit from the reuse of several components (for instance, the *core* of the services architecture presented in [18] could be reused for all developed applications). A problem these solutions can manifest is the adaptation cost to slight changes in the requirements. As an example, an application developed to analyse students data could need severe changes to be able to focus the analysis in other domain aspects, such as course activities or exams.

Generic Applications for Non-expert Users. These applications offer high level solutions to execute some data mining tasks without the intervention of an expert. A representative of this group is *Oracle Predictive Analytics* [4]. This solution offers several procedures, which can be applied to data contained in a table from an Oracle database. For instance, the EXPLAIN procedure allows to find the most relevant columns of a table when we want to infer - or *explain* - another column from the table. This command could be used to obtain those columns which best explain a CourseOutcome column in a Students table, giving us some highlights of the relevant indicators to pay attention to during a course.

The commands in [4] do not require any special configuration, therefore they can be applied to different domains indistinctly. Nevertheless, their generic approach might hamper the quality of their results, as the analysis techniques are not tuned for the details of the domain where they are applied.

After this state-of-the-art analysis, we studied the following idea: first, we would encapsulate some data mining processes into components that could be reused, such as the procedures contained in the *Oracle Predictive Analytics* solution. However, we must be able to prepare or change these components for specific cases, as it happened with the services of [18]. Second, we would develop query languages to invoke these data mining components. As we want the business experts to become the final users of these languages, their syntax would need to allow the definition of a data mining process through high-level primitives and familiar vocabulary of the application domain, and consequently hiding the data mining techniques' associated complexity. A query written with these languages would be used to generate a code script, which will execute the developed data mining components in order to answer the question provided by the business user.

As an initial case study, we explored this idea by developing a DSL which supported a set of data mining processes for the educational domain. Next section describes this case study, and enumerates the reasons that drove us to develop an infrastructure for the definition of these data mining DSLs.

3   A DSL for the Analysis of Educational Data: Experience and Challenges

For this DSL, the objective was to analyse data from the educational domain. The DSL was devised for teachers to get insights of their courses, using for the

```
00 show_profile of Students;
01 show_profile of Students with courseOutcome=fail;
02 find_reasons_for courseOutcome=fail of Students;
```

Fig. 1. Examples of queries written with the educational DSL.

analysis the information stored in the e-learning environment that hosted the course, such as Moodle [13]. These insights would then be used to improve the performance of the analysed courses.

Two data mining processes were supported. First one of them extracted profiles from a data set allowing, for instance, to separate students into different groups according to their characteristics. The second one tried to highlight the causes of a concrete event taking place. In the educational domain, this event could refer to students failing the course, withdraws, or low grades in a task, among others.

These analysis processes were coded into Java snippets, which used algorithms from the Weka [6] data mining library. Then, a query-based DSL was developed to execute the defined snippets from a high-level perspective. Figure 1 shows some examples of the kind of queries allowed by the DSL.

The first query (Fig. 1, Line 00) invoked the profile extraction process by using the primitive show_profile, with the objective of grouping the course students according to the information contained in a Students entity.

The second query profiles the students again, but not all of them (Fig. 1, Line 01). A filter is applied by using the with keyword, which in this case limits the analysis to those students who have failed the course (course_outcome = fail), and thus tries to find different behaviours that lead to the same negative result.

In the third query, we want to find causes that best explain the event of failing a course (Fig. 1, Line 02). For this, we use the find_reasons_for primitive, introducing the same condition that was used before in the filter (course_outcome = fail) as the event to study.

The described queries show the two main components that define the syntax of our DSL. The first one is a set of primitives, which determine the analysis task to apply on each case. The objective of each primitive can be understood or easily explained to business experts in order to employ them.

The second one comprises entities from the analysed domain, that allow the user to indicate the data to analyse on each query. In order to perform an analysis, we need a link from the entities that are used in the DSL and the data sources over which we want to apply the analysis processes. In our case, there is a mapping that relates each entity to a dataset formatted in *ARFF* (tabular format accepted in the Weka suite).

The DSL also included capabilities that helped the teacher to create syntactically and semantically correct queries. For instance, the entity name introduced in the query has to be valid, this is, a mapping between the provided entity name and an available dataset has to exist. To achieve this, the language contained error-checking capabilities which validated and informed the user about any present mistakes in the query. Moreover, proposals of valid terms from the domain were provided, such as existing entities to analyse, through content assistants.

The development was carried out by following a model-driven approach. The DSL's abstract syntax was specified through an *Ecore* metamodel, and a concrete textual syntax was defined with the *Xtext* [5] framework. For the analysis step, the queries formulated with the DSL were used to generate code that parametrized and executed the previously created snippets. The code generation was performed with the *Epsilon* [10] model management suite.

This case study revealed two important problems of this approach: (1) it is difficult to define data mining processes that can perform well across different domains, and (2) the definition of such a DSL for non-expert users is a challenging task, which can incur in important development costs. In this work, we face the second of these problems. The first one is a well-known problem in the data mining field, which usually involves defining specific analysis tasks for each domain and target. Nevertheless, there is some research focus in alleviating this problem, for instance, with *meta-learning* approaches [11]. In the following, we will assume that the invoked data mining processes by our languages are appropriate, either because they are reusable, or because they have been specifically developed for the domain being studied on each case.

Regarding the second problem, the development of the educational DSL exposed that several components of the language could be designed in a generic way, and later get personalized for a specific domain. As this generic components would be shared among the developed DSLs, the generation cost of each one of them would be cheaper. Based on this, we developed an infrastructure to generate analysis DSLs from a generic perspective, which constitutes the main contribution of this work. Next section presents this infrastructure.

4   An Infrastructure for the Development of DSLs for Data Mining

The infrastructure description has been organised into two blocks: (1) DSL definition, where the components that conform a language, from the lexical and syntactical elements to the final editor, are presented; and (2) queries execution, which completes the DSL description by indicating how the queries written with the DSL are answered via the execution of a data mining process.

To facilitate the description of these blocks, an example where a DSL is developed for the analysis of clinical data is used throughout the rest of the paper. The domain of this example is introduced below.

4.1   Case Study: Indicator Analysis of Diabetes Disease

This DSL analyses information coming from the clinical field, where a group of patients is tested for diabetes [15]. For each patient, data regarding different indicators, such as blood pressure, age, or diabetes occurrence in ancestors is collected, along with the result of the test (positive or negative). These data could be used, among other things, to find conditions that provoke the apparition of a diabetes disease. This analysis task might be invoked with the following query: find_reasons_for test_result = positive of Diabetes_Results.

Other possible analyses could involve the obtention of patient groups, according with the captured indicators, or the ranking of most relevant indicators when determining if a patient has or does not have diabetes.

Next section describes how the grammar and the components of the DSL editor are defined.

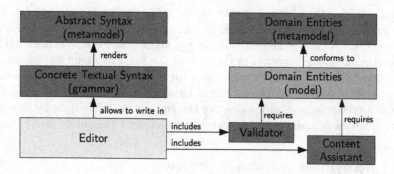

Fig. 2. Overview of the DSL syntax and editor components. (Color figure online)

4.2   DSL Syntax and Editor Definition

As previously introduced, the syntax in our DSLs has two main components: (1) the different commands that determine the task analysis to perform, and (2) the domain entities and attributes that are selected for the analysis.

In the educational case study, the grammar of the DSL controlled the domain terms which could be introduced in the queries, such as the valid entity names to be analysed. This provoked that rules regarding the commands invocation and other rules for domain terms were interleaved in the grammar, making difficult the extraction of reusable parts to create a new DSL applied to a different domain.

To overcome this, a different approach was followed for the infrastructure. The syntax of the languages was generalized, to make it applicable in different domains. Therefore, the previously controlled domain terms in the grammar are now free fields, this is, they can be filled with any value. To keep ensuring that the introduced query is correct, it is checked by means of an external validator. Figure 2 displays the components that this new DSL structure contains with their relations. The abstract and a concrete textual syntax of the languages are used to provide an editor, which also gets error checking and assistance capabilities with the help of an *entities model*. These components are explained below.

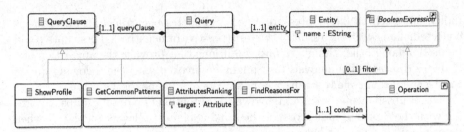

Fig. 3. Generic abstract syntax.

A fragment of the abstract syntax of the DSLs can be found in Fig. 3. Each `Query` written with a DSL has a `QueryClause`, which indicates the analysis task to perform. Each clause might require extra attributes to be specified, such as the `condition` that is required in the case of the `Find_Reasons_For` clause.

The `QueryClause` task is executed over the selected `Entity` from the domain. This entity is specified by introducing a `name` and, optionally, it is possible to focus the analysis on a specific subset of the entity's available data by providing a `filter`, which is based on a boolean expression over the entity attributes.

$$
\begin{array}{lll}
\langle query\rangle & ::= & \langle queryClause\rangle \text{ 'of' } \langle entity\rangle \\
\langle queryClause\rangle & ::= & \langle showProfile\rangle \\
& \mid & \langle findReasonsFor\rangle \\
& \mid & \langle attributesRanking\rangle \\
& \mid & \langle getCommonPatterns\rangle \\
\langle entity\rangle & ::= & \langle name\rangle \text{ ('with' } \langle booleanExpression\rangle)? \\
\langle showProfile\rangle & ::= & \text{'show\_profile'} \\
\langle findReasonsFor\rangle & ::= & \text{'find\_reasons\_for' } \langle operation\rangle \\
\langle attributesRanking\rangle & ::= & \text{'attributes\_ranking\_for' } \langle attribute\rangle \\
\langle getCommonPatterns\rangle & ::= & \text{'get\_common\_patterns'}
\end{array}
$$

Fig. 4. Simplified grammar of the DSLs.

This abstract syntax is used in the definition of a concrete textual syntax that constitutes the grammar of our DSLs family. Figure 4 shows a simplified version of the Xtext grammar in BNF format. A query starts by introducing a command keyword, which determines the selected `QueryClause` for the analysis. For instance, the `attributes_ranking_for` keyword would be used to choose the `AttributesRanking` clause. Any extra required information for each clause is specified next to the command, such as the `operation` of a `FindReasonsFor` clause. Then, the information about an entity is specified. First, its `name` is introduced, which is a string field. Optionally, it is possible to define a filter, by using the `with` keyword and a `booleanExpression` as commented before.

Neither the abstract syntax nor the grammar contain any reference to specific domains. Therefore, they can be used to generate different analysis languages.

However, the control of the free fields, such as the entity's **name** attribute, is still necessary. This control is achieved with an external validator, which checks the introduced domain terms against a model to test if they are valid. This model corresponds to the *entities model* component in Fig. 2 (orange component), and contains the information about the available domain entities and the characteristics of their attributes.

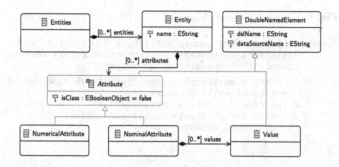

Fig. 5. Metamodel used to define the available entities in the domain.

Each entities model conforms to a metamodel, which is depicted in Fig. 5. In the metamodel, we can see that there exists a set of **Entity** objects, which have a name and a list of attributes. These attributes can have different types, such as numeric (**NumericalAttribute**) or categorical (**NominalAttribute**). For the categorical attributes, also, a set of the possible **values** they might take is also registered.

This entities model allows the validator to check the correctness of the generated query, at different levels. For instance, it can check if an introduced entity exists by looking for its name among the existent entities in the model. More fine-grained controls are also available, such as if the selected entity has an attribute specified in the filter or, moreover, if the boolean operation that is being applied to an attribute makes sense regarding its type (as an example, a *moreThan* operation applied to a categorical attribute, such as *sex*, would be an invalid operation). This validator also makes sure that the introduced query is syntactically correct, according to the grammar of the DSL.

The validator was implemented by using the capabilities of Xtext. It offers the possibility to define check functions in Java or Xtend language, which get triggered over different elements in the grammar. As an example, in Fig. 6, a validation function checks whether the introduced entity name corresponds to an available entity in the domain. First, it looks for its name among the existent entities in the model by using the **entitiesProvider** object (Fig. 6, lines 02–04). If it does not find it, it shows an error with an explanation message (Fig. 6, lines 05–07).

Additionally, the entities model is also used by a content assistant module, in order to provide terms proposals when writing the query. Figure 7 shows the

```
00  @Check
01  def checkEntityName(Entity entity) {
02    if (!entitiesProvider.entities.exists[
03          e | e.name.equals(entity.name)
04       ]) {
05      error("Entity with name '" + entity.name +
06          "' does not exist",
07          EdmdslPackage::eINSTANCE.entity_Name)
08    }
09  }
```

Fig. 6. Check function which validates the name of an entity.

```
00  override public void completeAttribute_Name(EObject model,
01        Assignment assignment, ContentAssistContext context,
02        ICompletionProposalAcceptor acceptor) {
03    val entity = entitiesProvider.findEntityByModel(model)
04    if (entity == null) { return }
05    for (attribute : entity.attributes) {
06      acceptor.accept(createCompletionProposal(
07          attribute.dslName, context))
08    }
09  }
```

Fig. 7. Assistant function that suggests attributes of an entity.

function that suggests attribute names when the user wants to apply a filter over the selected entity. For that purpose, it first looks for the entity in the model (Fig. 6, line 03), and then transverses its lists of attributes generating a proposal for each one of them (Fig. 6, lines 05–08).

It is important to remark that both the validator and the assistant have been developed in a generic way, because the domain information they require to work with is obtained from an entities model. Therefore, if we want to use them in a DSL for another domain, we would need to modify the entities model, but the already defined validation and proposal functions will remain the same.

This provision of a new entities model is the only change needed in the components shown in Fig. 2 when one wants to obtain a DSL with an editor for a different domain, as all blue components in the figure can be reused. This reduces the number of components which must be defined and, therefore, the development time of the new language.

4.3   DSL Semantics: Queries Execution

The last step to complete the infrastructure description corresponds to the DSL semantics. Each query gets a meaning by being translated to a data mining process, which tries to answer it. The translation is completely transparent to the final user, who will only introduce the query and receive the results of the analysis.

We will use an example query for explanation purposes during the section. This example will be the one mentioned earlier, where we looked for causes that provoked a positive diabetes test in our case study. The query would be as follows: `find_reasons_for test_result = positive of Diabetes_Results`.

Figure 8 shows the steps that take place in the translation. As introduced in Sect. 3, the query is converted through model transformations into Java code, which executes data mining algorithms from the Weka library in order to obtain the desired answer. The input of this translation is the model of the written query (Fig. 8, left). This model is provided by the Xtext editor, and conforms to the abstract syntax metamodel that was described in the previous subsection.

The mining processes which get executed for each query might vary depending on the DSL domain. For instance, it is possible that the mining task of grouping data in a domain could be better answered by executing the Kmeans clustering algorithm, while for another domain it would be preferable to execute a distinct type of algorithm, such as DBSCAN. Besides, it could also be necessary to apply algorithms contained in data mining libraries other than Weka, such as R or KNIME.

To support the mentioned variability, instead of directly generating a specific Java snippet for each query, we introduced an intermediate step in the form of a *Data Procedure* metamodel (Fig. 8, middle). It represents an abstract analysis process over data, which is independent of the DSL syntax and of the data mining platforms. A fragment of this metamodel is shown in Fig. 9 (left).

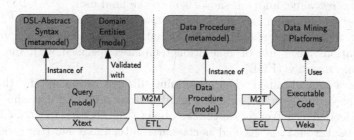

Fig. 8. Transformation process of a query written with the DSL, including the tools involved on each stage.

A data procedure operates over a `DataSource`, which is the equivalent to the `Entity` present in the abstract syntax metamodel. There is an inheritance hierarchy of data procedures, which groups them according to the data mining technique they represent. For each class representing a procedure, the appearing attributes represent input parameters that must be provided to perform the analysis.

For instance, a `Classification` procedure requires a `className` string, which determines the attribute from the source data over which to perform the classification task. Moreover, the `J48Rules` procedure, apart from the `className` of its superclass, also requires a `classValue`, to obtain those rules which describe the causes behind the selected `className` attribute taking the value indicated by `classValue`.

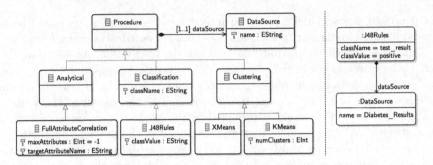

Fig. 9. Left: metamodel of a generic data procedure; right: resulting procedure model of the M2M transformation over the example query.

Therefore, the first step of the translation that takes place is a *model-to-model* (M2M) transformation, from the query model generated by the editor, to a generic data procedure (Fig. 8, left to middle). This transformation is expressed in the *Epsilon Transformation Language* (ETL). The example query, which used a `find_reasons_for` clause, would get transformed into a `J48Rules` procedure, which is depicted in Fig. 9, right. It will look for rules in a *J48* classification tree [12], where the attribute *test_result* from the data source *Diabetes_Results* takes a *positive* value, and will show them to the final user.

In order to obtain an executable snippet, the data procedure model is used as input in a *model-to-text* (M2T) transformation (Fig. 8, middle to right). This transformation makes use of generation templates specified with the *Epsilon Generation Language* (EGL).

The Java code obtained when performing this generation step for the example data procedure can be seen in Fig. 10, left to middle. First, the selected dataset is loaded as a Weka's `Instances` object (Fig. 10, lines 01–02). Then, the attribute `test_result` is selected as class attribute, and a `J48` tree is built over the instances data (Fig. 10, lines 03–05). Classification rules are extracted from this tree and, from those, the ones which have a `positive` value in the consequent are selected (Fig. 10, lines 06–07). Finally, the resulting rules are shown to the user (Fig. 10, line 08).

In Fig. 10, right we can see one of the obtained rules by executing the code snippet. This rule determines that, if the `plasma_glucose_concentration` and `body_mass_index` indicators exceed some limit, there is a high probability that the result of the diabetes test is positive. For each rule, metrics about its support and confidence are provided. The support indicates that these excessive indicator values happen in about 12% of the analysed data, of which in ~87% of the cases the test result was positive.

Now that the complete transformation process has been described, we can enumerate more clearly the benefits that the introduction of an intermediate model in the translation provides:

```
    // data obtention
01 DataSource source = new DataSource(
       "data/diabetesResults.arff");
02 Instances ins = source.getDataSet();
03 ins.setClass(ins.attribute("test_result"));
    // rules generation
04 J48 j48 = new J48();
05 j48.buildClassifier(ins);
06 RuleSet ruleSet = j48.toRules();
07 ruleSet = ruleSet.filterByConsequent("positive");
    // results visualization
08 RulesVisualizer.show(ruleSet);
```

```
IF (body_mass_index > 29.9 AND
    plasma_glucose_concentration > 157)
THEN result = tested_positive

Support: 11.979%, Confidence: 86.957%
```

Fig. 10. Left: resulting code of the M2T generation applied over the example procedure model; right: an example of the rules obtained when running the generated code.

1. The translation of a query into a mining process gets simplified, because the M2M transformation does not need to be aware of the technicalities involved when working with the mining platforms.
2. Changes in the DSL would only affect the M2M transformation step, leaving the code generation templates unchanged.
3. If we want to change which mining process gets invoked for a specific command in the DSL, we can do so by modifying the M2M transformation to select another data procedure. If the new mining process already existed in the templates and in the data procedure metamodel, that is the only necessary modification to perform the substitution.
4. Any change of the mining platform where a mining process is implemented would only require modifying the M2T generation templates, while the DSL and the data procedure metamodel would remain unaltered.

Next section summarizes the contributions and future research lines of this work, and concludes the paper.

5   Summary and Future Work

In this paper we presented, as main contribution, an infrastructure for the efficient development of domain-specific languages for the execution of data mining processes. These DSLs are oriented towards users with limited to no experience in the application of data mining techniques, thus contributing to the *democratisation* of data mining.

The work was motivated by a previous development of a DSL in the educational domain, where these languages exhibited potential to hide the complexity of the data mining techniques. However, some problems were detected, being one of them the associated cost the development of this kind of languages might involve. The described infrastructure allows to create DSLs starting from a generic solution, which gets specialized into the final domain with modular changes that are easy to introduce. As a consequence, less work is required to obtain a final DSL, which reduces its development time.

As future work, more mining tasks and case studies will be introduced, in order to test and improve the infrastructure. In addition, other non-textual types of interfaces for the final user applications, such as visual DSLs, will be studied.

Acknowledgements. This work has been partially funded by the Government of Cantabria (Spain) under the doctoral studentship program from the University of Cantabria, and by the Spanish Government under grant TIN2014-56158-C4-2-P (M2C2).

References

1. Abadi, D., et al.: The Beckman report on database research. SIGMOD Rec. **43**(3), 61–70 (2014)
2. Balcázar, J.L.: Parameter-free association rule mining with yacaree. In: Extraction et Gestion des Connaissances (EGC), Brest (France), pp. 251–254 (2011)
3. Berthold, M.R., Cebron, N., Dill, F., Gabriel, T.R., Kötter, T., Meinl, T., Ohl, P., Sieb, C., Thiel, K., Wiswedel, B.: KNIME: the Konstanz information miner. SIGKDD Explor. Newsl. **11**(1), 26–31 (2009)
4. Campos, M., Stengard, P., Milenova, B.: Data-centric automated data mining. In: Fourth International Conference on Machine Learning and Applications (ICMLA 2005), vol. 2005, pp. 97–104 (2005)
5. Eysholdt, M., Behrens, H.: Xtext: implement your language faster than the quick and dirty way. In: Companion to the 25th Annual Conference on Object-Oriented Programming, Systems, Languages, and Applications (SPLASH/OOPSLA), Reno/Tahoe (Nevada, USA), pp. 307–309, October 2010
6. Hall, M., et al.: The WEKA data mining software: an update. SIGKDD Explor. Newsl. **11**(1), 10–18 (2009)
7. Jalali, S., Wohlin, C.: Systematic literature studies: database searches vs. backward snowballing. In: Proceedings of the 2012 6th ACM_IEEE International Symposium on Empirical Software Engineering and Measurement (ESEM), pp. 29–38 (2012)
8. Kamsu-Foguem, B., Tchuenté-Foguem, G., Allart, L., Zennir, Y., Vilhelm, C., Mehdaoui, H., Zitouni, D., Hubert, H., Lemdani, M., Ravaux, P.: User-centered visual analysis using a hybrid reasoning architecture for intensive care units. Decis. Support Syst. **54**(1), 496–509 (2012)
9. Kitchenham, B., Charters, S.: Guidelines for performing systematic literature reviews in software engineering. Technical report EBSE 2007–001, Keele University and Durham University Joint Report (2007)
10. Kolovos, D.S., Paige, R.F., Rose, L.M., Williams, J.R.: Integrated model management with epsilon. In: France, R.B., Kuester, J.M., Bordbar, B., Paige, R.F. (eds.) ECMFA 2011. LNCS, vol. 6698, pp. 391–392. Springer, Heidelberg (2011). doi:10.1007/978-3-642-21470-7_33
11. Lemke, C., Budka, M., Gabrys, B.: Metalearning: a survey of trends and technologies. Artif. Intell. Rev. **44**(1), 117–130 (2015)
12. Quinlan, J.R.: C4.5: Programs for Machine Learning. Morgan Kaufmann Publishers Inc., San Francisco (1993)
13. Rice, W.: Moodle E-Learning Course Development. Packt Publishing, Birmingham (2006)
14. Schrage, M.: Stop Searching for That Elusive Data Scientist. Harvard Business Review. https://hbr.org/2014/09/stop-searching-for-that-elusive-data-scientist/

15. Smith, J.W., et al.: Using the ADAP learning algorithm to forecast the onset of diabetes mellitus. In: Proceedings of the Annual Symposium on Computer Application in Medical Care, pp. 261–265, November 1988

16. Sweney, M.: Netflix gathers detailed viewer data to guide its search for the next hit. The Guardian. http://www.theguardian.com/media/2014/feb/23/netflix-viewer-data-house-of-cards

17. de la Vega, A., García-Saiz, D., Zorrilla, M., Sánchez, P.: Towards a DSL for educational data mining. In: Sierra-Rodríguez, J.-L., Leal, J.P., Simões, A. (eds.) SLATE 2015. CCIS, vol. 563, pp. 79–90. Springer, Cham (2015). doi:10.1007/978-3-319-27653-3_8

18. Zorrilla, M., García-Saiz, D.: A service-oriented architecture to provide data mining services for non-expert data miners. Decis. Support Syst. **55**, 399–411 (2013)

Continuous Process Compliance Using Model Driven Engineering

Fahad Rafique Golra[1(✉)], Fabien Dagnat[1], Reda Bendraou[2],
and Antoine Beugnard[1]

[1] IMT Atlantique, IRISA, Université Bretagne Loire, 29238 Brest, France
fahad.golra@imt-atlantique.fr
[2] LIP6/Université Pierre et Marie Curie, Sorbonne Universités, Paris, France

Abstract. Software development methods and standards have existed for decades and the software industry is often expected to follow them, especially when it comes to critical systems. They are of vital importance for establishing a common frame of reference and milestones for software life-cycle planning, development, monitoring and evaluation. However, there is hardly any (semi-)automatic method that ensures the compliance of *de-facto* processes to the adopted *de-jure* standards throughout the development life cycle *i.e.* from specification to enactment. We argue that compliance assurance should be dealt by the process modeling methodologies implicitly to facilitate correct by construction approach for process development. This article presents a framework for modeling software development processes that ensures their continuous compliance to an adopted standard from specification to execution.

1 Introduction

Software development standards define the structure and flow of activities to achieve the objectives efficiently, reduce development risks and promote trust towards external organizations [1]. Compliance of software development processes to these standards is often ensured manually, usually at design time [2]. Different approaches allow translation of design level process models to executable models (*e.g.* [3]). Such approaches can ensure the correctness of a process model for a specific modeling language, but can not guarantee compliance to a process standard. Compliance assessment process is not fully automated because of the way standards are described in a natural language. So it requires considerable human effort to assess compliance to a specific standard. Software development processes are dynamic in nature and often evolve over time. Design time compliance assessment techniques need to be implemented in an active manner, so that all modifications and their repercussions in the process model are evaluated against the standard as the process is being modified.

While some approaches rely on design time assessment of conformance [2], others resort to runtime assessment mechanisms [4,5]. Design time compliance assessment overlooks the possibility of runtime evolution of the processes.

© Springer International Publishing AG 2017
Y. Ouhammou et al. (Eds.): MEDI 2017, LNCS 10563, pp. 42–56, 2017.
DOI: 10.1007/978-3-319-66854-3_4

Whereas runtime assessment gives us a late feedback on the design of the processes being used in the organization. Some artifact based process compliance approaches even wait till the availability of the artifacts to give the feedback as to whether the process is compliant or not [6]. We argue that an approach that can continuously guide a process engineer for the development of processes from design time to their enactment can provide a viable solution for the IT industry. It would solve various issues that arise from using multiple approaches of process compliance assessment in different phases of process development life cycle.

A process modeling approach that separates specification phase process models from their corresponding implementation phase models, seems an interesting base for our approach [7]. As a natural extension to this approach, we have added the process enactment capability. A metamodel for executable process models is defined using a bi-layered approach. In this approach, the modeling elements of a single metamodel are partitioned in two conceptual layers *i.e.* abstract and concrete levels. It defines the modeling elements related to process standards at the abstract level and the ones related to process models at the concrete level. Mappings between the two layers are exploited to realize the notion of compliance to standards. The novelty of our approach is to (1) define a methodology that integrates the compliance requirements of the standards with a process model inside a single model, (2) expand the coverage of process compliance from design till enactment phases of process development life cycle and offer it in a single approach, (3) define a methodology where abstractly specified standards can continuously guide the development and enactment of concrete processes.

The rest of this paper is organized as follows. First, we present the key concepts of process compliance and introduce an running example from our case study in Sect. 2. Then, in Sect. 3, we explain our process modeling approach. In Sect. 4, we describe our methodology for continuous process compliance. Then, Sect. 5 discusses the state of the art in process compliance management. Finally, we conclude this paper in Sect. 6.

2   Process Compliance

Like all other models in MDE, the language for defining *process models* is defined through metamodels. The primary objective of formally specifying processes is their consistent execution to achieve the intended goals. *Process enactment* is the runtime phase for process models, where humans (or tools) carry out the tasks prescribed in them. *Process trace* records the sequence of activities and the artifacts that were created during their execution. This allows an organization to analyze the runtime behavior of a process to assess its quality and propose any improvement for it, if needed. Different standardization organizations and regulatory bodies define a set of minimum norms that need to be followed so that they can assure that a certain process fulfills a degree of soundness. Compliance to *standards* ensures that processes and practices being followed in an organization are in accordance with adopted/agreed set of norms. These standards can be used either to improve the processes being followed by an organization or to evaluate a specific software provider.

5.10.5 Conducting maintenance reviews

5.10.5.1 Maintenance reviews

a. The maintainer shall conduct joint reviews with the organization authorizing the modification to determine the integrity of the modified system.
EXPECTED OUTPUT: Joint review reports.

5.10.5.2 Baseline for change

a. Upon successful completion of the reviews, a baseline for the change shall be established.
EXPECTED OUTPUT: Baseline for changes.

Fig. 1. Sample activity from ECSS-ST-40C Standard [8]

A software provider may adopt a standard either for improving its internal processes or to assure its clients about the soundness of its processes. This assurance to clients is at times mandatory, specially if working for critical software systems. The norms described in a standard affect the way different tasks are carried out in a compliant organization. In this paper, we use a running example of ECSS-ST-40C [8] that extends a widely adopted ISO/IEC standard, 12207:2008 [9]. It is a software development standard for space engineering by European Cooperation for Space Standardization. A software sub-contractor working with European Space Agency (ESA) needs to follow ECSS-ST-40C Standard to provide a space mission software. For example, for conducting a maintenance review, ESA's sub-contractor needs to follow the *Conducting maintenance reviews* activity in *software maintenance process* of the ECSS standard (Sect. 5.10.5 [8]). This activity from the standard, shown in Fig. 1, illustrates that the compliant organization is constrained to ensure some minimum requirements. For example, it must (1) perform maintenance reviews (completeness assessment), (2) allocate a person in charge of these reviews who meets a certain criteria of a maintainer (capability assessment), (3) produce specific artifacts like joint review report and baseline for changes (artifact assessment), and (4) ensure that baseline of changes should be produced after the maintenance reviews (flow assessment).

For a software contractor to show that it is compliant to a specific standard, a *process compliance assessment* must be performed by a recognized body. But before presenting itself for assessment, it needs to make sure that its internal processes are actually in compliance with the adopted standard. Software industry needs a process compliance management approach that can handle the processes in different phases of process life cycle i.e. from design to their enactment and even post-enactment analysis based on process trace. This can be carried out using a mixture of forward and backward assessment approaches [10]. Forward assessment is a pre-emptive approach used either before the execution of the process i.e. design time or during the execution. Backward assessment approaches either use the traces produced by the process enactment or rely on the assessment of the produced artifacts against their specifications.

3   Process Modeling Methodology

We believe that methods and tools should assist process designers to create, manipulate or improve software development processes in a manner that compliance to standards becomes an implicit part of the routine. We have developed a metamodel, that has served as a basis for tool implementations. Figure 2 presents an excerpt from the complete metamodel, which can be consulted here [11]. This metamodel uses two layers of abstraction *i.e.* abstract level and concrete level. The abstract level defines the abstract notions of process design and the concrete level defines the corresponding concrete implementations. It is important to note here that both these layers are conceptual and do not mean that the user needs to develop two different models. This separation of modeling notions in abstract and concrete levels is within a single model. The abstract level suits process standards that are normally defined on the basis of dataflow and do not provide implementations. The user process models are modeled at the concrete level, which provides the modeling notions to deal with concrete implementations of the software development processes. An implementation relationship between the two layers is used to concretize the concepts of compliance. The process model developed using this metamodel can be seen as a single model that captures the structure and behavior of both processes and standards. There is no explicit mapping between the concrete process and the abstract process, because it is implicitly defined through the elements that they contain.

Our metamodel defines a process as an assembly of activities. Processes are inherently hierarchical in nature. This hierarchy is managed through the concept of primitive and composite activities. A composite activity contains a process which gathers a sub-assembly of activities. Whereas a primitive activity specifies or implements the procedure for performing the activity, depending on whether the activity is manual or (semi-)automatic. This hierarchy of activities is defined

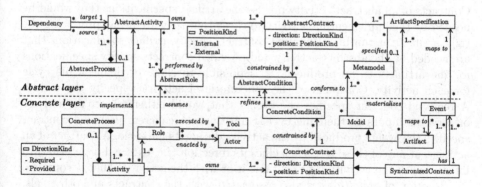

Fig. 2. Fragment of the core metamodel

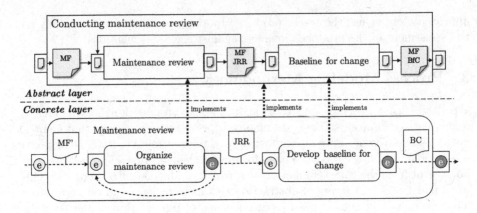

Fig. 3. *Conducting maintenance reviews* activity

both at the abstract level and at the concrete level. *Abstract activities* define the higher level specifications for an activity, much like the ones stated in standards. Abstract activities can not be enacted/executed directly, because they lack the necessary implementation details. *Activities* at the concrete level provide complete implementations of the activity, which makes them enactable (by humans) or executable (by tools). These details pertain to approach, schedule, resource planning, refined milestones, objectives and execution status of the activities during runtime. Figure 3 shows the *conducting maintenance review* abstract activity with both its sub-activities at the abstract level. This activity is implemented by a user process activity, *maintenance review*, at the concrete level. A mapping between an activity of concrete level (*e.g. develop baseline for change*) and the corresponding abstract activity (*baseline for change*) of this process model describes the implementation relationship between them.

Each activity (whether at abstract or concrete level) defines contracts that serve as interfaces for interaction. The notion of *contract* is used to bind the components (activities) using *Design by Contract* [12]. These contracts ensure that all interactions to/from an activity are well-specified and can be monitored. Contracts of an abstract activity precise the artifact specifications that would be needed by the implementing activity to check that they are using/producing the right artifacts at runtime. Required contracts specify artifact specifications that are needed by the abstract activity and provided contracts specify specifications for the artifacts to be produced. It is possible to chose or define a life cycle for each activity. Contracts of the concrete level activities specify the events. A required contract specifies the events that would either trigger an activity or serve as inputs to their life cycle transitions. A concrete provided contract specifies the events produced by the activity during its life cycle. A contract of an activity, at any of these levels, specifies its direction (*i.e.* external or internal) to interact with the activity that contains it or with the activities that it contains.

A notion of *conditions* is also associated with the contracts at both levels. This serves for specifying the pre/post conditions associated with an activity.

Defining conditions at both levels allows the refinement of conditions specified at the abstract level. Various software standards specify these conditions for the activities, which can be translated to the conditions at the abstract level. This refinement of conditions at the concrete level provides the possibility to further constrain the interactions of a specific implementation of an abstract activity.

Dependencies between the abstract activities are explicitly defined, because the processes specified in the standards are generally based on the concept of flow between the activities. This flow is usually implicitly defined in standards, where the artifacts produced by one activity are required by the next. We capture this data-flow through the concept of dependencies and artifact specifications provided by the contracts at the abstract level. Some standards are very specific about the artifacts being produced and go as far as pointing to a metamodel, in case the produced artifact is a model. We treat every artifact in our approach as model, whether its metamodel is explicitly defined or not. For example, a document file (*e.g.* docx) does not seem to have a metamodel, but the XML based structure of that document is indeed defined by an implicit metamodel. Activities at the concrete level do not specify this dependency because they are implemented using an event management system. Activities are responsible for creating artifacts at the concrete level, but they specify events in their contracts to notify other activities that they have for example, produced an artifact. We try to capture the control flow of the process during runtime at the concrete level, which is constrained by the data flow specified at the abstract level.

Software standards usually specify a role that is responsible for performing each assigned activity. We translate the role described by the standard as *abstract role* at the abstract level in our metamodel. This abstract role is also refined to the concrete level as *role*. A concrete level role is described by the process model, which depends on the *work breakdown structure* of the compliant organization. Their roles might not be the same as that of a specific standard, because they might be following multiple standards. The role defined in the process model is constrained by the abstract role for its capabilities. This role in the process model can either be played by an actor (human agent) or a tool (software agent), depending on the nature of the activity.

4   Continuous Process Compliance

We propose continuous process compliance through the use of correct by construction approach that we call *compliance by construction*. It allows to guarantee compliance from the process design time till their monitoring and even during the runtime evolution. To implement this vision, we opted for the development of reference standard models from existing process standards. One important aspect of our methodology is to integrate the modeling elements of this reference process standard in the user process models. A process standard is translated into the abstract level of a process model only once for each standard. This partial process model is then reused multiple times for the development of process models that need to be compliant with this standard.

Each activity in a process has two facets: its static structure and its dynamic behavior. The structure of an activity is defined by its associated roles, properties[1], objectives (see footnote 1), *etc.*, whereas the behavior through its corresponding states and outputs to various conditions and inputs (see footnote 1). The behavior helps in deciding the execution sequence of activities, which may be guided by data (required or produced artifacts) or control (execution dependencies). Continuous process compliance takes both structural and behavioral facets of the process and maps the corresponding notions by associating the elements of the concrete level activities to that of abstract activities (where process standards are specified). The mapping between the modeling elements of the two levels is carried out at the design time. While the abstract level of the model remains the same, the concrete level of the process model is transformed to get the runtime process model used for process enactment. During process enactment, the mapping between the two levels help in ensuring runtime compliance to process standards.

4.1   Design-Time Compliance Management

A process model is developed by reusing an already developed partial process model from an adopted process standard at the abstract level (Sect. 3). This partial process model is then enriched with the defined processes of the compliant organization. The constructs of the standard model are accessible to this process model during the development, which are used for developing a compliant process. This form of compliance, ensured at the development phase of process life cycle, is called the design-time compliance management in our methodology. For design-time compliance, we exploit the mappings between the concrete and abstract levels of our process metamodel to perform consistent checks concerning compliance of contracts, capacity and hierarchy of activities.

Contractual Compliance: For making an activity compliant to its corresponding abstract activity, we need to ensure compliance between their contracts. A contract of abstract activity consists of artifact specifications and a contract of concrete level activity contains events (Sect. 3). The contractual compliance between them is ensured using following assessments.

– *Interface assessment:* Generally, the standards define the input and output artifacts of the activities that are placed in a sequence/flow such that a later activity uses the artifact(s) produced by the former activities. For standards translated at the abstract level of the model, these interactions between the abstract activities are realized through artifact specifications. However the activities from the user process model either produce or listen to events, through their contracts. So the compliance of interfaces for an activity is to ensure that the events produced and listened by it are compliant to the artifact specifications of the corresponding abstract activity. A state machine

---

[1] Concepts not included in the excerpt of metamodel are accessible here [11].

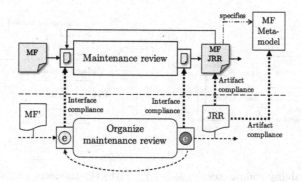

Fig. 4. Contractual compliance

related to each artifact specification is available in the abstract contract. In our example, shown in Fig. 4, the *maintenance review* abstract activity from the standard is implemented by *organize maintenance review* activity in the user process model. The required contract of the concrete level activity listens to the events related to *maintenance file*. The process designer may choose to trigger this activity with an event that confirms the availability of maintenance file. The execution of this activity should produce the *joint review report* at runtime. On creation of this artifact, *organize maintenance review* activity fires an event, which could be used by subsequent activities. In this scenario, the process designer should make sure that this activity would listen for an event compliant to *maintenance file* and produce an event compliant to *joint review report*. Following checks are needed to ensure the contractual compliance between the concrete and abstract activities.

1. The *required events* of the concrete activity are a subset of events specified in the required artifact state machine.
2. The events specified in the provided artifact state machine are a subset of the *provided events* of the concrete activity.

– *Artifact assessment:* Standards define the input and output artifacts of their activities through artifact specifications. This difference between the artifact and its specification is important in our methodology. The artifact specification is modeled at the abstract level, whereas the actual artifact at the concrete level. We consider each artifact as a model that conforms to its metamodel. Sometimes the metamodel of an artifact is implicit. When the metamodel is explicit, the artifact specification points to it. In such a case, (artifact) model can be checked against the metamodel to verify its structure and properties, using existing model checking techniques. In our example, as shown in Fig. 4, the *joint review report* produced by the *organize maintenace review* activity is checked against its specification (*MF JRR*). The standard does not provide a metamodel in our example, but in case it did, *joint review report* would have to be checked against it as well.

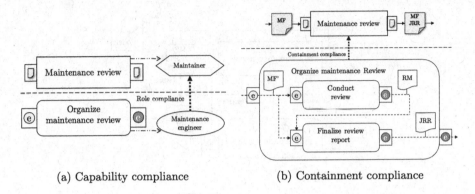

(a) Capability compliance   (b) Containment compliance

Fig. 5. Capability and containment

Capability Compliance: Activities specified in the standard are associated to the abstract roles that perform them. An abstract role is a set of capabilities that are required from the person, team or tool performing a specific activity. Software vendors normally define their own roles, according to their particular team structures. The mapping between the role at concrete level and the abstract role is translated as a *responsibility assignment matrix (RAM)*. This matrix ensures that the concrete level role complies with all the capability requirements specified by the standard. In our example, the ECSS standard defines a *maintainer* abstract role, as shown in Fig. 5a. The concrete role that is responsible for performing the compliant activity is *maintenance engineer*. The mapping between the maintenance engineer and the maintainer is translated to the RAM, which maps each capability of the concrete level role to the abstract role.

Containment Compliance: Each activity realizes a given abstract activity. A process designer adds the implementation details to an activity during its development while maintaining its compliance to the corresponding abstract activity. Adding these implementations can either involve enriching the activity directly or making it a composite activity, hence adding further activities deep in its hierarchy. The milestones set by an abstract activity are further refined in the concrete level activity. This refinement can introduce intermediate goals that can be set as objectives for the sub-activities, when implemented as a composite activity. Figure 5b shows the *maintenance review* abstract activity from our example. It is implemented by *organize maintenance review* composite activity containing two sub-activities: *conduct review* and *finalize review report*. For *organize maintenance review* activity to remain compliant to its abstract activity, its sub-activities have to respect the compliance as well. Our metamodel (Sect. 3) defines a *position* and a *direction* for every contract. *Organize maintenance review* activity listens to the required events from its *external required contract*. Once an event triggers the activity, it is passed on to the sub-activities through its *internal provided contract*. The sub-activities produce the planned artifacts and fire the concerned events, which are moved up in the hierarchy in the same fashion. Containment compliance ensures both the contractual and capability compliance for the contained activities. Contractual compliance is assured when:

1. The events required by the sub-activities are a subset of events provided by the *internal provided contract* of the parent activity.
2. The events required by the *internal required contract* of the parent activity are a subset of events fired by the sub-activities.

Capability compliance is assured in the hierarchy, by automatically associating the role of parent activity to the roles of sub-activities. It is important to note that multiple roles can be associated with an activity. The role who performs an activity can be different from the role who supervises it.

4.2   Runtime Compliance Management

Runtime assurance of compliance depends on the state of the user defined process during its enactment. The state of a process is defined by the collective state of all the activities that it contains. The state of a particular activity depends on its defined state machine and the events that it has consumed at a particular time. When an activity changes its state, it can fire events that can be consumed by other activities. In this event-based enactment paradigm for the processes, the compliance of a user process to a standard at runtime is assessed though the compliance of flow, conditions, traceability, completeness and capacity.

Flow Compliance: Processes are defined as a (partially) ordered set of activities. The order of activities is due to the dependence of certain activities over others, which comes from the handshake of data, artifacts or control. The order in which the activities are enacted in a user process model needs to conform to the standard. A compliant order of enactment for the activities is ensured through the runtime assessment of data-flow and control-flow of the process.

– *Data-flow assessment:* In a process standard, activities are defined in a sequence such that the artifacts produced by an activity are required by the following activities. This dependence of one activity over another, based on the artifacts, is captured at the abstract level of our process model through the notion of *contract* and *dependency*. The contracts at the abstract level of the process model require and provide *artifact specifications*. When an abstract activity (of standard process) requires the artifact specification that is produced by another, this dependence is explicitly stated by the use of *dependency* (Sect. 3). However, the user process model uses an event driven paradigm for enactment. Events at the concrete level map to the artifact specifications. A data-flow dependence between two activities translates to the events through the mappings between events and artifact specifications. In our example, shown in Fig. 6a, once the *organize maintenance review (OMR)* activity starts its execution, event related to *joint review report (JRR)* can be fired. However, events that map to *maintenance file (MF)* can not be

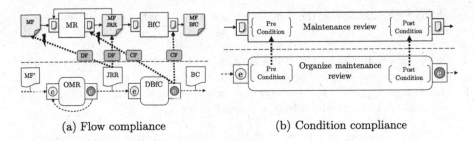

(a) Flow compliance   (b) Condition compliance

Fig. 6. Flow and condition compliance

fired anymore. OMR activity allows multiple iterations, but the subsequent executions also require events related to JRR.

– *Control-flow assessment:* Some activities are only meant to execute some operations without creating an artifact. For such activities, if their order of execution is not constrained by the standard, the event-driven paradigm allows a reactive mechanism to order them according to the execution state of the process. In case, they are constrained by the standard, compliance becomes mandatory. In this case, the events use the notion of *dependency* at the abstract level to order the execution sequence. In our example, in Fig. 6a, the dependence of *develop baseline for change (DBfC)* activity on OMR is dictated by data-flow, however the control-flow decides the number of iterations for OMR and subsequent transfer of control to DBfC.

Conditions Compliance: Apart from specifying the input and output artifacts of an activity, process standards can also constrain them by specifying pre and post conditions. These conditions are translated into the *abstract condition* at the abstract level of our metamodel[2]. Conditions specified at the concrete level of the model are the refinement of the abstract conditions. The mapping between the conditions of *organize maintenance review* and *maintenance review* shows their refinement in Fig. 6b. For the user process model to be compliant with the standard, all abstract conditions should be implemented at the concrete level. Concrete conditions may further constrain the user activities based on their specific implementation details, however they can not relax the conditions.

Traceability Compliance: The runtime compliance management uses the execution trace of the process model for the following assessments.

– *Traceability assessment:* Contrary to other approaches, our approach incorporates the modeling elements of the standards at the abstract level of the model and the user process maps to them at design time. Modeling elements of the standard don't execute at runtime, however user process activities can

---

[2] Conditions are further refined into pre and post conditions in the metamodel [11].

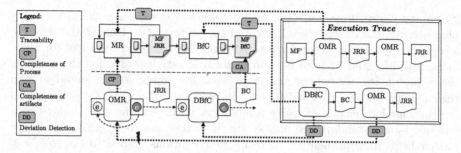

Fig. 7. Traceability and completeness compliance

trace back to them. This allows to evolve the user process in a compliant manner, even during the runtime. In our example, shown in Fig. 7, a traceability link is maintained between *OMR* and *MR*. During the execution of the process, *OMR* activity can be replaced by *OMR'*. However, for the user process to stay compliant, *OMR'* needs to follow the design time compliance assessments *i.e.* contractual, capability and containment compliance.

– *Deviation Detection:* The traceability links allow to map the runtime process to the adopted standard. The runtime order of execution for the activities is generated using a set of execution constraints from the specific runtime conditions (execution history of activities through process trace) and the defined dependencies. A constraint analyzer detects the any violated constraints if the process enactment deviates from the defined process. In our example, shown in Fig. 7, lets imagine a case where the project manager wants to re-enact OMR after the execution of DBfC, because he is not satisfied with the results. This is contrary to the defined process. A violated constraint in this case may put the compliance of runtime user process to the adopted standard at risk. Thus runtime deviation detection triggers the design-time compliance assessment for the modified part of the process before the actual execution of the forced deviation. Then it helps user to pinpoint the exact conflicts by stating which constraints will be violated by this specific user decision. In this case, the user is notified that the order of execution of OMR and DBfC is against the adopted standard.

Completeness Compliance: Compliance to a standard is not ensured, unless the user process guarantees to execute all the activities defined by the standard. The mappings between the user process elements and the elements of the standard, established at design-time, help ensure the completeness of compliance at runtime. Figure 7 shows the mappings from the activities (*OMR*) to the abstract activities (*MR*) and artifacts (*BC*) to the artifact specifications (*MF BfC*). These mappings are used for a continual runtime assessment for process enactment. For a compliant user process, it needs to guarantee that at least one concrete activity is enacted for each abstract activity of the process standard.

Capacity Compliance: *Capability compliance* at design time checks the mapping between the concrete level *role* and the *abstract role*. Role at the concrete level is enacted by an *actor* for manual activities, executed by a *tool* for automatic activities and by both for semi-automatic activities. During the runtime, the *responsibility assignment matrix* of capability compliance is reused to map the competences of actors and tools to the corresponding role. These mappings are then used to ensure capacity compliance, such that the competences constrained by the standard are fulfilled by the actors and tools. This compliance further helps in implementing the concrete conditions related to the roles *e.g.* two activities X and Y can not be enacted by the same maintenance engineer.

5   Related Work

With process standards becoming increasingly popular as a mean to guarantee the quality of a software deliverable, we see multiple approaches that deal with the challenges of compliance assessment for user processes to the adopted standards. We classify these approaches in three categories: rule-based, artifact-based and reference model based approaches. Rule based approaches include multiple proposals for formal modeling of business rules both by academia (*e.g.* [5,10]) and industry (e.g. ILOG by IBM). A closely related approach models control objectives for monitoring the execution behavior of the user processes [2]. These approaches focus on the backward assessment of the process model, hence even if they detect noncompliance in some part of the process, that part needs to be re-modeled and re-enacted. They do not offer any support during the initial development phases of the process models.

Out of different approaches that assure compliance management for process models, there are some that offer artifact based compliance [6]. They model the deliverables expected from the activities by a standard. Then the artifacts developed by the user process model are verified against the expected deliverables (artifact specifications). Just like rule-based approaches, the problem is that the artifacts are produced late in a project. In case of noncompliance, the process needs to be modified and considerable effort of process design and execution is wasted. Having the compliance assured at design time, we use this kind of compliance as a secondary assessment method for the quality control of the artifacts. Reference model based approaches develop a reference model from the adopted standard [13,14]. They use different model checking approaches for assessing the compliance of the user process against the developed reference model. These approaches are closest to our methodology, as we also model the constructs of a given software process standard. However, we do not translate the standard as a different model, we put its constructs within the process model at an abstract level. This allows us to support compliance not only in design and development phases, but all along the process development life cycle.

A limitation of our approach is that modeling elements of the abstract model (process standard) becomes part of the user process model. Even though it offers the benefits of active compliance assessment, it makes the process model 'heavier'. It might seem as combining the concepts from both process standard and the user process in a single model might make the development of process models even more complex. Actually, an already modeled process standard serves as a partial model for developing any process model that needs to comply with that standard. Our prototype guides the user through process development using the modeling elements of the process standard. Hence the effort for the development of a process model is in fact reduced.

6 Conclusion

We have presented a model driven approach to continuous process compliance for a complete coverage of process development life cycle. We proposed a methodology for modeling the constructs of a user process model and a given standard in a single process model. Constructs from the user process and the standard are modeled in two different levels within this model. We create mappings between these two abstraction levels and use them to ensure compliance of the user process model to an adopted standard. This compliance is assessed both at design time and at the runtime. At design time, we concentrate on the structural elements of the process model, whereas at runtime, we focus on constraining its execution behavior according to the compliance requirements of the standard. Hence we provide an overall methodology for the development of process models using compliance by construction and then verify the compliance during the runtime. The current prototype implementation of our methodology supports a single standard for the moment. We are working towards the compliance of a user process model to multiple standards simultaneously. Our vision is to provide a methodology where software vendors can define their processes in an intuitive way and compliance to the quality standards becomes part of this routine.

References

1. Wüllenweber, K., Beimborn, D., Weitzel, T., König, W.: The impact of process standardization on business process outsourcing success. Inf. Syst. Front. **10**(2), 211–224 (2008). doi:10.1007/s10796-008-9063-x
2. Sadiq, S., Governatori, G., Namiri, K.: Modeling control objectives for business process compliance. In: Alonso, G., Dadam, P., Rosemann, M. (eds.) BPM 2007. LNCS, vol. 4714, pp. 149–164. Springer, Heidelberg (2007). doi:10.1007/978-3-540-75183-0_12
3. Ouyang, C., Dumas, M., Breutel, S., ter Hofstede, A.: Translating standard process models to BPEL. In: Dubois, E., Pohl, K. (eds.) CAiSE 2006. LNCS, vol. 4001, pp. 417–432. Springer, Heidelberg (2006). doi:10.1007/11767138_28
4. El Kharbili, M., Stein, S., Pulvermüller, E.: Policy-based semantic compliance checking for business process management. In: MobIS Workshops, vol. 420, pp. 178–192. Citeseer (2008)
5. Rozinat, A., van der Aalst, W.M.P.: Conformance checking of processes based on monitoring real behavior. Inf. Syst. **33**(1), 64–95 (2008)
6. Emmerich, W., Finkelstein, A., Montangero, C., Antonelli, S., Armitage, S., Stevens, R.: Managing standards compliance. IEEE Trans. Softw. Eng. **25**(6), 836–851 (1999)

7. Golra, F.R., Dagnat, F.: Generation of dynamic process models for multi-metamodel applications. In: 2012 International Conference on Software and System Process (ICSSP), pp. 48–57. IEEE, June 2012
8. ECSS, Requirements & Standards Division: Space Engineering - Software, ECSS-E-ST-40C (2009)
9. ISO/IEC: Systems and Software Engineering - Software Life Cycle Processes, ISO/IEC 12207, IEEE Std 12207-2008 (2008)
10. El Kharbili, M., Stein, S., Markovic, I., Pulvermüller, E.: Towards a framework for semantic business process compliance management. In: Proceedings of GRCIS (2008)
11. Golra, F.R.: A refinement based methodology for software process modeling. Ph.D. thesis, Télécom Bretagne, Université de Rennes 1 (2014)
12. Meyer, B.: Applying 'design by contract'. Computer **25**(10), 40–51 (1992)
13. Chung, P.W., Cheung, L.Y., Machin, C.H.: Compliance flow - managing the compliance of dynamic and complex processes. Knowl.-Based Syst. **21**(4), 332–354 (2008)
14. Panesar-Walawege, R., Sabetzadeh, M., Briand, L.: A model-driven engineering approach to support the verification of compliance to safety standards. In: 22nd International Symposium on Software Reliability Engineering (ISSRE), pp. 30–39, November 2011

An Approach to Automated Two-Phase Business Model-Driven Synthesis of Data Models

Drazen Brdjanin[(✉)], Danijela Banjac, Goran Banjac, and Slavko Maric

University of Banja Luka, Patre 5, 78 000 Banja Luka, Bosnia and Herzegovina
{drazen.brdjanin,danijela.banjac,goran.banjac,slavko.maric}@etf.unibl.org

Abstract. The paper proposes an approach to automated two-phase business model-driven synthesis of the conceptual database model. Unlike the existing approaches, which are characterised by the direct synthesis of the target model based on business process models represented by concrete notations (e.g. BPMN or UML activity diagram), the proposed approach is characterised by the introduction of a domain specific language (DSL) as an intermediate between different concrete business modelling notations and the target data modelling notation. Thus, the data model synthesis is split into two phases: (i) extraction of specific concepts from the source business process model and their DSL-based representation, and (ii) automated generation of the target data model based on the DSL-based representation of the extracted concepts. Such an indirect approach could simplify the target data model synthesis and facilitate modifications of the required generator, since all synthesis rules are implemented by one generator that is independent of different source notations in contrast to the existing approaches that require different generators for each source business modelling notation.

Keywords: Activity diagram · Business process model · BPMN · Class diagram · Data model · DSL · Model-driven · Synthesis · UML

1 Introduction

Data models are essential to any information system. The process of data modelling is not straightforward. It is often time consuming and requires many iterations before the final model is obtained. Therefore, automatic synthesis of data models is very appealing and has been the subject of research for many years. Although the idea of model-driven synthesis of data models (MDSDM) is almost 30 years old, surveys [6,21] show that only a small number of papers present the implemented automatic model-driven generator of the data model.

The existing MDSDM approaches are characterised by the direct synthesis (Fig. 1 left) of the data model based on business process models (BPMs) represented by concrete notations such as BPMN [16] or UML activity diagram [17]. The direct synthesis introduces dependency of the generation process from the source notation, because different source notations require different generators.

© Springer International Publishing AG 2017
Y. Ouhammou et al. (Eds.): MEDI 2017, LNCS 10563, pp. 57–70, 2017.
DOI: 10.1007/978-3-319-66854-3_5

Furthermore, these generators depend on changes of notations, which are caused by metamodel changes and/or vendor specific implementations as well.

In this paper we propose an approach that enables automated synthesis of the conceptual database model (CDM) independently of different source BPM notations. We identified concepts that are common for BPMs (objects, participants, tasks, etc.), which have the semantic potential that enables the automated CDM synthesis. Based on the identified semantic potential, a domain specific language (DSL) called *Business Model Representation Language* (BMRL) is defined for the representation of those characteristic BPM concepts. With the introduction of BMRL, the CDM synthesis is split into two phases (Fig. 1 right). In the first phase, specific concepts are to be extracted from the source BPM and represented by BMRL. Such an extraction can be easily implemented for different BPM notations. In this paper we use two different BPM extractors (one for BPMN and another for UML activity diagram). In the second phase, the target CDM is to be generated based on the BMRL-based representation of the extracted concepts. This generator is to implement a rather complex set of rules, which are dependent of simple and unique BMRL concepts, but independent of different source BPM notations. If some modifications of the generation rules are necessary, then only this generator is to be modified. Therefore, the introduction of a DSL could facilitate the modifications of the required tools and simplify the target CDM synthesis.

The paper is structured as follows. After the introduction, the second section presents the related work. The proposed approach for the two-phase business-model driven synthesis of the CDM is elaborated in the subsequent sections. The third section presents the semantic capacity of BPMs for the automatic CDM synthesis. The first phase of the CDM synthesis is discussed in the fourth section, while the second phase is analysed in the fifth section. The final section concludes the paper.

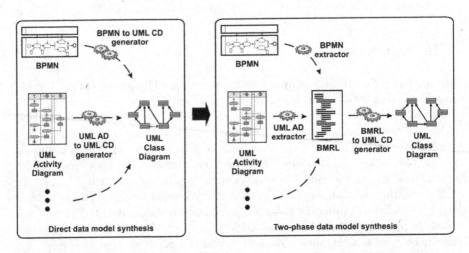

Fig. 1. Transition from direct (one-phase) to two-phase data model synthesis

2   Related Work

The survey [6] shows that the current MDSDM approaches can be classified as: *function-oriented*, *process-oriented*, *communication-oriented*, and *goal-oriented*. Process-oriented models (POMs) constitute the largest category of models used as a source for MDSDM. Although the first data model synthesis based on a POM (A-graph) was proposed by Wrycza [23] in 1990, the boom of these approaches was influenced by the development of metamodel-based notations, particularly UML activity diagram and BPMN, as well as model-to-model (M2M) transformation languages ATL [13] and QVT [15].

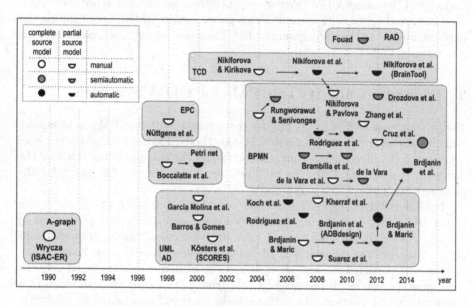

Fig. 2. Overview of POM-based approaches for MDSDM

The survey [6] shows that POMs, used as a basis for data model synthesis, have been represented by seven different notations: UML activity diagram, BPMN, GRAPES-BM/TCD, Petri Net, RAD (Role Activity Diagram), EPC (Event-driven Process Chain) and A-graph. Although there are more than 35 papers considering POMs as a source for the MDSDM (due to the paper length restrictions, those approaches are shown in Fig. 2, while the complete overview can be found in [6]), the survey shows that the semantic capacity of POMs has still not been sufficiently identified to enable automatic synthesis of the complete target data model. Furthermore, the majority of the approaches enable (semi)automated generation of the target model with modest *recall* (automatically generated percentage of the target model) and *precision* (measure showing the percentage of correct automatically generated concepts).

The majority of all POM-based approaches are based on guidelines and informal rules that do not enable automated MDSDM. The formal rules that enable automated MDSDM are presented in [5,8,9], and partially in [11,12,14,18–20]. The large majority of all proposals are based on an incomplete source model, i.e. single diagram, although a real model contains a finite set of diagrams. Only three papers [9,12,23] take the complete source model as the basis for MDSDM.

The first set of formal rules for automatic synthesis of the initial CDM based on UML activity diagrams was initially proposed in [5], and thereafter extended [8] to cover automatic CDM synthesis based on collaborative BPMs represented by BPMN. We additionally improved this set based on experiences gained in two controlled experiments [4,7]. The results of the experiments [4,7] imply that the specified transformation rules enable the automated generation of the majority of the target CDM (average completeness and precision are over 80%). This improved set of rules is used in this paper for the BMRL specification and implementation of the corresponding BPM extractors and UML class diagram generator as well.

3   Semantic Capacity of BPMs for CDM Synthesis

The previous research [4,5,7,8] implies that several common BPM concepts have semantic capacity for the automatic CDM synthesis. This section provides a brief overview of the identified semantic capacity and the corresponding rules for the direct automatic MDSDM (Fig. 3). They constitute the starting point for the proposed two-phase CDM synthesis.

Typical BPM concepts that enable automatic generation of classes in the target CDM are: *participants, roles, objects, message flows,* and *activations of existing objects.* Participants (may) have different roles. Participants and their roles are represented differently in BPMs (pools/lanes, partitions/subpartitions). All types of participants, and all their roles as well, are to be mapped into the corresponding classes in the target CDM (rule T_1). During the execution of a business process, participants perform tasks (actions) and exchange messages. Each different type of objects, and message flows as well, is to be mapped into the corresponding class in the target CDM (T_2). Each task/action may have a number of input and output objects that can be in different states. The objects can be *generated* in the given process, or *existing* – created in some other process. An activation represents the fact that some existing object constitutes the input in a task that changes its state. Activated objects have the semantics similar to that of generated objects and need to be represented with a corresponding class (activation class) (T_3).

There are several common patterns in BPMs, which enable automatic generation of associations in the target CDM. They enable generation of three types of associations: *participant-participant, participant-object,* and *object-object. Participant-participant* associations originate from the fact that a participant may have different roles. This implies that the class representing a pool should have associations with classes representing corresponding lanes (T_4). Process patterns having semantic potential for the generation of *participant-object* associations are: creation and subsequent usage of generated objects (T_5), exchange of messages (T_6), and activation and subsequent usage of activated objects (T_7). Every mentioned fact is to be represented by corresponding association(s) with multiplicities 1:* or 0..1:*. There are two bases for the generation of *object-object* associations: (i) activation (T_8), which is represented with an association between the class that represents the existing object and the class that represents its activation, and (ii) tasks having input and output objects of different types (T_9), where the association end multiplicities depend on the nature of the objects (if they are generated, non-activated existing or activated existing objects).

4   Phase I: DSL-Based Representation of BPM Concepts

The first phase of the data model synthesis includes the extraction of important concepts from the source BPM and their DSL-based representation. In this section we present: specification of the implemented DSL, and implementation of BPM extractors.

4.1   DSL Specification

DSL is a computer programming language of limited expressiveness focusing on a particular domain. Programming languages, including DSLs, consist of three main elements: concrete syntax, abstract syntax and semantics [22]. The concrete syntax defines the notation with which users can express programs (it may be textual, graphical, tabular or combined). The abstract syntax is a data structure that can hold the semantically relevant information expressed by a program (most often represented like a tree or graph). There are two kinds of semantics. The static semantics is defined by the set of constraints and/or type system rules to which programs have to conform, while the execution semantics refers to the meaning of a program once it is executed [22].

Based on the identified semantic capacity of BPMs for MDSDM, we implemented a DSL named *Business Model Representation Language* (BMRL). For its specification we used Xtext [3] framework. Xtext belongs to parser-based approaches, in which a grammar specifies the sequence of tokens that forms structurally valid programs. In such systems, users interact only with the concrete syntax, while the abstract syntax tree (AST) is constructed from the concrete syntax of a program [22]. Xtext relies on Eclipse Modeling Framework (EMF) [10] models for internal AST representation.

The grammar used for the BMRL specification is shown in Fig. 4, while the Ecore metamodel of the implemented language is shown in Fig. 5. A BMRL program contains an arbitrary number of abstract elements (AbstractElement): PackageDeclaration, Import, Object, ObjectReference, IOObjectReference, Task and GeneralizedParticipant. Each business process participant can be represented by the Participant element. Participants can have roles (Role), and each role can have subroles. The Participant and

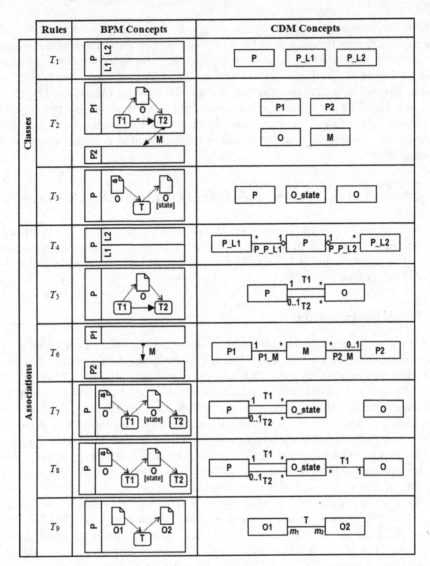

Fig. 3. Mapping of BPM concepts into CDM concepts

Role elements have the name attribute. Participants (or participants with specified roles) perform tasks (Task). The Task element has the name attribute. Also, each task can have inputs and outputs which are represented by input/output specification elements (IOObjectReference). Each different type of object is represented by the Object element. For each object type, one or more references (ObjectReference) can be specified, since objects can be in different states (represented by the state attribute). The fact whether the given reference represents a reference to an object generated in the given BPM, or reference to an existing object, is denoted by the `existing` attribute. The `IOObjectReference` references one of the `ObjectReference` elements and specifies its multiplicity. BMRL supports the use of packages (`PackageDeclaration`) and imports (`Import`) in order to avoid name clashes.

```
grammar org.unibl.etf.BMRL with org.eclipse.xtext.common.Terminals
generate bMRL "http://www.etf.unibl.org/bmrl2cd/BMRL"
Model:
    (elements+=AbstractElement)*;
PackageDeclaration:
    'package' name=QualifiedName '{' (elements+=AbstractElement)* '}';
AbstractElement:
    PackageDeclaration | Import | GeneralizedParticipant | Object |
    ObjectReference | Task;
QualifiedName:
    ID ('.' ID)*;
Import:
    'import' importedNamespace=QualifiedNameWithWildcard;
QualifiedNameWithWildcard:
    QualifiedName '.*'?;
GeneralizedParticipant:
    Participant | Role;
Participant:
    'participant' name=ID;
Role:
    'role' name=ID ('(' superRole=[Role|QualifiedName] ')' | 'of'
            participant=[Participant|QualifiedName]);
Object:
    'object' name=ID;
ObjectReference:
    'objectReference' name=ID 'references' object=[Object|QualifiedName]
                    ('[' state=ID ']')? (existing?='existing')?;
IOObjectReference:
    reference=[ObjectReference|QualifiedName]
                'multiplicity' multiplicity=Multiplicity;
Task:
    'task' name=ID '{'
    'actor' ':' actor=[GeneralizedParticipant|QualifiedName]
    ('input' '(inputObjects+=IOObjectReference)* '}')?
    ('output' '{' (outputObjects+=IOObjectReference)* '}')? '}';
Multiplicity:
    INT | '-1';
```

Fig. 4. BMRL grammar

4.2 BPM Extractors

As previously described, the first phase includes the extraction of important concepts from the source BPM and their representation according to the implemented DSL. This extraction and generation of the corresponding BMRL code can be implemented in different ways, either by using general purpose or specialized transformation languages.

We used Acceleo [1] for the implementation of extractors. Up to now, we implemented two extractors – one for BPMN and another one for UML activity diagrams. Due to the paper length restrictions, we provide only the rules

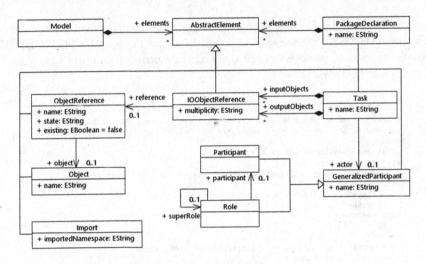

Fig. 5. BMRL metamodel

Table 1. Rules for extraction of BPM concepts from UML activity diagrams and their BMRL representation

Source concept in AD	Target BMRL concept
`ap:ActivityPartition`	`p:Participant` `    {p.name=ap.name}`
`sp:ActivityPartition` `    {sp=ap.subpartition}`	`r:Role` `    {r.name=sp.name ∧ r.participant=p}`

`on:CentralBufferNode`
`    {¬isEmpty(on.incoming)}`
	`o:Object`
	`    {o.name=on.name}`
	`or:ObjectReference`
	`    {or.object=o ∧ or.existing=false ∧`
	`    or.name=concat(on.name,on.inState.name) ∧`
	`    or.state=on.inState.name}`

`on:CentralBufferNode`
`    {isEmpty(on.incoming)}`
	`o:Object`
	`    {o.name=on.name}`
	`or:ObjectReference`
	`    {or.object=o ∧ or.existing=true ∧`
	`    or.name=concat('Existing',on.name,on.inState.name) ∧`
	`    or.state=on.inState.name}`

`oa:OpaqueAction`
`    {¬isEmpty(oa.incoming) ∨`
`    ¬isEmpty(oa.outgoing)}`
	`t:Task`
	`    {t.name=oa.name ∧`
	`    t.actor=GeneralizedParticipant(oa.inPartition.name) ∧`
	`    t.inputObjects=ioo:IOObjectReference[0..*]`
	`        {ioo.reference=ObjectReference(oa.incoming.source.name)`
	`        ∧ ioo.multiplicity=oa.incoming.weight} ∧`
	`    t.outputObjects=ioo:IOObjectReference[0..*]`
	`        {ioo.reference=ObjectReference(oa.outgoing.target.name)`
	`        ∧ ioo.multiplicity=oa.outgoing.weight}}`

for the extraction of concepts from UML activity diagrams and their BMRL-based representation (Table 1). This simple set of rules enables the extraction of: participants and their roles, generated and existing objects, as well as actions

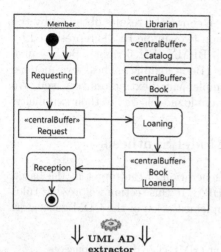

<table>
<tr><td>

```
participant Librarian
participant Member
object Book
object Request
object Catalog
objectReference ExistingCatalog_
    references Catalog existing
objectReference ExistingBook_
    references Book existing
objectReference Request_
    references Request
objectReference Book_Loaned
    references Book[Loaned]
task Requesting {
  actor: Member
  input { ExistingCatalog_ multiplicity 1 }
  output { Request_ multiplicity 1 } }
task Loaning {
  actor: Librarian
  input { ExistingBook_ multiplicity 1
          Request_ multiplicity 1 }
  output { Book_Loaned multiplicity 1 } }
task Reception {
  actor: Member
  input { Book_Loaned multiplicity 1 }
  output { } }
```

</td><td>

```
participant Librarian
participant Member
object Book
object Request
object Catalog
objectReference ExistingBook_
    references Book existing
objectReference ExistingCatalog_
    references Catalog existing
objectReference Book_
    references Book
objectReference Request_
    references Request
objectReference Book_Loaned
    references Book[Loaned]
objectReference Request_Received
    references Request[Received]
task Loaning {
    actor: Librarian
    input { ExistingBook_ multiplicity 1
            Request_Received multiplicity 1 }
    output { Book_Loaned multiplicity 1 } }
task Issuing {
    actor: Librarian
    input { Book_Loaned multiplicity 1 }
    output { Book_ multiplicity 1 } }
task Requesting {
    actor: Member
    input { ExistingCatalog_ multiplicity 1 }
    output { Request_ multiplicity 1 } }
task Reception {
    actor: Member
    input { Book_ multiplicity 1 }
    output { } }
task ReceiveMessage_Request {
    actor: Librarian
    input { Request_ multiplicity 1 }
    output { } }
```

</td></tr>
</table>

Fig. 6. BMRL representation of sample BPMs: UML AD (left) and BPMN (right)

having input and/or output objects. Figure 6 shows the results obtained by the applications of the implemented extractors on two simple BPMs represented by the UML activity diagram (Fig. 6 left) and BPMN (Fig. 6 right). Both source models represent the same business process (Book loaning). These two models, simple though they may be, illustrate the implemented extractors very well. We have omitted a detailed description of the sample models due to their simplicity.

5   Phase II: DSL-Based Data Model Synthesis

The second phase includes the automatic generation of the target model based on the BMRL representation of the source BPM. In this section we present: rules for the automatic CDM generation, and implementation of the CDM generator.

Table 2. Mapping of BMRL concepts into UML class diagram concepts

Source BMRL concepts	Target UML CD concepts	Rules
`p:Participant`	`ep:Class` `{ep.name=p.name}`	T_1
`r:Role` `{r.participant=p}`	`er:Class` `{er.name=concat(r.participant.name,r.name)}`	T_1

	`rpr:Association`
	`{rpr.name=concat(r.participant.name,er.name) ∧`
	`rpr.memberEnd.source=ep ∧`
	`multiplicity(rpr.memberEnd.source)=1 ∧`
	`rpr.memberEnd.target=er ∧`
	`multiplicity(rpr.memberEnd.target)=*}`
		T_4

`o:Object`	`eo:Class` `{eo.name=o.name}`	T_2

`t:Task,`
`in:IOObjectReference[0..*],`
`out:IOObjectReference[0..*]`
`{in=t.inputObjects ∧`
`out=t.outputObjects ∧`
`in.reference.existing=true ∧`
`in.reference.object=`
`   out.reference.object}`
	`ea:Class`
	`{ea.name=concat(in.reference.object.name,`
	`             out.reference.state)}`
		T_3

	`rpa:Association`
	`{rpa.name=t.name) ∧`
	`rpa.memberEnd.source=(ep ∨ er) ∧`
	`multiplicity(rpa.memberEnd.source)=1 ∧`
	`rpa.memberEnd.target=ea ∧`
	`multiplicity(rpa.memberEnd.target)=*}`
		T_7

	`roa:Association`
	`{roa.name=t.name) ∧`
	`roa.memberEnd.source=eo ∧`
	`multiplicity(roa.memberEnd.source)=1 ∧`
	`roa.memberEnd.target=ea ∧`
	`multiplicity(roa.memberEnd.target)=*}`
		T_8

`t:Task,`
`in:IOObjectReference[0..*],`
`out:IOObjectReference[0..*]`
`{in=t.inputObjects ∧`
`out=t.outputObjects ∧`
`∄in | in.reference.object=`
`      out.reference.object}`
	`rgc:Association`
	`{rgc.name=t.name) ∧`
	`rgc.memberEnd.source=(ep ∨ er) ∧`
	`multiplicity(rgc.memberEnd.source)=1 ∧`
	`rgc.memberEnd.target=eo ∧`
	`multiplicity(rgc.memberEnd.target)=*}`
		T_5
		T_6

Table 3. Mapping of BMRL concepts into UML class diagram concepts

Source BMRL concepts	Target UML CD concepts	Rules

`t:Task,`
`in:IOObjectReference[0..*]`
`  {in=t.inputObjects ∧`
`  in.reference.existing=false}`
	`ru:Association`
	`  {ru.name=t.name) ∧`
	`  ru.memberEnd.source=(ep ∨ er) ∧`
	`    multiplicity(ru.memberEnd.source)=0..1 ∧`
	`  ru.memberEnd.target=(eo ∨ ea) ∧`
	`    multiplicity(ru.memberEnd.target)=*}`
		T_5
		T_6
		T_7

`t:Task,`
`in:IOObjectReference[0..*],`
`out:IOObjectReference[0..*]`
`  {in=t.inputObjects ∧`
`  out=t.outputObjects ∧`
`  in.reference.object≠`
`    out.reference.object}`
	`roo:Association[n]`
	`  {roo.name=t.name) ∧`
	`  roo.memberEnd.source=(eo ∨ ea) ∧`
	`    multiplicity(roo.memberEnd.source)=sm ∧`
	`  roo.memberEnd.target=(eo ∨ ea) ∧`
	`    multiplicity(roo.memberEnd.target)=tm}`
	
	$n = \begin{cases} 1, \text{ in.multiplicity} \in \{1, *\} \\ \text{in.multiplicity, otherwise} \end{cases}$
	
	$\text{low(sm)} = \begin{cases} 0, \text{ in.multiplicity} = * \vee \\ \quad \exists r \in \text{in} \mid \text{r.reference.object} = \\ \qquad \text{out.reference.object} \wedge \\ \qquad \text{r.reference.existing} = \text{false} \\ 1, \text{ otherwise} \end{cases}$
	
	$\text{high(sm)} = \begin{cases} *, \text{ in.multiplicity} = * \\ 1, \text{ otherwise} \end{cases}$
	
	$\text{low(tm)} = 0$
	
	$\text{high(tm)} = \begin{cases} *, \text{ out.multiplicity} \neq 1 \vee \\ \quad \text{in.reference.existing} = \text{true} \\ 1, \text{ otherwise} \end{cases}$
		T_9

5.1 Rules for Automatic CDM Generation

The rules for the automatic generation of the UML class diagram (target CDM), based on the BMRL representation of the source BPM, are given in Tables 2 and 3. The first two columns contain source and target concepts, while the third column contains the labels of the respective mapping rules illustrated in Fig. 3.

5.2 CDM Generator

The previously specified rules constitute the basis for the implementation of the target CDM generator. The generator can be implemented in different ways. In our case, it is implemented as an automatic Xtend-based [2] generator in the Eclipse integrated development environment (as well as the implemented BPM extractors). The implementation is dependent on simple BMRL concepts, but independent of different source BPM notations. Due to the paper length restrictions, we omit the implementation details.

Figure 7 shows the visualization result of the automatically generated CDMs obtained by the application of the implemented generator on BMRL-based representation of the sample BPMs (used in the previous section). The automatically generated CDMs are equal to the CDMs that are obtained by the

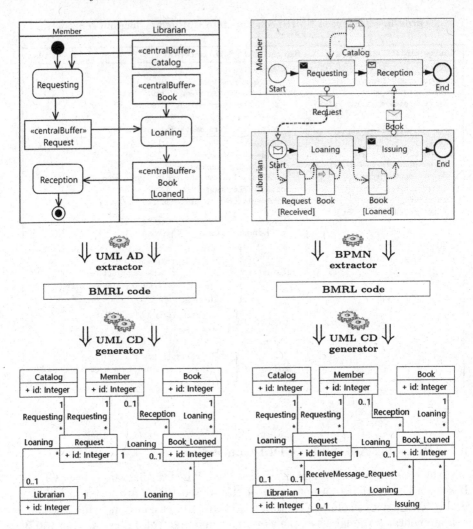

Fig. 7. Automatically generated UML class diagrams (bottom) representing the CDMs, which are generated based on BMRL representation of sample BPMs (top)

application of the direct generators [8,9]. This fact indicates that the implemented tools (Acceleo-based extractors + Xtend-based CDM generator) provide the same MDSDM functionality as the existing direct generators [8,9]. Due to the paper length restrictions, we do not provide a detailed analysis and evaluation of the automatically generated CDMs. However, the results of the controlled experiments [4,7] are very promising. They imply that the specified transformation rules enable the automated generation of the majority of the target CDM (the average completeness and precision are over 80%).

6   Conclusion

In this paper we proposed an approach that enables automated generation of the conceptual database model independently of different starting BPM notations. We identified BPM concepts having semantic potential for the automated CDM synthesis, and we specified a simple DSL named Business Model Representation Language (BMRL) for the representation of those characteristic concepts.

By the introduction of DSL, the data model synthesis is split into two phases. In the first phase, the specified concepts are extracted from the source BPM and represented by BMRL. This phase is dependent on different starting notations. In order to illustrate the proposed approach, we implemented two automatic Acceleo-based extractors and applied them to two sample business process models represented by UML activity diagram and BPMN. In the second phase, the BMRL-based representation of the extracted BPM concepts is used for the automated generation of the target CDM. Based on the set of formal rules for the automatic synthesis, we implemented an Xtend-based automatic CDM generator, which is independent of different source BPM notations.

The proposed approach has several advantages over the existing approaches, since it enables the splitting of the CDM synthesis into two decoupled phases. The first phase only deals with the extraction of the characteristic concepts from the source BPM independently of the target CDM synthesis, while the second phase only deals with the target CDM synthesis independently of the source BPM extraction. This approach reduces the CDM synthesis dependency on the source BPM notations that are caused by the metamodel changes and/or vendor specific implementations as well. If some source BPM notation is changed, then only the corresponding BPM extractor is to be changed. If some modifications of the generation rules are necessary, then only the CDM generator is to be modified, while the BPM extractors remain unchanged. Thus, the proposed approach facilitates the implementation of the required tools and simplifies the target CDM synthesis.

The future work will focus on further identification of the semantic capacity of BPMs for automated CDM design and additional improvement of the implemented DSL and implemented tools as well. Our intention also is to implement necessary BPM extractors to cover other source business modelling notations.

References

1. Acceleo. http://www.eclipse.org/acceleo/
2. Xtend. http://www.eclipse.org/xtend/
3. Xtext. http://www.eclipse.org/Xtext/
4. Banjac, D., Brdjanin, D., Banjac, G., Maric, S.: Evaluation of automatically generated conceptual database model based on collaborative business process model: controlled experiment. In: Stojanov, G., Kulakov, A. (eds.) ICT Innovations 2016. AISC. Springer, Heidelberg (2016, in press)
5. Brdjanin, D., Maric, S.: An approach to automated conceptual database design based on the UML activity diagram. Comput. Sci. Inf. Syst. **9**(1), 249–283 (2012)

6. Brdjanin, D., Maric, S.: Model-driven techniques for data model synthesis. Electronics **17**(2), 130–136 (2013)
7. Brdjanin, D., Banjac, G., Banjac, D., Maric, S.: Controlled experiment in business model-driven conceptual database design. In: Reinhartz-Berger, I., Gulden, J., Nurcan, S., Guédria, W., Bera, P. (eds.) BPMDS/EMMSAD -2017. LNBIP, vol. 287, pp. 289–304. Springer, Cham (2017). doi:10.1007/978-3-319-59466-8_18
8. Brdjanin, D., Banjac, G., Maric, S.: Automated synthesis of initial conceptual database model based on collaborative business process model. In: Bogdanova, M.A., Gjorgjevikj, D. (eds.) ICT Innovations 2014: World of Data. AISC, vol. 311, pp. 145–156. Springer International Publishing, Cham (2015)
9. Brdjanin, D., Maric, S.: Towards the automated business model-driven conceptual database design. In: Morzy, T., Harder, T., Wrembel, R. (eds.) Advances in Databases and Information Systems. AISC, vol. 186, pp. 31–43. Springer, Heidelberg (2012)
10. Budinsky, F., Steinberg, D., Merks, E., Ellersick, R., Grose, T.: Eclipse Modeling Framework. Pearson Education, Boston (2003)
11. Cruz, E.F., Machado, R.J., Santos, M.Y.: From business process modeling to data model: a systematic approach. In: Proceedings of QUATIC 2012, pp. 205–210. IEEE (2012)
12. Cruz, E.F., Machado, R.J., Santos, M.Y.: Deriving a data model from a set of interrelated business process models. In: Proceedings of ICEIS 2015, pp. 49–59 (2015)
13. Jouault, F., Allilaire, F., Bezivin, J., Kurtev, I.: ATL: a model transformation tool. Sci. Comput. Program. **72**(1–2), 31–39 (2008)
14. Koch, N., Zhang, G., Escalona, M.J.: Model transformations from requirements to web system design. In: Proceedings of ICWE 2006, pp. 281–288. ACM (2006)
15. OMG: MOF 2.0 Query/View/Transformation Specification, v1.0. OMG (2008)
16. OMG: Business Process Model and Notation (BPMN), v2.0. OMG (2011)
17. OMG: Unified Modeling Language (OMG UML), v2.5. OMG (2015)
18. Rodríguez, A., Fernández-Medina, E., Piattini, M.: Analysis-level classes from secure business processes through model transformations. In: Lambrinoudakis, C., Pernul, G., Tjoa, A.M. (eds.) TrustBus 2007. LNCS, vol. 4657, pp. 104–114. Springer, Heidelberg (2007). doi:10.1007/978-3-540-74409-2_13
19. Rodríguez, A., Fernández-Medina, E., Piattini, M.: Towards obtaining analysis-level class and use case diagrams from business process models. In: Song, I.-Y., et al. (eds.) ER 2008. LNCS, vol. 5232, pp. 103–112. Springer, Heidelberg (2008). doi:10.1007/978-3-540-87991-6_15
20. Rodriguez, A., Garcia-Rodriguez de Guzman, I., Fernandez-Medina, E., Piattini, M.: Semi-formal transformation of secure business processes into analysis class and use case models: an MDA approach. Inf. Softw. Technol. **52**(9), 945–971 (2010)
21. Sepúlveda, C., Cravero, A., Cares, C.: From business process to data model: a systematic mapping study. IEEE Lat. Am. Trans. **15**(4), 729–736 (2017)
22. Voelter, M., Benz, S., Dietrich, C., Engelmann, B., Helander, M., Kats, L., Visser, E., Wachsmuth, G.: DSL engineering - designing, implementing and using domain-specific languages (2013)
23. Wrycza, S.: The ISAC-driven transition between requirements analysis and ER conceptual modelling. Inf. Syst. **15**(6), 603–614 (1990)

Modular Term-Rewriting Framework for Artifact-Centric Business Process Modelling

Bartosz Zieliński[✉]

Department of Computer Science, Faculty of Physics and Applied Informatics,
University of Łódź, Pomorska 149/153, 90-236 Łódź, Poland
bzielinski@uni.lodz.pl

Abstract. A plethora of formalisms is used to express various dimensions of business processes such as data and organization models, orchestration of tasks, and so on. Traditionally, those dimensions are treated as largely independent. Artifact centric models, however, require tighter integration between components. Thus, it is desirable to base a formal semantics of business process constructs on a mathematical formalism which is capable of expressing all or most of the dimensions of interest and their mutual dependence for the purpose of effective simulation and verification. We propose such a specification framework based on term rewriting and implemented in Maude system. Its important feature is the ability to specify the semantics in a piecewise, extensible manner reminiscent of aspect oriented approaches to business process modelling.

1 Introduction

A plethora of formalisms is used to express various dimensions of business processes such as data and organisation models, orchestration of tasks, and so on. In traditional, task centric approaches those dimensions were treated as separate concerns. Artifact-centric models (see e.g., [2,7,9]), however, are built around "business entities with lifecycles" [10] and activities (services) are defined in terms of the changes to artifact's contents and the stage of its' lifecycle, and hence require tighter integration between components. Thus, it is desirable to found a formal semantics of business process constructs on a mathematical formalism which is capable of expressing all or most of the dimensions of interest and their mutual dependence for the purpose of effective simulation and verification. A further beneficial feature is the ability to specify the behaviour of models in a piecewise, extensible manner, where, if need arises, one can clarify and extend the meaning of a construct with new aspects reusing the existing specification instead of starting from scratch (c.f., [3,4] and other aspect oriented approaches to business process modelling).

This paper proposes a specification framework for artifact centric business processes which has those features, based on *conditional term rewriting* [14, 15] and *membership equational logic* [13]. We also provide a proof of concept implementation in the Maude system [6] (if one decides to use term rewriting at all, Maude with its high performance implementation and a host of mature analysis and verification tools is the obvious choice).

© Springer International Publishing AG 2017
Y. Ouhammou et al. (Eds.): MEDI 2017, LNCS 10563, pp. 71–78, 2017.
DOI: 10.1007/978-3-319-66854-3_6

Comparison with Previous Work. Conditional term rewriting modulo a limited set of equational axioms which include associativity, commutativity and unitality subsumes many formalisms used for specification of business processes. For example it is well known that coloured (and other types of) Petri nets (cf. [20]) as well as process algebras (cf. [21]) are naturally represented as rewriting systems. Rewriting logic was also proposed as a general logical framework capable of expressing other logics, see e.g., [12].

Rewriting logic is a logic of concurrent systems having states and evolving by means of transitions [12]. Hence it has many advantages over the usual predicate logic when modelling of dynamic systems is concerned. Most notably, it makes the frame problem, plaguing the planning systems, trivial [11].

One of the main inspirations for our work is the aspect oriented approach to business process modelling (see, e.g., [3,4]) where we try to solve the same problem—of defining the semantics of business process constructs in a piecewise manner and factoring out common cross-cutting concerns—but we use term rewriting instead of UML metamodels. An advantage of our approach is much greater simplicity—UML is very complex and requires the use of other logical formalisms anyway, e.g., in case of the OCL. On the other hand, UML comes with graphical notation and a number of code generation and analysis tools.

An alternative and popular approach to formalizing business processes is to use predicate calculus (and Prolog or Datalog to make it executable). For example, book [5] presents an elegant lightweight approach to formalization of artifact-centric business processes. Predicate calculus is well understood and often translates straightforwardly to and from natural language presentations, and it perfectly fits data modelling. On the other hand, while it can be used to model changing state of business process as witnessed by numerous papers, such descriptions are not so natural and, as remarked above, care must be taken to provide frame axioms. Here we believe that rewriting systems are much more suitable. Let us remark that Maude is really a functional-logic language [1] hence some techniques of logic programming are available for Maude. Moreover, rewriting based systems offer much richer algebraic structure than logic programming systems. This structure may be fruitfully exploited. For example, having a state described as a sea of "pieces" combined together with an associative and commutative operator with identity, one can write matching patterns which explicitly mention only relevant components and abstract away others. This idea was successfully employed in matching logic and K-framework [17–19], which is another source of inspiration for the present paper. Note that in matching logic the ACI rewriting is used to enable extending the described language with new constructs without breaking or modifying the existing semantics, whereas here we are rather interested in enriching semantics of given constructs.

Finally, Maude system was already many times used for specification of semantics of business process models, e.g., in [8].

Term Rewriting. *An algebraic signature* $\Sigma = (\Sigma_S, \Sigma_F)$ consists of a finite poset of sorts Σ_S (sorts are like type names, and the order corresponds to subtyping) and a finite set Σ_F of function signatures of the form $f : s_1 s_2 \ldots s_n \to$ s, where f is a function symbol and s_i's are sorts in Σ_S. Constants have signatures $c :\to s$. Note that Maude supports the so-called mixfix syntax—underscores in the function name correspond to consecutive arguments, as in, e.g., $\_ + \_$. We denote by $T_\Sigma(X)$ the set of "type safe" terms in the signature Σ and variables X. A conditional rewrite rule is an expression of the form $l \Rightarrow r$ if C where $l, r \in T_\Sigma(X)$ and C is a condition (conjunction of equality, rewriting and sort membership assertions). A set $\mathcal{R}$ of rewrite rules defines a binary relation $\_ \Rightarrow_\mathcal{R} \_$ on terms as follows: $t \Rightarrow_\mathcal{R} s$ iff there exists a position p of t and a substitution σ such that $t|_p = \sigma(l)$, $s = t[\sigma(r)]_p$ and $\sigma(C)$ is satisfied. In Maude, rewriting relations are defined modulo equational theories $\mathcal{E} = \mathcal{B} \cup \mathcal{A}$ (i.e., rewritings are really between classes of terms modulo equations). Equational theories are split into equations $\mathcal{B}$ implemented as left to right simplifications into canonical forms (the rewriting system defined by $\mathcal{B}$ is assumed terminating and confluent), and a handful of equational properties such as associativity, commutativity and identity axioms which are implemented directly and are specified as equational attributes of operators in the signature.

2   Labelled Transition Systems, KCells and Maude

Operational semantics is often described in terms of labelled transition systems.

Definition 1. *A labelled transition system $\mathcal{T} = (\mathcal{S}_\mathcal{T}, \mathcal{L}_\mathcal{T}, \to_\mathcal{T})$ consists of a set of states $\mathcal{S}_\mathcal{T}$, a set of transition labels $\mathcal{L}_\mathcal{T}$ and a transition relation $\to_\mathcal{T} \subseteq \mathcal{S}_\mathcal{T} \times \mathcal{L}_\mathcal{T} \times \mathcal{S}_\mathcal{T}$. We write $s \xrightarrow{\lambda} t$ whenever $(s, \lambda, t) \in \to_\mathcal{T}$.*

Depending on the application, transition labels may correspond to user actions or software events. Often $\mathcal{S}_\mathcal{T}$ and $\mathcal{L}_\mathcal{T}$ are quotients of term algebras, and transition relation is defined with conditional rules determining possible transitions from $s \in \mathcal{S}_\mathcal{T}$ in terms of the structure of s and the transitions from s's components. This is a typical situation for process algebras (see e.g., [16]), and we use a variation of the same idea. The basic signature Σ^0 of our framework contains:

- Sort Action for transition labels, sort KCell for hierarchical, independent components of state, and sorts Tag and Tags for KCell tags and their lists. The notion of KCell's was taken from matching logic and K-framework [17].
- Constructors for non-atomic KCells. A KCell is either atomic, multiset of or complex KCell. Multisets of KCells are constructed with associative, commutative empty binary operator $\_$ with unit none (i.e., none is a KCell and $K_1 K_2$ is a KCell when K_1 and K_2 are). Complex KCells are of the form $\langle K \rangle_{\bar{t}}$ where K is a KCell and $\bar{t} = t_1 t_2 \ldots t_n$ is a list of tags constructed with an empty associative operator. Framework instances must extend Σ^0 with constructors of atomic KCells encapsulating domain dependent data terms.
- Sorts and operators implementing ternary transition relation as binary single-step rewriting relation by attaching the transition label to the target term. Following [21] we represent transitions $K \xrightarrow{\lambda} K'$ as rewrites $K \Rightarrow \{\lambda\}K$.

Terms of the form $\{\lambda\}K$ are given the supersort of KCell and frozen attribute to prevent further rewrites. In what follows we mostly use ternary transition relations for better readability. Reachability analysis is supported by multi-step transitions represented with trace terms. Explicitly, given $K_1 \xrightarrow{\lambda_1} K_2 \xrightarrow{\lambda_2} K_3 \xrightarrow{\lambda_3} \cdots \xrightarrow{\lambda_{n-1}} K_n$ we represent it as the multi-step rewrite

$$\{\mathsf{nil}\}^* K_1 \Rightarrow \{\lambda_1\}^* K_2 \Rightarrow \{\lambda_1\lambda_2\}^* K_3 \Rightarrow \cdots \Rightarrow \{\lambda_1\lambda_2\ldots\lambda_{n-1}\}^* K_n.$$

The basic idea is that states of business processes consist of independent, perhaps hierarchical, components, each of which adds some aspect to the behaviour. Thus, transitions of complex KCells are defined through transitions of their components. Moreover, utilizing ACI matching we can improve the modularity of rules by abstracting away irrelevant components as "catch all" variables in patterns. KCell tags denote included aspects. The behaviour of $\langle K\langle C\rangle\rangle_{\bar{t}s}$ is the result of extending $\langle K\rangle_{\bar{t}}$ with aspect s implemented with component $\langle C\rangle$. The extension is described with rules of the form:

$$\frac{\langle KR\rangle_{\bar{t}} \xrightarrow{\lambda_1} \langle K'R'\rangle_{\bar{t}} \quad \langle C\rangle \xrightarrow{\lambda_2} \langle C'\rangle}{\langle\langle C\rangle KR\rangle_{\bar{t}c} \xrightarrow{\theta} \langle\langle C'\rangle K'R'\rangle_{\bar{t}c}},$$

where K, K' are variables of sort KCell matching abstracted away part of the original (unextended) state, R and R' are patterns of the relevant parts of unexpanded state, λ_1, λ_2 and θ are transition label terms which might depend on R, R', C and C', and, finally, $\bar{t}$ is a tag list pattern. Examples presented in the next section should clarify the meaning of the above general considerations.

3   Stepwise Enrichment of the Lifecycle Model

As an example we consider a stepwise enrichment of a publication's lifecycle implemented as a finite state machine. Publication is drafted by author, reviewed, revised and, if accepted it is edited by a copy editor. After checking with author it is published either after explicit author's confirmation or timeout:

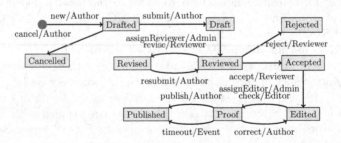

Labels of transitions consist of action's name and the role of action's initiator connected by binary operator _/_. Finite automatons are implemented in

Maude as labelled transition systems using methods from the preceding section. We encapsulate states and transition labels into terms of sort KCell and Action, respectively, with constructors $\langle \_ \rangle$ and $[\_]$. There is a rule for each lifecycle transition, e.g., $\langle \text{Drafted} \rangle \xrightarrow{[cancel/Author]} \langle \text{Cancelled} \rangle$.

While this simple specification might suffice in some situations, the executable semantics of the lifecycle is clearly underspecified. Neither the meaning of role annotations, nor of timeout action labels is defined. Also, loops in the state machine diagram mean that the publication might never reach terminal state, while we expect publications to have finite lifecycles. In the remainder we address those issues by piecewisely enriching the lifecycle model.

First, we add counters to limit the number of executions of selected transitions. Counter terms are of the form $\lambda_1/n_1; \lambda_2/n_2; \cdots ; \lambda_n/n_k$ where λ_i's are actions, n_i's are natural numbers, $\_; \_$ is an associative commutative operator, and they indicate that λ_i has no more than n_i executions left. Operator $\langle \_ \rangle$ encapsulates counters as KCells. Let undefined(λ, C) be false iff action term λ appears in counter term C. Then the behaviour of counters as well as their coupling with other KCells can be defined with the following rules:

$$\frac{\text{undefined}(\lambda, C)}{\langle C \rangle \xrightarrow{\lambda} \langle C \rangle}, \qquad \frac{}{\langle \lambda/(n+1); R \rangle \xrightarrow{\lambda} \langle \lambda/n; R \rangle}, \qquad \frac{\langle K \rangle_{\bar{t}} \xrightarrow{\lambda} \langle K' \rangle_{\bar{t}} \quad \langle C \rangle \xrightarrow{\lambda} \langle C' \rangle}{\langle K \langle C \rangle \rangle_{\bar{t}c} \xrightarrow{\lambda} \langle K' \langle C' \rangle \rangle_{\bar{t}c}}.$$

Here $\bar{t}$ is some list of tags, tag c corresponds to counters, C is an arbitrary counter term and K is an arbitrary multiset of K-cells. Note that the nature of K (and the tags $\bar{t}$ related to K) is completely abstracted away. Hence counters may be attached to any complex KCell's corresponding to arbitrary business process constructs, and not just to lifecycles.

Next, we add the semantics of random, exponentially distributed timeouts. Let $\mathcal{E}(n, B)$ return n-th element of a pseudorandom sequence of numbers distributed according to the exponential distribution $F(x; B) = 1 - e^{-x/B}$. Timeout aspect KCells are of the form $\langle n : b \rangle$ where n is the first unused position in the random number sequence and b is the boolean indicating if the current state is timeouted (if true). Transition labels for timeout KCells are of the form $[\lambda, \Gamma]$ where λ is a transition label and Γ (of sort TiData) is either a pair $[B, M]$ of real numbers, or constant $\perp$. Let timeout? : Action $\rightarrow$ Bool be a predicate returning true iff its argument is a timeout transition (in a domain specific form), and let

$$n \leftarrow [B, M] = (n + 1) : (\mathcal{E}(n, B) > M), \qquad n \leftarrow \perp = n : \text{false}$$

The behaviour of timeouts is defined with the rule $\dfrac{\text{timeout?}(\lambda)=b}{\langle n{:}b \rangle \xrightarrow{[\lambda, \Gamma]} \langle n \leftarrow \Gamma \rangle}$.

Timeouts are coupled to the state machine by associating to. each state s a value $\pi(s)$ of sort TiData. The states s where $\pi(s) = [B, M]$ are called timeoutable. Upon entering timeoutable state a value is drawn from the exponential distribution. If it is larger than the threshold M associated to the given state, the state is timeouted (i.e., timeout KCell becomes $\langle n : \text{true} \rangle$). A timeouted state can perform only timeout action. Non-timeouted state can perform any possible transition apart from a timeout action (t is a tag corresponding to timeouts):

$$\frac{\langle K\langle s\rangle\rangle_{\bar{t}} \xrightarrow{\lambda} \langle K'\langle s'\rangle\rangle_{\bar{t}} \quad \langle T\rangle \xrightarrow{[\lambda,\pi(s')]} \langle T'\rangle}{\langle K\langle s\rangle\langle T\rangle\rangle_{\bar{t}t} \xrightarrow{\lambda} \langle K'\langle s'\rangle\langle T'\rangle\rangle_{\bar{t}t}.} \tag{1}$$

In the case of our example lifecycle the only timeoutable state is Proof and timeout?(λ) iff $\lambda = [\mathsf{timeout/Event}]$. Note that timeouts can enrich any extension of basic states, as the above rules allow for any additional KCells.

Finally, we show how to extend the system to deal with multiple documents and give semantics to the role annotations by introducing a simple data model.

We represent each document as a complex KCell of the form $\langle d|K\rangle_{\bar{t}}$ where d is a document identifier (of sort DocId), K is a multiset of KCells and $\bar{t}$ is a list of tags). It is assumed that $\langle d|K\rangle_{\bar{t}}$ behaves in the same way as $\langle K\rangle_{\bar{t}}$, identifier d distinguishes distinct document KCells. In order to add role based access control modelling capabilities we extend transition labels to include information about a principal performing an action and we implement a simple relational data model holding information about principals and their possible and active roles.

(Human) principals and roles have sorts Person and Role, respectively. Facts are represented with function symbols into Data sort. Facts are combined into multisets (also of sort Data) using an associative, commutative empty operator understood as "and", and they are encapsulated into KCells using constructor $\langle \_\rangle : \mathsf{Data} \to \mathsf{KCell}$. We define the following fact constructors:

- $[\_ : \_] : \mathsf{Person\ Role} \to \mathsf{Data}$. $[p : R]$ means that person p can have the role R.
- do $: \mathsf{Person\ Role} \to \mathsf{Data}$. Facts constructed with do are meant to be placed inside document K-cells. $\langle d|\langle \mathrm{do}(p,R)D\rangle K\rangle_{\bar{t}}$ matches the document KCell such that p plays the role R for document d.

For convenience we introduce constructors $p : \mathsf{Qid} \to \mathsf{Person}$ and $d : \mathsf{Nat} \to \mathsf{DocId}$ which construct terms of sorts Person and DocId from Maude's quoted identifiers and natural numbers, respectively. A full state of the system is now represented by a higher order KCell (tagged with d) which contains a data cell with some shared information (such as possible roles for principals) as well as zero or more document KCells. An example of a KCell describing a system with several documents is presented below:

$$\langle\langle d(0)|\langle \mathsf{Rejected}\rangle\langle \mathrm{do}(p('\mathsf{Adam}),\mathsf{Reviewer})\mathrm{do}(p('\mathsf{Bart}),\mathsf{Author})\rangle\rangle\rangle_s$$
$$\langle d(1)|\langle \mathsf{Drafted}\rangle\langle \mathrm{do}(p('\mathsf{Adam}),\mathsf{Author})\rangle\rangle\rangle_s$$
$$\langle ['\mathsf{Adam} : \mathsf{Reviewer}]['\mathsf{Adam} : \mathsf{Author}]['\mathsf{Bart} : \mathsf{Author}]['\mathsf{Bart} : \mathsf{Reviewer}]\rangle\rangle_d$$

Thus, there are two documents, one drafted, the other rejected. Document $d(0)$ was authored by $p('\mathsf{Bart})$ and reviewed by $p('\mathsf{Adam})$ who also authored $d(1)$. In addition to documents, the top KCell contains a data KCell with information about possible roles of principals.

Finally, we extend the transition labels to include information on document affected and principal performing the action:

$$[\_ : \_ : \_] : \mathsf{Person\ DocId\ Action} \rightarrow \mathsf{Action}.$$

The complete set of rules describing the behaviour of multidocument KCells include document creation rules and many others. Here we give as an example the rule for assigning reviewers:

$$\frac{p_1 \neq p_2 \quad \langle K \rangle_{\bar{t}} \xrightarrow{[\mathsf{assignReviewer/Admin}]} \langle K' \rangle_{\bar{t}}}{\langle\langle d | K \mathsf{do}(p_1, \mathsf{Author})\rangle_{\bar{t}} \langle [p_2 : \mathsf{Reviewer}][p_3 : \mathsf{Admin}] Z \rangle\rangle_d \xrightarrow{[p_3 : d : [\mathsf{assignReviewer/Admin}]]}}$$
$$\langle\langle d | K' \mathsf{do}(p_1, \mathsf{Author})\mathsf{do}(p_2, \mathsf{Reviewer})\rangle_{\bar{t}} \langle [p_2 : \mathsf{Reviewer}][p_3 : \mathsf{Admin}] Z \rangle\rangle_d$$

4 Conclusion

In the paper we have demonstrated how one can utilize rewriting modulo associativity commutativity, and identity (ACI) to create an extensible, modular testing framework in which the semantics of various aspects of (artifact centric) business process model can be described. ACI simplifies matching in which one only explicitly mentions relevant components and abstracts away others. This enables a modular and layered architecture of our framework in which a given construct is given semantics in a piecewise (and often independent) manner (cf. [3,4]), where different pieces correspond to different aspects of the process (data, lifecycle, security, etc.). The framework was implemented in Maude system. This allows us to use standard tools of Maude for verification of various properties of the model. Thus, we can perform reachability analysis, or check satisfaction of a temporal logic formula. Because of the piecewise manner in which we describe semantics of various constructs, such analysis can be naturally performed at varying levels of abstraction.

References

1. Antoy, S., Hanus, M.: Functional logic programming. Commun. ACM **53**(4), 74–85 (2010)
2. Bhattacharya, K., Caswell, N.S., Kumaran, S., Nigam, A., Wu, F.Y.: Artifact-centered operational modeling: lessons from customer engagements. IBM Syst. J. **46**(4), 703–721 (2007)
3. Cappelli, C., Leite, J.C., Batista, T., Silva, L.: An aspect-oriented approach to business process modeling. In: Proceedings of the 15th Workshop on Early Aspects, EA 2009, pp. 7–12. ACM, New York (2009)
4. Cappelli, C., Santoro, F.M., Cesar Sampaio do Prado Leite, J., Batista, T., Luisa Medeiros, A., Romeiro, C.S.: Reflections on the modularity of business process models: the case for introducing the aspect-oriented paradigm. Bus. Process Manag. J. **16**(4), 662–687 (2010)

5. Chen-Burger, Y.H., Robertson, D.: Automating Business Modelling: A Guide to Using Logic to Represent Informal Methods and Support Reasoning. Springer Science and Business Media, Heidelberg (2006)
6. Clavel, M., Durán, F., Eker, S., Lincoln, P., Martí-Oliet, N., Meseguer, J., Talcott, C.: The maude 2.0 system. In: Nieuwenhuis, R. (ed.) RTA 2003. LNCS, vol. 2706, pp. 76–87. Springer, Heidelberg (2003). doi:10.1007/3-540-44881-0_7
7. Cohn, D., Hull, R.: Business artifacts: a data-centric approach to modeling business operations and processes. Bull. IEEE Comput. Soc. Tech. Comm. Data Eng. **32**(3), 3–9 (2009)
8. El-Saber, N., Boronat, A.: BPMN formalization and verification using maude. In: Proceedings of the 2014 Workshop on Behaviour Modelling-Foundations and Applications, p. 1. ACM (2014)
9. Hull, R.: Artifact-centric business process models: brief survey of research results and challenges. In: Meersman, R., Tari, Z. (eds.) OTM 2008. LNCS, vol. 5332, pp. 1152–1163. Springer, Heidelberg (2008). doi:10.1007/978-3-540-88873-4_17
10. Hull, R., Damaggio, E., Fournier, F., Gupta, M., Heath III, F.T., Hobson, S., Linehan, M., Maradugu, S., Nigam, A., Sukaviriya, P., Vaculin, R.: Introducing the guard-stage-milestone approach for specifying business entity lifecycles. In: Bravetti, M., Bultan, T. (eds.) WS-FM 2010. LNCS, vol. 6551, pp. 1–24. Springer, Heidelberg (2011). doi:10.1007/978-3-642-19589-1_1
11. Marti-Oliet, N., Meseguer, J.: Action and change in rewriting logic. In: Pareschi, R., Fronhöfer, B. (eds.) Dynamic Worlds, vol. 12, pp. 1–53. Springer, Heidelberg (1999). doi:10.1007/978-94-017-1317-7_1
12. Martí-Oliet, N., Meseguer, J.: Rewriting logic as a logical and semantic framework. In: Gabbay, D.M., Guenthner, F. (eds.) Handbook of Philosophical Logic, vol. 9, pp. 1–87. Springer, Heidelberg (2002). doi:10.1007/978-94-017-0464-9_1
13. Meseguer, J.: Membership algebra as a logical framework for equational specification. In: Presicce, F.P. (ed.) WADT 1997. LNCS, vol. 1376, pp. 18–61. Springer, Heidelberg (1998). doi:10.1007/3-540-64299-4_26
14. Meseguer, J.: Conditional rewriting logic as a unified model of concurrency. Theor. Comput. Sci. **96**(1), 73–155 (1992)
15. Meseguer, J., Rosu, G.: The rewriting logic semantics project. Theor. Comput. Sci. **373**(3), 213–237 (2007)
16. Milner, R. (ed.): A Calculus of Communicating Systems. LNCS, vol. 92. Springer, Heidelberg (1980)
17. Roşu, G., Ellison, C., Schulte, W.: Matching logic: an alternative to Hoare/Floyd logic. In: Johnson, M., Pavlovic, D. (eds.) AMAST 2010. LNCS, vol. 6486, pp. 142–162. Springer, Heidelberg (2011). doi:10.1007/978-3-642-17796-5_9
18. Ştefănescu, A., Ciobâcă, Ş., Mereuta, R., Moore, B.M., Şerbănută, T.F., Roşu, G.: All-path reachability logic. In: Dowek, G. (ed.) RTA 2014. LNCS, vol. 8560, pp. 425–440. Springer, Cham (2014). doi:10.1007/978-3-319-08918-8_29
19. Stefănescu, A., Park, D., Yuwen, S., Li, Y., Roşu, G.: Semantics-based program verifiers for all languages. In: Proceedings of the 2016 ACM SIGPLAN International Conference on Object-Oriented Programming, Systems, Languages, and Applications. pp. 74–91. ACM (2016)
20. Stehr, M.O., Meseguer, J., Ölveczky, P.C.: Representation and execution of petri nets using rewriting logic as a unifying framework. Electron. Notes Theor. Comput. Sci. **44**(4), 140–162 (2001)
21. Verdejo, A., Martí-Oliet, N.: Implementing CCS in maude 2. Electron. Notes Theor. Comput. Sci. **71**, 282–300 (2004)

Systems and Software Assessments

The Stability of Threshold Values for Software Metrics in Software Defect Prediction

Goran Mauša[(✉)] and Tihana Galinac Grbac

Faculty of Engineering, University of Rijeka, Vukovarska 58, 51000 Rijeka, Croatia
goran.mausa@riteh.hr, tihana.galinac@rireh.hr

Abstract. Software metrics measure the complexity and quality in many empirical case studies. Recent studies have shown that threshold values can be detected for some metrics and used to predict defect-prone system modules. The goal of this paper is to empirically validate the stability of threshold values. Our aim is to analyze a wider set of software metrics than it has been previously reported and to perform the analysis in the context of different levels of data imbalance. We replicate the case study of deriving thresholds for software metrics using a statistical model based on logistic regression. Furthermore, we analyze threshold stability in the context of varying level of data imbalance. The methodology is validated using a great number of subsequent releases of open source projects. We revealed that threshold values of some metrics could be used to effectively predict defect-prone modules. Moreover, threshold values of some metrics may be influenced by the level of data imbalance. The results of this case study give a valuable insight into the importance of software metrics and the presented methodology may also be used by software quality assurance practitioners.

Keywords: Software metrics · Threshold · Data imbalance · Software defect prediction

1 Introduction

There are many different software metrics and each describes the program code from a different perspective [1,2]. Software metrics that describe the object oriented code can be used to quantify its quality [3]. One of the most direct attributes of software quality is the number of defects that need to be handled after the implementation phase. Software defect prediction (SDP) is the research area that investigates the possibility to use these metrics to classify the software modules that contain defects. Contradictory results have been reported across studies that evaluated the classification accuracy of various software metrics [4]. There are indications that the choice of the prediction model has lower impact on accuracy than the choice of metrics [5]. However, certain software metrics proved to be efficient for defect prediction [6]. Moreover, some metrics exhibit threshold effect, i.e. a relationship can be identified between a metric's threshold value and the occurrence of defects [7]. Threshold is the level of a metric, above

© Springer International Publishing AG 2017
Y. Ouhammou et al. (Eds.): MEDI 2017, LNCS 10563, pp. 81–95, 2017.
DOI: 10.1007/978-3-319-66854-3_7

which we classify the module to be faulty, i.e. to contain defects, and non-faulty otherwise.

Software defects are generally not distributed according to any probability distribution that could be described with a particular mathematical model [8]. That is why SDP community turned to machine learning methods. However, there is not any prediction model that is the best in all the application contexts [9]. Furthermore, most machine learning methods exhibit performance deterioration in high levels of data imbalance [10]. Data imbalance is the phenomenon in which one class of data greatly outnumber the other class or classes of data. The class that represents faulty software modules is outnumbered in SDP, making data imbalance its inherent feature [11]. Recent studies experimented with the use of genetic programming algorithms for classification, i.e. building the prediction model in SDP, and achieved some promising results [12]. The multi-objective framework of genetic programming improves the generalization ability by forming ensembles of diverse classifiers [13]. These algorithms combine all the metrics in a decision tree structure and train the prediction models using multiple fitness functions sensitive to data imbalance. In such configuration, every software metric is one additional dimension in the search space. Having a large search space with too many dimensions reduces the probability of finding the optimal solutions in any heuristic optimization algorithm [14]. Furthermore, these algorithms may be further improved by incorporating certain domain knowledge [15]. This may be done by using a predefined initial populations or by fine tuning its configuration.

This paper aims to empirically validate the stability of threshold values of software metrics for SDP. We replicate the threshold derivation model from the studies performed by [7,16]. The stability of threshold values is examined in terms of rate of significance, spread of threshold values and the difference of central tendency between different datasets. The results of this case study research provides us with insight into the importance of individual software metric for SDP. This valuable domain knowledge will be used to improve the genetic algorithm configuration that achieved promising results in spite of data imbalance [12]. Software metrics not significant for defects prediction will be excluded and the significant ones will be given higher priority in the decision making process. Moreover, the threshold values of metrics that prove to be effective in prediction will be regarded as reference points in a multivariate model configuration. That is why it is important to perform a large scale case study and include all the possible software metrics, whereas previous research focused mainly on a small number of object-oriented metrics [7,17]. This paper performs this study on 49 different metrics that are calculated according to the systematically defined collection procedure for SDP research [18].

The remainder of this paper is structured as follows: Sect. 2 presents an overview of related work; Sect. 3 describes the details of the case study we have conducted; Sect. 4 shows and discusses the results that we have obtained; Sect. 5 gives a conclusion and explains our future work intentions.

2   Related Work

Many studies searched for software metrics with strong association to software defect prediction. Majority of these studies concentrated on a small number of object oriented metrics like: coupling between objects ('CBO'), response for class ('RFC'), weighted method per class ('WMC'), depth of inheritance tree ('DIT') and number of children ('NOC') [7]. Their results indicated that metrics like 'CBO', 'WMC' and 'RFC' were often significant for SDP and other metrics like 'DIT' and 'NOC' were rarely significant [7,16]. A recent replicated study involved other metrics like: lack of cohesion between objects ('LCOM'), maximum or average cyclomatic complexity ('MAXCC', 'AVCC') or lines of code ('LOC') and demonstrated that they may also be significant [16].

On the other hand, fewer studies experimented with threshold derivation [16]. That does not mean that practitioners do not use it. The senior software developers usually determine the threshold values based on their experience [19]. Their decision making process cannot be replicated nor reused and it is highly biased. Hence, researchers proposed several methods to perform it systematically. The most popular are the Bender method which is based on logistic prediction model and the method which is based on receiver operating curve (ROC) [16].

In most classification applications that suffer from data imbalance, the minority class is usually the one that is more important to find and this posses a problem to most classification algorithms [20]. The fact that defects in large and complex software systems are distributed according to the Pareto principle [11,21,22] makes data imbalance an inherent feature of SDP. The rate of faulty software modules is always lower than the rate of modules that are non-faulty and we refer to it as the level of imbalance in the rest of this paper. Different methods were proposed to deal with data imbalance. The ones that take into account the misclassification costs of unequally distributed classes were generally the most successful [12,23]. In this paper we analyze whether data imbalance has an impact on threshold derivation method as well and use the proper evaluation metrics to take that into account.

3   Case Study

The goal of this paper is to empirically validate the stability of threshold values in different contexts. We want to see whether there are metrics significant for defect prediction with stable threshold values so that the practitioners could use them in software quality assurance. The threshold values are calculated by using the logistic regression model and Bender method, and evaluated by using the decision tree binary classification. The proposed methodology examines individually the strength of each metric for defect prediction. The stability of threshold values is examined in datasets with varying levels of imbalance by using 10-fold cross-validation. We used Matlab R2014a to perform the case study calculations.

3.1   Data

We use 14 datasets of two open source projects from the Eclipse community: JDT and PDE. Each dataset represents one release and there are 7 subsequent releases of each project in this case study. We used the BuCo Analyzer tool [24] to collect the datasets. BuCo is a tool that implements systematically defined data collection procedure [18]. The tool performs linking between bugs and commits using a technique that is based on regular expression [25]. The effectiveness of the linking is expressed by linking rate, i.e. the ratio of bugs that are linked to at least one commit. We present the linking rate, the number of reported bugs, the number of Java files, the ratio between non-faulty and faulty files and the number of software metrics for each dataset in Table 1.

Table 1. Datasets used in this study

Eclipse JDT project					
tool plug-ins that support the development of any Java application					
Release	Linking Rate	Bugs	Files	Non-Faulty : Faulty	Metrics
2.0	48.4%	4276	2397	54.1% : 45.9%	50
2.1	64.4%	1875	2743	68.1% : 31.9%	50
3.0	70.9%	3385	3420	61.4% : 38.6%	50
3.1	80.6%	2653	3883	67.3% : 32.7%	50
3.2	84.9%	1879	2233	63.5% : 36.5%	50
3.3	88.7%	1341	4821	76.2% : 23.8%	50
3.4	90.0%	989	4932	81.5% : 18.5%	50
Eclipse PDE project					
tools to create, develop, test, debug, build and deploy Eclipse plug-ins					
Release	Linking Rate	Bugs	Files	Non-Faulty : Faulty	Metrics
2.0	22.3%	561	576	80.7% : 19.3%	50
2.1	27.4%	427	761	83.7% : 16.3%	50
3.0	33.6%	1041	881	68.8% : 31.2%	50
3.1	51.6%	769	1108	67.8% : 32.2%	50
3.2	69.2%	546	1351	53.8% : 46.2%	50
3.3	85.3%	727	1713	56.3% : 43.7%	50
3.4	80.9%	963	2144	71.5% : 28.5%	50

3.2   Methodology

The methodology of this case study is presented in Fig. 1. In the first phase we sample the datasets into 10 equally distributed folds, according to the stratified sampling strategy of 10-fold cross-validation. We use the 10-fold cross-validation to validate the stability of the results that are going to be obtained in the following releases. The training dataset contains 9 folds and the testing dataset contains the remaining fold. This process is repeated 10 times, each time with

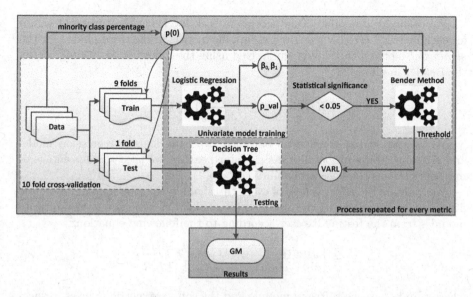

Fig. 1. Methodology of this case study

different fold as the testing dataset but with equal ratio between the minorty
and the majority class.

The following three phases belong to the threshold derivation model. The univariate logistic regression model is built for each dataset separately in the second
phase. The logistic regression model is presented with the following equation [26]:

$$P(X) = \frac{e^{\beta_0 + \beta_1 \cdot X}}{1 + e^{\beta_0 + \beta_1 \cdot X}} \tag{1}$$

where β_0 is the free coefficient, β_1 is the regression slope coefficients for predictor
X, X represents a particular metric and $P(X)$ is the probability that a module
is faulty. The coefficients β_0 and β_1 define the curvature and the non-linearity
of the logistic regression output curve.

Base probability **p(0)** is the cutoff value that is required to transform probability $P(X)$ into binary variable. It is often set to 0.5 [27], but it can be tuned to
account for data imbalance present in the dataset [3]. Using the percentage of the
majority class as the base probability accounts for the higher probability that a
randomly selected module is non-faulty [3]. This is also applicable to the Bender method in the following phase so the majority class percentage is forwarded
there. An intermediate step in the methodology is also the analysis of statistical significance. The null-hypothesis states there is no relationship between
the logistic regression model of a particular metric and the defect-proneness of
the examined software modules. This step forwards the metrics for which the
null-hypothesis is rejected to the following phase.

We calculate the value of an acceptable risk level, i.e. the threshold values for each metric THR_j, where j represents the metric, in the third phase. For the *significant* metrics, thresholds are derived using the following equation given by the Bender method [28]:

$$THR_j = \frac{1}{\beta_{1,j}}(ln(\frac{p_0}{1-p_0}) - \beta_{0,j}), \tag{2}$$

where β_0 and β_1 are coefficients obtained from the logistic regression model and $p(0)$ is the base probability. As explained earlier, we used the percentage of majority class as the base probability ($p_0 = p(0)$) [16].

We evaluate the effectiveness of every threshold in the fourth phase. A simple decision tree is built using the obtained threshold values to classify the software modules from the testing dataset according to the following equation:

$$Y_i = \begin{cases} faulty & if\ X_{i,j} > THR_j \\ non-faulty & if\ X_{i,j} > THR_j \end{cases}, \tag{3}$$

where i and j are the software module and the software metric indexes, respectively. In our study, the granularity level of software modules is the file level. The software metrics in our study describe the size and complexity of source code (like lines of code, cyclomatic complexity), the usage of object oriented principles (inheritance, encapsulation, abstraction and polymorphism), the design of source code (like coupling and cohesion), the programming style (like number of comments, blank lines of code) and more. The full list of metrics and their descriptions that we have used can be found in [12]. Then we compare the output of prediction with the actual values and evaluate its performance. The following subsection describes this in more details.

3.3   Evaluation

General importance of each metric for the defect prediction is evaluated upon building the model based on logistic regression. We test the statistical significance in a univariate model by making the opposite null-hypothesis that there is no relationship between the calculated coefficient and the defect-proneness of the modules. If the p-value is lower than 0.05, we reject the null-hypothesis and conclude that the observed metric is significant for prediction.

A more precise evaluation of the metrics that are statistically significant for prediction is done after building the decision trees. There are four possible outcomes when performing binary classification and they are present with the confusion matrix in Table 2. The faulty software modules constitute the positive (1) class, while non-faulty ones constitute the negative (0) class.

There are various evaluation metrics that can be computed using the true positive (TP), true negative (TN), false positive (FP) and false negative (FN) predictions. In this paper, we use the *geometric mean accuracy* (GM) to evaluate the performance of the decision tree classifier that is based on calculated level

Table 2. Confusion matrix for binary classification

Actual Value:	Predicted Value:	
	Faulty (1)	Non-Faulty(0)
Faulty(1)	**TP**	**FN**
Non-Faulty(0)	**FP**	**TN**

of threshold for each metric. GM is calculated as the geometric mean using the following equation:

$$GM = \sqrt{TPR \cdot TNR}, \tag{4}$$

where TPR (true positive rate) and TNR (true negative rate) are calculated as:

$$TPR = TP/(TP + FN), \\ TNR = TN/(TN + FP). \tag{5}$$

Its values are within a range of [0,1], higher results indicating better performance. The main advantage of this evaluation metric is its sensitivity to class imbalance [29]. We adopt the interpretation that metrics which achieve $GM > 0.6$ are considered effective for prediction [7,16].

4   Results

The first step in our case study was to build an univariate logistic regression model for each metric. We used a function built in the Matlab system for that. The statistical significance of computed coefficients is one of the outputs of that function. Metrics that had $p\text{-}value > 0.05$ were not considered relevant for defect prediction and were reject from following analysis. Table 3 presents how many times the null-hypothesis was rejected in each of the analyzed releases. The maximum number of times a metric could be significant is 10 because we used 10-fold cross-validation. Column named *sum* presents the average rate of significance in the project. The table is vertically divided in two parts, left part representing JDT releases and right part representing PDE releases. The metrics are placed in rows and we categorized several types of metrics in the table based on their summed values:

– Metrics significant in every release of both projects are marked **bold**,
– Metrics significant in majority of releases of both projects are not marked,
– Metrics rarely significant in both projects are marked in dark gray color,
– Metrics significant in every release of one project and rarely significant in the other are marked in light gray color.

Threshold values are calculated and evaluated in terms of GM each time a metric is considered significant. We have analyzed the distribution of GM values for all the datasets. Due to a great number of datasets and space limit, we

Table 3. Rate of rejecting the null-hypothesis in all datasets

Project:	JDT								PDE							
Release:	2.0.	2.1.	3.0.	3.1.	3.2.	3.3.	3.4.	sum	2.0.	2.1.	3.0.	3.1.	3.2.	3.3.	3.4.	sum
'LOC'	10	10	10	10	10	10	10	100%	10	10	10	10	10	10	10	100%
'SLOC_P'	10	10	10	10	10	10	10	100%	10	10	10	10	10	10	10	100%
'SLOC_L'	10	10	10	10	10	10	10	100%	10	10	10	10	10	10	10	100%
'MVG'	10	10	10	10	10	10	10	100%	10	10	10	10	10	10	10	100%
'BLOC'	10	10	10	10	10	10	10	100%	10	10	10	10	10	10	10	100%
'C_SLOC'	10	10	10	10	10	10	10	100%	10	10	10	10	10	10	10	100%
'CLOC'	10	10	10	10	10	10	10	100%	0	0	0.1	3	0	5	10	27%
'CWORD'	10	10	10	10	10	10	10	100%	0	0	0.1	0	5	10	10	37%
'HCLOC'	0	3	0	0	0	0	0	4%	8	0	0	0	0	0	10	26%
'HCWORD'	10	9	0	0	0	0	9	40%	7	0	10	0	0	0	10	39%
'No_Methods'	10	10	10	10	10	10	10	100%	10	10	10	10	10	10	10	100%
'LCOM'	0	0	0	0	0	0	0	0%	10	10	8	10	10	10	10	97%
'AVCC'	10	10	10	10	10	10	10	100%	10	10	10	10	10	10	10	100%
'NOS'	10	10	10	10	10	10	10	100%	10	10	10	10	10	10	10	100%
'HBUG'	10	10	10	10	10	10	10	100%	10	10	10	10	10	10	10	100%
'HEFF'	10	10	10	10	10	10	10	100%	10	10	10	10	10	10	10	100%
'UWCS'	10	10	10	10	10	10	10	100%	10	10	10	10	10	10	10	100%
'INST'	10	10	10	10	10	10	10	100%	10	10	10	10	10	10	10	100%
'PACK'	10	10	10	10	10	10	10	100%	10	10	10	10	10	10	10	100%
'RFC'	10	10	10	10	10	10	10	100%	10	10	10	10	10	10	10	100%
'CBO'	10	10	10	10	10	10	10	100%	0	0	0	0	0	0	0	0%
'MI'	10	10	10	10	10	10	10	100%	10	10	10	10	6	0	0	66%
'CCML'	10	10	10	10	10	10	10	100%	3	0.1	10	10	10	10	10	77%
'NLOC'	10	10	10	10	10	10	10	100%	10	10	10	10	10	10	10	100%
'F_IN'	10	10	10	10	10	10	10	100%	0	0	0	0	0	0	0	0%
'DIT'	0	0	0.1	0	5	0	10	23%	0	0	0.1	0	0	0	0	1%
'MINC'	10	10	10	10	10	10	10	100%	10	10	10	10	10	10	10	100%
'S_R'	0	0	0	0.1	0	6	10	24%	0	0	0	0	0	0	0	0%
'R_R'	10	10	10	10	10	10	10	100%	10	0	6	10	10	10	10	80%
'COH'	0	0	0	0	10	0	10	29%	10	6	0	0	0	0	5	30%
'LMC'	10	10	10	10	10	10	10	100%	10	10	10	10	10	10	10	100%
'LCOM2'	10	10	10	10	9	10	10	99%	10	10	8	10	10	10	10	97%
'MAXCC'	10	10	10	10	10	10	10	100%	10	10	10	10	10	10	10	100%
'HVOL'	10	10	10	10	10	10	10	100%	10	10	10	10	10	10	10	100%
'HIER'	10	10	10	10	10	10	10	100%	10	10	10	10	10	10	10	100%
'NQU'	10	10	10	10	10	10	10	100%	10	10	10	10	10	10	10	100%
'FOUT'	0	0	2	0	0	5	10	24%	0	0	2	0.1	0	0	0	4%
'SIX'	0	0	0	0.1	8	0	10	27%	0	0	0	0	0	0	0	0%
'EXT'	10	10	10	10	10	10	10	100%	0	0	2	10	10	10	10	60%
'NSUP'	10	10	10	10	10	10	10	100%	10	0	8	10	10	10	8	80%
'TCC'	10	10	10	10	10	10	10	100%	10	10	10	10	10	10	10	100%
'NSUB'	0	0	3	0.1	2	9	10	36%	0	0	0	0	0	0	0	0%
'MPC'	10	10	10	10	10	10	10	100%	0	0	2	10	10	10	10	60%
'NCO'	10	10	10	10	10	10	10	100%	10	10	10	10	10	10	10	100%
'INTR'	10	10	10	10	10	10	10	100%	10	2	10	10	10	10	10	89%
'CCOM'	10	10	10	10	10	10	10	100%	10	10	10	10	10	10	10	100%
'HLTH'	10	10	10	10	10	10	10	100%	10	10	10	10	10	10	10	100%
'MOD'	10	10	10	10	10	10	8	97%	3	0	0	0	0	0	0	4%

present the distribution of results only for all releases together. The box and whisker plots is given in Figs. 2 and 3. The central mark presents the median, the box is interquartile range, the whiskers extend to the non-outlier range, and outliers are plotted individually. Due to a great number of metrics, we omitted the ones that did not have 100% rate of significance in the previous analysis. The majority of presented metrics is considered effective, according to the ($GM > 0.6$) interpretation. Figure 2 presents the results obtained from the releases of JDT project. From the size of the box, we can see that the majority of metrics exhibits rather stable prediction performance. The best performing metrics achieve GM value above 0.7. Figure 3 presents the results obtained from the releases of PDE project. Comparing to the JDT project, the size of the box is wider and, hence, the performance of metrics is less stable. However, the best performing metrics achieve admirable GM values above 0.8.

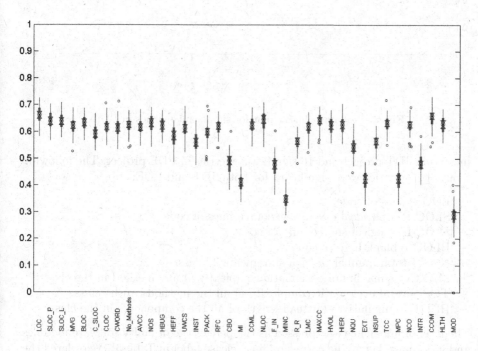

Fig. 2. Box and whisker plot for significant metrics in JDT

The threshold values of metrics that are significant in terms of statistical test ($p\text{-}value < 0.05$) and prediction performance ($GM > 0.6$) are given in Tables 4 and 5. We presented the mean and the standard deviation (in brackets) of threshold values for each release. The metrics are placed in rows and the releases are placed in columns. The threshold values of metrics 'HEFF' and 'HVOL' in Table 5 need to be multiplied by 10^4. In both projects combined, 21 different metrics were significant for defect prediction. There are 13 significant

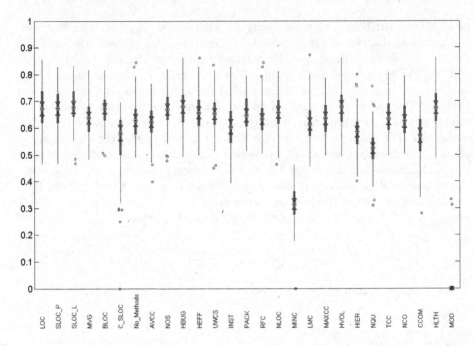

Fig. 3. Box and whisker plot for significant metrics in PDE

metrics in JDT project and 16 significant metrics in PDE project. The following 8 out of 21 metrics were significant for both JDT and PDE:

- 'LOC' - lines of code,
- 'SLOC-P' - physical executable source lines of code
- 'SLOC-L' - logical source lines of code
- 'BLOC' - blank lines of code
- 'NOS' - total number of Java statements in class
- 'MAXCC' - maximum cyclomatic complexity of any method in the class
- 'TCC' - total cyclomatic complexity of all the methods in the class
- 'HLTH' - cumulative Halstead length of all the components in the class

The level of imbalance is expressed as the percentage of faulty software modules and it is shown below the corresponding release label in Table 5. We ordered the releases in the table according to the level of imbalance to get an insight into the effect of data imbalance on threshold values. The standard deviation of each threshold is at least two orders of magnitude lower than its mean value. Hence, we conclude that the threshold values are very stable within the 10 folds of each release.

4.1   Discussion

In this paper we wanted to analyze the impact of data imbalance on the stability of threshold values. For the JDT project, all the thresholds have the lowest

Table 4. Threshold values for significant metrics (ordered by level of imbalance)

Project:	JDT						
Release:	2.0.	3.0.	3.2.	3.1.	2.1.	3.3.	3.4.
Imbalance:	46%	38%	36%	33%	32%	24%	18%
'LOC'	160.50 (0.95)	199.08 (2.03)	208.10 (1.29)	200.68 (1.71)	202.59 (1.77)	191.19 (1.36)	201.32 (1.53)
'SLOC_P'	100.84 (0.98)	123.23 (1.45)	132.70 (1.31)	127.80 (1.24)	129.40 (1.28)	118.00 (1.18)	122.79 (1.05)
'SLOC_L'	75.21 (0.73)	91.92 (1.02)	99.20 (1.10)	96.14 (0.92)	96.79 (0.98)	88.11 (0.86)	91.89 (0.77)
'BLOC'	18.51 (0.16)	21.50 (0.19)	24.16 (0.15)	23.37 (0.14)	23.12 (0.26)	20.73 (0.13)	22.60 (0.13)
'No_Methods'	9.01 (0.06)	10.34 (0.14)	10.80 (0.11)	10.61 (0.09)	10.57 (0.12)	10.00 (0.10)	9.94 (0.07)
'NOS'	61.84 (0.63)	74.16 (1.03)	78.67 (0.90)	75.65 (0.89)	77.65 (0.84)	71.56 (0.78)	71.99 (0.60)
'CCML'	39.22 (0.29)	48.83 (0.57)	45.05 (0.52)	43.07 (0.55)	44.80 (0.48)	46.70 (0.41)	48.95 (0.75)
'NLOC'	83.45 (0.75)	99.01 (1.41)	104.66 (1.13)	100.16 (1.18)	103.65 (1.04)	95.61 (0.89)	96.56 (0.75)
'MAXCC'	5.00 (0.04)	5.55 (0.07)	5.67 (0.04)	5.21 (0.03)	5.66 (0.04)	5.41 (0.03)	5.56 (0.03)
'TCC'	20.41 (0.19)	24.26 (0.35)	25.67 (0.23)	24.58 (0.27)	25.26 (0.23)	23.36 (0.24)	23.47 (0.17)
'NCO'	6.35 (0.05)	7.50 (0.12)	7.67 (0.10)	7.24 (0.07)	7.58 (0.10)	7.30 (0.08)	7.20 (0.07)
'CCOM'	14.67 (0.14)	16.74 (0.31)	16.27 (0.24)	15.96 (0.17)	16.93 (0.18)	16.87 (0.15)	16.55 (0.24)
'HLTH'	471.22 (5.37)	570.77 (8.74)	612.52 (6.13)	583.54 (6.66)	596.74 (6.47)	547.53 (6.43)	557.38 (5.04)

Table 5. Threshold values for significant metrics (ordered by level of imbalance)

Project:	PDE						
Release:	3.2.	3.3.	3.1.	3.0.	3.4.	2.0.	2.1.
Imbalance:	46%	44%	32%	31%	28%	19%	16%
'LOC'	143.16 (1.61)	146.49 (1.31)	154.70 (1.41)	151.88 (1.90)	141.68 (1.46)	147.51 (2.45)	165.59 (2.55)
'SLOC_P'	100.93 (1.29)	106.67 (1.13)	116.54 (1.27)	113.39 (1.59)	102.29 (1.23)	116.43 (2.22)	124.41 (1.99)
'SLOC_L'	73.27 (0.95)	78.37 (0.86)	84.05 (0.92)	81.55 (1.10)	75.72 (0.91)	85.88 (1.57)	89.29 (1.44)
'MVG'	15.09 (0.21)	16.47 (0.19)	16.88 (0.23)	16.51 (0.40)	15.76 (0.22)	15.62 (0.28)	17.39 (0.37)
'BLOC'	13.98 (0.12)	14.76 (0.12)	14.06 (0.14)	14.40 (0.15)	15.20 (0.13)	12.25 (0.22)	15.14 (0.18)
'NOS'	62.35 (0.73)	64.99 (0.72)	68.76 (0.83)	67.60 (0.86)	63.09 (0.75)	69.93 (1.26)	73.21 (1.38)
'HBUG'	0.80 (0.01)	0.84 (0.01)	0.89 (0.01)	0.86 (0.01)	0.82 (0.01)	0.87 (0.02)	0.93 (0.02)
'HEFF' [E+4]	2.78 (0.05)	2.99 (0.05)	3.01 (0.05)	2.93 (0.06)	2.98 (0.05)	2.78 (0.07)	3.09 (0.09)
'UWCS'	14.09 (0.15)	14.15 (0.12)	15.18 (0.17)	15.10 (0.20)	13.69 (0.16)	16.09 (0.18)	15.81 (0.23)
'PACK'	6.97 (0.07)	8.09 (0.06)	8.06 (0.07)	7.23 (0.08)	8.52 (0.08)	8.44 (0.11)	8.38 (0.11)
'RFC'	9.32 (0.10)	9.71 (0.07)	9.86 (0.11)	9.74 (0.09)	9.44 (0.08)	10.01 (0.13)	9.82 (0.09)
'NLOC'	85.34 (1.02)	88.03 (0.97)	95.47 (1.12)	93.38 (1.22)	85.03 (0.93)	95.49 (1.75)	101.91 (1.93)
'MAXCC'	4.41 (0.04)	4.63 (0.05)	4.53 (0.05)	4.49 (0.08)	4.55 (0.03)	4.25 (0.06)	4.57 (0.05)
'HVOL' [E+4]	2.41 (0.03)	2.52 (0.03)	2.66 (0.03)	2.57 (0.04)	2.45 (0.03)	2.61 (0.05)	2.80 (0.07)
'TCC'	19.24 (0.23)	20.53 (0.21)	20.62 (0.26)	20.19 (0.32)	20.04 (0.22)	19.52 (0.32)	20.99 (0.34)
'HLTH'	476.37 (6.10)	497.55 (5.54)	526.96 (6.21)	510.47 (7.13)	484.96 (5.97)	520.08 (10.17)	552.55 (11.50)

values in the most balanced dataset (release 2.0.) and rather stable value in the remaining datasets. Considering that JDT 2.0. is the earliest release and its liking rate is the lowest, the more emphasized difference may not be caused by data imbalance. For the PDE project, almost all the thresholds have the lowest values in the most balanced dataset (release 3.2.). Unlike the JDT 2.0., PDE 3.2. release is not the earliest nor does it have the lowest linking rate. Moreover, some metrics in PDE project exhibit a predominantly increasing rate of threshold values with higher levels of imbalance (for example 'LOC', 'SLOC-P', 'HLTH'). That is why we suspect that the data imbalance may have an impact on the threshold values for some metrics, after all. On the other hand, some metrics have a rather stable threshold value regardless of imbalance ('No_methods' 'MAXCC', 'NCO' and 'CCOM' for JDT and 'HBUG', 'UWCS', 'MAXCC', 'RFC' and 'TCC' for PDE).

Some of the metrics that are significant in both projects do have similar threshold values. For example, the range of threshold values for 'NOS' is [61–79] for JDT and [62–74] for PDE; for 'SLOC-P' it is [100–132] for JDT and [100–125] for PDE. On the other hand, some of the metrics are more diverse between the two projects which we have analyzed. For example, the maximum threshold value for 'LOC' is 202 for JDT and only 165 for PDE; for 'HTLT' it is 612 for JDT and 552 for PDE.

Our metrics 'No_Methods' and 'NSUB' are also known as 'WMC' and 'NOC' in related studies. The mean of threshold value of 'WMC' in related research varies from 10.49 [16], 13.5–13.94 [17] up to 23.17 [7]. The mean threshold value of 'No_Methods' varies from 9 to 10.8 in JDT and from 9.18 to 9.88 in PDE, which is similar to [16]. Although this metric passes the statistical significance criterion in every dataset, its GM value was lower than 0.6 for some datasets in PDE. Another metric that is often significant in related studies is 'CBO'. We obtained the same results for JDT, but the completely opposite results for PDE, where it was never significant. On the other hand, 'RFC' was found statistically significant both in our case study and in related research. However, the threshold values were 9.2–11.02 for JDT, 9.3–10.01 for PDE in our case study and 26.82 [16], around 40 [17] or 41.77 [7] in related studies. The 'DIT' metric was rarely significant in related studies and our case study confirmed this.

All of these examples confirm that general threshold values are hard to find and cross-project SDP is still difficult to achieve. Instead, we may only find generally significant or insignificant metrics. This case study also shows somewhat unexpected results. Software metrics that present very important features of object oriented code and its design, like for example cohesion or coupling, seam to be less often significant to defect prediction. This shows that most of previous research intentions that focused on a smaller number of intuitively important metrics offered a narrow view of this complex problem. That is why we believe this methodology should to be used to gain additional knowledge that can be used to improve the multivariate defect prediction models.

5   Conclusion and Future Work

This paper replicated the methodology for deriving the threshold values of software metrics which are effective for SDP. Afterwards, we analyzed the rate of metrics' significance, the spread of threshold values and we compared the central tendency of these values among different datasets. Unlike previous studies, our focus was not on finding generally applicable threshold values. Instead, we analyzed the stability of thresholds for within-project defect prediction. For that purpose we tested the metrics using a statistical test of significance and cross-validated the geometric mean accuracy of defect prediction. The results revealed that all the metrics that passed the two significance criteria had stable threshold values within the same release of a project. Data imbalance may have influenced the threshold values of some metrics, for which we noticed different values in the most balanced datasets and an increasing trend of values. Some of the derived thresholds were stable regardless of data imbalance and some were stable even across different projects. However, the results and the discussion pointed out that practitioners need to use the presented methodology for their specific projects because it is difficult to obtain general conclusions with regard to threshold values.

It is important to discuss the threats to construct, internal and external validity of this empirical case study. Construct validity is threaten by the fact that we do not posses industrial data. However, we used carefully collected datasets from large, complex and long lasting open source projects. The choice of threshold derivation model is a threat to internal validity, so we have used a model that was used and replicated in related studies. The main disadvantage of this case study is the inability to discover strong evidence regarding the influence of data imbalance on the stability of derived threshold values. Finally, the external validity is very limited by the diversity of data we have used. The results of this case study are reflecting the context of open source projects, in particular from the Eclipse community. We used only two projects and both are quite central for the Eclipse community. Our future work will expand the number of datasets and combine the results of this case study with our previous research in evolving co-evolutionary multi-objective genetic programming (CoMOGP) classification algorithm for SDP. We plan to use the calculated rate of significance for better definition of the weights that are assigned to each metric in the CoMOGP. We also plan to use the estimated threshold values for building the decision tree in the CoMOGP. Instead of taking the absolute value of each metric, we will use the distance of its value from the threshold. That way, we hope to achieve a more focused CoMOGP and improve the prediction results.

Acknowledgments. This work is supported in part by Croatian Science Foundation's funding of the project UIP-2014-09-7945 and by the University of Rijeka Research Grant 13.09.2.2.16.

References

1. Chidamber, S.R., Kemerer, C.F.: A metrics suite for object oriented design. IEEE Trans. Softw. Eng. **20**(6), 476–493 (1994)
2. Briand, L.C., Daly, J.W., Wust, J.K.: A unified framework for coupling measurement in object-oriented systems. IEEE Trans. Softw. Eng. **25**(1), 91–121 (1999)
3. Basili, V.R., Briand, L.C., Melo, W.L.: A validation of object-oriented design metrics as quality indicators. IEEE Trans. Softw. Eng. **22**(10), 751–761 (1996)
4. Radjenović, D., Heričko, M., Torkar, R., Živković, A.: Software fault prediction metrics: a systematic literature review. Inf. Softw. Technol. **55**(8), 1397–1418 (2013)
5. Arisholm, E., Briand, L.C., Johannessen, E.B.: A systematic and comprehensive investigation of methods to build and evaluate fault prediction models. J. Syst. Softw. **83**(1), 2–17 (2010)
6. Shatnawi, R., Li, W.: The effectiveness of software metrics in identifying error-prone classes in post-release software evolution process. J. Syst. Softw. **81**(11), 1868–1882 (2008)

7. Shatnawi, R.: A quantitative investigation of the acceptable risk levels of object-oriented metrics in open-source systems. IEEE Trans. Softw. Eng. **36**(2), 216–225 (2010)
8. Galinac Grbac, T., Huljenić, D.: On the probability distribution of faults in complex software systems. Inf. Softw. Technol. **58**, 250–258 (2015)
9. Hall, T., Beecham, S., Bowes, D., Gray, D., Counsell, S.: A systematic literature review on fault prediction performance in software engineering. IEEE Trans. Softw. Eng. **38**(6), 1276–1304 (2012)
10. He, H., Garcia, E.A.: Learning from imbalanced data. IEEE Trans. Knowl. Data Eng. **21**(9), 1263–1284 (2009)
11. Galinac Grbac, T., Runeson, P., Huljenić, D.: A second replicated quantitative analysis of fault distributions in complex software systems. IEEE Trans. Softw. Eng. **39**(4), 462–476 (2013)
12. Mauša, G., Galinac Grbac, T.: Co-evolutionary multi-population genetic programming for classification in software defect prediction: an empirical case study. Appl. Soft Comput. **55**, 331–351 (2017)
13. Graning, L., Jin, Y., Sendhoff, B.: Generalization improvement in multi-objective learning. In: The 2006 IEEE International Joint Conference on Neural Network Proceedings, pp. 4839–4846 (2006)
14. Eiben, A.E., Smith, J.E.: Introduction to Evolutionary Computing. Springer, Heidelberg (2003)
15. Martin, W.N., Lienig, J., Cohoon, J.P.: Island (migration) models: evolutionary algorithms based on punctuated equilibria. Handb. Evol. Comput. **6**, 1–15 (1997)
16. Arar, O.F., Ayan, K.: Deriving thresholds of software metrics to predict faults on open source software. Expert Syst. Appl. **61**(1), 106–121 (2016)
17. Shatnawi, R.: Deriving metrics thresholds using log transformation. J. Softw.: Evol. Process **27**(2), 95–113 (2015). JSME-14-0025.R2
18. Mauša, G., Galinac Grbac, T., Dalbelo Bašić, B.: A systemathic data collection procedure for software defect prediction. Comput. Sci. Inf. Syst. **13**(1), 173–197 (2016)
19. Oliveira, P., Valente, M.T., Lima, F.P.: Extracting relative thresholds for source code metrics. In: Proceedings of CSMR-WCRE, pp. 254–263 (2014)
20. Weiss, G.M.: Mining with rarity: a unifying framework. SIGKDD Explor. Newsl. **6**(1), 7–19 (2004)
21. Andersson, C., Runeson, P.: A replicated quantitative analysis of fault distributions in complex software systems. IEEE Trans. Softw. Eng. **33**(5), 273–286 (2007)
22. Fenton, N.E., Ohlsson, N.: Quantitative analysis of faults and failures in a complex software system. IEEE Trans. Softw. Eng. **26**(8), 797–814 (2000)
23. Bhowan, U., Johnston, M., Zhang, M., Yao, X.: Evolving diverse ensembles using genetic programming for classification with unbalanced data. IEEE Trans. Evol. Comput. **17**(3), 368–386 (2013)
24. Mauša, G., Galinac Grbac, T., Dalbelo Bašić, B.: Software defect prediction with bug-code analyzer - a data collection tool demo. In: Proceedings of SoftCOM 2014 (2014)
25. Mauša, G., Perković, P., Galinac Grbac, T., Štajduhar, I.: Techniques for bug-code linking. In: Proceedings of SQAMIA 2014, pp. 47–55 (2014)
26. Hastie, T., Tibshirani, R., Friedman, J.: The Elements of Statistical Learning: Data Mining, Inference and Prediction, 2nd edn. Springer, Heidelberg (2009)
27. Zimmermann, T., Nagappan, N.: Predicting defects using network analysis on dependency graphs. In: Proceedings of the 30th International Conference on Software Engineering. ICSE 2008, pp. 531–540. ACM, New York (2008)

28. Bender, R.: Quantitative risk assessment in epidemiological studies investigating threshold effects. Biometrical J. **41**(3), 305–319 (1999)
29. Bhowan, U., Johnston, M., Zhang, M., Yao, X.: Reusing genetic programming for ensemble selection in classification of unbalanced data. IEEE Trans. Evol. Comput. **18**, 893–908 (2013)

Big Data DBMS Assessment: A Systematic Mapping Study

Maria Isabel Ortega$^{(\boxtimes)}$, Marcela Genero, and Mario Piattini

Institute of Technology and Information Systems,
University of Castilla-La Mancha, Ciudad Real, Spain
misabel.ortega2@alu.uclm.es,
{marcela.genero,mario.piattini}@uclm.es

Abstract. The tremendous prosperity of big data systems that has occurred in recent years has made its understanding crucial for both research and industrial communities. Big Data is expected to generate an economy of 15 billion euros over the next few years and to have repercussions that will more or less directly change the way in which we live. It is, therefore, important for organizations to have quality Database Management Systems (DBMSs) that will allow them to manage large volumes of data in real time and according to their needs. The last decade has witnessed an explosion of new Database Management Systems (DBMSs) which deal not only with relational Data Bases but also with non-relational Data Bases. Companies need to assess DBMS quality in order, for example, to select which DBMS is most appropriate for their needs. The main research question formulated in this research is, therefore, *"What is the state of the art of Big Data DBMS assessment?"*, which we attempt to answer by following a well-known methodology called "Systematic Mapping Studies" (SMS). This paper describes an SMS of papers published until May 2016. Five digital libraries were searched, and 19 papers were identified and classified into five dimensions: quality characteristics of Big Data DBMSs, techniques and measures used to assess the quality characteristics, DBMSs whose quality has been measured, evolution over time and research methods utilized. The results indicate that there are several benchmarks, which are principally focused on the performance of MongoDB and Cassandra, and that the interest in Big Data DBMS quality is growing. Nonetheless, more research is needed in order to define and validate a quality model that will bring together all the relevant characteristics of DBMSs for Big Data and their respective measures. This quality model will then be employed as a basis on which to build benchmarks for DBMSs, covering not only the diversity of DBMSs and application scenarios and types of applications, but also diverse and representative real-world data sets.

Keywords: Big data · DBMS · Quality · Benchmark

1 Introduction

The technological advances we have been experiencing in recent years, such as cloud computing, the Internet of Things and social networks, have led to a continuous increase in data, which are accumulating at an unprecedented rate. The term Big Data

© Springer International Publishing AG 2017
Y. Ouhammou et al. (Eds.): MEDI 2017, LNCS 10563, pp. 96–110, 2017.
DOI: 10.1007/978-3-319-66854-3_8

was coined to represent the large amount and many types of digital data, including documents, images, videos, audio and websites. All of the aforementioned technologies were the forerunners to the arrival of what has been called the Big Data era.

Big Data is expected to generate an economy of 15 billion euros over the next few years, and it will have very many repercussions that will change the way in which we live to a greater or lesser extent. This future, which is so impressive as regards numbers and seems so promising, signifies that the appearance of Big Data has attracted the attention of industry, academia and governments.

In fact, the McKinsey Global Institute [1] estimated that data volume was growing by 40% per year, and would grow to 44 times its initial size between 2009 and 2020. However, the volume of data is not the only important characteristic. Most of the tech industry follows Gartner's '3Vs' (Volume, Velocity and Variety) model to define Big Data [3], and Dijcks [2] recently added one more characteristic to this model: Value. Many other authors also propose that Veracity should be considered.

It is, therefore, important for organizations to have quality Database Management Systems (DBMSs) that will allow them to manage large volumes of data in real time and according to their needs.

For all of the above reasons, the last decade has witnessed an explosion of new Database Management Systems (DBMSs) which deal not only with relational data bases but also with non-relational data bases (NoSQL databases). And companies need to assess quality characteristics for the current and emerging DBMSs in order, for example, to compare which is more appropriate according to the actual needs.

The main research question formulated in this research is, therefore, *"What is the state of the art of Big Data DBMS assessment?"* which we attempt to answer by following a well-known methodology called "Systematic Mapping Studies" (SMS). A systematic mapping study provides an objective procedure with which to identify the nature and extent of the research that is available to answer a particular research question. These kinds of studies also help to identify gaps in current research in order to suggest areas for further investigation. They therefore also provide a framework and background in which to appropriately develop future research activities [1].

The remainder of the paper is organized as follows. Section 2 presents a brief discussion of related work. This is followed by an outline of the SMS and a description of the activities of the SMS process in Sect. 3. Section 4 presents the complete procedure followed to develop the SMS, whilst the main results obtained are presented in Sect. 5. The paper concludes with a discussion of the results and outlines future work.

2 Related Work

To the best of our knowledge, the relevant literature contains no systematic literature reviews (SLR) or SMS that tackle Big Data DBMS quality. It is, however, true that there are some works whose aim is to provide the state of art regarding different issues related to Big Data:

- Mathisen et al. [2] presents a systematic mapping review that provides an overview of empirical papers dealing with Big Data and categorizes them according to the

3 V's. These authors conclude that no systematic review of empirical work has been carried out to date in the field of Big Data.

- Ruixan [3] presents a bibliometrical analysis of the Big Data research in China. They conclude that research based on Big Data now has an outline, although most papers that present the theoretical step of the research lack sufficient practical sustenance, and they consequently recommend intensifying efforts based on both theory and practice.
- Jeong and Ghani [4] carried out a review of semantic technologies for Big Data, concluding that their analysis shows that there is a need to put more effort into suggesting new approaches. They also note that tools need to be created with the purpose of encouraging researchers and practitioners to realize the true power of semantic computing and support them as regards solving the crucial issues of Big Data.
- Wang and Krishnan [5] present a review whose aim is to provide an overview of the characteristics of clinical Big Data. They describe some commonly employed computational algorithms, statistical methods, and software tool kits for data manipulation and analysis, and discuss the challenges and limitations in this field.
- Polato et al. [6] conducted a systematic literature review to assess research contributions to Apache Hadoop. The objective was to detect possible gaps, providing motivation for fresh research, and outline collaborations with Apache Hadoop and its environment, categorizing and quantifying the central topics dealt with in literature.
- Hashem et al. [7] assessed the rise of Big Data in cloud computing, studying research challenges focused on scalability, availability, data integrity, data transformation, data quality, data heterogeneity, privacy, legal and regulatory issues, and governance. Finally, they provided an overview of open research topics that require substantial research efforts.

The literature review presented in this paper is different from those mentioned above in that it tackles Big Data DBMS quality, which has not been researched to date. Moreover, this literature review has been carried out in a systematic and rigorous manner, following the guidelines provided in [8, 13].

3   SMS Outline

A systematic mapping study consists of three activities: planning, execution, and reporting [8]. Each of these activities is divided into several steps. The first step when developing an SMS is the definition of the review protocol, which establishes a controlled procedure with which to conduct the review. The execution activity includes data retrieval, study selection, data extraction, and data synthesis. Finally, the reporting activity presents and interprets the results.

3.1 Planning the Review

The aim of this SMS is to gather all existing proposals regarding the assessment of the quality characteristics of DBMSs for Big Data. To this end, the following research question was formulated:

"What is the state of the art of the Big Data DBMS assessment?"

As this question is too broad to answer, we have split it into five research questions, which are shown in Table 1.

Table 1. Research questions

Research questions	Main motivation
RQ1. Which quality characteristics of Big Data DBMSs have been investigated by researchers?	To identify the quality characteristics of DBMSs with which to manage Big Data that have been addressed by researchers, and map them onto the quality characteristics proposed in ISO/IEC 25010 [9]
RQ2. Which techniques and quality measures are used to assess the quality characteristics?	To identify which quality assurance techniques for Big Data DBMSs have been used and which measures have been proposed to assess the quality characteristics of Big Data DBMSs
RQ3. Which DBMSs have been evaluated by researchers and how is the data represented in them?	To identify which DBMSs have been evaluated and what kind of data representation is used
RQ4. How has the research into the quality of Big Data DBMSs evolved over time?	To discover the importance that has been placed on empirical studies on the topic of Big Data DBMS quality over time
RQ5. What research methods have been used to investigate the quality of Big Data DBMSs?	To determine whether or not the research has been validated. Also, to discover which research method was used to validate it

3.2 Search Strategy

The research question was decomposed into individual elements related to the technology (technology acceptance model), the study type (evaluation) and the response measure (correlation with actual effort) used, in order to obtain the main search terms. Secondly, key words obtained from known primary studies were assessed in order to obtain other main terms. Synonyms for the main terms were then identified. Finally, the search string was constructed using the Boolean "AND" to join the main terms and the Boolean "OR" to include synonyms. This process enabled the main search terms and alternative terms (spellings, synonyms and terms related to the major terms) to be defined, as is shown in Table 2.

The final search string was: "("Database Management System" OR DBMS OR Warehouse OR "Data system") AND (evaluat* OR measur* OR assess* OR test* OR

Table 2. Search string terms

Main terms	Alternative terms
Database management system	("Database management system" OR DBMS OR warehouse OR "data system")
Evaluate	(evaluat* OR measur* OR assess* OR test* OR analys* OR select* OR compar* OR adquisi* OR implement* OR benchmark)
Big data	("Big Data" OR "NewSQL" OR "No SQL" OR NoSQL)

analys* OR select* OR compar* OR adquisi* OR implement* OR benchmark) AND ("Big Data" OR "New SQL" OR "No SQL" OR NoSQL))".

The search was performed in digital libraries that contain a wide variety of computer science journals. The search was specifically performed in Scopus database, Science@Direct, IEEE Digital Library, Springer database and ACM Digital Library. As we wished to guarantee the reliability of the elements that would be studied, we analyzed only journal papers, workshop papers and conference papers. Table 3 summarizes the search strategy defined.

Table 3. Search strategy

Databases	Scopus Science@Direct (subject computer science) IEEE digital library ACM digital library Springer database
Target items	Journal papers Workshop papers Conference papers
Search applied to	Title Abstract Keywords
Language	Papers written in English
Publication period	Until May 2016 (inclusive)

3.3 Selection Criteria and Procedure

The intention of this SMS was to discover all papers that present any research related to Big Data DBMS Quality, that are written in English and have been published until May 2016. The start of the publication period was not established because we wished to discover since when Big Data DBMS quality proposals have existed. Papers were excluded according to the selection criteria shown in Table 4.

The study selection procedure was executed with the final string defined above, and was conducted in two stages. In the first stage, the selection of the studies was executed by reviewing the title, the abstract and the keywords of the studies; only those papers that dealt with Big Data DBMS quality were selected. The set of papers selected in the first stage was used as the basis for the second stage, which consisted of reading the full texts of these papers and applying the inclusion and exclusion criteria.

Table 4. Inclusion and exclusion criteria

Inclusion criteria	Journals, conferences and workshop papers Papers written in English Papers published until May 2016 (inclusive)
Exclusion criteria	Papers not focusing on DBMS quality Papers focusing on data quality Papers available only in the form of abstracts or PowerPoint presentations Duplicate papers (the same paper in different databases) Papers in which Big Data DBMS quality is mentioned only as a general introductory term, or in which there are no proposals related to quality among the paper's contributions

3.4 Data Extraction and Synthesis Procedure

A set of five dimensions was used to classify the research, based on the research questions described above. This classification scheme was developed prior to the first round of data extraction and was subsequently refined after the pilot data had been extracted and analyzed. The possible categories are based on the results found during the review. A summary of the classification scheme is presented in Table 5. The detailed classification scheme is available at http://alarcos.esi.uclm.es/DBMS-BigData-Quality.

Table 5. Summary of the classification scheme

Dimensions	Categories
Quality characteristic	Product quality in use model: efficiency Product quality model: performance efficiency, adaptability, availability and usability
Techniques and measures	YCSB, YCSB ++, LUBM, TPCX-HS, BigDataBench and Others
DBMS	MongoDB, Cassandra, Riak, HBase, Neo4j, Hadoop, Redis, CouchDB, MySQL, Phoenix, Spark, Hive, Pig, Oracle and DB2
Time evolution	The year of the publication
Research method	Proposal, evaluation, validation, philosophical, opinion or personal experience [10]

4 Conducting the Review

The SMS was carried out by following all the steps of the protocol defined previously. Nonetheless, as the definition of the protocol is iterative, we have made some modifications to it during the execution. The version of the protocol presented in the previous section is the final one.

The SMS was completed in 9 months, and this period included the time needed for planning, conducting and reporting. 957 papers were initially founded. We found 430 studies in Scopus, 382 studies in ACM, 3 studies in Science Direct and 142 studies in IEEE. No studies were found in Springer.

After applying the inclusion and exclusion criteria and reviewing the title and abstract of each paper, the number of papers selected was reduced to 86. As will be observed, we selected 58 studies form Scopus, 19 studies form ACM, 2 studies form Science Direct and 7 studies form IEEE.

17 papers were also subsequently excluded because they were duplicated (the same paper in a different database). As is shown in Fig. 1, we removed 15 studies from Scopus and 2 studies from ACM.

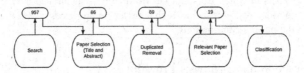

Fig. 1. Selection process

Inclusion and exclusion criteria were applied to the full text and 40 more papers were discarded. The final 19 papers were analyzed and their results were synthesized and interpreted. Figure 1 shows the selection process employed. The list of the primary studies selected is available at http://alarcos.esi.uclm.es/DBMS-BigData-Quality.

Table 6 summarizes the chronology of activities rigorously performed to carry out the SMS. The identification and selection of studies took place between February 2016 and November 2016. This period included the protocol refinement.

Table 6. Review outline

Chronology	Step	Activities	Outcome
March 2016	Planning	Protocol development	Reviewed protocol
May 2016	Conducting	Data retrieval	Metadata information of 957 papers
		Paper selection (title and abstract)	Metadata information of 86 papers selected
		Removal of duplicates	Metadata information of 69 papers selected
		Extraction of files of the papers	Repository of papers (69 papers)
July 2016	Planning	Protocol improvement Pilot data extraction	Data extraction form (classification scheme refined), 69 papers reviewed
August 2016	Conducting	Paper selection, classification (full text)	Data extraction form complete, 19 papers classified
		Data synthesis	
November 2016	Reporting	Report on the stages and activities undertaken during the development of the SMS	Final report of the SMS

5   Reporting Results and Data Synthesis

In this section, the answers to each of the questions formulated in Sect. 3 are presented and interpreted, in addition to which the dimensions covered by the questions are combined.

5.1   RQ1. Which Quality Characteristics of Big Data DBMSs Have Been Investigated by Researchers?

The process used to match the characteristics in the ISO/IEC 25010 standard [9] with the characteristics investigated in the paper is described as follows. The full text of the paper was read in order to search for quality characteristics, and we then looked at the standard for the characteristics that best matched the characteristics found in the paper. In the review of the full text of the selected papers, it was found that in the majority the authors used several terms to refer to the quality characteristics being researched. These terms were analyzed until the characteristics that best fitted them was found in the standard.

The results obtained for RQ1 revealed that most of the papers selected addressed only one quality characteristic or sub-characteristic. We found that the quality model most frequently investigated is the product quality model. The characteristics of the quality product model most frequently researched were performance efficiency (89.47%), distantly followed by usability (10.53%) the adaptability sub-characteristic. The reliability was most frequently researched through the use of the availability sub-characteristic, with the same amount of appearances as those of the usability characteristic (5.26%). Table 7 shows which paper evaluates each characteristic.

Table 7. Distribution of papers per characteristics of the ISO 25010 product quality model

Characteristic	Reference
Performance efficiency	[P01] [P02] [P03] [P04] [P05] [P06] [P08] [P09] [P10] [P11] [P13] [P14] [P15] [P16] [P17] [P18] [P19]
Usability	[P12]
Adaptability	[P06] [P07]
Availability	[P09]

We also found that only one article researched quality in use characteristics (efficiency (5.26%)). Table 8 shows which characteristic(s) or sub-characteristic(s) are evaluating each paper.

Table 8. Distribution of papers per characteristics of the ISO 25010 quality in use model

Characteristic	Reference
Efficiency	[P09]

These results could be explained by the fact that researchers are principally concerned with the rapid treatment of large volumes of data with the purpose of obtaining the value of the data, which is why they might research performance efficiency. Surprisingly, the security characteristic, which is usually crucial when selecting a Big Data DBMS in order to assess the privacy and integrity of the information, has not been addressed as regards the security of Big Data DBMSs.

5.2 RQ2. Which Techniques and Quality Measures Are Used in Order to Assess the Quality Characteristics?

Benchmarking provides us with the possibility of evaluating quality characteristics by comparing them with a standard. Various standards have been imposed in order to measure the quality of Big Data DBMSs, among others, and particularly to measure the performance of DBMSs. In conceptual terms, a big data benchmark aims to generate application-specific workloads and tests capable of processing big data with the 5 V properties (volume, velocity, variety, value and veracity) [11] in order to produce meaningful evaluation results [12].

The SMS revealed that most of the benchmarks that have been carried out are proposal of benchmarks (53.63%). These are followed by the Yahoo! Cloud Serving Benchmark (YCSB) at 31.58%, which is very distantly followed and with the same result of utilization by YCSB++ (5.26%), LUBM benchmark (5.26%), TPCx-HS (5.26%) and BigDataBench (5.26%). The results show the lack of consensus as regards the use of a benchmark when the intention is to ensure Big Data DBMS quality. At this point, the importance of achieving standardization is tangible, in order to ensure that all systems are measured with the same established criteria that will facilitate their comparison (Table 9).

Table 9. Metrics and techniques per primary studies

Reference	Technique	Metrics
[P01]	YCSB	*Latency*: relating time spend with the number of operations per second
[P02]	YCSB	*Latency*: relating time spend with the number of operations per second
[P03]	Proposal of benchmark	*Resource Utilization*: memory, CPU utilization, Garbage Collection (GC) statistics, heap memory usage, IO wait, disk read and write throughput, disk usage, OS load, etc. *Datastore*: Read and write throughput, pending read and write requests count, read and write latency, compactions completed, pending compactions, etc.
[P04]	LUMB benchmark	*vertical joins*: Cost (q, sdb) = |T|, where |T| is the number of pages in the table T. If an index is defined in the triple table, cost (q, sdb) = P (index) + sel(t) * |T|,

(continued)

Table 9. (*continued*)

Reference	Technique	Metrics
		where P(index) is the cost of index scanning and sel(t) is the selectivity of the triple pattern t as defined in [13] *binary joins*: the selection is made in the property tables. Cost q, sdb) = |T p| where Tp is the property table of the property of the query triple pattern. With an index on the selection predicate, cost(q,sdb) = P(index) + sel∗|Tp|, where sel is the selectivity of the index *horizontal joins*: the selection targets the tables of the class domain of the property of the query triple pattern. Cost(q,sdb) = Tcp∈dom(p)(|Tcp|), where Tcp are the tables corresponding to the classes domain of the property of the query triple pattern. If there is an index defined in the selection predicate, cost(q, sdb) = T cp∈dom(p)(P (index) + sel ∗ |T cp|) where sel is the index selectivity
[P05]	Proposal of benchmark benchmark	*general statistics (STATS)*: the algorithm counts the numbers of vertices and edges in the graph and computes the mean local clustering coefficient *breadth-first search (BFS)*: the algorithm traverses the graph starting from a seed vertex, and first visits all the neighbors of a vertex before moving to the neighbors of the neighbors *connected components (CONN)*: for each vertex, the algorithm determines the connected component it belongs to *community detection (CD)*: the algorithm detects groups of nodes that are more strongly connected to each other than they are connected to the rest of the graph *graph evolution (EVO)*: the algorithm predicts the evolution of the graph according to the "forest fire" model
[P06]	YCSB and YCSB++	Not specified
[P07]	Proposal of benchmark	*Load balancing*
[P08]	Proposal of benchmark	Not specified
[P09]	TPCx-HS	*Performance (HSph@SF):* the effective sort throughput of the benchmarked configuration: •HSph@SF = SF /(T /3600) Where: •SF is the Scale Factor •T is the total elapsed time for the run-in seconds *Price-performance metric:* •\$/HSph@SF = P HSph @ SF

(*continued*)

Table 9. (*continued*)

Reference	Technique	Metrics
		Where: •P is the total cost of ownership of the system being tested *System Availability Date:* when the benchmarked systems are generally available to any customer *TPCx-HS Energy Metrics:* expected to be accurate representations of system performance and energy consumption. The approach and methodology are explicitly detailed in this specification and the TPC Benchmark Standards, as defined in TPC- Energy
[P10]	YCSB	*Speed limit on a single node:* workload operations which consist of update heavy, read heavy, read only, read latest, short ranges and read-modify-write *Latency*: relating time spent with the number of operations per second *Workloads*: workload operations which consist of 95% of read and 5% of update sent by each client on non-master nodes
[P11]	YCSB	*Latency*: relating time spent with the number of operations per second
[P12]	YCSB	*Latency*: relating time spent with the number of operations per second
[P13]	Proposal of benchmark	*Latency*: relating time spent with the number of operations per second
[P14]	Proposal of benchmark	*RPS in short*: the number of processed requests per second Latency: relating time spent with the number of operations per second *OPS in short*: number of operations per second *DPS in short*: data processed per second *MIPS*: million instructions per second *MPKI*: MIS-Predictions per 1000 Instructions (branch prediction)
[P15]	BigDataBench	Not specified
[P16]	Proposal of benchmark	*Latency*: relating time spent with the number of operations per second
[P17]	Proposal of benchmark	Not specified
[P18]	Proposal of benchmark	Not specified
[P19]	Proposal of benchmark	*Query response time, tuning overhead, data arrival to query time, storage size* and *monetary cost*

5.3 RQ3. Which DBMSs Have Been Evaluated by Researchers and How Is the Data Represented in Them?

The results show that Cassandra (36%) and MongoDB (31%) stand out as the dominant DBMSs. They are followed by Hadoop (26%) and HBase (21%). There are other DMBSs that make a medium number of appearances in the papers, such as MySQL (15%), Riak (15%), Hive (10%), Redis (10%) and Neo4j (10%). The DBMSs which appear the least are Pig (5%), Spark (5%), Phoenix (5%), CouchDB (5%), Google (5%), Graph (5%), Giraph (5%), DB2 (5%) and Oracle (5%) (Fig 2).

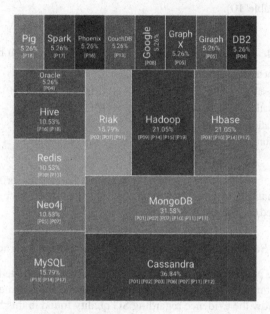

Fig. 2. Percentage of DBMSs evaluated in the primary studies

At this point, we should highlight the lack of maturity of the systems, thus making the use of larger and more complex systems such as Apache Hadoop, unnecessary. It is also noteworthy that more conventional DBMSs, such as Oracle or DB2, appear to be falling behind and giving way to new systems as a first alternative.

5.4 RQ4. How Has the Research into the Quality of Big Data DBMSs Research Evolved Over Time?

The question shows the apparent evolution of the quality of Big Data DBMS over time. It can be observed that it has been rising. This may be owing to the ever-growing weight of Big Data systems in our society and therefore to the importance of their efficiency and reliability. In the year 2016, only 1 item has been found concerning the quality of Big Data systems. This is probably because the review was finalized in May of that year and many of the referenced articles had not yet been published.

5.5   RQ5. What Research Methods Have Been Used to Investigate the Quality of Big Data DBMSs?

This question was answered by using the classification of research approaches proposed by Wieringa et al. [10], as recommended in Petersen et al. [14]. The scheme also presents the classification of non-empirical research, which contains the categories of proposal papers, evaluation papers, validation papers, philosophical papers, opinion papers and personal experience papers. The results showed that proposal (42%) stood out as the dominant research method. The second most common research method used was evaluation (32%); in third place was validation (16%), and finally in last place was opinion (1.0%) (Table 10).

Table 10. Distribution of papers per characteristics by research method

Characteristic	Reference
Proposal	[P05] [P06] [P07] [P08] [P10] [P12] [P13] [P18]
Evaluation	[P01] [P02] [P03] [P04] [P11] [P15]
Validation	[P14] [P16] [P19]
Opinion	[P09] [P17]

The results of this classification show that almost half of the primary studies are proposals or evaluations in laboratory contexts, and it is therefore evident that more validation is needed in industrial settings.

5.6   Combining Several RQs and Additional Information Extracted

Figure 3 shows the combination of the quality characteristics evaluated in the SMS, the quality characteristic, the DBMS, the research method and the techniques. The aim of this section is to show the evidence regarding SG quality found in this SLM, combining some research questions with additional information extracted from primary studies. This figure shows that, of the 19 studies analyzed:

- 9 of the primary studies focused on evaluating the performance efficiency and none of them used any of the existing standard benchmarks.
- The DBMSs which have been most frequently used to evaluate any of the quality characteristics are: MongoDB, Cassandra and Hadoop. Moreover, these DBMSs are principally used to ensure the performance efficiency of the DBMSs.
- The most frequently evaluated and modified benchmark is the YCBS benchmark. However, most of the primary studies are proposals and additionally proposed new techniques or benchmarks with which to assess the quality of Big Data DBMSs.

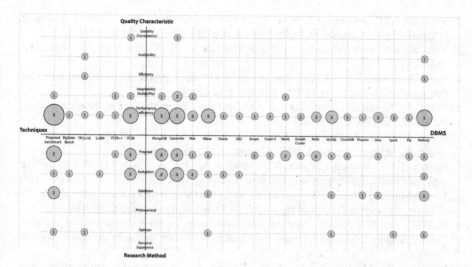

Fig. 3. Combination of quality characteristic, DBMSs, research method and techniques

6 Conclusions

Several efforts have been made in recent years to assess Big Data DBMS quality, but further work is needed. In this work we have, therefore, identified the different proposals regarding Big Data DBMS quality, in an attempt to answer the questions raised based on five facets: the quality characteristic investigated (Q1), the techniques and metrics used to assess the quality characteristics (Q2), the DMBSs used (Q3), the evolution of quality research over time (Q4) and the research method (Q5).

The results of the systematic mapping study presented in the previous sections allow us to state that there is an increasing interest in Big Data DBMS quality assessment. However, much still needs to be done. Thus, as future work we shall continue to advance in this line of work. We shall define and validate a quality model for Big Data DBMSs, integrating different exiting proposals, while in the long term we intend to build benchmarks based on the quality model that will cover not only the diversity of DBMSs and application scenarios and types of applications, but also diverse and representative real-world data sets.

Acknowledgements. This work has been funded by the SEQUOIA project (Ministerio de Economía y Competitividad and Fondo Europeo de Desarrollo Regional FEDER, TIN2015-63502-C3-1-R).

References

1. Budgen, D., Turner, M., Brereton, P., Kitchenham, B.: Using mapping studies in software engineering. In: Proceedings of PPIG, pp. 195–204 (2008)

2. Mathisen, B.M., Wienhofen, L.W.M., Roman, D.: Empirical big data research: a systematic literature mapping. Journal of ArXiv preprint arXiv:1509.03045 (2015)
3. Yang, R.: Bibliometrical analysis on the big data research in China. J. Digit. Inf. Manag. **11**, 383–390 (2013)
4. Jeong, S.R., Ghani, I.: Semantic computing for big data: approaches, tools, and emerging directions (2011–2014). ACM TIIS **8**, 2022–2042 (2014)
5. Wang, W., Krishnan, E.: Big data and clinicians: a review on the state of the science. Proc. JMIR Med. Inform. **2**, e1 (2014)
6. Polato, I., Ré, R., Goldman, A., Kon, F.: A comprehensive view of Hadoop research—a systematic literature review. J. Netw. Comput. Appl. **46**, 1–25 (2014)
7. Hashem, I.A.T., Yaqoob, I., Anuar, N.B., Mokhtar, S., Gani, A., Khan, S.U.: The rise of "big data" on cloud computing: review and open research issues. J. Inf. Syst. **47**, 98–115 (2015)
8. Kitchenham, B., Charters, S.: Guidelines for performing systematic literature reviews in software engineering. Technical report, EBSE Technical report EBSE-2007-012007
9. ISO/IEC: ISO/IEC 25010 - Systems and software engineering - Systems and software Quality Requirements and Evaluation (SQuaRE) - System and software quality models (2010)
10. Wieringa, R., Maiden, N., Mead, N., Rolland, C.: Requirements engineering paper classification and evaluation criteria: a proposal and a discussion. J. Requirements Eng. **11**, 102–107 (2006)
11. IBM: IBM big data platform (2016). http://www-01.ibm.com/software/data/bigdata/
12. Tay, Y.: Data generation for application-specific benchmarking. J. VLDB Challenges Vis. (2011)
13. Stocker, M., Seaborne, A., Bernstein, A., Kiefer, C., Reynolds, D.: SPARQL basic graph pattern optimization using selectivity estimation. In: Proceedings of the 17th International Conference on World Wide Web, pp. 595–604 (2008)
14. Petersen, K., Vakkalanka, S., Kuzniarz, L.: Guidelines for conducting systematic mapping studies in software engineering: an update. J. Inf. Softw. Technol. **64**, 1–18 (2015)

Assessment of the SEMCO Model-Based Repository Approach for Software System Engineering

Brahim Hamid[(✉)]

IRIT, University of Toulouse, 118 Route de Narbonne,
31062 Toulouse Cedex 9, France
hamid@irit.fr

Abstract. We have developed a methodological tool support for software development based on the reuse of dedicated subsystems, that have been pre-engineered to adapt to a specific domain. This paper proposes an empirical evaluation of the proposed approach through its practical application to a use case in the railway domain with strong security and dependability requirements, followed by a description of a survey performed among domain experts to better understand their perceptions regarding our approach. The case study enables us to determine that our approach centered around a model-based repository of patterns leads to a reduction in the number of steps in the engineering process or to their simplification. The survey assists in assessing whether domain experts agree on the benefits of adopting the model-based repository approach in a real industrial context.

Keywords: Modeling artifact · Model-based repository · Model repository · Metamodel · Model-driven engineering · Software system engineering

1 Introduction

Repositories of modeling artifacts have recently gained increased attention as a means of encouraging reuse in software engineering. In fact, repository-centric development processes are more widely adopted in software system development than are other approaches, such as architecture-centric or pattern-centric development processes. According to Bernstein and Dayal [1], a repository is a shared database of information regarding engineered artifacts. In our work, we go one step further: we conceptualize a model-based repository to support the specifications, definitions and packaging of a set of modeling artifacts. During system development lifecycles, modeling artifacts may be used in various forms such as domain models, design patterns, component models, code modules, test and code generators [3]. However, the question remains of when and how to integrate modeling artifacts into the software-intensive system development process. Closely related to our vision is the approach of [8,12] that autonomously locates

© Springer International Publishing AG 2017
Y. Ouhammou et al. (Eds.): MEDI 2017, LNCS 10563, pp. 111–125, 2017.
DOI: 10.1007/978-3-319-66854-3_9

and delivers task-relevant and personalized components into the current software development environment.

The envisioned modeling framework consists of two main pillars: solid theory and proven principles. The first pillar offers an integrated conceptual design for the specification and development of a model-based repository and its contents; the second pillar offers a concrete and coherent methodology for the development of software systems based on the repository. We have developed a System and software Engineering with Multi-COncerns (SEMCO) framework [5,6] to assist system and software developers in the domain of resource constrained systems to capture, implement and document distributed system applications. SEMCO aims at supporting model- and pattern-based development approaches by defining and providing several artifacts types representing the different related engineering concerns (Security, Dependability, Safety and Resources) and architectural information. The approach relies on an MDE tool suite called SEMCOMDT to support the methodology and thus, in our context, to support the automated construction of and access to the model-based repository. The foundation of SEMCOMDT is a collection of Domain-Specific Modeling Languages (DSMLs) built on an integrated repository of modeling artifacts working as a group, each one relevant to a particular key concern. The resulting tool chain supports two categories of users: developers who reuse existing artifacts from the repository and developers of artifacts to be stored in the repository.

This work provides evidence of the SEMCO benefits and applicability through the example of a representative industrial case from the FP7 TERESA project[1] by applying the approach to Pattern-Based System Engineering (PBSE). Modeling artifacts derived from the model repository and associated with domain-specific models can assist developers in integrating in-development application building blocks with pre-defined modeling artifact building blocks. Empirical evaluation of the proposed approach, using Key Performance Indicators (KPIs), is presented through its practical application to a use case in the railway domain. KPI is an industry term that refers to a type of performance measurement, to evaluate the success of a particular activity, project or product. The second evaluation step is performed using a survey to better understand the perceptions of practitioners regarding our findings. Based on the background of our research project partners', we started with an existing approach, such as the Technology Acceptance Model (TAM) [2]. For instance, we have identified a set of measures to evaluate our solutions, which produced the definition of a set of hypotheses. Then, we enhanced the TAM using the ISO-9126's quality-in-use dimensions, i.e., effectiveness, productivity, safety and satisfaction. In some cases, we employed the factors developed in Rogers' theory of innovation diffusion [9], which were involved in technology adoption: (1) Trialability; (2) Compatibility; (3) Relative advantage; (4) Observability; and (5) Complexity. We designed a research strategy that is focused on testing these hypotheses by performing and reporting empirical studies, following the guidelines described in [11]

---

[1] http://www.teresa-project.org/.

(e.g., construct a set of research questions, design of questionnaires, data collection, using statistical tools for data analysis and threat to validity).

The remainder of this paper is organized as follows. Section 2 provides theoretical background and SEMCO. In Sect. 3, we present an empirical evaluation of our approach via a railway case study in framework of the TERESA project and a survey. Finally, Sect. 4 presents our conclusions and suggests possible directions for future work.

2 Motivations and Theoretical Background

A software system architect must work at multiple different levels. Integrating all the subsystems and accounting for the associated software requirements in a seamless fashion is quite a challenge given the various critical requirements and uncertainties associated with them. We propose a solution for software development based on the reuse of dedicated subsystems, so-called modeling artifacts that have been pre-engineered to adapt to a specific domain. We use MDE to develop a repository of models and a methodology for developing software systems based on this repository.

MDE promotes models as first-class elements. A model can be represented at different levels of abstraction, and the concept of MDE is based on (1) the metamodeling techniques used to describe these models and (2) the mechanisms used to specify the relations between them. Domain-Specific Modeling (DSM) [4] in software engineering is a methodology in which models are used to specify applications within a particular domain. Several DSM environments exist, including the open-source Eclipse Modeling Framework (EMF) [10] and its extended version Eclipse Modeling Framework Technology (EMFT)[2]. Note, however, that our vision is not limited to the EMF platform. EMF offers a set of tools to specify metamodels in Ecore and to generate other representations of these metamodels.

The proposed approach consists of six main steps (the numbers in parentheses below correspond to those indicated in Fig. 1):

- The first step (1) is the creation of a conceptual model of the repository.
- The second step (2) is the creation of a set of DSMLs for the specification of modeling artifacts.
- Using the DSMLs and the conceptual model of the repository, a software engineering expert defines the model and builds the repository (3).
- Using the DSMLs, a modeling artifact expert, with the help of the system and software engineering expert, defines the modeling artifacts and begins populating the repository (4).
- Then, a domain process expert adapts the modeling artifacts into a form that is suitable for the system development process (5). For instance, they might be adapted for use within a certain development environment.
- Finally, a domain engineer reuses the resulting modeling artifacts that have been adapted and transformed for the given engineering environment (development platform) to develop a domain application (6).

---

[2] https://eclipse.org/modeling/emft/.

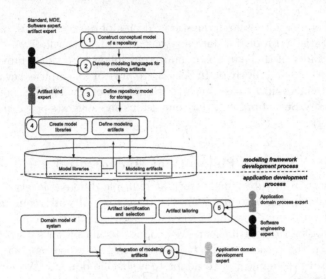

Fig. 1. Methodology for the creation of the model-based repository modeling framework

The first two steps (1 and 2) are performed once for a given set of domains. The inputs to these steps are expertise, standards and best practices from software system engineering. Step 3 is performed once for a given set of domains. Step 4 is performed once per application domain. Step 5 is performed once for each development environment. Performing Step 4 requires knowledge of software engineering, whereas Step 5 requires knowledge of both software engineering and the system development process for a specific application domain. Step 6 is performed once for every system in the application domain. This step requires the availability of knowledge of the specific target system and dedicated tools that are customized for a given development platform.

3   Empirical Assessment

In this section, we first report on an industrial case study performed in the railway domain (Sect. 3.1) and then present a description of a survey performed among TERESA domain experts (Sect. 3.2).

3.1   Case Study

Our case study is aimed at investigating the feasibility of our approach and the level of effort involved in its application using Key Performance Indicators (KPIs). A performance indicator or key performance indicator (KPI) is an industry term referring to a type of performance measurement. KPIs are commonly used to evaluate the success of a particular activity, project or company. In the context of the TERESA project, we evaluated our approach in the construction of an engineering discipline that is adapted to RCES by combining MDE and a model-based repository of S&D patterns and their related property models.

3.1.1   Case Selection

The *Safe4Rail* system is composed of (1) a *Clock* which generates a periodic event to trigger the system to estimate the current position and speed and to supervise that the train complies with the current track restrictions, (2) a *Environmental Conditions* to represent the physical interaction between environment (train, track, others) with the sensors of the system, (3) a *Balise* which represents a balise installed on the track to supply to the train supervision system with new information regarding the current position and the track conditions, (4) a *Safe Train Interface* which represents the actuators for the application and (5) a *Supervision System*. In turn, the *Supervision System* is composed of (a) a *BaliseReader* to detect and read the information provided by the balise on the rail, (b) a *Supervision*, as the main component of the system, which is responsible of carrying out the functionality of the system and (c) *Sensors* to provide the actual position and speed of the train and the track conditions to the system.

To illustrate our study, two different railway industry scenarios will be considered: (1) Railway manufacturing group which is divided in subsidiary companies specialized in the development of train and railway infrastructure systems and (2) An SME that develops safety related embedded systems. This company has a proven experience in the development of safety related embedded systems, but accounts scarce experience in the railway domain. Therefore, the estimations given for the railway domain provide two values with associated argumentation:

1. *Large and complex safety systems*, such as on-board ERTMS/ETCS, and
2. *Intermediate safety systems*, such as traction control safety supervision.

3.1.2   Research Questions

The purpose of our study was to address the following two research questions:

- **RQ1:** *Does the proposed approach reduce the effort involved in developing a new application (design and implementation)?* To answer **RQ1**, we evaluate whether the approach leads to a reduced number of steps in the engineering process or to their simplification, and we assess whether the domain experts agree on the benefits of adopting the approach in a real industrial context for the development of new applications.
- **RQ2:** *Is the effort involved to engineer a new version of an existing application to add a security or dependability property acceptable?* For **RQ2**, we measure the ability of the approach to integrate security and dependability solutions into existing products.

3.1.3   Data Collection Procedure

The procedure used for developing the case study closely followed the approach described in Sect. 2. Given a repository requirements, a conceptual model is built that fulfill these design requirements. The next step is the creation of a set of Domain-Specific Modeling Languages (DSMLs) for the specification of modeling artifacts. In the context of our experiment, we have developed System and

Software Engineering Pattern Metamodel (SEPM) [7] and Generic PRoperty Metamodel (GPRM) [13] to model pattern and property models, respectively. Using the DSMLs and the conceptual model of the repository, a software engineering expert defines the model and builds the repository. This work was done by the author. Then, the modeling artifact expert, with the help of the system and software engineering expert, defines the modeling artifacts and begins populating the repository. Then, a domain process expert adapts the modeling artifacts into a form that is suitable for the system development process. Finally, a domain engineer reuses the resulting modeling artifacts that have been adapted and transformed for the given engineering environment to develop a domain application.

For the purpose of our study, we have developed SEMCOMDT [3](SEMCO Model Development Tools) as an MDE tool chain to support all steps of our approach using EMFT. All metamodels used are specified using EMF. To create model instances of the proposed metamodel, we choose to use a tree-structured concrete syntax provided by EMFT. It provides graphical, but not-diagrammatic notations, to specify Ecore models. The SEPM's concrete syntax is described using a mixed syntax combining structured-tree syntax and a UML-based diagrammatic syntax. The structure of the repository is derived from the repository structure model and implemented using Java and the Eclipse CDO[4] framework. This work was done by the two Phd students.

In the following, KPIs are presented with an estimated target value submitted at the beginning of the case studies, and real values are estimated upon completion of the case studies. Both values are averages because the individual values highly depend on certain factors, such as the size of the project, the product requirements, the expertise of the engineering team, the use of the approach facilities and the availability of the appropriate patterns. In both cases, KPIs are estimated based on previous knowledge of implementing such systems or equivalents. A description of the considered constraints and assumptions is discussed below.

- *(K1) Overall engineering cost.* Cost to develop a new application (design and implementation) with dependability requirements using a target reduction of 10% to 20% (on average).
- *(K2) Percentage of reused code.* Amount of code reused from existing patterns in a new development with dependability requirements using a target reduction of 20% to 60% (on average).
- *(K3) Engineering time.* Time to develop a new application (design and implementation) with dependability requirements using a target reduction of 10% to 25% (on average).
- *(K4) Re-engineering time.* Time to engineer a new version of an existing application to add a dependability property with an estimated target reduction of 40% (on average).

---

[3] http://www.semcomdt.org.
[4] http://www.eclipse.org/cdo/.

- *(K5) Errors in reused code.* Number of errors appearing in code reused from patterns using a target value of 10 as a factor of the probability of errors in reused code with respect to new code.
- *(K6) Code quality.* Readability and compliance of the reused code with the required standard with an estimated target value of compliance of 100%.
- *(K7) Maintenance cost.* Total cost and effort associated with bugs being detected after deployment using a target reduction of 10% to 20% (on average).
- *(K8) Incident response.* Time and effort for identifying affected products from reused code/concepts with an estimated target reduction of 30% to 50% (on average).

3.1.4   Case Study Results and Discussion

Here, we discuss the results of the case study focusing on answering the research questions that we presented in Sect. 3.1. The creation of the conceptual model of the repository required approximately 4 person months. The creation of the DSMLs for the modeling artifacts took approximately 6 person months. The construction of the model of the repository and the implementation of the MDE tool chain took 6 person months. The construction of the domain model took another 3 person months. The process of populating the repository took one month. The proposed tool chain is designed to support the proposed metamodels, and hence, the tool chain and the remainder of the activities involved in the approach may be developed in parallel. This activity needs to be performed only once for a given set of domains. We expect the effort for the creation of a DSMLs and the development of tools to be less on future applications, as we had to address several technical details in relation to using EMFT and CDO in our first application.

A comparison of the resulting KPIs in the two cases is shown in Fig. 2, where the estimated KPI values for the newly proposed approach at the end of the case study are presented. From this comparison, it appears that using the security and dependability pattern-based approach brings significant advantages in S&D engineering, especially for intermediate safety systems.

RQ1. *Does the proposed approach reduce the effort involved in developing a new application (design and implementation)?* With regard to the overall engineering cost, we estimate that the development of large and complex systems (ERTM-S/ETCS), respectively intermediate systems, is reduced by an average of 12.5%, respectively 30% (**K1**). The overall engineering cost is reduced as follows. During the safety concept, system architecture, software architecture and module detailed design phases, a reduction in the time to formalize and document the design is observed using already-developed design patterns that include all necessary safety information and reducing the effort required to document detailed descriptions by hand. Moreover, a reduction in the time and effort associated with verification is also observed because the design patterns are already verified and provide a common understanding for both designers and verifiers. Finally,

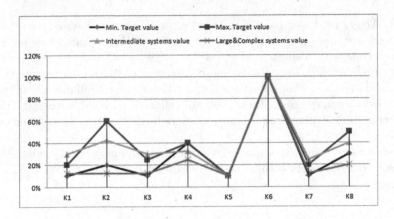

Fig. 2. Intermediate, large & complex safety systems

a reduction in the time and effort associated with RAMS[5] analysis is observed because the design patterns are already verified and provide a common understanding for both designers and RAMS engineers. With regard to the percentage of reused code, we estimate that during the development of large and complex systems (ERTMS/ETCS), resp. intermediate systems, code is reused at an average of 12.5%, respectively 43% (**K2**). The selected case study, namely, ERTMS/ETCS on-board railway signaling acting as a large and complex safety system, is a representative SIL4 safety embedded system in which multiple design patterns can be instantiated. However, ERTMS/ETCS is a highly complex system in which most of the software application implements the safety and functional requirements established by the standard for interoperability. Selected and integrated design patterns provide the safety skeleton and safety architectural foundation of the system (key foundation), where the system-specific application is deployed and executed. However, the ratio between system-specific software and software that can be provided by design patterns is less than 0.1.

This is a paradox because other safety subsystems of the train that perform intermediate complexity safety functions might be developed with a much smaller set of design patterns, although the ratio of design-pattern-based safety software compared to system-specific safety software might be at least one to one. For example, the safety function of a railway traction system (SIL2) acting as an intermediate safety system has an intermediate complexity. It must compare already acquired current, voltage and temperature measurements with given minimum and maximum thresholds and perform a small set of coherency checks on the measurements.

RQ2. *Is the effort involved to engineer a new version of an existing application to add a security or dependability property acceptable?* With regard to the re-engineering, we estimate that the development of large and complex systems (ERTMS/ETCS), respectively intermediate systems, is reduced by an average

---

[5] Stands for Reliability, Availability, Maintainability, and Safety.

of 25%, respectively 33% (**K4**). After developing the demonstrator and considering the previous estimation of **K2** (percentage of reused code) and that safety design patterns provide key foundational patterns for the development of safety systems, we estimate that the maintenance cost is reduced in large and complex (ERTMS/ETCS), resp. intermediate systems, by an average of 12.5%, respectively 25% (**K7**). Moreover, we estimate that the time and effort for incident response is reduced in large and complex (ERTMS/ETCS) systems, resp. intermediate systems, by an average of 20%, resp. 40% (**K8**). An example is the reduction of complex incident responses associated with the operation of safety replicas (e.g., data agreement, safety communication layer, etc.) that require a considerable amount of time to be analyzed and solved.

3.2 Survey

After the completion of our case study, we conducted an experiment where we presented our approach and the solution of our case study in order to collect feedback from industry practitioners through a survey. The case study enables us to determine that the model-based repository approach leads to a reduced number or to a simplification of the engineering process steps, whereas the survey assists in assessing whether domain experts agree on the benefit of adopting the proposed approach in a real industrial context. In the following, we present and discuss the design and results of this survey.

3.2.1 Context and Description of the Methodology for Experimentation

The approach, its corresponding tool suite and the solution of our case study presented in Sect. 3.1 were proposed to the industry practitioners for evaluation through a survey. The purpose of this survey is to give an overview of the design of a software architecture of a small but sufficiently complex system that we will use to illustrate the model-based repository approach we propose.

All participants attended the TERESA MDE workshop in Toulouse, where the experiment was initiated. Six security experts (SEC) participated in the survey: four from the TERESA domains and two from other domains. Five dependability experts (DEP) also participated in the survey: three from the TERESA domains and tow from another domain. In addition, five software engineering (SEN) experts participated in the survey: two from the TERESA domains and three from other domains. All participants were recognized as experts in their domains with a high level of skill in security or dependability who had already participated in the development of several projects related to their skills. All participants were already familiar with S&D patterns and modeling tools. Overall, 62% of the participants had over two years of S&D engineering experience and a further 19% had at least one year of experience with S&D engineering.

The objective of the survey was to determine whether domain experts agree on the benefits of adopting our approach in a real industrial context. For that, we proposed to use the factors developed in Rogers' theory of innovation diffusion [9], involved in technology adoption: (1) Trialability; (2) Compatibility; (3) Relative advantage; (4) Observability; and (5) Complexity. To address these factors we have developed a simple questionnaire, containing 20 questions (some questions were used to measure more than one factor), to capture the information required. Precisely, we focus on (1) the perceived usefulness of the approach itself; (2) the perceived usefulness of the conceptual models, the execution of the approach and the tool suite as a means of building and reusing modeling artifacts; and (3) the willingness to use a model-based repository approach in future related activities. Next, the participants were asked to scale their satisfaction on a scale from 1 to 5, 1 being the lowest value of satisfaction or the greatest difficulty (meaning *Not Useful at All, Very Difficult, Very Probably Not*) and 5 being the highest value of satisfaction regarding the presented concepts or the greatest ease in realizing a solution to the given question (meaning *Extremely Useful, Very Easy, Definitely*). We calculated the averages of the values provided by the participants.

3.2.2   The Questionnaire

The questionnaire was divided into three parts. The first section, which consisted of *Q1–Q5*, as shown below, concerned the perceived usefulness of the approach itself.

- *Q1: Do you think that a model-based repository approach is a good idea?*
- *Q2: Do you think that a model-based repository approach helps to maintain focus without being distracted by other aspects of software engineering?*
- *Q3: Is the information provided by the model-based repository approach useful for defining meaningful 'units of solution'?*
- *Q4: Does the model-based repository approach reduce the effort involved in developing a new application (design and implementation)?*
- *Q5: Do you think that a model-based repository approach avoids the re-invention of existing solutions?*

The second section, *Q6–Q14*, addressed the conceptual models, the execution of the approach and the tool suite as a means of building and reusing modeling artifacts.

- *Q6: Were the presented conceptual models easy to understand?*
- *Q7: Overall, how easy to follow were the steps of our approach?*
- *Q8: Was the presented tool -suite easy to use?*
- *Q9: Did you find the models easy to use for engineering your application?*
- *Q10: Did you find it easy to define new security and dependability patterns?*
- *Q11: Do you think that the tool provided for tailoring security and dependability patterns is easy to use?*
- *Q12: Do you think that the tools provided for the integration of security and dependability patterns is easy to use?*

- *Q13: How easy was it to integrate the tool suite into your favorite development environment?*
- *Q14: Does the presented tool suite provide useful assistance in the development of secure and dependable applications?*

The last section, *Q15–Q20*, concerned the participants' willingness to use a model-based repository approach in future related activities.

- *Q15: Would you see value in adopting the presented approach at your company?*
- *Q16: Would you like to define other kinds of reusable modeling artifacts in the future?*
- *Q17: Would you like to install other SEMCO plugins in the future?*
- *Q18: Would you like to use the approach in the future?*
- *Q19: Would you like to customize various SEMCO plugins in the future?*
- *Q20: Would you like to extend various features of the approach in the future?*

3.2.3   Experiment Conduct

Because of the technical and administrative problems encountered in the design, implementation and deployment of repository software, we performed this group of tasks in a pre-processing step prior to the study. Thus, in our experiment, we considered only a pre-defined model-based repository. In our case, the repository server application is hosted on a machine at the University of Toulouse. Once the service was initialized, we proceeded to the repository initialization. A Java-based GUI application enabled the creation of the repository structure as well as the initialization and management of compartments and users. Each of the participants was given a login and password to manage her/his artifacts. The second element of the SEMCO environment is the client tool suite, which is provided as a set of Eclipse plugins. The client tool suite consists of a set of modeling artifact editors, helpers for depositing artifacts into and retrieving them from the repository, and the required repository interfaces. The installation is finalized by setting the preferences on the client to point to the correct repository. The experiment included five tasks: SEMCO plugin installation, property model development, pattern development, pattern tailoring and pattern integration.

For each task, a set of materials was provided to the participants at the beginning of the experiment: the SEMCO tool suite and its accompanying installation and user documentation, a detailed textual description of the patterns and their properties, a detailed requirements document, and a conceptual model of the system under development in the form of UML diagrams. Finally, the participants were given a subjective post-experiment questionnaire consisting of a set of questions, as described previously, and space for comments. In addition, they were provided with a sheet presenting the instructions for each task (e.g., what properties to specify and what patterns to develop, when to take note of the time, and so on).

Training of the Participants. During the TERESA MDE workshop in Toulouse, the participants were trained to use the method and the SEMCO tool suite.

The training was conducted in two sessions on the same day. The first session was 3 h long and was managed by two instructors. The first instructor introduced MDE and presented a pattern-based development methodology and how it might be used to support the development of secure and dependable applications. In addition, a 1-h practice session on Eclipse and the EMFT environment was presented by the second instructor as a laboratory exercise. During the second hour-long session, several operating examples were introduced to the participants, with detailed explanations, by two additional instructors who participated in the development of the SEMCO tool suite.

Execution of the Experiment. The experiment was conducted in the context of the TERESA project regarding the development of secure and dependable applications. The participants were grouped according to whether they possessed expertise in the related domains. To improve and simplify the evaluation of the results, the participants were asked to use only tools and methods that were presented during the training sessions. However, they were allowed to use their own resources, predominantly those related to the description of patterns in their domain. Before they started, a general description of the objective of the study was presented (30 min). Portions of these evaluation studies were performed internally, whereas other studies were outsourced. The participants were given 2 h on site to complete the installation tasks (performed during the TERESA MDE workshop in Toulouse). Then, a 6-month outsourced evaluation was conducted to complete the other tasks.

Data Collection. The questionnaire was uploaded online using Google Docs, and the link to the questionnaire was forwarded to the participants. All of the registered participants received the questionnaire link in this manner. At the time of the survey, twelve participants were members of the TERESA project. The data collection process began in January 2013 and continued for 6 months, and ultimately, a sample of sixteen usable responses was collected. As the first step of the analysis, the mean scores corresponding to the participant's responses were calculated.

3.2.4 Survey Results and Discussion

After the data were collected, data analysis was conducted to determine the answers to the research questions. The following presents an overview of the results of our experiment. The purpose of the first question was to assess the first impressions of the participants. This answer was used as a baseline and as a measure of whether they were prepared and motivated to perform the subsequent steps of the experiment.

Of the participants in the experiment, 75% of them thought that the approach would be extremely useful, and the remaining 25% thought that the approach would be very useful. After being presented with a high-level description of the approach, 31% of the participants perceived the approach as being extremely useful for maintaining focus without being distracted by other aspects of software engineering, whereas 69% thought it would be very useful. Based on the collected responses, 56% of participants found the approach very useful for defining meaningful units of solution, and the remaining 44% found it extremely useful. We can also conclude that 69% of the participants found the approach to be very useful for development through reuse, and 75% of them found the approach to be very useful for development for reuse.

When presented with the conceptual models of the approach, 50% of the participants perceived the approach as being very easy to understand, whereas the remaining 50% thought it was easy to understand. The results reveal also that 31% of the participants perceived the approach as very easy to follow, whereas 56% thought it was easy, and the remaining 13% experienced average difficulty. Regrading the tool support, 51% of the participants found the tool suite very easy to use; meanwhile, 19% experienced average difficulty in using the tool suite. With regards to integrating the provided tool-suite into other development environment, 38% of the participants indicated that it is seldom easy, 56% experienced average difficulty in integrating the tool-suite, whereas the remaining participants (6%) found it difficult. However, the current tool suite based on EMFT was expected to be useful. A total of 31% of the participants believed that the tool-suite would be extremely useful for the development of secure and dependable applications, and a further 44% thought that it would be very useful. The remaining 25% of the participants thought that the tool suite would be useful.

With regards to the adoption of the approach, 63% of the participants thought that there was definitely value in adopting the approach, and a further 31% thought that the approach was very probably worth adopting. Regarding the extent to which the participants indicated that they would likely use the model-based repository approach in the future for the development of other kinds of systems, 19% Of the them indicated that they would definitely continue their application of the approach, whereas 63% said that they would very probably do so.

In summary, the answers received in our survey suggest that the proposed approach was overall regarded as easy to learn and to follow. Moreover, the participants thought that it would be beneficial to use within their context. These responses indicate that model-based repository approaches to the development of software systems should be investigated further. We believe that these experimental results may be generalized to other pattern-based development approaches and, in a broader scope, to other model-based development approaches, as the patterns were provided as models for the application developers.

4   Conclusion and Future Work

The proposed model-based approach for software application development relies on a repository of models and focuses on the problem of software system engineering through a design philosophy that fosters reuse. This approach was evaluated in the context of the TERESA project for application to a repository of S&D

patterns and property models. Following the specification, design, implementation and deployment of an S&D pattern repository, pattern designers can define property and pattern models and store them in the repository. System designers can then reuse existing patterns from the repository through identification and tailoring mechanisms, leading to simpler and more seamless designs with higher quality and reduced cost. By means of the practical demonstration provided by our case study, we can validate the feasibility and effectiveness of the proposed specification and design frameworks. We also conducted a survey of industry practitioners among TERESA members and other security, dependability and software engineering experts. The preliminary evidence indicates that users are satisfied with the notion of a development approach centered around a model-based repository of patterns and, in a broader context, a model-based repository of modeling artifacts. However, the results also highlight one of the main challenges, namely, the design of an automated search functionality to allow the user to derive the necessary modeling artifacts from an analysis of the requirements for a project.

In our future work, we plan to study the automation of the model search and tailoring tasks. Our vision is for modeling artifacts to be inferred from the browsing history of users and constructed from a set of already developed applications. We would also like to study the integration of our tools with other MDE tools. For that purpose, we need to implement other kinds of software and means of generating validated artifacts, such as programming language code and certification artifacts, that are capable of producing a restrictive set of artifacts that comply with domain standards.

References

1. Bernstein, P.A., Dayal, U.: An overview of repository technology. In: Proceedings of the 20th International Conference on Very Large Data Bases, VLDB 1994, pp. 705–713. Morgan Kaufmann Publishers Inc. (1994)
2. Davis, F.: Perceived usefulness, perceived ease of use, and user acceptance of information technology. MIS Q. **13**(3), 319 (1989)
3. Frakes, W., Kang, K.: Software reuse research: status and future. IEEE Trans. Softw. Eng. **31**(7), 529–536 (2005)
4. Gray, J., Tolvanen, J.-P., Kelly, S., Gokhale, A., Neema, S., Sprinkle, J.: Domain-specific modeling. In: Fishwick, P. (ed.) Handbook of Dynamic System Modeling, Chap. 7, pp. 1–20. Chapman & Hall/CRC, Boca Raton (2007)
5. Hamid, B.: A model-driven methodology approach for developing a repository of models. In: Ait Ameur, Y., Bellatreche, L., Papadopoulos, G.A. (eds.) MEDI 2014. LNCS, vol. 8748, pp. 29–44. Springer, Cham (2014). doi:10.1007/978-3-319-11587-0_5
6. Hamid, B.: Modeling of secure and dependable applications based on a repository of patterns: the SEMCO approach. Reliab. Digest, IEEE Reliab. Soc. Special Issue Trustworthy Comput. Cybersecur. **1**(1), 9–17 (2014)

7. Hamid, B., Gürgens, S., Jouvray, C., Desnos, N.: Enforcing S&D pattern design in RCES with modeling and formal approaches. In: Whittle, J., Clark, T., Kühne, T. (eds.) MODELS 2011. LNCS, vol. 6981, pp. 319–333. Springer, Heidelberg (2011). doi:10.1007/978-3-642-24485-8_23. ACM/IEEE International Conference on Model Driven Engineering Languages and Systems (MODELS)
8. Katalagarianos, P., Vassiliou, Y.: On the reuse of software: a case-based approach employing a repository. Autom. Softw. Eng. **2**(1), 55–86 (1995)
9. Rogers, E.: Diffusion of Innovations, 5th edn. Free Press, New York (2003)
10. Steinberg, D., Budinsky, F., Paternostro, M., Merks, E.: EMF: Eclipse Modeling Framework 2.0, 2nd edn. Addison-Wesley Professional (2009). ISBN 0321331885
11. Wohlin, C., Runeson, P., Höst, M., Ohlsson, M., Regnell, B., Wesslén, A.: Experimentation in Software Engineering: An Introduction. Kluwer Academic Publishers, Norwell (2000)
12. Ye, Y., Fischer, G.: Reuse-conducive development environments. Autom. Softw. Eng. **12**(2), 199–235 (2005)
13. Ziani, A., Hamid, B., Trujillo, S.: Towards a unified meta-model for resources-constrained embedded systems. In: 37th EUROMICRO Conference on Software Engineering and Advanced Applications (SEAA), pp. 485–492. IEEE (2011)

Self-adaptive Architecture for Ensuring QoS Contracts in Cloud-Based Systems

Esma Maatougui[✉], Chafia Bouanaka, and Nadia Zeghib

LIRE Laboratory, University of Constantine 2-Abdelhamid Mehri,
Constantine, Algeria
{esma.maatougui, chafia.bouanaka,
nadia.zeghib}@univ-constantine2.dz

Abstract. Elasticity, as a key characteristic of Cloud-based systems, allows a rapid adjustment of the allocated resources capacity according to the time-varying workload. However, relying only on elasticity features does not seem sufficient to ensure the quality of service (QoS) requirements of modern applications. Furthermore, uncertainty that emerges while selecting the elasticity policy to be applied in a given context to ensure the desired QoS in cloud-based systems is a challenging task. Hence, the problem to be addressed in the present paper is to define a model allowing cloud architecture to dynamically and efficiently determine the elastic strategy to be applied to ensure QoS contracts in cloud-based systems in the presence of uncertainty. The paper introduces a hybrid approach that combines elasticity advantages and an appropriate mechanism for runtime monitoring and preservation of QoS requirements for cloud-based systems. We mainly focus on non-deterministic selection of the elasticity strategies based on the quality aspects. The formal model implementing our approach is defined using PSMaude which allows specifying nonfunctional requirements, strategies and probabilistic systems features.

Keywords: Self-adaptive systems · Quality of service (QoS) · MAPE-loop · Cloud computing · Elasticity · PSMaude

1 Introduction

Self-adaptation has been proposed as an effective approach to tackle the increasing complexity of managing software systems runtime adaptation in many application domains, such as cloud-based, cyber-physical and mobile systems. Such systems should be able to dynamically adapt their structure and/or behaviour in order to continuously ensure the required QoS. However, self-adaptive software systems (SAS) operate in uncertain environments, making the adaptation operation extremely complex [1].

Cloud computing, as an emerging discipline, is an application domain of self-adaptability that involves non-determinism while selecting adaptation strategies or more precisely elasticity strategies. However, relying only on elasticity features does not seem sufficient to ensure the QoS requirements of modern cloud-based applications, which are specific to the underlying applications themselves and expressed in predefined QoS contracts [6]. Therefore, cloud-based applications while utilizing the

© Springer International Publishing AG 2017
Y. Ouhammou et al. (Eds.): MEDI 2017, LNCS 10563, pp. 126–134, 2017.
DOI: 10.1007/978-3-319-66854-3_10

flexibility feature of cloud environments, e.g. cloud elasticity, should be entangled with intelligent software, i.e., autonomic manager, that continuously monitors application behavior and automatically adjusts resource allocations to meet the predefined QoS contracts [7]. Besides, the autonomic manager might deal with uncertainty to be encountered while selecting the elasticity strategies. Consequently, handling uncertainty in self-adaptive software systems and especially cloud-based ones has become an important and challenging issue in the software engineering discipline.

   To deal with such challenges, this paper introduces a novel hybrid approach that combines autonomic systems and elasticity management to efficiently and continuously determine the elasticity strategy that ensures QoS contracts of cloud-based systems. The idea is to exploit the cloud elasticity characteristic for improving the quality of cloud-based applications by relying on the self-adaptive systems capabilities to deal with uncertainty and non-determinism and ensure QoS contracts through the MAPE [2] control loop.

   To capture the uncertain behavior and probabilistic aspects of elasticity strategies in Cloud based-systems, we define a formal model that supports their specification and management. We propose a probabilistic approach for quality-aware self-adaptive systems based on feedback control mechanism to formally specify, drive and analyze cloud-based systems. In order to additionally infuse non-determinism for representing the multiplicity in elasticity actions, we resort to probabilistic strategies, which form the basis of our approach. We model the main system processes and specify the required properties using PSMaude [3] (Probabilistic Strategy Maude).

   The rest of the paper is organized as follows: Sect. 2 presents our approach to model quality-aware cloud-based systems. Section 3 illustrates the proposed approach through a realistic case study; the TeleAssistance system. Finally, some concluding remarks and ongoing work round up the paper.

2 Our Approach

We propose in this section our hybrid approach that augments cloud-based systems with self-adaptability employing the MAPE-loop model as the underlying model for ensuring QoS contracts of cloud services. Our approach is described by sketching out a reference architecture (see Fig. 1). In a more generic view, the proposed model is composed of (1) the managed system and (2) the Autonomic manager represented by the MAPE loop.

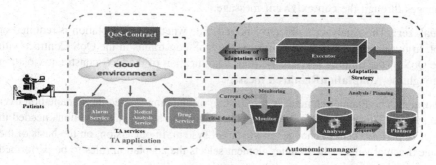

Fig. 1. Reference architecture for quality-aware cloud-based systems

The managed part may be a software system deployed in a cloud environment (we consider the TA application which will be presented in Sect. 3). The autonomic manager is the core element of the model, it supervises the managed system and performs corrective actions to adapt the cloud resources in a way to meet the desired QoS, i.e., decisions are made on the basis of non-functional requirements. A formal model for designing and specifying the managed system was already proposed in [5]. In the present work, we define the autonomic manager that is parameterized with probabilistic adaptation strategies and based on quality aspects to manage uncertainty and resolve the nondeterministic choice of the elasticity mechanism. The desired QoSs of the cloud-based system are expressed as QoS contracts which must be monitored and preserved at runtime. These concepts need to maintain a formal model that supports their specification and management and can provide the appropriate level of abstraction to describe dynamic changes in our reference architecture. Therefore, we propose a formal approach for designing, specifying and analyzing QoS-aware Cloud-based software using self-adaptive vision.

2.1 Formal MAPE-Loop for Quality-Aware Self-adaptive Systems

We define a formal specification of SASs and specially the managing system represented by the MAPE-loop to support the adaptation mechanism using PSMaude.

Adopting PSMaude, we refer the interested readers to [3] for more details, as the semantic basis is motivated by the fact that: PSMaude supports the probabilistic quantification of nondeterminism in a wide class of probabilistic rewrite theories [3]. Furthermore, the different ways in which the nondeterminism is quantified are specified in a modular way, since probabilistic strategies are defined on top of the "base" nondeterministic (and possibly probabilistic) model. The proposed approach enables the following modeling methodology: (1) all possible adaptation actions that can take place are modeled as rewrite rules. Each action is associated with a precondition specifying the rule applicability conditions, and an **adaptation cost** (which is incurred whether the system succeeds or not). (2) We quantify the uncertainty of the adaptation planner with probabilistic terms in probabilistic rewrite rules. Then, (3) we define the probabilistic strategies on top of our base model. The MAPE-loop elements can be expressed naturally as subset of rewrite rules as follows:

Monitor: The Monitor supervises the sensed context changes in both internal and external environments. It notifies relevant context events to the analyzer based on these changes through the **contextEvent** message.

Analyzer: The Analyzer's objective is to decide whether an adaptation is required or not. In our case, the Analyzer compares the QoS constraints in the QoS Contract with the QoS of the running service, yielding a notification of the QoS constraint violation through the **AdaptationRequired** message.

Planner: The Planner element is responsible of planning the required adaptation over the system. This element constructs a plan containing all adaptation actions needed in order to perform certain changes in the target system. In our vision, on the basis of the context actual values, the Planner element selects the adaptation rules to be performed to regulate the QoS parameters. The planner builds a list of adaptation rules (i.e., structural and/or behavioral adaptation) that are weighted with different probabilities in order to quantify the uncertainty and generates the **ApplyAdaptationRule** message. The Planner is defined in PSMaude as a probabilistic rewrite rule as follows:

```
prl [planner] :
        AdaptationRequired(CTXV )
    => ApplyAdaptationRule(S:String )
 with probability S:String := (("AdpRule1") -> 1/4;
                              ("AdpRule2") -> 2/4 ;
                              ("AdpRule3") -> 1/4 ) .
```

After building the list of adaptation rules, we define a probabilistic strategy for the planner element to resolve the non-deterministic choice while selecting the adaptation rule to be applied in three steps: We initially define the strategy **RuleStrat** affecting a weight to each candidate rewrite rule at each stage of the execution. Then, we define the strategies of context which are uniformly random for all states. Furthermore, we define the substitution strategy that models the probability of selecting an adaptation action which is inversely proportional to its cost. The probabilistic strategy of the planner is defined in PSMaude as follows:

```
psdrule RuleStrat := given state: CF:Configuration
                      is: ( planner ) -> 1 .
psdcontext CtxStrat := given state:  CF:Configuration    rule: planner
is: uniform .
psdsubst SubstStrat := given state: CF:Configuration
                ApplyAdaptationRule(XS: String )
                rule: planner
                context: CTX:Configuration
              is: { S: String <- XS } -> (1 /(1 + Cost(XS))) .
psd selfStrat := < RuleStrat | CtxStrat | SubstStrat > .
```

Executor: it is responsible of executing the adaptation plan. Its purpose is to translate every step of the plan to an adaptation rule and to guarantee its correct execution over the target system.

2.2 Hybrid Approach for Quality-Aware Cloud-Based System

To bring the ability of quality-aware self-adaptability to cloud-based systems, we implement a generic MAPE loop that is parameterized with probabilistic adaptation strategies.

Our previous research work [5] defines a model for designing and specifying the managed part of quality-aware self-adaptive systems. This model is designed with a focus on the separation of concerns between the specification of QoS contracts; defining user quality requirements, and software components quality parameters. To implement the proposed approach, we have combined the Model Driven Engineering (MDE) technique and a formal method in order to provide an intuitive modeling notation, supporting a graphical view, but still maintaining a rigorous syntax and semantics. The key idea of the approach is to define a meta-model for a SAS then use a model-to-text transformation engine to generate a Maude formal specification. The obtained code is then executed using the Maude tools.

A cloud-based application may be viewed as a set of components requiring or providing services, each one with a predefined QoS. Furthermore, cloud-based application QoS requirements are expressed as a QoS contract. QoS contracts comprise a number of QoS constraints that might be satisfied and preserved by the cloud services. These QoS constraints are specified for each of the different context conditions to be faced by the cloud-based application while it is running. At runtime, once these conditions occur in the execution context of the cloud-based application, the respective QoS constraints must be monitored, and their fulfillment enforced. To accomplish this, we model the adaptation strategy as a pair of elements: an action associated with the notification of events that violate their contracted QoS constraints. In cloud-based applications, adaptation strategies are defined by the well-known elasticity mechanisms.

The correlation and interaction between the MAPE elements activities and the cloud-based application is built as follows:

- The monitor element gathers information from the running system, the sensed context changes and QoS of the running components of the cloud-based application.
- Based on the monitor' outputs, the analyzer element compares the actual service QoSs with QoS constraint relative to the sensed context and QoS of the running component yielding a notification of QoS constraint violation; in this case, the application of an elasticity policy is required.
- Based on the received notification, the planner element builds a list of possible elasticity strategies with different probabilities in order to quantify the uncertainty in systems' elasticity.
- The selected elasticity strategy is automatically executed by the PSMaude engine.

3   Case Study: The TeleAssistance Cloud-Based System

We consider a cloud-based application for remote diagnoses and monitoring of patients to motivate the need for a probabilistic self-adaptive model to ensure QoS attributes of the proposed services. The TeleAssistance (TA) cloud-based application provides health support to chronic condition sufferers within the comfort of their homes. One can visualize this environment as a "cloud" where sensors connected to legacy medical devices are plugged to operate, i.e. to collect and transmit data. The computer resources available in the cloud, shared via Virtual Machines (VMs) deployed on physical servers (see the left-hand part of Fig. 1), are configured to receive, store, process, and distribute the information. These resources are provided as on demand services; that users (patients, analysis labs, pharmacies…) can consume.

The TA takes periodical measurements of the patient vital parameters and employs a third-party medical service to analyze them by sending a "vitalParamsMsg" message; containing the patient's vital parameters to the **Medical Laboratory service** (LAB) and invoking the "analyzeData" service. The LAB element is in charge of analyzing the data, it replies by sending a result value stored in a variable

analysisResult. The patient analysis results may trigger the invocation of a pharmacy service to deliver new medication or an adjustment of his/her medication dose or the invocation of an alarm service leading to, e.g., the intervention of a **First-Aid Squad** (FAS) comprising doctors, nurses and paramedics to consult the patient at home. To alert the squad, the TA invokes the alarm service of the FAS. Accordingly, the TA system incorporates the following abstract services: **Alarm Service, Medical Analysis Service, Drug Service.** Different providers could be involved in providing concrete implementations of the already described abstract services, each one with its own QoS values and can experience different environmental changes (e.g., changes in workload). As an example, the Alarm Service could be provided by several Cloud providers, with different costs, performance and reliability characteristics.

In distributed environments as the cloud one, each tier in a multi-tiers application, composed of concrete services $\{S_1, S_2, ... S_i\}$ may have multiple replicas deployed on different VMs. The replica of a tier running on a VM is assumed to have the replicas of its services running on the same VM [4]. In this work, we refer to the replicas of concrete services as service-instances. In addition, since services are deployed in a highly dynamic, elastic and on-demand environment like cloud, it is desirable to manage their QoS. To accomplish this, we define QoS contracts between the TA application and its clients (patients), which comprise a number of QoS constraints that might be satisfied and preserved by cloud service providers. The violation of quality contracts necessarily leads to the demand for an adaptation strategy.

In the following subsections we illustrate our approach through the design and formal specification of the TA system in two steps: The first step presents formal specification of the TA Cloud-based System structure and QoS contracts respectively. The second step consists of formally specifying dynamics of the TA system, the elasticity strategies in particular.

3.1   Formal Specification of TA Cloud-Based System Structure

The TA Cloud-based system constitutes the managed system layer where we identify three types of components: **Patient (PA)**, **Medical Analysis Laboratory (LAB)** and **First-Aid Squad (FAS)**. We model the TA Cloud-based system state as a configuration of objects and messages. The initial state of our TA Cloud-based System is expressed in PSMaude as a collection of objects (see Listing 1).

Listing 1. TA system components.

```
op SelfConf : -> Configuration .
eq SelfConf =
--------------------------------------------------------------------
< 'TA_System : FonctionnelSystem | Components : 'PA 'LAB 'FAS >
< 'PA : Component | Cname : "PA_Comp" , QualityAttribute : 'Q1 , ProvidedInterfaces : 'PA_Interface >
< 'PA_Interface : ProvidedInterface | ProvidedServices : 'SendVitalParam 'L >
< 'SendVitalParam : Service | Servicename : "SendVitalParam" , QualityAttribute : 'Q1 , isActive : true , Parameters:'vital_Param >
< 'LAB : Component | Cname : "LAB_Comp" , QualityAttribute : 'Q2 , ProvidedInterfaces : 'LAB_I 'PL >
< 'LAB_I : ProvidedInterface | ProvidedServices : 'ChangeDrug 'ChangeDoses 'SendAlarm >
< 'ChangeDrug : Service | Servicename : "ChangeDrug" , QualityAttribute : 'QC , isActive : false , Parameters : 'PL >
< 'ChangeDoses : Service | Servicename : "ChangeDoses" , QualityAttribute : 'QD , isActive : false , Parameters : 'PL >
< 'SendAlarm : Service | Servicename : "SendAlarm" , QualityAttribute : 'QS , isActive : false , Parameters : 'PL >
< 'FAS : Component | Cname : "FAS" , QualityAttribute : 'Q3 , ProvidedInterfaces : 'FAS_I 'PL >
< 'FAS_I : ProvidedInterface | ProvidedServices : 'FASs 'L2 >
< 'FASs : Service | Servicename : "FAS" , QualityAttribute : 'Q3 , isActive : false , Parameters : 'PL >
< 'Q1 : QualityAttribute | name : "ResponseTime" , value : 40.0 >
< 'Q2 : QualityAttribute | name : "ResponseTime" , value : 20.0 >
< 'Q3 : QualityAttribute | name : "ResponseTime" , value : 60.0 >
```

We also identify the patient's vital parameters and specially the **glucose** level as a context influencing system behavior that is sensed by the home device: glucometer. The **glucose** level is expressed as follows:

Listing 2. patient's vital parameters Context.

```
< 'CTXS1 : ContextSonsor | SonsorID : "Glucometer" , Type : PhysicalSonsor , context : 'Glucose >
< 'Glucose : Context | ContextID : "Glucose" , ContextValue : "3,25" , Flag : true >
```

In the TA system, we are concerned with the analysis of the performance quality parameter in terms of the response time. In addition, since the TA system services are hosted on the Cloud, we might consider service reliability in terms of the number of service failed invocations ("high reliability" QoS requirement may lead to the selection of services with minimal failure rate) and the cost of the service invocation ("low cost" QoS requirement may lead to selecting minimal-cost services). For this reason, we identify the **TA_Contract** that comprises three QoS Properties: **Performance**, **Reliability** and **Cost**. Each QoS Property needs one or more metrics to be quantitatively measured. We identify Response time, the Number of service invocation failures and Cumulative service invocation cost. For the **"glucose"** context we propose three QoS constraints, QosC1: The response time in the context **Glucose** of the running service must not exceed 30 s, QosC2: The number of service failed invocations of the running service in the **"glucose"** context must not exceed 5, QosC3: The Cumulative service invocation cost do not exceeds 50. The QoS contract representing the QoS requirements for TA Cloud-based system is defined as follows:

Listing 3. TA QoS_Contract

```
< 'TA_Contract : QosContract | name : "TA_Contract" , QosProperties : 'P1 'P2 'P3 >
--------------------------------------------------------------
< 'P1 : QosProperty | name : "Performance" , Weight : hight , Qosmetrics : 'PM >
< 'PM : QosMetric | idMetric : "ResponseTime" , QosContraints : 'C1 >
< 'C1 : QosConstraint | value : 30.0 , operator : "<" , contextValue : 'Glucose >
--------------------------------------------------------------
< 'P2 : QosProperty | name : "Reliability" , Weight : hight , Qosmetrics : 'RM >
< 'RM : QosMetric | idMetric : "Nb_FailedSer" , QosContraints : 'C2 >
< 'C2 : QosConstraint | value : 5.0 , operator : "<" , contextValue : 'Glucose >
--------------------------------------------------------------
< 'P3 : QosProperty | name : "Cost" , Weight : hight , Qosmetrics : 'CM >
< 'CM : QosMetric | idMetric : "CumCost" , QosContraints : 'C3 >
< 'C3 : QosConstraint | value : 50.0 , operator : "<=" , contextValue : 'Glucose >
```

Furthermore, to reflect the hierarchical structure of cloud systems we consider the cloud architecture as a collection of objects that conforms to a well defined structural hierarchy.

Listing 4. Cloud architecture specification.

```
class DataCenter | loadbalancer : Oid , servers : OidListe .
class LoadBalancer | connected : Bool .
class Server | NbrVm : Nat , NbrReq : Nat , vms : OidListe, state : State , Cout : Nat .
class Vm | NbrService : Nat , NbrReq : Nat , services : OidListe, state : State , Cout : Nat .
```

3.2   QoS-Based Monitoring of the TA System

To validate the proposed model, we present now a scenario of QoS violation and expect its reaction. We consider a scenario of sending the patient's data (glucose level) to the lab that should reply in less than 30 min. However, the response time of the running service "SendVitalParam" is equal to 40 min. In this case, the analyzer detects a violation of the QoS Constraint and notifies the planner that an adaptation is required. The planner element builds a list of possible elasticity strategies with different probabilities (Fig. 2) in order to quantify the uncertainty in systems' elasticity. As possible elasticity strategies, we have: Replication-of-service, Change-Service-Instance, migrate-Service. For better system performance, one could think to equilibrate the workload so that, e.g., users may get services with the least workload. For this reason, we have weighed the "Replication-of-service" elasticity strategy with a higher probability since it allows adding a new instance with no workload of a given service.

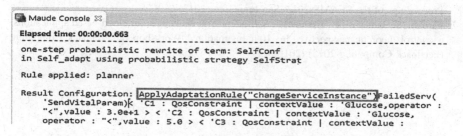

Fig. 2. A probabilistic strategy application

The probabilistic strategies of the planner element select "ChangeServiceInstance" as a best action to be applied (see Fig. 2) in terms of the least cost.

4   Conclusion

We have introduced a hybrid approach that combines elasticity advantages and the MAPE-loop as an appropriate mechanism for runtime monitoring and preservation of QoS requirements in cloud-based systems. The approach establishes a clear separation of concerns between the managed system (cloud-based applications) and the managing one. We have implemented a generic formal MAPE-Loop that is parameterized with probabilistic adaptation strategies and based on quality aspects in Cloud-based applications. We have used PSMaude, a probabilistic extension of Maude, to address the challenge of self-adaptability in cloud-based systems.

As future work, we intend to rigorously verify the behavior of model-based SASs via statistical model checking, with a focus on the analysis of probabilistic rewrite theories.

References

1. Ghezzi, C., Pinto, L., et al.: Managing non-functional uncertainty via model-driven adaptivity. In: Proceeding of ICSE 2013 the International Conference on Software Engineering, San Francisco, CA, USA (2013)
2. Kephart, J.O., Chess, D.M.: The vision of autonomic computing. Computer $36(1)$, 41–50 (2003)
3. Bentea, L., Ölveczky, P.C.: A probabilistic strategy language for probabilistic rewrite theories and its application to cloud computing. In: Martí-Oliet, N., Palomino, M. (eds.) WADT 2012. LNCS, vol. 7841, pp. 77–94. Springer, Heidelberg (2013). doi:10.1007/978-3-642-37635-1_5
4. Chen, T., Bahsoon, R.: Symbiotic and sensitivity-aware architecture for globally-optimal benefit in self-adaptive cloud. In: Proceedings of the SEAMS 2014, pp. 85–94 (2014)
5. Maatougui, E., Bouanaka, C., Zeghib, N.: Toward a meta-model for quality-aware self-adaptive systems design. In: Proceedings of the 3rd International Workshop ModComp @ MODELS, Saint-Malo, France (2016)
6. Chen, T., Bahsoon, R.: Self-adaptive and sensitivity-aware QoS modeling for the cloud. In: Proceedings of the SEAMS 2013, San Francisco (2013)
7. Farokhi, S., Jamshidi, P., Brandic, I.: Self-adaptation challenges for cloud-based applications: a control theoretic perspective. In: 10th International Workshop on Feedback Computing (Feedback Computing 2015) (2015)

Modeling and Formal Methods

Contextualization and Dependency in State-Based Modelling - Application to Event-B

Souad Kherroubi and Dominique Méry[(⊠)]

Université de Lorraine, LORIA UMR CNRS 7503, Campus Scientifique - BP 239,
54506 Vandœuvre-lès-Nancy, France
dominique.mery@loria.fr

Abstract. Context-awareness is an important feature in system design. We argue that in proof systems and conceptual modelling this notion should be precisely highlighted. Since we focus on conceptual modelling, understandability and clarity are provided precedence for reasoning about proofs done. In this paper, we introduce a new definition for proof context in state-based formalisms with an application in the Event-B modelling language. Furthermore, we introduce a dependency relation between two Event-B models. The contextualization of Event-B models is based on knowledge provided from domains that we classified into constraints, hypotheses and dependencies, according to their truthfulness in proofs. The dependency mechanism between two models makes possible to structure the development of systems models, by organizing phases identified in the analyzed process. These ideas are inspired by works based on the modelling of situations in situation theory that emphasize capabilities of type theory with regard to situation modelling to represent knowledge. Our approach is illustrated on small case studies, and have been validated on a development of design patterns for voting protocols.

1 Introduction

System design is based on various informal, semi-formal and formal methods and techniques. Techniques based on abstraction [19] facilitate this conception, giving more or less precise views of these systems. The relevant acquisition of domain knowledge allows a better understanding and communication of the problem to solve. In fact, a conceptual model must integrate the *intention* of the designer and must give a clear, correct and complete view of the system using an unambiguous semantics. Contextualism focuses precisely on the details of each particular application, as well as on the modelling process itself. These details define a context and constitute the unique identity of each modelling task. The contextualization is an abstraction mechanism that provides a separation between the collected data. It makes possible to solve the problem related to the differences in perception between different actors in the system, thus facilitating the organization and rationalization of the perspectives of the same reality.

This work was supported by grant ANR-13-INSE-0001 (The IMPEX Project http://impex.gforge.inria.fr) from the Agence Nationale de la Recherche (ANR).

© Springer International Publishing AG 2017
Y. Ouhammou et al. (Eds.): MEDI 2017, LNCS 10563, pp. 137–152, 2017.
DOI: 10.1007/978-3-319-66854-3_11

The context in the formal verification of system is an advantage: whereas the use of the context in the downstream development phases makes it possible to situate the developed systems in space and time [20], its use during the upstream of the development process improves the validation of the produced systems [10]. Such a validation is determined by measuring the relationship between the representation of the real system and a model with respect to the intended use cases (configurations and scenarios) of the model.

The "*context*" has been widely recognized as important according to the various research topics. For instance, in the context of security, integrating the knowledge contained in attack patterns with limited knowledge related to the target system vulnerabilities and potential threats depends strongly on the context of its application [6]. The context is used to assess the impact and the *plausibility* of these attacks. The reliability of a system is based on a systematic approach to recovery requirements and strategies [14], by identifying, detecting, and correcting risks and threats, and developing secure mechanisms while helping designers to choose the appropriate countermeasures to reduce attackers abilities. Thus, the validation of the assumptions made by designers is performed on the modelling of threats associated with their contextual information in order to protect the system against unauthorized modification of data or disclosure of information. The context is therefore a key element in the choice of the security patterns to be applied.

Logics and ontologies are two main research directions, where the notion of context has taken a large place. Barlatier [8] shows that this notion is not absolute and the context is always defined with respect to a focus, an activity, an intentional concept i.e.: an action, ... etc. Contexts are formal objects constructed incrementally from an existing one which corresponds to the "*context lifting*" (see for instance, McCarthy [15]). The situation appears as a new parameter in predicates and thus, predicates depend on a situation. Otherwise, the treatment of partiality and the ability to cope with dynamic information [3] based on the framework of situation theory are relevant for modelling the contexts. Typed situations behave as models that validate some information fragments called *infons* [9]. In situation theory, contexts are defined as a combination of situations involving facts and constraints involving types [5].

At the proof-theoretical level, the context allows to establish and validate trust relationships that provide valid interpretations in a specific domain for certification purposes. We are interested in the contextualization and the context of proof in the Event-B formalism [1]. The Event-B method is a structuring framework that ensures, through its language, a formal model of systems. The behavioral specifications in this formalism follow an assertional approach described by means of contexts and machines. Rather than considering contexts as formal objects like McCarthy, we adopt the Barlatier approach [8] which considers context as minimal knowledge being part of a system focused on proof, by assimilating the Event-B models to concepts in the ontological meaning. The context is thus an integral part of the proof and constrains its semantics. We propose to decompose the context in Event-B into: *constraints, hypotheses* and *dependencies*, depending on whether the knowledge is acquired, supposed and deduced in a proof system. We define this new mechanism of dependency between Event-B models, where the property of termination with stability, is a necessary condition for its establishment. A correspondence with situation theory is established: a situation corresponds to the state of the system in Event-B, and the facts establish a logical interpretation which defines the state of the system. These represent the values in the sets (the content of the Event-B sets), the values of the constants as well as the values of the variables defined in the machines. The constraints correspond to the static properties defined in Event-B contexts. This mechanism is then defined by a combination of states and static properties of Event-B contexts. The dependency is a measurable relationship taking values from existing facts in a situation that requires the definition of a new proof obligation.

This paper is organized as follows. Section 2 reports related works on the context in the literature. We briefly present the Event-B modelling language in Sect. 3 and what is the context in this formalism. Section 4 gives the definition of dependency between Event-B models as well as two examples. Finally, Sect. 5 concludes our works and gives perspectives.

2   Contextualization and Dependency

The notion of context is important in two main general topics namely logic and ontologies: a first view is logic-based and its origins are works of McCarthy [15] and the second one is based on ontologies.

McCarthy [15] introduces this notion as a *generalization* of a collection of *assumptions*. He describes *contexts* as a *first class citizens*. The basic relation is a meta-predicate $ist(c, p)$ stating that the proposition p is true in the context c. Context's axiomatization defined in its approach is extended by defining a *specialization* mechanism between two contexts *specializes(c_1, c_2)* whose truth value is true, if the context c_1 has more assumptions than c_2.

Others works are based on situation theory [5,9]. The context is considered as a combination of grounding situations and rules, which govern the relations within the context. It is represented by situation type supporting two kinds of infons (a primitive concept in situation theory): factual infons to establish facts, and constraints that correspond to parametric conditionals [3].

The main primitive concepts in situation theory [9] are infons and situations. The infon is the basic unit that embodies the information. Infons are represented by $\ll R, a_1, a_2, ... a_n, i \gg$, where R denotes a relation with n-arguments; $a_1, ..., a_n$ are appropriate objects representing the arguments of R respectively, those that denote spatial locations, individuals, relations situations, infons, ... and are represented by i; i denotes infon's polarity which characterizes the state of truth of this information unit. Consider the following example $\langle\langle On, AC system, t, 1\rangle\rangle$ representing an infon which defines an air conditioning system at a time t. This infon indicates all situations where the system is operating (On). The situations make certain infons factual i.e.: $s \models \iota$: states that the infon ι is true in the situation s. The symbol $\models$ states a validity relation between situations and infons which allow to capture the semantics of a situation. Such validity expresses a dependency relationship between situation and infons. In situation theory context defines the domain of quantification [9] that corresponds to the uniformities of Barwise shared by infons. Systematic constraints between types of situations allow a situation to contain information about another situation. Given a parameter $\dot{x}$, a finite set I of infons containing $\dot{x}$, so a type abstraction defined by $[\dot{x}|s \models \bigwedge_{\iota \in I} \iota]$ is the type of all situations in which $\dot{x}$ depends on objects of a particular type so that all conditions in I are obtained.

To illustrate the way in which a situation can be represented, here is the study of a concrete example. Given an individual invited person to a seminar located in a particular lounge of a hotel.

$$S_0 = [\dot{s} \mid \dot{s} \models << Located, seminar28, Hotel\_Pierre\_le\_Grand, \dot{t}, 1 >>]$$
$$S_1 = [\dot{s} \mid \dot{s} \models << Located, Pierre, Hotel\_Pierre\_le\_Grand, \dot{t}, 1 >>]$$
$$B = [\dot{s} \mid \dot{s} \models << Participates, Pierre, seminar28, \dot{t}, 1 >>]$$

The parametric conditionals which expresses a constraint is defined as follows: $C = \{S_0 \Rightarrow S_1 | B\}$, which means that, if a seminar takes place in a given hotel (S_0), then it is possible to infer that a person is also in that hotel (S_1) because it participates in the seminar (B). B is a set of conditions for which the constraint C expresses an information.

Barlatier [8] unifies both approaches based on logic and those based on ontologies. His main notion is an ontological concept denoted by a type:—(i) A *fact* denotes the objects in relation; (ii) A *situation* S is described by a collection of facts f_i, such that $S = \{f_1, ..., f_n\}$.

A contextualized action is considered as a function that maps one or many extracted arguments from context within a symbol used by action. Barlatier claims that the context is continually updated by successive actions. Since it can not be considered outside of the use of an action, the description of a context must rely on this dependency by establishing an *explicit* link between the action and the context. Thus, the structure of the context is described by an aggregation of predicates expressing properties and constraints related by contextualized actions in a situation. The formalism defined by Barlatier is based on constructive intuitionistic logic and Extended Calculus of Constructions ECC (that he has extended to take into account constants and sub-typing) and the situation theory. The ability to use context is expressed by the notion of dependent types.

This correspondence between the dependent types and contexts is justified by the fact that a context is not absolute concept, but it is related to an activity (which may correspond to a verification activity in our case). Otherwise, the context is perceived as a *'universal moment'* [11] from an ontological point of view, i.e.: a concept whose existence depends on intentional concepts. These are materialized by actions. Thus, the link between context and intention is expressed through a functional dependency represented by a dependent type.

3   Modelling in Event-B

An Event-B model is built with two main ingredients: a specification language based on set theory and predicate logic and a refinement mechanism that allows correct-by-construction development. An Event-B model $\mathcal{M}$ is composed of contexts and machines. A context $\mathcal{T}h$ specifies the static part of a model and includes carrier sets s, constants c, axioms and theorems $\mathcal{P}$ that establish constraints and properties of static elements. A machine describes the dynamic of the system by means of a finite list of variables x describing the state of the system, possibly modified by a list of events $\{e_0, ..., e_n\}$. The change of state must preserve properties called *invariants* $\mathcal{I}nv$ which must be maintained whenever events in the system are observed. An event is defined by a condition (guards) under which the event can be observed, actions that define the evolution of the state values in the model for the next state.

In the Event-B formalism, a situation $\mathcal{S}$ is called a state, and a state includes variables values, as well as values of sets and constants.

Definition 1 *(Configuration of Event-B model). The configuration of a model $\mathcal{M}$ in a domain $\mathcal{D}$, and we denote $config(s, c) \in \mathcal{D}$, is the values of the sets s $(\mathcal{I}_s \subseteq \mathcal{D})$, union the values of the constants c $(\mathcal{I}_c \subseteq \mathcal{D})$.*

Definition 2 *(Context). Given the Event-B's proof system, the context $\mathcal{C}xt$ is the minimal knowledge related to the behavior of any action in the system satisfying the safety properties in a given situation.*

The minimal knowledge is divided into three categories explained in the following.

Context as Constraints - The meaning of a model and its properties depends on the context of its conceptualization. The semantic aspect of a conceptualization is the point of view based on the model, its properties and its context, which addresses the foundations of the system according to the existing form, structure and facts of a particular domain. These features are called constraints. They correspond to the different concepts, roles and values of the concept attributes of the domain in study. Constraints can be physical (i.e. they exist in nature) such as the structure of the human body, the temperature in the atmosphere; or they are fully conceived by human or artificial as artifacts. For instance, the currency, the different types of vote (majoritarian voting, preferential voting, cumulative voting, ...) which make it possible to compute and give meaning to the result of an election, are constraints that define the context in which the proof is carried out. Constraints are expressed in Event-B by the structures defined in the context, namely, sets, constants, axioms and theorems that establish their typing and their static characteristics or properties. We denote these constraints by the form $C\text{-}AX$ and $C\text{-}TM$ to illustrate axioms and theorems in a context of an Event-B model.

Context as Hypotheses - Assumptions on environment also situate the systems to verify. These are established by the designers. Assumptions are not always verified but only assumed, accepted or supposed. They are reflected in a restriction on the abilities of the corrupt behavior (these are expressed in Event-B machines), and on constraints that can be defined in the Event-B contexts. In the example of voting protocols we studied, the objectives of each voting protocol as well as the type of the attacks described determine whether the proofs are successful or not. The use of cryptographic primitives to ensure the construction of secure voting guaranteeing the required properties is based on assumptions about difficulties in performing computations or solving some problems. In the context of the Belenios system [7] whose development is based on the version of Helios with credentials and zero-knowledge proofs, the proof scheme is constructed on the assumptions that the registration authority and the bulletin board are not simultaneously dishonest, and thus providng the correctness of the voting scheme is made under these trust assumptions. We [12] have shown that these kinds of assumptions can be expressed in Event-B models, possibly by refinement, by adding new variables, events and properties in the machines. Hypotheses on constraints are restrictions on static elements defined in Event-B contexts. Many voting protocols have succeeded in proving properties by making assumptions about the format of the ballots. Thus, proofs are only possible using binary values of ballots (i.e. 1/0, yes/no, ...). These restrictions are expressed by adding new constants and axioms in the Event-B contexts. We note the hypotheses on the constraints in the Event-B contexts by H-AX and H-TM to illustrate the additional axioms and theorems in the contexts of an Event-B model. The hypotheses on the environment are illustrated by variables, invariants properties and additional events in machines.

Context as Dependencies - McCarthy has shown that predicates that define the context are parametrized by situations, thus defining a *context lifting* in his work. While the ontological point of view demonstrates that a context is a *moment universals*[1] [11]. Barlatier has established a correspondence between set theory and ontologies, namely, ontological concepts (i.e. types) are interpreted as sets of elements and roles as relations between the elements of different concepts. Starting from this observation, and by comparing with the situation theory, where situations are interpreted as states in the Event-B formalism, and the constraints as the elements defined in the Event-B contexts, we can express this type of context by a dependency relation between the Event-B models. This relation results from the combination of situations (of the values of states in the Event-B formalism) and of constraints expressed in Event-B contexts by confusing this *moment universals* with the termination which requires the stability property. This type of context can be illustrated by voting systems.

The achievement of the voting process [12] consists mainly of three phases: *(1) The preparation phase*: At the end of this phase, the lists of nominated candidates, as well as the registered voters entitled to vote shall be drawn up. The establishment of these lists depends on the local laws of each country; *(2) the vote registration phase*: This phase allows all eligible voters to express their choice on the basis of the list of nominated reprentatives in the previous phase; Thus, by using the voters list,the elector must authenticate himself as an eligible voter and cast his vote individually; *(3) The tallying phase*: It covers the counting and results of the reports arising from the recording phase. At the end of these phases,

---

[1] A moment is an individual that existentially depends on other individuals.

the interpretation of the results depends on the method of voting adopted which constrains the final decision. Each phase of the vote depends on the previous one. This notion of dependency exemplifies the parties integrated into the entire voting system (*"Whole"*), assuring them a separate existence independent of the *"Whole"*. This distinction between *"Parts"* and *"Whole"* is important for verifying safety properties on the models (components) of one part independently of the others. These Part-Whole relations are derived from the mereologies. The mereologies are formal ontologies based on the dependency theory [18] which describes a differential semantics of qualified objects that assures them their own existence.

The notion of *existential dependency* [13] states a general principle as follow: *Let the predicate ϵ denote existence. We have that an individual x is existentially dependent on another individual y iff, as a matter of necessity, y must exist whenever x exists, or formally $ed(x, y) \overset{def}{=} \Box(\epsilon(x) \Rightarrow \epsilon(y))$.*

The constraints dependencies are expressed by *D-AX* and *D-TM* to illustrate dependent axioms and theorems in the contexts of an Event-B model.

We have sketched the contextualization in Event-B, and we will describe the notion of dependent Event-B models in order to enrich the structuring techniques in this formalism. As refinement is the main mechanism used in the Event-B formalism, we will explain at the end of the next section how this mechanism is used to contextualize the systems under study allowing conceptual models to have a better semantic integration and thus a good reasoning.

4   Dependency of Models

The dependency between two Event-B models $\mathcal{M}_1$ and $\mathcal{M}_2$ is informally defined as follows: *(i)* the Event-B contexts of $\mathcal{M}_1$ and $\mathcal{M}_2$ may be related i.e.: *(ii)* some variables of the first model $\mathcal{M}_1$ are *transformed* into *constants* in the target model $\mathcal{M}_2$; *(iii)* the predicate characterizing the termination of the first model implies the constraints defined in the Event-B context of the second component. In this case, there is no sharing of variables, and a component corresponds to an abstract Event-B model and possibly a set of models that refine this abstract one, and it is requested that the refinement level for each phase must be sufficiently elaborate so that the set of constants in the Event-B context of the phase that follows the current one finds its correspondent (variable) in the last refinement of the phase on which it depends.

Our reasoning is that an Event-B model is considered as an ontological concept as argued by Barlatier. Thus, we speak about models and their logic interpretation with a specific valuation belonging to the domain. Thus, individuals concern the valuation.

In the following, we adopt notations [4,16], which expresses relationnal models and their extension to the temporal aspects following TLA.

4.1 Relational Models for Event-B

Given two Event-B models $\mathcal{M}_i$, with $i \in 1..2$ defined by:

$$\mathcal{M}_i \triangleq (\mathcal{T}h_i(s_i, c_i), x_i, Val_i, \mathcal{I}nit_i(x_i), \{e_{i0}, ..., e_{in_i}\})$$

- $\mathcal{T}h_i(s_i, c_i)$ is the Event-B context that defines all elements and static properties of the model $\mathcal{M}_i$;
- the state space is the set of all possible values of the variables Val_i;
- $\mathcal{P}_i(s_i, c_i) \triangleq AX(s_i, c_i) \cup TM(s_i, c_i)$ are the statiques or the *constraints* on the sets s_i and constants c_i of the model $\mathcal{M}_i$. We note $\mathcal{C}_i(s_i, c_i)$ to express the dependent constraints defined in the Event-B which express the dependent axioms $D - AX(s_i, c_i)$ and theorems $D - TM(s_i, c_i)$;
- the set of initial states $\mathcal{I}nit_i$;
- a set of events $\{e_{i0}, ..., e_{in_i}\}$;
- $Spec(\mathcal{M}_i) \triangleq \mathcal{I}nit_i(x_i) \wedge \Box[NEXT_i]_{x_i} \wedge L_i$ with $NEXT_i \triangleq \exists e.e \in \{e_{i0}, ..., e_{in_i}\} \wedge BA(e)(x_i, x'_i)$; x'_i is the value of variables after the observation of the event e; $\Box[NEXT_i]$ means that all state pair satisfies the relation $NEXT$ and the values of variables remain the same or change; and L_i is a conjunction of weak and strong fairness constraints on the combinations of events e_i of the model $\mathcal{M}_i$;

A fair execution trace $tfair(\mathcal{M}_i, L_i)$ generated by a model $\mathcal{M}_i$ is defined by an infinite sequence of values:

$$\mathcal{T}race(\mathcal{M}_i) \triangleq \{\sigma_0\sigma_1\sigma_2...\sigma_j\sigma_{j+1}... \mid \sigma_0 \in \mathcal{I}nit_i \wedge \forall j \in \mathbb{N}.(\sigma_j, \sigma_{j+1}) \in NEXT_i\}$$

that satisfies the specification $Spec(\mathcal{M}_i)$ and is noted by $\sigma \models Spec(\mathcal{M}_i)$. To define the termination property with stability, it is necessary to add to the definition of the *Leads to*[2] operator [4] the stability property the following definition: This definition expresses that we inevitably reach a future where the property Q will be verified and will remain true on all paths that will follow. The termination property is defined as follows:

Definition 3 (*Stable termination*). *A specification $Spec(\mathcal{M}_i)$ of a model $\mathcal{M}_i$ under the fairness assumptions L_i satisfies the termination property in Q, if the following property is satisfied in Q:*

$$\forall i.(i \geqslant 0 \wedge P(\sigma_i) \Rightarrow \exists j.(j \geqslant i \wedge Q(\sigma_j) \wedge \forall k.(k \geqslant j \wedge Q(\sigma_k))))$$

Q is the predicate that characterizes the set of terminal states of the $\mathcal{M}_i$ model denoted by $\mathcal{T}_i$ in the following.

The stability implies that the predicate that characterizes the final states will remain true for all reachable states afterwards. A proof of the progression by definining a variant on a well-founded order is necessary to show convergence in the system [4].

---

[2] Leads to: Under the fairness assumptions L of the model $\mathcal{M}$, the specification of the model $Spec(\mathcal{M})$ satisfies the property $P \rightsquigarrow Q$, if for all traces $\sigma \in tfair(\mathcal{M}, L)$, the following property holds: $\forall i.(i \geqslant 0 \wedge P(\sigma_i) \Rightarrow \exists j.(j \geqslant i \wedge Q(\sigma_j)))$.

Definition 4 *(Dependency between two Event-B models). The two models $\mathcal{M}_i$, with $i \in 1..2$ (i.e.: $\mathcal{M}_1$ and $\mathcal{M}_2$) are dependent, and we say that the model $\mathcal{M}_2$ contextually depends on the model $\mathcal{M}_1$ with respect to the property of termination $\mathcal{T}_1$ and we denote $Dep(\mathcal{M}_1, \mathcal{T}_1, \mathcal{M}_2, v_1, c_{21})$, if:*

1. *$Spec(\mathcal{M}_1) \models \mathcal{I}nit_1 \rightsquigarrow \mathcal{T}_1$ and $\mathcal{T}_1$ is the predicate characterizing the set of final states at the stability of the model $\mathcal{M}_1$;*
2. *$Spec(\mathcal{M}_1) \models (\forall x_1, x_1'.(\mathcal{T}_1(x_1) \wedge NEXT_1(x_1, x_1') \Rightarrow \mathcal{T}_1(x_1')));$*
3. *the dependent context extends the source context i.e.: $\mathcal{T}h_2(s_2, c_2)$ extends $\mathcal{T}h_1(s_1, c_1);$*
4. *there is a non-empty subset v_1 of all set of variables x_1 ($v_1 \subseteq x_1$) in the first model $\mathcal{M}_1$ such that the following property is verified:*

$$\mathcal{T}h_2(s_2, c_2) \models (\mathcal{T}_1(x_1) \wedge v_1 = c_{21} \wedge c_2 = c_{21} \cup c_1 \cup c_{22}) \Rightarrow \mathcal{C}_2(s_2, c_2),$$

with c_2 is the set of constants c_1 defined in the context of the first model $\mathcal{M}_1$ and which is obtained by extension of the context $\mathcal{T}h_1$ according to the item 3, union the variables v_1 issued from the machine of the first model $\mathcal{M}_1$, to which the constants c_{22} are added newly introduced in the Event-B context of the second model $\mathcal{M}_2$. The values of these (c_{22}) can be defined according to the values of the variables v_1 in the first model.

Concretely, a model $\mathcal{M}_2$ depends on an other model $\mathcal{M}_1$, if the predicate characterizing the set of terminal states of the first model $\mathcal{M}_1$ allows to satisfy the **initial configuration** of the $\mathcal{M}_2$ defined by the content of sets, and values of constants of the context $\mathcal{T}h_2(s_2, c_2)$. $\mathcal{T}h_2(s_2, c_2)$ is the structure definining the Event-B context of the second model i.e., all static properties (axioms and theorems) in conjunction that establish the typing and the constraints of dependent and independent of the situations, while $\mathcal{C}_2$ are the constraints that must be satisfied by all final states of the first model i.e., which dependent on situations. These situations are added to the context of the second Event-B model, in conjunction with the properties that are independent of the situations linked to the first model. This approach reflects the fact that at the stabilization of the first phase, no modification can be made on these elements as variables, since the latter in the first component maintain their values at the termination. We then apply to the operator defining the predicate of the static constraints which takes the list of sets and constants defined in the context depending on, the new values of the variables defined in the first model. The consistency in Event-B is defined by the set of proof obligations. The proof obligation to prove the dependency mechanism between two models $\mathcal{M}_1$ and $\mathcal{M}_2$ which must be discharged is defined as follows.

Definition 5 *(Proof obligation of dependencies between $\mathcal{M}_1$ and $\mathcal{M}_2$).*
$$\mathcal{T}h_1(s_1, c_1), Inv(s_1, c_1, x_1), v_1 \subseteq x_1, c_{21} \subseteq c_2, \mathcal{T}_1(x_1) \vdash \mathcal{C}_2(s_2, c_2)(v_1/c_{21})$$

The contexts[3] become in partonomic relation as defined by Barlatier[4] [8], where a context Cxt_1 is a part of another context Cxt_2, if Cxt_1 contains at least all the constraints verified in Cxt_2. The second model becomes dependent on the first one.

Case Studies 1: Example of an Experiment - We illustrate required mechanisms using an experiment process. An experiment requires the collection of data and the processing of collected data to produce an indicator. We do not care what is the experiment and we consider the example as illustrating the phasing of two processes namely collecting and interpreting. The process COLLECTING is simply collecting data from sensors and storing them in a file; there are possible invalid data, which are not stored in the file. One assumes that there is a filter which is stating when a datum is valid or not. The process interpreting is applying an analysis of the results which are stored in store at the end of the process collecting. The problem is to evaluate the value of $sum(store)$ when store is computed. The problem is clearly decomposed into two phases and is first expressed by a machine stating the two different computations: (1) The process collecting is producing the final value of $store$; (2) The process interpreting is retoruning a value which is the value of the summation of all the values of $store$. First, we define the initial context that helps to define the specification of the problem to solve. We define the function sum which is returning the value of the summation of data of a given set. We do not care what is exactly sum and what we are really computing.

The small example is illustrating our methodology for analysing this class of problems. The machine $exp0$ is simply describing the two phases for producing the required result, namely $s = sum(store)$, when the process is completed.

```
CONTEXT data0
SETS    data, PHASES
CONSTANTS    valid, tmax, val, sum, collecting, interpreting, final
AXIOMS
    axm1 : valid ⊆ data
    axm2 : tmax ∈ N
    axm3 : tmax ≠ 0
    axm4 : val ∈ N × data → N
    axm5 : sum ∈ ℙ(N × data) → N
    axm6 : sum(∅) = 0
    axm7 : ∀i, e·i ↦ e ∈ N × data ⇒ sum({i ↦ e}) = val(i ↦ e)
    axm8 : ∀p, i, e·p ⊆ N × data ∧ e ∈ data ∧ i ∈ N
                ⇒ sum(p ∪ {i ↦ e}) = sum(p) + val(i ↦ e)
    axm7 : partition(PHASES, {collecting}, {interpreting}, {final})
```

Each event (collecting and interpreting) is describing a pre/psot specification that is supposed to be developed in another session. Now, we develop two separate models that are modelling the two processes collecting and interpreting.

---

[3] We will talk, indifferently, about Event-B contexts or models in partonomic relation.
[4] In his work, Barlatier is interested only in the dependency-based *"Part-Whole"* relationships.

```
MACHINE exp0
SEES data0
VARIABLES    store, phase, s
INVARIANTS
    inv1 : store ⊆ N × data
    inv2 : phase ∈ PHASES
    inv3 : s ∈ N
    inv4 : phase = final ⇒ s = sum(store)
EVENTS
EVENT INITIALISATION
    BEGIN
        act1 : store := ∅
        act2 : phase := collecting
        act3 : s := 0
    END
EVENT collecting
    WHEN
        grd01phase = collecting
    THEN
        act1 : phase := interpreting
        act2 : store : |(store' ⊆ N × data ∧ ran(store') ⊆ valid)
    END
EVENT interpreting
    WHEN
        grd1 : phase = interpreting
    THEN
        act1 : phase := final
        act2 : s := sum(store)
    END
```

Each event corresponds to a phase and defines a required *liveness* property which is derived from the definition of the process experimenting. The main liveness property can be simply stating that the experiment starts and ends after a time which is explicitly stated in the experiment requirements.

- $at(\text{experimenting}) \land store = \emptyset \land s = 0 \land t = t0 \rightsquigarrow after(\text{experimenting}) \land s = sum(store) \land t = tf$ and the process experimenting is decomposed into the two processes coresponding to models:

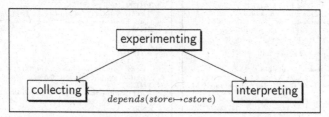

→ phase *collecting*: $at(\text{collecting}) \land store = \emptyset \land s = 0 \rightsquigarrow after(\text{collecting}) \land (store \subseteq \mathbb{N} \times data \land ran(store) \subseteq valid)$

- phase *interpreting*: $at(\text{interpreting}) \land (store \subseteq \mathbb{N} \times data \land ran(store) \subseteq valid) \rightsquigarrow after(\text{interpreting}) \land s = sum(store)$

The **depends** operation is expressing that the variable *store* has a final value which is used as an constant *cstore* in the model interpreting. The validity of the **depnds** operation is based on checking that the final value of *store* is satisfying the properties of *cstore*, which are defined as *axioms* in the development of interpreting. The **depends** operation is based on the definition and the proof of *liveness* properties and we are using the approach in [16] for combining and integrating the two phases.

Case Study 2: ERP Management System - The example presented here concerns the management of inventories by purchases and sales of articles, and a deferred accounting of revenues and expenditures. This modelling is a simplified representation and it does not describe all the management details in an ERP system. The first model denoted by $\mathcal{M}\_sp$ is described by a context *sales_purchases_cxt* and a machine *sales_purchases_machine*. The system manages purchaes (*buy* event) and the sales (*sale* event) of articles. Sales are performed according to the prices fixed in the context, while purchases are fixed by the market. The imputation of the deferred accounting entries allows to transactions to be counted only at the time of the execution of the transfer operations.

```
CONTEXT  sales_purchases_cxt
SETS
    ARTICLES
CONSTANTS
    deferred_period, prices_art
AXIOMS
    axm1 : deferred_period ∈ ℕ1
    axm2 : prices_art ∈ ARTICLES → ℕ1
```

The journal of accounting entries for sales and purchases is configured on a deferred basis according to a closing period market *"deferred period"* noted *deferred_period*. Purchases and sales can be performed during this period (*grd3*).

This period is decremented by the convergent event *"forward_time"* which decrementes the expression of the variant defined in this first machine, and is under a weak fairness assumption. The printing of the various sales and purchases operations is done through the two variables *incomings* and *expenses* respectively.

```
MACHINE  sales_purchases_machine
SEES  sales_purchases_cxt
INVARIANTS
    inv1 : period ∈ 0 .. deferred_period
    inv2 : sold_art ⊆ ARTICLES
    inv3 : incomings ∈ sold_art → ℕ
    inv4 : purchased_art ⊆ ARTICLES
    inv5 : expenses ∈ purchased_art → ℕ
    inv6 : purchased_art ∩ sold_art = ∅
    inv7 : ∀art, p·(art ↦ p ∈ incomings
        ⇒art ↦ p ∈ prices_art)
VARIANT
    deferred_period − period
EVENTS
EVENT forward_time  convergent
    WHEN
        grd1 : period ∈ 0 .. (deferred_period − 1)
    THEN
        act1 : period := period + 1
    END
```

```
EVENT sale
    ANY art
    WHERE
        grd1 : art ∈ ARTICLES
        grd2 : art ∉ sold_art ∧ art ∉ purchased_art
        grd3 : period ∈ 0 .. (deferred_period − 1)
    THEN
        act1 : sold_art := sold_art ∪ {art}
        act2 : incomings(art) := prices_art(art)
    END
EVENT buy
    ANY art, p
    WHERE
        grd1 : art ∈ ARTICLES ∧ p ∈ ℕ1
        grd2 : art ∉ purchased_art ∧ art ∉ sold_art
        grd3 : period ∈ 0 .. (deferred_period − 1)
    THEN
        act1 : purchased_art := purchased_art ∪ {art}
        act2 : expenses(art) := p
    END ...
```

The *closure* of an operation period implies that the accounting of the income and expenditure can *begin* when the value of the *period* variable will be equal to *deferred_period* i.e., at the stability of the first component. This is expressed by the dependency relation between the two models. Accounting is described by the model $\mathcal{M}\_accounting$ defined by the machine *accounting_machine* which sees the context *accounting_cxt* depending on the machine *sales_purchases_machine*. This context extends the first one *sales_purchases_cxt* and contains all the constants defined as variables in this latter (*sales_purchases_machine*) with constant *period* having as value *deferred_period* in the dependent context. We note the dependency between the two models by:

$Dep(\mathcal{M}\_sp, period = deferred\_period, \mathcal{M}\_accounting, v_1, c_{21})$, with: v_1 all variables defined by the invariants *inv1, ... ,inv7* in the first machine; and c_{21} corresponds to the same elements, but defined as constants in the dependent context *accounting_cxt*, to which we add the following constraint: $axm11$: $period = deferred\_period \Rightarrow (purchased\_art \neq \varnothing \lor sold\_art \neq \varnothing)$. The dependent constraint in this example is $period = deferred\_period \land axm11$. The accounting consists of the computation using the variable *balance*, which is initialized to 0, of the difference between the *incomings* and *expenses* by means of the constant *total* defined in the dependent context as a function that allows to sum the values of arguments that it takes.

```
MACHINE accounting_machine / * dependent machine * /
SEES accounting_cxt / * dependent context * /
INVARIANTS
   inv1 : balance ∈ ℤ ∧ accounted ∈ BOOL
   inv2 : period = deferred_period ∧ accounted = FALSE
      ⇒balance = 0
EVENT accounting
   WHEN
      grd1 : accounted = FALSE
   THEN
      act1 : balance := total(incomings) − total(expenses)
      act2 : accounted := TRUE
   END
```

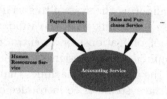

Fig. 1. ERP management system

This relation can be generalized to any number of Event-B models, as shown in the diagram of Fig. 1. If we take for instance, the example of management system, it is then possible to define a dependency between *Human Ressources Service* and *Payroll Service*, and between this last service and the *Accounting Service*. Thus, the dependency relation is irreflexive, antisymmetric and transitive as argued by Barlatier in his works.

4.2   Contextualizing Systems vs. the Refinement of Event-B Models

The case study [12] illustrates how refinement mechanism in its various forms (horizontal and vertical) contextualizes the target systems and provides a good compromise between expressiveness and rigorous reasoning. Refinement can be seen as a *a posteriori* approach, where implicit knowledge can be explicit by integration into abstract models, thus avoiding some conflicts and ambiguities. Implicit semantics play an important role in the identification and evaluation of the functionalities of the studies systems.

Our investigations show that as long as there are semantically equivalent relations between constraints, refinement mechanism remains a good integration approach for the verification of systems that reconciles the different views of different actors and parties involved in the system. The examples [2,17] illustrate this point of view. The work [2] deals with the design of an avionics system, where the part that produces information such as altitude and flight speed communicates them to the party responsible for their display via a unidirectional channel. These data are exchanged by converting values expressed in inches, meter and kilometer using constants, axioms defined in Event-B contexts. While the component responsible for calculating this information expresses the altitude in inches and the speed in meters per hour, their display is carried out in meters and kilometers per hour respectively. The system [17] estimates wheel speed in kilometers per hour, while the calculation for determining ground speed is estimated in miles hour. This example also introduces conversion constants between the various units used to express the requirements. The context treated in the various cases cited corresponds to the *context of constraints*.

Accordingly, the carrier sets and logic quantifiers on which the Event-B is based also allow a good parameterization of the models for the verification by an automatic construction of invariants on systems covering enough behaviors to conceive design patterns. The instantiation of the obtained patterns consists in configuring the system to specify the values of the sets in Event-B contexts, this case has a link with the validation issues and does not give rise to additional proof obligations; or to introduce other refinements for the specific needs or requirements of designers. The refinement in the Event-B formalism is defined by the addition of machines that refine other machines to better define behaviors in the systems or to introduce other behaviors that do not exist in the abstract models. This approach requires the use of Event-B contexts that defined the static aspects in the models. Often, it is done by extension of these Event-B contexts that one can integrate new concepts, useful mechanisms for system functionalities. This method has a great advantage that consists in factoring the efforts of proofs to be realized for possible re-use of the proofs and therefore of the developed models.

Contrary to what we have claimed in the above, when no interpretation exists between the constraints to elaborate the semantic of the context, refinement via different extensions between the Event-B contexts is possible. The example of the voting systems that we developed in [12] illustrates this case. Different elections have different modes/types of voting and voting theory analyses the advantages and disadvantages of each. Each type of voting has no interpretation semantically equivalent in the other. Therefore, each type is defined in a different Event-B context.

5   Conclusion

The *context lifting* of McCarthy involves situations or times. In addition, the partonomic relations between contexts in [8] express a change of structures which corresponds to a change of models in our case. The context as knowledges is a notion which depends on space and time, it can therefore be defined as a dependency between models in Event-B, where the termination as defined i.e.: with persistence must be established. The principle of dependencies is a dual principle to the principle of invariance in Event-B machines, claiming that states are constrained by invariants in order to establish safety in a proof system. We have applied this mechanism to the voting protocols [12]. We have developed a voting system as an Event-B composition via the dependency mechanism. The models in our development are described by means of Event-B contexts and machines linked by refinement describing the constants and the dynamic of the system. The advantages of such a modelling is that this manner to design makes proofs to be realized easier, and allows to express/verify properties separately.

We have, for instance, expressed Eligibility, no double voting, confidentiality, in the recording phase; and the Verifiability in the tallying phase. Moreover, this modelling approach makes it possible to exploit the dependent Event-B contexts for validating ontologies. Future works will explore the use of the dependency relationship, when developing technical systems, and questions related to the mechanisation of the depends relation over Event-B components.

References

1. J.-R. Abrial. Modeling in Event-B: System and Software Engineering. Cambridge University Press, 2010
2. Ameur, Y.A., Méry, D.: Making explicit domain knowledge in formal system development. Sci. Comput. Program. **121**, 100–127 (2016)
3. Akman, V., Surav, M.: The use of situation theory in context modeling. Comput. Intell. **13**(3), 427–438 (1997)
4. Andriamiarina, M.B.: Développement d'algorithmes répartis corrects par construction. Thèse, Université de Lorraine, October 2015
5. Barwise, K.J.: Conditionals and conditional information. In: Traugott, E., ter Meulen, A., Reilly, J., Ferguson, C. (eds.) On Conditionals, pp. 21–54. Cambridge University Press, Cambridge (1986)
6. Benaissa, N., Méry, D.: Cryptographic protocols analysis in event B. In: Pnueli, A., Virbitskaite, I., Voronkov, A. (eds.) PSI 2009. LNCS, vol. 5947, pp. 282–293. Springer, Heidelberg (2010). doi:10.1007/978-3-642-11486-1_24
7. Cortier, V., Fuchsbauer, G., Galindo, D.: BeleniosRF: a strongly receipt-free electronic voting scheme. IACR Cryptology ePrint Archive 2015:629 (2015)
8. Dapoigny, R., Barlatier, P.: Modeling contexts with dependent types. Fundam. Inform. **104**(4), 293–327 (2010)
9. Devlin, K.: Logic and Information. Cambridge University Press, Cambridge (1991)
10. Dhaussy, P., Boniol, F.: Mise en œuvre de composants MDA pour la validation formelle de modèles de systèmes d'information embarqués. Ingénierie des Systèmes d'Information **12**(5), 133–157 (2007)
11. Costa, P.D., Almeida, J.P.A., Pires, L.F., Guizzardi, G., van Sinderen, M.J.: Towards conceptual foundations for context-aware applications. In: Roth-Berghofer, T.R., Schulz, S., Leake, D.B. (eds.) AAAI Workshop on Modeling and Retrieval of Context 2006, WS-06-, AAAI Technical Report, pp. 54–58, Menlo Park, CA, USA, 2006. AAAI Press
12. Gibson, J.P., Kherroubi, S., Méry, D.: Applying a dependency mechanism for voting protocol models using event-B. In: Bouajjani, A., Silva, A. (eds.) FORTE 2017. LNCS, vol. 10321, pp. 124–138. Springer, Cham (2017). doi:10.1007/978-3-319-60225-7_9
13. Guizzardi, G.: Ontological foundations for structural conceptual models. Number 15 in Telematica Instituut Fundamental Research Series. University of Twente, 2005. ISBN 90-75176-81-3 ISSN 1388-1795
14. Kotonya, G., Sommerville, I.: Requirements Engineering: Processes and Techniques. Wiley, Hoboken (1998)
15. McCarthy, J.: Notes on formalizing context. In: Proceedings of the 13th International Joint Conference on Artifical Intelligence, IJCAI 1993, vol. 1, pp. 555–560. Morgan Kaufmann Publishers Inc., San Francisco (1993)

16. Méry, D., Poppleton, M.: Towards an integrated formal method for verification of liveness properties in distributed systems with application to population protocols. Softw. Syst. Model. (SoSyM) (2015). https://doi.org/10.1007/s10270-015-0504-y
17. Méry, D., Sawant, R., Tarasyuk, A.: Integrating domain-based features into event-b: a nose gear velocity case study. In: Bellatreche, L., Manolopoulos, Y. (eds.) MEDI 2015. LNCS, vol. 9344, pp. 89–102. Springer, Cham (2015). doi:10.1007/978-3-319-23781-7_8
18. Miéville, D.: Un développement des systèmes logiques de stanislaw lesniewski. Peter Lang (1984)
19. Mylopoulos, J.: Information modeling in the time of the revolution. Inf. Syst. **23**(3), 127–155 (1998)
20. Sutcliffe, A.G., Fickas, S., Sohlberg, M.M.: PC-RE: a method for personal and contextual requirements engineering with some experience. Requir. Eng. **11**(3), 157–173 (2006)

Formal Modelling of Domain Constraints in Event-B

Linda Mohand-Oussaid and Idir Ait-Sadoune[✉]

LRI, CentraleSupelec, Paris-Saclay University,
Plateau du Moulon, Gif-sur-Yvette, France
{linda.mohandoussaid,idir.aitsadoune}@centralesupelec.fr

Abstract. When designing a hardware or a software system, the integration of domain constraints becomes a determining factor to ensure a great match with the system requirements. This domain knowledge is most often modelled using ontologies that allow to express the domain data properties. In this paper, we propose an approach to integrate domain ontologies into a system development process based on Event-B. It consists to annotate Event-B models using the ontology concepts, this assumes a formalization of the domain ontology in the Event-B method. Therefore, we propose an extensible generic transformation approach which develops an Event-B specification based on an ontology described in an ontological language. The integration of the Event-B description of a domain ontology allows to constrain the system under design with the domain ontology and to validate domain properties.

Keywords: Domain constraints · Ontologies · Formal specification · Event-B · Theorem proving

1 Introduction

In critical systems, the usefulness of a formal development process is well established, formal approaches allow to specify and validate different aspects: intrinsic characteristics of the system under development like structure or behaviour and extrinsic properties related to context or domain. In order to achieve the validation of these two last classes of properties, it is necessary to integrate specific representations of context and domain.

For domain specifications, designers rely on consensual domain representations that capture knowledge into a formal semantic conceptualization: a domain ontology. The integration of ontologies into a formal development process requires describing these ontologies into a formal language supporting the expression of ontology semantics and allowing the validation of significant properties. One way to integrate these ontologies into a specific formal method development process is to express the ontologies languages constructs into the target formal language by means of a transformation rules. To be valid, these rules must preserve semantics during transformation.

© Springer International Publishing AG 2017
Y. Ouhammou et al. (Eds.): MEDI 2017, LNCS 10563, pp. 153–166, 2017.
DOI: 10.1007/978-3-319-66854-3_12

In this paper, we present a generic approach to integrate domain description formalized by ontologies (OWL [13], PLIB [14], RDFS [6], ...) into an Event-B formal development process [1]. The proposed approach is conducted by transformation rules that define for each ontological concept, the corresponding Event-B formalisation leading to build Event-B contexts expressing ontology concepts. This approach is implemented by the OntoEventB Eclipse/Rodin plug-in [2] that has been developed to automatically support the formalisation of ontologies using set theory and predicate logic supported by the Event-B method.

Our paper is structured as follows. In Sect. 2, we present our approach to integrate domain constraints in Event-B development process. In Sect. 3, we describe the ontology transformation approach. In Sect. 4, we detail some representative transformation rules. In Sect. 5, we illustrate our approach on a simple access control case study. In Sect. 6, we present an overview of existing approaches for domain constraints integration into formal modelling processes. Finally, we conclude and give some perspectives to this work.

2   Domain Constraints Integration Approach

This paper deals with domain constraints integration into a system development process based on Event-B. During an Event-B development process, the system behaviour is modelled by a machine, a set of variables whose values change within events. The variables are usually typed by predefine or built Event-B sets defined in a static component, the context.

Regardless the describing language, ontologies share a set of modelling concepts to describe domain constraints. An ontology describes individuals (instances) grouped into collections called classes (concepts). Classes are characterized by typed attributes and linked to other classes using properties. A class can be built by combining other classes using algebraic operators or by constraining a class using a logical predicate established on a property. Classes can be linked by inheritance relationships. Ontology modelling languages use set theory and predicate logic to describe ontologies, they involve deduction mechanisms to infer new assertions and answer queries about ontology components.

In order to integrate domain ontologies in Event-B development process, we propose to formalize the ontology as a system data model within a context component. Thus, the machine variables take their values in ontology concepts and inherit domain constraints. The proposed integration approach is operated in a three steps process (see Fig. 1).

1. *Formalization step.* A first step in the development process consists to formalize the system in the Event-B method. This leads to develop the machine component modelling the system behaviour using variables and events.
2. *Transformation step.* During this step, the domain ontology is translated into the Event-B formalism. An ontology is translated into an Event-B context using sets, constants and axioms. The transformation process is detailed in Sect. 3.

3. *Annotation step.* Once the context describing the ontology obtained, the integration of domain constraints is carried out by annotating machine variables by ontology context entities. The annotation step is illustrated in the case study section.

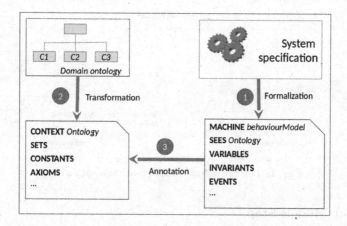

Fig. 1. Domain constraints integration in an Event-B development process

3   Ontology Transformation into Event-B Contexts

The development of a transformation approach emerges as a natural choice for the expression of an ontology description in the Event-B language. This approach allows to transform an ontology described into an ontology language into an Event-B specification. It takes as inputs the constructs used to describe an ontology in the different ontology languages and as outputs Event-B language constructions. The transformation approach is based on correspondences between ontology languages and the Event-B language semantics. The development of a such transformation approach (see Fig. 2) involves two distinct tasks:

1. Establish a pivot model (see Sect. 3.2) summarizing ontology concepts used in the different languages. This model describes relationships between specific languages concepts and generic concepts. The pivot model allows to federate common languages concepts into generic ones leading to generic transformation rules set on generic concepts rather than specific languages ones.
2. Develop for each pivot model concept the corresponding Event-B construct by establishing semantics mappings [9].

The obtained transformation approach is based on a three successive step process. Input Models step, Pivot Model step and Output Models step (Fig. 2).

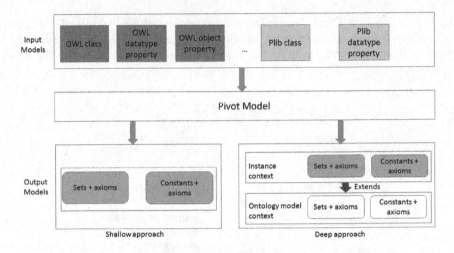

Fig. 2. The proposed transformation approach

3.1 Input Models Step

The Input Models step is devoted to treat the input models described using different ontology description languages such as OWL, Plib ... It browses the input models files in order to extract ontological concepts descriptions intended to be processed in the Pivot Model step.

3.2 Pivot Model Step

Following the receipt of the different ontological concepts derived from the Input Model step, the specific concepts are translates within the *Pivot Model* step into generic Pivot Model concepts (classes, properties and data types). After this first translation step, the obtained generic concepts are ready to be treated by the next process handled by the Output Model component.

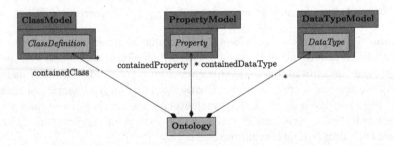

Fig. 3. The main concepts of the Pivot Model.

The Pivot Model step is based on an intermediate operational model which summarizes the common pertinent concepts used by ontology description languages: the Pivot Model,. It defines generic concepts integrating all specific concepts that can be received from the Input Model step. The Pivot Model can be extended to integrate others specific concepts that can be identified if a new language is added as input model in the Input Models step. Figure 3 presents an UML model showing the generic concepts defined in the proposed *Pivot Model*. An *Ontology* is defined by a set of classes (defined in the *ClassModel* part), a set of properties (defined in the *PropertyModel* part), and a set of data types definition (defined in the *DataTypeModel* part).

The *ClassModel* part (Fig. 4) of the *Pivot Model* presents the *class* concept that is described by a set of *properties*. This model defines also that a class can be sub-class of others classes (*subclassOf* definition), a class can be equivalent to others classes (*equivalentClassOf* definition) and/or a class can be disjoint with others classes (*disjointWith* definition). The *ClassModel* model defines five types of classes: *ItemClass* for defining new named class, *EnumeratedClass* for defining an enumerated class (list of individuals that are the instances of the defined class), *CombinationClass* for defining a new class that can be a combination of others classes (using *union, intersection* and *complement* operators), *restriction-Class* for defining a class of individuals that satisfy a restriction (like in OWL language), and *CaseOfClass* for defining a class that can be a particular case of another class (like *subClassOf* definition but without importing all properties of the mother class).

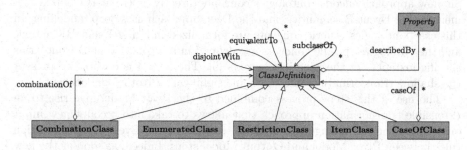

Fig. 4. The *ClassModel* model.

The *PropertyModel* part (Fig. 5) of the *pivot Model* defines the *Property* concept that can be described by its domain (optional if property is not linked to a class definition) and its range. This model defines also that a property can be sub-property of others properties (*subPropertyOf* definition), a property can be equivalent to others properties (*equivalentTo* definition) and/or a property can be inverse of other property (*inverseOf* definition). The *PropertyModel* model defines three categories of properties: *NonDependentProperty* for defining independent properties, *DependentProperty* for defining dependent properties and *ConditionProperty* for defining properties on which *DependentProperty* depends. The range of *Property* concept is formalized by the *DataType* class defined in the *DataTypeModel* part of the *pivot model* that supports the definition of primitive types, collection types and classes instances that instantiates the *ClassDefinition* class defined in the *ClassModel* model.

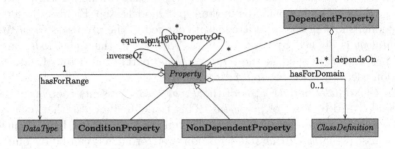

Fig. 5. The *PropertyModel* model.

3.3 Output Model Step

The Output Model step starts by receiving the generic concepts computed during the Pivot Model step; they are translated into Event-B Context elements (sets, constants and axioms). This process uses transformation rules, proposed in the IMPEX project, that formalize each ontological concept by an Event-B definition. Two approaches have been developed (Shallow [9] and Deep [8]). The Shallow approach encodes ontologies concepts directly as Event-B Context elements using Event-B semantics, and the Deep approach uses deep modelling. In this case, ontologies generic concepts are formalized in a first Event-B Context, and the ontologies specific concepts are defined in a second Event-B Context as specific instances of the generic Contexts [9]. The Sect. 4 is devoted to present the shallow transformation rules for some significant Pivot Model concepts.

The use of this steps process combined to the Pivot Model give rise to an extensible transformation approach that allows to take into account new input ontology description languages without redefining the Event-B formalization rules between Pivot Model and Output Model steps. Indeed, as soon as the new concepts defined by these new languages are translated into generic concepts of the Pivot model, they will be directly formalized in the Event-B Context elements without redefining new transformation rules.

4 From Ontology to Event-B Context

This section is dedicated to describe transformation rules from Pivot Model to Event-B constructs. The concepts: class, type and property are the primitive concepts for the description of an ontology in our Pivot Model, they are formalized into Event-B contexts using: constants, sets and axioms. Due to paper length limitation, we choose to present the shallow transformation rules for the most representative Pivot Model concepts organized into two categories, a first one describing Pivot Model components and a second one devoted to relations characterizing ontologies concepts.

4.1   Pivot Model Components Transformation Rules

In this section we present some transformation rules in Event-B for Pivot Model components illustrated by: item class, non dependent property, restriction and intersection combination class concepts.

Item Class. For a given *itemclass* identified by its name *Class*, the corresponding Event-B context defines a set *Class*, subset of the Thing set (abstract set corresponding to the root class Thing).

```
SETS Thing
CONSTANTS Class
AXIOMS
axm : Class ⊆ Thing
```

Non Dependent Property. For a given non dependent property identified by its name *Property*, its domain and range classes (*Class1* respectively *Class2*), the corresponding Event-B context defines a relation *Property* from *Class1* to *Class2* (the respectively corresponding sets to *Class1* and *Class2* classes).

```
CONSTANTS
Class1
Class2
Property
AXIOMS
axm : Property ∈ Class1 ↔ Class2
```

Restriction. The restriction concept considers a property and defines a restricted population of individuals from the property domain satisfying a constraint on the property range.

The value restriction is a type of restriction which defines a subclass of the property domain containing elements whose relational image is equal to a value. The value restriction defined on the *Property* property and the *val* value is modelled in Event-B by the domain of the range restriction defined on the *Property* relation on the *val* singleton set.

```
CONSTANTS
Property
Restriction
val
AXIOMS
axm : Restriction = dom(Property ▷ {val})
```

Intersection Class. The intersection class is a combination class built from at least two classes, containing individuals that are instances of the two classes. The intersection class obtained by combining the two classes *Class1* and *Class2* is modelled in Event-B as a set *IntersectionClass*, intersection of the two sets corresponding to the classes *Class1* and *Class2*.

```
CONSTANTS
Class1
Class2
IntersectionClass
AXIOMS
axm : IntersectionClass = Class1 ∩ Class2
```

4.2   Pivot Model Relations Transformation Rules

The Pivot Model relations express semantic relationships between entities. In this section we present transformation rules in Event-B for two representative Pivot Model relations: classes subsumption and equivalence relations.

Subsumption. The Subsumption relationship between two classes states that the first class (subclass) is a subclass of the second one (mother class). It is a fundamental relationship that construct a class inheritance hierarchy. In the proposed approach, the Subsumption relationship defined from a subclass *SubClass* to a mother class *MotherClass* is modelled as a set inclusion relationship between the corresponding sets to the subclass and the mother class.

```
CONSTANTS
SubClass
MotherClass
AXIOMS
axm : SubClass ⊆ MotherClass
```

Equivalence. The equivalence relationship between two classes states that the two classes have precisely the same instances. The equivalence relationship between the classes *Class* and *EquivalentClass* is defined in Event-B using the set equality relationship between the corresponding sets to the equivalent classes.

```
CONSTANTS
Class
EquivalentClass
AXIOMS
axm : Class = EquivalentClass
```

4.3   The *OntoEventB* Tool

The proposed ontology transformation approach in Event-B is fully supported by the *OntoEventB* RODIN plug-in that automatically produces the Event-B formalization related to an ontology (OWL, Plib or RDFS). The *OntoEventB* tool implements the proposed Shallow and Deep approaches, it takes as input an ontology description file and generates, according to the selected approach (shallow or deep approach), the corresponding Event-B Context. The actual version of *OntoEventB* plug-in treats only OWL files but we expect to extend it to treat other ontologies description formats like Plib. To use *OntoEventB* plug-in in your RODIN platform instance, you must install it using this update site link[1]. This article [12] describes the *OntoEventB* plug-in installation and using processes.

---

[1] OntoEventB update site: http://wdi.supelec.fr/OntoEventB-update-site/.

5   Case Study

We illustrate our domain constraints integration approach by means of a simple access control system example that administers users access to a given institution resources according to the access control policy. A user can access a resource only if he is authorized. Access authorizations are described by pairs (user, resource).

The institution has three resources:

- *Kiosk*. corresponding to interactive terminals providing general information to all users;
- *Computer*. related to computers used by registered institution employees;
- *Server*. corresponding to servers hosting institution databases, applications and messaging.

The used domain ontology *AccessControl* is a role based access policy ontology. A Pivot Model description of this ontology, which can be derived from an OWL, Plib or RDFS ontology is given below, it classifies institution users into four roles (a set of users sharing the same access permissions to resources).

- *Public*. External users that are authorized to access only *Kiosks*.
- *Registered*. Internal registered users that are authorized to access *Kiosks* and *Computers*.
- *Admin*. Internal super users that are authorized to access *Kiosks*, *Computers* and *Servers*.
- *Guest*. External users such as trainees that are assimilated to registered users and are authorized to access *Kiosks* and *Computers*.

The AccessControl ontology introduces two classes: *User* representing institution users and *Resource* for institution resources, the *Resource* class is an enumerated class defined by its three values corresponding to the resources categories: *Kiosk*, *Computer* and *Server*. A property *Authorization* from *User* to *Resource* modelling that a User is allowed to access a Resource is modelled. Three values restrictions *authorizedOnKiosk*, *authorizedOnComputer* and *authorizedOnServer* are defined on the *Authorization* property and respectively the values *Kiosk*, *Computer* and *Server*. Four classes corresponding to the user roles: *Public*, *Registred*, *Admin* and *Guest* are defined in terms of the previously defined value restrictions. *Public* is equivalent to the *authorized OnKiosk* class. *Registred* is equivalent to the intersection of *authorizedOnKiosk* and *authorizedOnComputer* classes, *Admin* is equivalent to the intersection of *authorizedOnKiosk*, *authorizedOnComputer* and *authorizedOnServer* classes. The guest role is defined a an equivalent class of *Registred*.

```
CLASS Resource
CLASS User
PROPERTY Authorization
    DOMAIN User
    RANGE Resource
CLASS authorizedOnComputer
    SUBCLASSOF User RESTRICTION ONPROPERTY Authorization HASVALUE Computer
CLASS authorizedOnKiosk
    SUBCLASSOF User RESTRICTION ONPROPERTY Authorization HASVALUE Kiosk
CLASS authorizedOnServer
    SUBCLASSOF User RESTRICTION ONPROPERTY Authorization HASVALUE Server
CLASS Admin
    EQUIVALENTCLASS
        INTERSECTIONOF authorizedOnComputer authorizedOnKiosk authorizedOnServer
CLASS Registred
    EQUIVALENTCLASS
        INTERSECTIONOF authorizedOnComputer authorizedOnKiosk
CLASS Guest
    EQUIVALENTCLASS Registred
CLASS Public
    EQUIVALENTCLASS authorizedOnKiosk
```

The development of the access control case study is carried out among three steps corresponding to the defined steps in Sect. 2.

Step 1. In this step, we describe an initial development of the users access process to the *Computer* resource.

The *accessControl* context models the access control policy, it defines the *Resource* and *User* sets, respectively related to the *Kiosk*, *Computer* and *Server* resources, and users. Users authorizations on resources are formalized using the *Authorization* relation from the *User* to the *Resource* sets.

```
CONTEXT accessControl
SETS Thing
CONSTANTS Resource User Kiosk Computer Server Authorization
AXIOMS
    axm1 : Resource ⊆ Thing
    axm2 : partition(Resource, {Kiosk}, {Computer}, {Server})
    axm3 : User ⊆ Thing
    axm4 : Authorization ∈ User ↔ Resource
```

The *AccessToComputer* machine formalizes the connection of a user to the *Computer* resource. It introduces the *connectedToComputer* variable containing all users connected to the *Computer* resource. The *connect_to_Computer* event connects one user to a computer resource by adding it to the *connectedToComputer* variable under the condition that he is authorized. Note that the condition of access to the *Computer* resource is explicitly defined by the guard $g2$ of the *connectedToComputer* event.

```
MACHINE AccessToComputer
SEES accessControl
VARIABLES connectedToComputer
INVARIANTS
        inv1 : connectedToComputer ⊆ User
EVENTS
    INITIALISATION
    BEGIN
            i1 : connectedToComputer := ∅
    END
    connect_to_Computer
    ANY user
    WHERE
            g1 : user ∈ User
            g2 : user ↦ Computer ∈ Authorization
    THEN
            a1 : connectedToComputer := connectedToComputer ∪ {user}
    END
```

If we have several resources to handle, and several users authorisations categories to define, we must precise all the policies explicitly as guards of events like in the previous model. This kind of information can be obtained from ontologies and we can use informations given by ontologies to easily handle this complexity. In our case, we use the *AccessControl* ontology defined at the beginning of this section.

Step 2. The integration of the *AccessControl* ontology in the *Computer* access process starts by the automatic generation of the *AccessControlOntology* context (see below). The *Resource* and *User* classes are formalized as subsets of the *Thing* set (*axm1* and *axm3* axioms). The enumerated class *Resource* containing the *Kiosk*, *Computer* and *Server* resources is defined as a partition (*axm2* axiom). The *Authorization* property is modelled as a relation from *User* to *Resource* (*axm4* axiom). The values restrictions *authorizedOnKiosk*, *authorized OnComputer* and *authorizedOnServer* are formalized using range restrictions (*axm5*, *axm6* and *axm7* axioms). User roles are formalized by sets intersection (*axm8*, *axm9*, *axm10* axioms). The equivalence relation between *Guest* and *Registred* classes is modelled using equality sets between the *Guest* and *Registred* sets.

```
CONTEXT accessControlOntology
SETS Thing
CONSTANTS Resource User Authorization Admin Public Guest Registered
            authorizedOnKiosk authorizedOnComputer authorizedOnServer
AXIOMS
    axm1 : Resource ⊆ Thing
    axm2 : partition(Resource, {Kiosk}, {Computer}, {Server})
    axm3 : User ⊆ Thing
    axm4 : Authorization ∈ User ↔ Resource
    axm5 : authorizedOnKiosk = (dom(Authorization ▷ {Kiosk}))
    axm6 : authorizedOnComputer = (dom(Authorization ▷ {Computer}))
    axm7 : authorizedOnServer = (dom(Authorization ▷ {Server}))
    axm8 : Admin = (authorizedOnServer ∩ authorizedOnKiosk ∩ authorizedOnComputer)
    axm9 : Registered = (authorizedOnKiosk ∩ authorizedOnComputer)
    axm10 : Public = authorizedOnKiosk
    axm11 : Guest = Registred
```

Now, all users authorisations categories are explicitly defined in the *access-ControlOntology* context that replaces the *accessControl* context defined in the first step.

Step 3. In this step, the *AccessToComputer* machine is modified by importing the *accessControlOntology* context in the SEES clause. The *AccessToComputer* machine is annotated by typing its variables using sets (concepts) defined by the *accessControlOntology* context (ontology) (the invariant *inv1*).

```
MACHINE AccessToComputer
SEES AccessControlOntology
VARIABLES connectedToComputer
INVARIANTS
        inv1 : connectedToComputer ⊆ authorizedOnComputer
EVENTS
    INITIALISATION
    THEN
            i1 : connectedToComputer := ∅
    END
    connect_to_Computer
    ANY user
    WHERE
            g1 : user ∈ authorizedOnComputer
    THEN
            a1 : connectedToComputer := connectedToComputer ∪ {user}
    END
```

We remark that in this case, the guard *g1* of the *connect_to_Computer* event is simplified because the access rules are defined in the context. This simplification affects also the proof process in the case of refinement. Indeed, if we want to prove that another category of user (*Registered* for example) can also connect to the same resource (*Computer*), it is enough to define a *connect_Registered_to_Computer* event that refines the *connect_to_Computer* event. In this case, the proof of the refinement is done automatically thanks to the axiom *axm9* of the context *AccessControlOntology*.

```
connect_Registered_to_Computer
    REFINES connect_to_Computer
    ANY user
    WHERE
            g1 : user ∈ Registered
    THEN
            a1 : connectedToComputer := connectedToComputer ∪ {user}
    END
```

6   Related Work

Integration of domain constraints into design processes has attracted lately great interest in the software engineering community. Many proposed approaches uses ontology descriptions as design models for these domain constraints. We focus in this overview on integration approaches devoted to formal developement processes: in [3,4], authors suggest to integrate domain constraints as a part of design models, they propose to model domain concepts using ontologies to annotate systems and to formalize the obtained design models in Event-B. In [15], an ontology axioms transformation into Z notation is proposed to express application domain rules. In [10], an integration of domain constraints is proposed for cyber-physical systems, it is performed by interpretation of computing platform components on real-world types to derive properties specification and validation. In [7], authors propose to define real-world systems semantics using domain ontologies. A domain specific description of the system is coupled to a domain ontology, the two are formalized into logic theories and conformity validation is conducted using the Alloy formal method. In [11], an Event-B specification of an OWL domain ontology is integrated to goal-based model during requirements engineering phase, this approach aims to construct a data structure for typing. In [8], domain knowledge is integrated to development process by annotation using two approaches: an MDE approach mixing ontology and OCL constraints and a theorem proving approach based on Event-B specifications. The proposed Event-B modelling approach for ontologies is based on an own definition of ontological constructs in an ontology model context combined to instantiation mechanisms. In [5], a derivation approach is proposed to generate Event-B models from OWL ontologies through the ACE controlled natural language.

In comparison with the approaches cited above, our approach is distinguished, on the one hand, by its genericity assured by the Pivot Model which federates the ontological description languages (OWL, Plib and RDFS) and ensures the integration of new languages, on the other hand, by the broad coverage of the ontological languages primitives allowing a total ontology support. Finally, our approach is tooled in order to automatically support the transformation of ontologies in Event-B.

7   Conclusion and Perspectives

In this paper, we propose to offer to a critical system designer a formal tooled approach to integrate domain data and constraints modelled by means of an ontological model into an Event-B development process. This approach consists to annotate Event-B machine variables with ontologies constructs, it involves, on the one hand, a pivot model capturing the semantics of ontological languages in an intermediate federating model which ensures genericity and flexibility of the proposed approach, the used pivot model allows to integrate in addition to the actual supported ontological languages (OWL, RDFS and Plib) new input languages without redefining transformation rules and supports different formal descriptions (actually two Event-B modelling approaches). On the other hand, transformation rules enabling to generate the Event-B context corresponding to the ontology. This approach has been fully automated and is supported by an Eclipse plug-in. We have shown throw a simple case study the contribution of integrating such domain constraint into a Event-B development process.

Acknowledgments. This work is supported by the French ANR-IMPEX project.

References

1. Abrial, J.R.: Modeling in Event-B: System and Software Engineering. Cambridge University Press, Cambridge (2010)
2. Abrial, J.R., Butler, M., Hallerstede, S., Hoang, T.S., Mehta, F., Voisin, L.: Rodin: an open toolset for modelling and reasoning in Event-B. Int. J. Softw. Tools Technol. Transfer **12**(6), 447–466 (2010)
3. Ait-Ameur, Y., Gibson, J.P., Méry, D.: On implicit and explicit semantics: integration issues in proof-based development of systems. In: Margaria, T., Steffen, B. (eds.) ISoLA 2014. LNCS, vol. 8803, pp. 604–618. Springer, Heidelberg (2014). doi:10.1007/978-3-662-45231-8_50
4. Ait-Ameur, Y., Méry, D.: Making explicit domain knowledge in formal system development. Sci. Comput. Program. **121**, 100–127 (2016)
5. Alkhammash, E.H.: Derivation of Event-B models from owl ontologies. In: MATEC Web of Conferences, vol. 76, p. 04008. EDP Sciences (2016)
6. Brickley, D., Guha, R.V.: RDF Vocabulary Description Language 1.0: RDF Schema, February 2004. http://www.w3.org/TR/rdf-schema
7. de Carvalho, V.A., Almeida, J.P.A., Guizzardi, G.: Using reference domain ontologies to define the real-world semantics of domain-specific languages. In: Jarke, M., Mylopoulos, J., Quix, C., Rolland, C., Manolopoulos, Y., Mouratidis, H., Horkoff, J. (eds.) CAiSE 2014. LNCS, vol. 8484, pp. 488–502. Springer, Cham (2014). doi:10.1007/978-3-319-07881-6_33
8. Hacid, K., Ait-Ameur, Y.: Strengthening MDE and formal design models by references to domain ontologies. a model annotation based approach. In: Margaria, T., Steffen, B. (eds.) ISoLA 2016. LNCS, vol. 9952, pp. 340–357. Springer, Cham (2016). doi:10.1007/978-3-319-47166-2_24
9. IMPEX Consortium: formal models for ontologies, June 2016
10. Knight, J., Xiang, J., Sullivan, K.: A rigorous definition of cyber-physical systems. Trustworthy Cyber-Physical Systems Engineering, p. 47 (2016)
11. Mammar, A., Laleau, R.: On the use of domain and system knowledge modeling in goal-based Event-B specifications. In: Margaria, T., Steffen, B. (eds.) ISoLA 2016. LNCS, vol. 9952, pp. 325–339. Springer, Cham (2016). doi:10.1007/978-3-319-47166-2_23
12. Mohand Oussaïd, L., Ait-Sadoune, I.: OntoEventB: Un outil pour la modélisation des ontologies dans B Événementiel. In: AFADL 2017, pp. 117–121, Montpellier, France, June 2017
13. W3C Web OWL Working Group: OWL 2 Web Ontology Language: Document Overview. W3C Recommendation (27 October 2009), available at http://www.w3.org/TR/owl2-overview/
14. Pierra, G.: Context-explication in conceptual ontologies: the PLIB approach. In: Proceedings of the 10th ISPE International Conference on Concurrent Engineering (CE 2003), Enhanced Interoperable Systems, vol. 26 (2003)
15. Vasilecas, O., Kalibatiene, D., Guizzardi, G.: Towards a formal method for the transformation of ontology axioms to application domain rules. Inf. Technol. Control **38**(4), 271–282 (2009). ISSN 1392-124X

Use of Tabular Expressions for Refinement Automation

Neeraj Kumar Singh[1]([✉]), Mark Lawford[2], Thomas S.E. Maibaum[2],
and Alan Wassyng[2]

[1] INPT-ENSEEIHT/IRIT, University of Toulouse,
Toulouse, France
nsingh@enseeiht.fr
[2] McMaster Centre for Software Certification,
McMaster University, Hamilton, Canada
{lawford,wassyng}@mcmaster.ca, tom@maibaum.org

Abstract. We aim to develop sound and effective techniques to automate formal modelling and refinement from tabular expressions using a *correct-by-construction* approach. In this work, we present a refinement strategy to generate formal models from tabular expressions, as they can be used in the Event-B modelling paradigm. The proposed refinement strategy permits us to develop an abstract model using tabular expressions and a series of Event-B models using refinement from the set of tabular expressions. Further the proofs associated with the refinement strategy used to generate the model are examined through the Rodin tools. Our work is an important step towards eliciting patterns of automatic refinement for Event-B models from tabular expressions and to meet the properties of *completeness* and *disjointness* in a rigorous manner. To assess the effectiveness of our proposed approach, we use a medical device case study: the *Insulin Infusion Pump (IIP)*.

Keywords: Tabular expression · Event-B · Refinement · Formal methods · Verification · Validation · Insulin Infusion Pump

1 Introduction

Requirement engineering (RE) provides a framework for a better understanding of system requirements by simplifying system complexity using formal and informal techniques. It plays an important role in analyzing system requirements, and functional and non-functional system behaviours to achieve the properties of consistency, unambiguity and completeness. Tabular expressions [1] support a technique for requirement engineering that uses (potentially complex) relations for documenting and analysing system requirements, in order to define them precisely and concisely. It is a visual representation of functions in a tabular layout that has a precise semantics and a formal notation. Moreover, this tabular representation of system requirements satisfies the important properties of *disjointness* and *completeness*.

© Springer International Publishing AG 2017
Y. Ouhammou et al. (Eds.): MEDI 2017, LNCS 10563, pp. 167–182, 2017.
DOI: 10.1007/978-3-319-66854-3_13

On the other hand, formal methods have been applied successfully to design and develop critical systems, such as avionics, medical and automotive [2,3]. In particular, formal methods have been used to check functional requirements and safety requirements by developing system models. In formal modelling, refinement plays an important role for handling a large complex system by developing the whole system incrementally, in which each incremental step can be used to introduce new functionalities while preserving the required safety properties.

Practicalities of performing automatic refinements are largely an open problem. It is, clearly, unrealistic to carry out such refinements entirely by hand, which is well illustrated by the complexity of the examples in [4,5]. Some refinement steps are, however, inherently difficult to automate. Our work highlights how automation is feasible to guide the refinement process.

Our primary contribution in this paper is to propose a refinement strategy that can help automate the process of formalizing system requirements from tabular expressions using a *correct-by-construction* approach. We show how the refinement strategy can be used to transform tabular expressions into formal models that aid in determining the correctness of functional behaviour, and the modelling structure of a system. The refinement approach allows us to build a formal model incrementally, where the first model represents only abstract behaviour, and the incremental models are enriched by more concrete behaviours. The generated formal models are used later to define safety properties and to check system consistency using formal verification. To achieve our goal, we select the Event-B modelling language that allows incremental refinement based on a *correct-by-construction* approach for generating formal models from tabular expressions.

To assess the proposed incremental refinement strategy in Event-B, we apply it to design and to formally specify an *Insulin Infusion Pump (IIP)*. First, the informal IIP requirements are described in tabular expressions that are used later for producing the formal models. In the IIP case study, we verify functional behaviours including various system operations, that are required to maintain insulin delivery, user profile management, and the calculation of required amounts of insulin. The complete formal development builds incrementally-refined models of IIP, formalizing the required functional behaviour by preserving its required safety properties. We also use the Rodin [6] tools to check the generated formal models. The added contributions of this article can be summarised as follows: (1) proposing a refinement strategy for generating formal models from tabular expressions; (2) discussing in detail opportunities and ramifications for automating the application of the refinement strategy; (3) presenting validation of the proposed refinement strategy by discharging the proof obligation of the generated models using Rodin tools; and (4) applying the refinement strategy to the *Insulin Infusion Pump (IIP)* case study.

The structure of the article is as follows. In Sect. 2, we review preliminary material: tabular expression and the modelling framework. Section 3 presents a refinement strategy for generating the formal models from tabular expressions. Section 4 presents an example that illustrates the application of the refinement strategy: the *Insulin Infusion Pump (IIP)*, including model analysis. Section 5 presents related work, and in Sect. 6, we conclude the paper and discuss with future work.

2   Preliminaries

2.1   Tabular Expressions

In the late 1970s, Parnas et al. [1,7] used tables to specify the software system requirements for expressing complex behaviours through organizing the relation between input and output variables. These tables were used simply to describe system requirements unambiguously. Parnas formally defined ten different types of tables for different purposes using functions, relations, and predicates [1]. Parnas also called these tables tabular expressions because the tables use mathematical expressions and recursive definitions. Some foundational works reported on formal semantics, table transformation, and composition of tables [8,9]. The formal semantics of tables specify the precise meaning that helps to maintain the same level of understanding when tables are used by various stakeholders. Similarly, table transformation can be used to derive a desired system behaviour under various system situations, and the composition of tables can be used to integrate different tables to obtain the final complex behaviour. These tables have been used in several safety-critical projects such as by Ontario Hydro for the Darlington Nuclear Shutdown Systems [10,11], and the US Naval Research Laboratory [12], etc.

Tabular expressions [7] are not only effective visually and as a simple approach to documenting system requirements by describing conditions and relations between input and output variables, they also facilitate preserving essential properties like *completeness* and *disjointness*, which are described as follows:

- **Disjointness:** *requires that the conditions (c_i) in columns (rows) do not overlap, which can be formalised as $\forall i, \forall j (i \neq j \Rightarrow \neg(c_i \wedge c_j))$.*
- **Completeness:** *requires that the conditions in columns (rows) cover all the input possibilities, which can be formalised as $(c_1 \vee c_2 \dots \vee c_n) \equiv TRUE$.*

In our work, for generating formal models from tabular expressions using our refinement strategy, we use *horizontal condition tables (HCT)*. An HCT table contains of a group of columns for input conditions and a group of columns for output results. However, the input column may be sub-divided to specify multiple sub-conditions. The tabular structure highlights the structure of predicates, and adjoining cells are considered to be ANDed so that can be interpreted in the tabular structure as a list of "*if-then-else*" predicates.

2.2   The Modelling Framework

In this section, we summarize the Event-B modelling language [13]. The Event-B language has two main components: *context* and *machine*. A *context* describes the static structure of a system, namely *carrier sets* and *constants* together with *axioms* and *theorems* stating their properties. A *machine* defines the dynamic structure of a system, namely *variables, invariants, theorems, variants* and *events*. Terms like *refines, extends*, and *sees* are used to describe the relation between components of Event-B models. Events are used in a *machine* to modify state variables by providing appropriate *guards*.

Modelling Actions over States. The event-driven approach of Event-B is borrowed from the B language [14]. An Event-B model is characterized by a list of *state variables* possibly modified by a list of *events*. An invariant $I(x)$ expresses required safety properties that must be satisfied by the variable x during the activation of events. An event is a state transition in a dynamic system that contains *guard(s)* and *action(s)*. A *guard*, a predicate built on the state variables, is a necessary condition for enabling an event. An *action* is a generalized substitution that describes the ways one or several state variables are modified by the occurrence of an event. There are three ways to define an event e. The first is BEGIN $x : |(P(x, x')$ END, where the *action* is not guarded and the action is always enabled. The second is WHEN $G(x)$ THEN $x : |(Q(x, x'))$ END, where the *action* is guarded by G, and the *guard* must be satisfied to enable the *action*. The last is ANY t WHERE $G(t, x)$ THEN $x : |(R(x, x', t))$ END, where the *action* is guarded by G, and it depends on the local state variable t for describing non-deterministic events. Event-B supports several kinds of proof obligations like invariant preservation, non-deterministic action feasibility, guard strengthening in refinements, simulation, variant, well-definedness etc.

Invariant preservation (see INV1 and INV2 below) ensures that each invariant is preserved by the INITIALIZATION event $Init(x)$ and other model events $BA(e)(x, x')$; non-deterministic action feasibility (FIS) shows the feasibility of the event e with respect to the invariant I; guard strengthening in a refinement ensures that the concrete guards in a refining event are stronger than the abstract ones; and simulation ensures that each action in a concrete event simulates the corresponding abstract action.

$$
\begin{aligned}
&INV1 : Init(x) \ \Rightarrow\ I(x) \\
&INV2 : I(x) \ \wedge\ BA(e)(x, x') \ \Rightarrow\ I(x') \\
&FIS \ \ \ : I(x) \ \wedge\ \mathsf{Grd}(e)(x) \ \Rightarrow\ \exists y.BA(e)(x, y)
\end{aligned}
$$

Model Refinement. A model can be refined to introduce new features or more concrete behaviour of a system. The Event-B modelling language supports a stepwise refinement technique to model a complex system. The refinement enables us to model a system gradually and provides a way to strengthen invariants thereby introducing more detailed behaviour of the system. This refinement approach transforms an abstract model to a more concrete version by modifying the state description. The refinement process extends a list of state variables by refining each abstract event to a corresponding concrete version, or by adding new events. These refinements preserve the relation between an abstract model and its corresponding concrete model, while introducing new events and variables to specify more concrete behaviour of the system. The abstract and concrete state variables are linked by *gluing invariants*. The generated proof obligations ensure that each abstract event is correctly refined by its concrete version. For instance, an abstract model AM with state variable x and invariant $I(x)$ is refined by a concrete model CM with variable y and gluing invariant $J(x, y)$. e and f are two events of the abstract model AM and concrete model CM, respectively. Event f refines event e. $BA(e)(x, x')$ and $BA(f)(y, y')$ are predicates of the events e and f, respectively. This refinement relation generates the following proof obligation:

$$I(x) \wedge J(x, y) \wedge BA(f)(y, y') \Rightarrow \exists x' \cdot (BA(e)(x, x') \wedge J(x', y'))$$

A set of new events introduced in a refinement step is viewed as hidden events, which are not visible to the environment of the system being modelled. These introduced events are outside of the control of the environment. Newly introduced events refine *skip* and are not observable in the abstract model. Any number of executions of an internal action may occur in between each execution of a visible action. This refinement relation generates the following proof obligation:

$$I(x) \wedge J(x, y) \wedge BA(f)(y, y') \Rightarrow J(x, y')$$

The refined model reduces the degree of non-determinism by strengthening the guards and/or predicates. The refinement of an event e by an event f means that the event f simulates the event e, which guarantees that the set of traces of the refined model contains (up to stuttering) the traces of the resulting model. The Rodin platform provides a set of tools to support project management, model development, proof assistance, model checking, animation and automatic code generation.

3   Refinement Strategy

A common way of constructing a formal specification is to start from a very simple abstract model that captures only basic system behaviour, and to add new features or system requirements to the abstract model to develop a concrete system by satisfying the additional requirements. An extension is a set of new features and system requirements that always zoom into a detailed system behaviour without changing the original abstract behaviour. We refer to this type of modelling method as *superpositioning* [15].

Superposition seems to be a good candidate in the field of formal modelling, because it allows us to construct a complicated formal specification by incremental refinement steps. Each new refinement step always focuses on a single design decision. In other words, it permits us to tackle one issue at a time, rather than having to make a joint design decision and settle a number of interrelated design questions [15].

Here, we describe a refinement strategy for generating formal models from documented system requirements. Our objective is to formalize tabular expressions and then define safety properties for the developed models to verify the documented system requirements. To produce formal models from tabular expressions is not an easy task due to no refinement relation among the tables, lack of techniques to support table compositions and implicit information about correct ordering of system behaviour. In order to produce formal models from tabular expressions, we propose a refinement strategy that allows us to construct a model progressively by traversing tabular requirements using a *correct-by-construction* approach. The proposed strategy can be suitable for any formal language that can support refinement based development. As mentioned, we use the Event-B modelling language, which supports refinement based progressive development. A formal definition of the transformation rule for the proposed refinement strategy is given below.

Definition 1. *Let T be a set of tabular expressions, in which each tabular expression satisfies the properties of disjointness and completeness. Then a transformation rule R is a function producing a new formal model M, defined according to the syntax of Event-B models for a given input model:*

$$R : T \times C \to M$$

where C contains a set of possible configurations (i.e., with/without refinement) of the transformation rule R.

Note that R is defined as a total function, i.e., it produces a new model for each input model t of tabular expressions and configurations c, i.e., when $(t, c) \in dom(R)$.

Figure 1 depicts a graphical layout of the refinement strategy. The refinement strategy for producing formal models from tabular expressions considers system requirements defined in tabular expressions to construct an abstract model and successive refinement models. A formal definition of the transformation rule using the refinement strategy for producing a formal model M from tabular expressions is defined below.

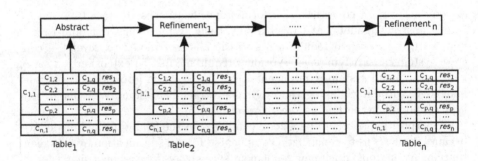

Fig. 1. Refinement strategy

Definition 2. *A refinement strategy is a transformation rule* $R : T \times C \rightarrow M$ *that constructs a model M for input tabular expressions and configuration (with/without refinement). The generated model M is defined as,*

$$M = AM \sqsubseteq CM_1 \sqsubseteq CM_2 \sqsubseteq \cdots \sqsubseteq CM_n$$
$$AM = t_1 \in T \wedge \Pi_{c_{1..n},res}(t_1)$$
$$CM_1 = AM \cup (t_2 \in T \wedge \Pi_{c_{1..n},res}(t_2))$$
$$CM_2 = CM_1 \cup (t_3 \in T \wedge \Pi_{c_{1..n},res}(t_3))$$
$$\cdots$$
$$CM_n = CM_{n-1} \cup (t_m \in T \wedge \Pi_{c_{1..n},res}(t_m))$$

where AM is an abstract model, $CM_1, CM_2, \ldots, CM_n$ are a series of concrete models, Π is a projection relation to select a table's column, $t_1, t_2, t_3, \ldots, t_m$ are a set of tables, $c_{1..n}$ is a set of columns of the table T, res is a set of output columns and $\sqsubseteq$ denotes a refinement relation. It is important to know that each table t of T contains a set of required variables, including type definitions, to describe system requirements in tabular form, which can be used during the process of model generation $(AM, CM_1 \ldots CM_n)$.

The generated formal model is composed of an abstract model and a list of refinement models. An abstract model is important because it tells us exactly what the system is supposed to do without telling us how. In this refinement strategy, we can start to design an abstract model from any tabular expression, and then we can select other tabular expressions in a sequential order to introduce a new system behaviour by applying refinement laws, and preserving abstract behaviour. In Fig. 1, each tabular expression is introduced at a new refinement level that is defined in Definition 2 as $CM_1 = AM \cup (t_2 \in T \wedge \Pi_{c_{1..n},res}(t_2))$. The *skip* refinement allows us to introduce other events to maintain state variables. Importantly, a new refinement level allows to introduce a set of new events. In this refinement strategy, we do not use any guard strengthening and action simulation refinement laws. By using *skip* refinement, we introduce a new set of events corresponding to the tabular expressions. To design a formal model from tabular expressions, we traverse a tabular expression, in which condition columns are used for defining the guard predicates and output columns are used for defining actions of the events. Each row of a tabular expression creates an event. For example, we can select a row from Table 2 to create the first event, and the second event can be created from the second row of Table 2. In fact, in both rows the first row of the condition column is common and can be used as a common guard for both events. At each refinement level, we always select a new tabular expression to introduce new features and system requirements. It should be noted that the total number of refinements will depend on the total number of tabular expressions, and sometimes a few tables can be formalized together. Moreover, to satisfy the refinement relation between two consecutive models, to develop a consistent model, and to prove all the generated proof obligations related to refinement, we need to identify a dependency order between the tables that can be used further to generate the formal models.

4   Case Study: The Insulin Infusion Pump

To assess the proposed refinement strategy for producing formal models from tabular expressions, we select a medical device case study: the *Insulin Infusion Pump (IIP)*. An insulin pump is a complex and software-intensive medical device that delivers an appropriate amount of insulin to patients whenever required. An insulin pump is an integration of several hardware components: a physical pump, a disposable reservoir, and a disposable infusion set. The pump system is made of a controller and a battery. The disposable infusion set includes a cannula for subcutaneous insertion, and a tubing system to interface the insulin reservoir to the cannula. An insulin pump can be programmed to release small doses of insulin continuously (basal), or a one shot dose (bolus) before a meal, to control the rise in blood glucose.

As far as we know, there are no published system requirements for an IIP, but several research publications provide informal requirements [16,17]. We used such informal descriptions as a basis for this work to identify the system requirements by formulating *use cases* and *hazard analysis*. These system requirements focus on the functional behaviour of an IIP without addressing design requirements, and human computer interaction (HCI) requirements.

4.1   Generating Tabular Expressions

In this section, we describe how tabular expressions can be produced from the informal requirements. The IIP system requirements are described in several tabular expressions that are used to check the important properties of *completeness* and *disjointness*. Note that the tabular expressions for IIP are derived manually from the given informal requirements. In this development, we define 49 tabular expressions, that are further grouped into eight main functionalities: power status, user operations, basal profile management, temporary basal profile management, bolus management, bolus delivery, reminder management, and insulin output calculator. These main functionalities form a group of several small sub-functions, that are also defined using tabular expressions. For instance, Tables 1 and 2 describe *power status* and *power on self test (POST)*, in which condition columns contain required conditions and the results columns show associated outputs of the variables. In Table 1, we use natural language descriptions for describing the required conditions and in Table 2 the first condition column depends on the previous state of the variable $c\_pwrStatus$. Similarly, in Table 2 the result column defines the value of control variable $c\_pwrStatus$. We derive several tabular expressions from informal requirements to specify the system requirements so as to meet the properties of *disjointness* and *completeness*. Note that, in our tabular expression, we used a naming convention that uses prefixes to distinguish different types of variables to improve readability of the developed tabular expressions.

Table 2. Tabular expression for power status

Condition		Result c_pwrStatus
c_pwrStatus$_{-1}$ = Standby	EXIST[M_pwrReq]	POST
	! EXIST[M_pwrReq]	NC
c_pwrStatus$_{-1}$ = POST	[POST] = Pass	Ready
	POST = Fail	Standby
c_pwrStatus$_{-1}$ = Ready	EXIST[M_pwrReq]	OffReq
	! EXIST[M_pwrReq]	NC
c_pwrStatus$_{-1}$ = OffReq	M_pwrResp = Accept	Standby
	M_pwrResp = Cancel	Ready

Table 1. Tabular expression for POST

Condition	Result POST
{ POST completed without problem }	Pass
{ POST completed and problems are detected }	Fail

4.2   Formalizing the Insulin Infusion Pump

In the IIP case study, we use the refinement strategy to produce formal models from tabular expression requirements. In this development approach, we initially ignore most of the system complexity, including various functional behaviours. All the tabular expressions are progressively modelled using the refinement strategy, by providing required safety properties to make the operations safe. Note that sometimes there is no specific order required in which to apply the refinements. In this case, any order can be chosen after developing an abstract model. However, sometimes this is not true due to dependency between tables. In fact, we need to choose a specific order of tables during the system development. Each table of the system requirements is introduced in a new refinement level. In this article, we include all elementary steps for describing the model development and refinement steps of an IIP and the complete formal specification is available for inspection in the appendix of a report [18], which is more than 1500 pages long.

Abstract Model: Power Status. Our abstract model of the IIP specifies only power status and related functionalities that control the power status, i.e., turning the system *on/off*. The tabular expressions of *power status* and *power on self test (POST)* are defined in Tables 1 and 2, which are used for modelling an abstract model of IIP. In order to start the formalization process, we need to define static properties of the system. An Event-B context declares three enumerated sets *e_pwrStatus*, *e_basicResp*, and *e_postResult* defined using axioms (*axm1–axm3*) for power status.

```
axm1 : partition(e_pwrStatus, {Standby_pwrStatus}, {POST_pwrStatus},
          {Ready_pwrStatus}, {OffReq_pwrStatus})
axm2 : partition(e_basicResp, {Accept_basicResp}, {Cancel_basicResp})
axm3 : partition(e_postResult, {Pass_postResult}, {Fail_postResult})
```

An abstract model declares a list of variables defined by invariants (*inv1–inv5*). A variable *POST_Res* is used to state the result of *power-on-self-test (POST)*, where the result 'pass' (*Pass_postResult*) means system is safe to turn *on*, and the result 'fail' (*Fail_postResult*) means system is unsafe to start. The next variable *post_completed* is used to show successful completion of POST of an IIP. The variable *c_pwrStatus* shows the current power status of the system.

The variable M_pwrReq is used to model a request for power on/off from the user, and the last variable $M\_pwrResp$ is used for modelling user responses to system prompts.

$$
\begin{aligned}
&inv1 : POST\_Res \in e\_postResult \\
&inv2 : post\_completed \in BOOL \\
&inv3 : c\_pwrStatus \in e\_pwrStatus \\
&inv4 : M\_pwrReq\_A \in BOOL \\
&inv5 : M\_pwrResp \in e\_basicResp
\end{aligned}
$$

We introduce 10 events (derived from Tables 1 and 2) for specifying a desired functional behaviour for controlling the power status of the IIP. These events include guards for enabling the given actions, and the actions that define the changes to the states of power status ($c\_pwrStatus$) and power-on-self-test ($POST\_Res$). Here, we provide only two events related to the power status and power-on-self-test in order to demonstrate the basic formalization process. An event $POST\_Completed$ is used to assign the pass result ($Pass\_postResult$) to $POST\_Res$, when $post\_completed$ is $TRUE$. This event is generated from Table 1. The light grey colour of the condition and result columns of Table 1 shows the conditions and actions that are translated equivalently to event $POST\_Completed$.

```
EVENT POST_Completed
  WHEN
    grd1 : post_completed = TRUE
  THEN
    act1 : POST_Res := Pass_postResult
  END
```

```
EVENT PowerStatus1
  WHEN
    grd1 : c_pwrStatus = Standby_pwrStatus
    grd2 : ∃x·x ∈ BOOL ∧ x = M_pwrReq
  THEN
    act1 : c_pwrStatus := POST_pwrStatus
  END
```

Similarly, another event $PowerStatus1$ is used to set $POST\_pwrStatus$ to $c\_pwr\text{-}Status$, when power status is $standby$, and there exists a power request from the user. The light grey colour of the condition and result columns of Table 2 presents the conditions and actions that are translated equivalently to event $PowerStatus1$. The remaining events are formalized in a similar way and are translated from the rows of Tables 1 and 2.

Since we do not have space for the detailed formalization, we summarise each refinement step of the IIP development in the following section.

4.3 A Chain of Refinements

For developing the whole system applying our refinement strategy, we used 7 main progressive development steps, which are defined as follows:

First Refinement: User Operations. This refinement introduces a set of operations, such as create, remove, activate and manage the basal profile, bolus profile, and reminders, performed by the user to program the IIP for delivering insulin. In this development, we cover all user interactions with the system, including user initiated commands and system responses. The formalised operations enable the delivery of a controlled amount of insulin according to the physiological needs of a patient.

Second Refinement: Basal Profile Management. This refinement introduces basal profile management to maintain a record and to store basal profiles defined by the user. In particular, we focus on the following operations: create a basal profile; remove a basal profile; check the validity of a selected basal profile; activate a basal profile; and deactivate a basal profile. Note that whenever a new basal profile activates, then the old basal profile deactivates automatically.

Third Refinement: Temporary Basal Profile Management. This refinement introduces temporary basal profile management that is similar to the basal profile management, which allows for activating, deactivating and checking the validity of a selected temporary basal profile.

Fourth Refinement: Bolus Preset Management. This refinement introduces bolus preset management, which includes creating and checking the validity of a new bolus preset, removal operation of an existing bolus preset, and activation of the selected bolus preset.

Fifth Refinement: Bolus Delivery. In this refinement, we introduce a bolus delivery mechanism that allows us to start bolus delivery, to calculate the required dose for insulin delivery, and to check the validity of the calculated bolus and manually entered bolus. Moreover, this refinement also ensures that the IIP always delivers a correct amount of bolus at the scheduled time.

Sixth Refinement: Reminder Management. In this refinement, we introduce reminder management that allows us to create and validate a new reminder, and to remove an existing reminder. This refinement covers all the necessary elements for describing the reminder management, and to verify the requirements of reminder management.

Seventh Refinement: Insulin Output Calculator. The last refinement models the insulin output calculator. It calculates the insulin required over the course of the day, the appropriate time segment, and the time steps for delivering the insulin. It also keeps track of the insulin delivered within the time segment. The infusion flow rate can be 0, if the system is *off*, and there is no active profile or the maximum amount of insulin has been delivered already.

4.4 Safety Properties

In our IIP case study, we introduce several safety properties (i.e., see *spr1*– *spr9*) to make sure that the formalized IIP system is consistent and safe. The first safety property (*spr1*) ensures that when *EnteredBasProfValid* is *TRUE*, an entered basal delivery rate is within the safe range. Similarly, when *Entered-BasProfValid* is *TRUE*, *spr2* ensures that the total amount of insulin delivered over a day is within the stated limit. *spr3* and *spr4* perform the same checks for the selected basal rate and amount when *SelectedBasalProfileIsValid* is *TRUE*. *spr5* and *spr6* perform the same checks for the temporary basal profile when *EnteredTemporaryBasalIsValid* is *TRUE*. *spr7* states that when *SelectedPre-setIsValid* is *TRUE*, the bolus rate of a selected bolus profile must be within the range of minimum bolus bound and maximum bolus bound. *spr8* ensures that when *EnteredBolusIsValid* is *TRUE*, the bolus rate of an entered bolus profile must be within the range of minimum bolus bound and maximum bolus bound. The last safety property ($spr9$) states that the total amount of insulin to output over the next time unit is less than or equal to the maximum daily limit of insulin that can be delivered.

$spr1 : EnteredBasProfValid = TRUE \Rightarrow (\exists x, y \cdot x \mapsto y = M\_basProf \wedge$
$\quad\quad (\forall i \cdot i \in index\_range \wedge i \in dom(y) \Rightarrow y(i) \geq k\_minBasalBound$
$\quad\quad \wedge y(i) \leq k\_maxBasalBound))$

$spr2 : EnteredBasProfValid = TRUE \Rightarrow (\exists x, y, insulin\_amount \cdot x \mapsto y = M\_basProf \wedge$
$\quad\quad insulin\_amount \in y\_insulinValue \wedge (\forall i \cdot i \in index\_range \wedge i \in dom(y) \Rightarrow$
$\quad\quad insulin\_amount = insulin\_amount + y(i) * k\_segDayDur) \wedge$
$\quad\quad insulin\_amount \leq k\_maxDailyInsulin)$

$spr3 : SelectedBasalProfileIsValid = TRUE \Rightarrow (\exists x, y \cdot x \mapsto y = M\_basActSelected \wedge$
$\quad\quad (\forall i \cdot i \in index\_range \wedge i \in dom(y) \Rightarrow y(i) \geq k\_minBasalBound$
$\quad\quad \wedge y(i) \leq k\_maxBasalBound))$

$spr4 : SelectedBasalProfileIsValid = TRUE \Rightarrow$
$\quad\quad (\exists x, y, insulin\_amount \cdot x \mapsto y = M\_basProf \wedge insulin\_amount \in y\_insulinValue \wedge$
$\quad\quad (\forall i \cdot i \in index\_range \wedge i \in dom(y) \Rightarrow insulin\_amount = insulin\_amount +$
$\quad\quad y(i) * k\_segDayDur) \wedge insulin\_amount \leq k\_maxDailyInsulin)$

$spr5 : EnteredTemporaryBasalIsValid = TRUE \Rightarrow \exists x, y, z \cdot x \mapsto y \mapsto z = M\_tmpBas \wedge$
$\quad\quad y \geq k\_minBasalBound \wedge y \leq k\_maxBasalBound)$

$spr6 : EnteredTemporaryBasalIsValid = TRUE \Rightarrow$
$\quad\quad (\exists x, y, z \cdot x \mapsto y \mapsto z = M\_tmpBas \wedge y * z \leq k\_maxDailyInsulin)$

$spr7 : SelectedPresetIsValid = TRUE \Rightarrow (\exists x, y \cdot x \mapsto y = M\_bolSelected \wedge$
$\quad\quad y \geq k\_minBolusBound \wedge y \leq k\_maxBolusBound)$

$spr8 : EnteredBolusIsValid = TRUE \Rightarrow (\exists x, y \cdot x \mapsto y = M\_bolus \wedge$
$\quad\quad y \geq k\_minBolusBound \wedge y \leq k\_maxBolusBound)$

$spr9 : c\_insulinOut \leq k\_maxDailyInsulin$

4.5   Model Analysis

In this section, we present the proof statistics by presenting detailed information about generated proof obligations. Event-B supports *consistency checking* which shows that a list of events preserves the given invariants, and *refinement checking* which makes sure that a concrete machine is a valid refinement of an abstract machine. This complete formal specification of an IIP contains 263 events, 16 complex data types, 15 enumerated types, and 25 constants for specifying the system requirements. The system requirements are described using 49 tabular expressions. The formal development of the IIP is presented through one abstract model and a series of seven refinement models. In fact, the refinement models are decomposed into several sub refinements. Therefore, we have a total of 43 refinement levels for describing the system behaviour. In this paper, we have omitted the detailed description of the 43 refinements by grouping them into the main components we used to present the formal specification of the IIP by applying the second refinement strategy to the group of tabular expressions.

Table 3 shows the proof statistics of the development in the Rodin tool. To guarantee the correctness of the system behaviour, we provide a list of safety properties in the last refinement model. This development resulted in 444 (100%) proof obligations, of which 342 (77%) were proved automatically, and the remaining 102 (23%) were proved interactively using the Rodin prover (see Table 3).

Table 3. Proof statistics

Model	Total number of POs	Automatic proof	Interactive proof
Abstract model	3	3 (100%)	0 (0%)
First refinement	22	22 (100%)	0 (0%)
Second refinement	98	82 (83%)	16 (17%)
Third refinement	26	25 (100%)	1 (0%)
Fourth refinement	52	45 (87%)	7 (13%)
Fifth refinement	54	54 (100%)	0 (0%)
Sixth refinement	66	60 (91%)	6 (9%)
Seventh refinement	123	51 (42%)	72 (58%)
Total	444	342 (77%)	102 (23%)

These interactive proof obligations are mainly related to automated refinement based model generation and complex mathematical expressions, simplified through interaction to provide additional information for assisting the Rodin prover. Other proofs needed only to simplify predicates.

5   Related Work

Since the late 1950s, tables have been used for analyzing computer code, and documenting requirements. Tables first appeared in the software literature in the 1960s [19]. Early tables included decision tables, transition tables, etc. Parnas and others introduced tabular expressions for developing the requirements document for the A-7E aircraft [20,21] in work for the US Navy. Parnas was the most influential person to apply tabular expressions in documenting software [1]. Later, tables were used by many others, including at Bell Laboratories, and the US Air Force. Starting in the late 1980s tabular notations were applied by Ontario Hydro in developing the shutdown systems for the Darlington Nuclear Plant [22]. Formal semantics of tabular expressions have been proposed by Parnas [1] and other researchers [8]. A slightly outdated survey on tabular expressions is available in [8]. Nalepa et al., have proposed eXtended Tabular Trees (XTT) [23] and HeKatE [24] for developing a complex rule-based system, where these approaches are used to ensure high density and transparency of visual knowledge.

Refinement enables the incremental development of a system to ensure that a refined model retains all the essential properties of an abstract model. The foundational work of formal reasoning about correctness and stepwise development using refinement was established by Dijkstra [25] and Hoare [26] and further developed by Back and von Wright [27], and Morgan [28]. The refinement calculus provides a formal stepwise approach for constructing a program from an abstract program to a concrete program by preserving essential properties. There are a few papers published on automating the refinement pattern [4] and principles for refinement [5]. In [4], the authors propose refinement patterns using syntactic model transformation, pattern applicability conditions and proof obligations for verifying correctness preservation. To handle the design complexity of applying Event-B refinement and consistency rules, one paper [5], presents refinement planning from an informal/semi-formal specification.

6   Conclusion

We have presented a refinement strategy that can automate the process of formalizing system requirements from tabular expressions using a *correct-by-*

construction approach. We used a refinement strategy to transform tabular expressions into formal models that determine the correctness of functional behaviour and modelling structure of a system. We also highlighted challenges for automation: primarily, composition of tabular expressions, use of sequential ordering of tables, and table traversing complexities. Due to the variety of layouts of tabular expressions, there are still open issues related to the automation of tables that ought to be supported, and hence we do not claim completeness at this stage. On the other hand, our results showed that the proposed refinement strategy can largely be automated to generate formal models from tabular expressions. Moreover, the proposed approach is scalable to handle large and complex systems, in which system requirements are presented in tabular form.

In order to apply a refinement strategy, we selected the Event-B modelling language, which allows incremental refinement based on a *correct-by-construction* approach, for generating formal models from tabular expressions. Further, the Rodin tools can be used to verify formally the produced model. To assess the effectiveness of our proposed refinement strategy, we used the *Insulin Infusion Pump (IIP)* as a case study. The IIP requirements are described in tabular expressions, which we used to produce formal models using incremental refinement steps. In order to guarantee the 'correctness' of the system behaviour, we provided a list of safety properties in the generated model. Each refined model was proven to guarantee the preservation of those safety properties. This method of model generation and verification from the defined tabular expression requirements facilitates systematic modelling of a formal model using incremental refinement to guarantee formal designing of system requirements including required properties of completeness, disjointness, and safety. Our complete formal development of this IIP is available in a 1500 page report [18].

Our future goal is to develop a tool based on the proposed refinement strategy to automate the process for generating formal models from tabular expressions, and to apply this approach on several large and complex case studies to automate formal reasoning for tabular system requirements to verify a desired behaviour under relevant safety properties. This automation will allow us to produce formal models automatically from tabular requirements. In fact, if the original requirements are modified later, then we can use the automation tool to produce the new modified formal models. In addition, our intension is to use the generated and proved Event-B models for producing source code in many languages using EB2ALL [2, 29].

References

1. Parnas, D.L.: Tabular representation of relations. Technical report, McMaster University (1992)
2. Singh, N.K.: Using Event-B for Critical Device Software Systems. Springer, New York (2013). doi:10.1007/978-1-4471-5260-6
3. Lee, I., Pappas, G.J., Cleaveland, R., Hatcliff, J., Krogh, B.H., Lee, P., Rubin, H., Sha, L.: High-confidence medical device software and systems. Computer **39**(4), 33–38 (2006)

4. Iliasov, A., Troubitsyna, E., Laibinis, L., Romanovsky, A.: Patterns for refinement automation. In: de Boer, F.S., Bonsangue, M.M., Hallerstede, S., Leuschel, M. (eds.) FMCO 2009. LNCS, vol. 6286, pp. 70–88. Springer, Heidelberg (2010). doi:10.1007/978-3-642-17071-3_4
5. Kobayashi, T., Ishikawa, F., Honiden, S.: Understanding and planning Event-B refinement through primitive rationales. In: Ait Ameur, Y., Schewe, K.D. (eds.) Abstract State Machines, Alloy, B, TLA, VDM, and Z. LNCS, vol. 8477, pp. 277–283. Springer, Heidelberg (2014). doi:10.1007/978-3-662-43652-3_24
6. Project RODIN: Rigorous open development environment for complex systems (2004). http://rodin-b-sharp.sourceforge.net/
7. Parnas, D.L., Madey, J., Iglewski, M.: Precise documentation of well-structured programs. IEEE Trans. Softw. Eng. 20(12), 948–976 (1994)
8. Janicki, R., Wassyng, A.: Tabular expressions and their relational semantics. Fundam. Inform. 67(4), 343–370 (2005)
9. Jin, Y., Parnas, D.L.: Defining the meaning of tabular mathematical expressions. Sci. Comput. Program. 75(11), 980–1000 (2010). (Special Section on the Programming Languages Track at the 23rd ACM Symposium on Applied Computing)
10. Archinoff, G., Hohendorf, R., Wassyng, A., Quigley, B., Borsch, M.: Verification of the shutdown system software at the Darlington nuclear generating station. In: International Conference on Control and Instrumentation in Nuclear Installations, Glasgow, UK (1990)
11. Wassyng, A., Lawford, M.: Lessons learned from a successful implementation of formal methods in an industrial project. In: Araki, K., Gnesi, S., Mandrioli, D. (eds.) FME 2003. LNCS, vol. 2805, pp. 133–153. Springer, Heidelberg (2003). doi:10.1007/978-3-540-45236-2_9
12. Heitmeyer, C., Kirby, J., Labaw, B., Bharadwaj, R.: SCR: a toolset for specifying and analyzing software requirements. In: Hu, A.J., Vardi, M.Y. (eds.) CAV 1998. LNCS, vol. 1427, pp. 526–531. Springer, Heidelberg (1998). doi:10.1007/BFb0028775
13. Abrial, J.: Modeling in Event-B: System and Software Engineering. Cambridge University Press, Cambridge (2010)
14. Abrial, J.: The B-book: Assigning Programs to Meanings. Cambridge University Press, Cambridge (2005)
15. Back, R., Sere, K.: Superposition refinement of reactive systems. Formal Aspects Comput. 8(3), 324–346 (1996)
16. Masci, P., Ayoub, A., Curzon, P., Lee, I., Sokolsky, O., Thimbleby, H.: Model-based development of the generic PCA infusion pump user interface prototype in PVS. In: Bitsch, F., Guiochet, J., Kaâniche, M. (eds.) SAFECOMP 2013. LNCS, vol. 8153, pp. 228–240. Springer, Heidelberg (2013). doi:10.1007/978-3-642-40793-2_21
17. Xu, H., Maibaum, T.: An Event-B approach to timing issues applied to the generic insulin infusion pump. In: Liu, Z., Wassyng, A. (eds.) FHIES 2011. LNCS, vol. 7151, pp. 160–176. Springer, Heidelberg (2012). doi:10.1007/978-3-642-32355-3_10
18. Singh, N.K., Wang, H., Lawford, M., Maibaum, T.S.E., Wassyng, A.: Report 18: formalizing insulin pump using Event-B. Technical report 18, McSCert, McMaster University, October 2014. https://www.mcscert.ca/index.php/documents/mcscert-reports
19. Cantrell, H.N., King, J., King, F.E.H.: Logic-structure tables. Commun. ACM 4(6), 272–275 (1961)
20. Heninger, K., Kallander, J., Parnas, D.L., Shore, J.E.: Software requirements for the A-7E aircraft. NRL Memorandum report 3876. Naval Research Laboratory (1978)

21. Parnas, D.L.: A generalized control structure and its formal definition. Commun. ACM **26**(8), 572–581 (1983)
22. Wassyng, A., Lawford, M., Maibaum, T.S.E.: Software certification experience in the Canadian nuclear industry: lessons for the future. In: EMSOFT, pp. 219–226 (2011)
23. Nalepa, G.J., Ligęza, A., Kaczor, K.: Formalization and modeling of rules using the XTT2 method. Int. J. Artif. Intell. Tools **20**(06), 1107–1125 (2011)
24. Nalepa, G.J., Ligęza, A.: The HeKatE methodology. Hybrid engineering of intelligent systems. Int. J. Appl. Math. Comput. Sci. **20**(1), 35–53 (2010)
25. Dijkstra, E.W.: A Discipline of Programming, 1st edn. Prentice Hall PTR, Upper Saddle River (1997)
26. Hoare, C.A.R.: An axiomatic basis for computer programming. Commun. ACM **12**(10), 576–580 (1969)
27. Back, R.J., von Wright, J.: Refinement Calculus: A Systematic Introduction, 1st edn. Springer-Verlag New York, Inc., New York (1998). doi:10.1007/978-1-4612-1674-2
28. Morgan, C.: Programming from Specifications. Prentice-Hall Inc., Upper Saddle River (1990)
29. Méry, D., Singh, N.K.: Automatic code generation from Event-B models. In: Proceedings of Second Symposium on Information and Communication Technology, pp. 179–188. ACM (2011)

Data Engineering

Bulk Insertions into xBR$^+$-trees

George Roumelis[1], Michael Vassilakopoulos[2], Antonio Corral[3]([✉]),
and Yannis Manolopoulos[1]

[1] Department of Informatics, Aristotle University of Thessaloniki,
Thessaloniki, Greece
{groumeli,manolopo}@csd.auth.gr
[2] Department of Electrical and Computer Engineering,
University of Thessaly, Volos, Greece
mvasilako@uth.gr
[3] Department of Informatics, University of Almeria, Almeria, Spain
acorral@ual.es

Abstract. Bulk insertion refers to the process of updating an existing
index by inserting a large batch of new data, treating the items of this
batch as a whole and not by inserting these items one-by-one. Bulk insertion is related to bulk loading, which refers to the process of creating a
non-existing index from scratch, when the dataset to be indexed is available beforehand. The xBR$^+$-tree is a balanced, disk-resident, Quadtree-
based index for point data, which is very efficient for processing spatial
queries. In this paper, we present the first algorithm for bulk insertion
into xBR$^+$-trees. This algorithm incorporates extensions of techniques
that we have recently developed for bulk loading xBR$^+$-trees. Moreover,
using real and artificial datasets of various cardinalities, we present an
experimental comparison of this algorithm vs. inserting items one-by-
one for updating xBR$^+$-trees, regarding performance (I/O and execution time) and the characteristics of the resulting trees. We also present
experimental results regarding the query-processing efficiency of xBR$^+$-
trees built by bulk insertions vs. xBR$^+$-trees built by inserting items
one-by-one.

Keywords: Spatial indexes · Bulk-inserting · xBR$^+$-trees · Query
processing

1 Introduction

Nowadays, the volume of available spatial data (e.g. location, routing, navigation, etc.) is continuously increasing world-wide. In many data-intensive spatial
applications, dealing with the problem of bulk-insertions of new large datasets
into an existing dataset is of particular interest. It is important to add newly

M. Vassilakopoulos, A. Corral and Y. Manolopoulos—Work funded by the MINECO
research project [TIN2013-41576-R].

© Springer International Publishing AG 2017
Y. Ouhammou et al. (Eds.): MEDI 2017, LNCS 10563, pp. 185–199, 2017.
DOI: 10.1007/978-3-319-66536-3_14

collected data into an existing dataset quickly, because new data are continuously being generated and added to existing datasets. The use of efficient spatial indexes is very important for performing spatial queries and retrieving efficiently spatial objects from datasets according to specific spatial constraints. An important aspect in the implementation of such spatial indexes is the time needed to build and update them from a given dataset [16].

If the dataset is *dynamic* (i.e. when insertions and deletions are interleaved), then we can devote efforts on creating and updating the spatial index in a way that permits the efficient execution of spatial queries. Furthermore, slow updates of spatial indexes can seriously degrade query response time, which is especially critical in modern interactive and data-intensive spatial database applications. There are three ways in which spatial indexes can be created or updated by a dynamic dataset. First, if the dataset has not been indexed yet, the spatial index can be built from scratch for the entire dataset (this process is known as *bulk-loading*). Second, if the dataset already has a spatial index and a large batch of data is to be added to the index, then the spatial index can be updated with all the new data at once (this process is known as *bulk-insertion*). Third, if the dataset already has an index and a small amount of data is to be added to the index, it can be more efficient to insert the new data items one by one into the existing spatial index (this process is known as *one-by-one-insertion* [7]). In this work, we present a method for speeding up the updating of a spatial index for the second situation (*bulk-insertion*).

In contrast to a bulk-loading algorithm, where a spatial index is built from scratch, a bulk-insertion algorithm aims at updating an existing index structure with a large set of new data. Thus, *bulk-insertion* refers to the process of updating an existing spatial index with a large new dataset, that is, of combining data that is already indexed by a disk-resident spatial index and data that has not yet been indexed. Bulk-insertion is necessary when a spatial index already exists and a large amount of new data needs to be added. An example of this process could be the following. If we are indexing data received from an earth-sensing satellite and new data from a specific region that spatially overlaps with the existing index have arrived, we need to insert these new data into the existing index. Loading indexes by inserting elements one-by-one is less efficient than executing specially designed bulk-insertion algorithms, with smart merging techniques. Bulk-insertion is therefore an interesting option for updating spatial indexes when chunks of new data are inserted as a whole. However, bulk-insertion methods in spatial indexes have not been studied in depth by the database research community.

In this paper, we study the efficiency of updating a Quadtree-based index structure when it already exists and a large amount of data is pending to be inserted. In particular, we focus on the xBR$^+$-tree [10], a balanced disk-based index structure for point data that belongs to the Quadtree family and hierarchically decomposes space in a regular manner. The xBR$^+$-tree improves the xBR-tree [14] in the node structure and the splitting process. Moreover, it outperforms xBR-trees and R*-trees with respect to several well-known spatial queries, such as Point Location, Window Query, K-Nearest Neighbor, etc. [10]. With this research work, we complete the design and implementation of methods to create and update an xBR+-tree from a dynamic dataset, since a new bulk-insertion method is proposed. That is, (1) in [11] a bulk-loading method is presented for xBR+-trees, (2) in [10] an efficient *one-by-one-insertion* procedure is defined and implemented for this new spatial index, and finally (3) in [13] a deletion algorithm is added to this index for removing object in a one-by-one fashion.

There are two important aspects of the bulk-insertion methods. First, the bulk-insertion itself should be fast enough and the storage utilization should not be degraded with respect to the existing spatial index (i.e. the quality of the structure should be preserved). Second, the spatial query performance should not be compromised by the bulk-insertion process. Keeping this in mind, in this paper, we present the first algorithm for bulk-insertion into xBR+-trees, for big datasets residing on disk and taking into account the previous important aspects. Moreover, using real and artificial datasets of various cardinalities, we present an experimental comparison of this bulk-insertion algorithm vs. the algorithm of loading items one-by-one in a existing xBR+-tree, regarding creation time and the characteristics of the tree created.

This paper is organized as follows. In Sect. 2 we review related work on bulk-insertion techniques and provide the motivation of this paper. In Sect. 3, we describe the most important characteristics of the xBR+-tree and the bulk-loading method for this recent spatial index. Section 4 presents our bulk-insertion method for the xBR+-tree. In Sect. 5, we discuss the results of our experiments. And finally, Sect. 6 provides the conclusions arising from our work and discusses related future work directions.

2   Related Work and Motivation

This section reviews previous bulk-insertion techniques, that consist of inserting a set of new data into an already existing spatial index at once rather than inserting one new data element at a time. The main target of the bulk-insertion process is to create a good enough spatial index in order to reduce the loading time, the query cost of the resulting index structure, or both. In [1] the bulk-insertion techniques are roughly classified into two categories: merge-based and buffer-based techniques.

- The *merge-based bulk-insertion* techniques are characterized by the following two steps: first, a new small spatial index is created from the new dataset (if has not been created yet) and second, the new small index is merged into the existing one to complete the bulk-insertion process.
- The *buffer-based bulk-insertion* techniques use the *buffer-tree* [2] as buffering technique for the bulk-insertion process.

Most of the bulk-insertion methods belong to the first category and concern the R-tree [1,3–5,8,15].

In [8], a bulk-insertion method in which new leaf nodes are built following the Hilbert-packed R-tree technique is proposed. The new leaf nodes are then inserted one-by-one into the existing R-tree using a dynamic R-tree insertion algorithm.

In [15], the *cubetree* is proposed, which is an R-tree-like structure for OLAP applications that uses a specialized packing algorithm. The bulk-insertion algorithm proposed in [15] works as follows. First, the new dataset to be inserted is sorted in the packing order. The sorted list is merged with the sorted list of objects in the existing dataset, which is obtained directly from the leaf nodes of the existing *cubetree*. A new *cubetree* is then packed using the sorted list resulting from merging.

In [3,4], a bulk-insertion technique for R-trees, called STLT (Small-Tree-Large-Tree), is proposed. The STLT technique constructs an R-tree (small tree) from the new dataset and inserts it into the existing R-tree (large tree). To insert a small tree into a large tree, it chooses an appropriate location to maintain the balance of the resulting large tree. That is, the root node of the small tree is then inserted into the appropriate place in the large R-tree, using a specialized algorithm that performs some local reorganization of the existing tree based on a set of proposed heuristics.

In [5], a variant of STLT, called GBI (Generalized Bulk Insertion), is presented. For this technique, the new input dataset is partitioned into a number of clusters by grouping spatially close data items into the same cluster. After clustering, from each of these clusters, R-trees are built. Finally, these R-trees are inserted into the existing R-tree one at a time. The data items not included in any cluster are classified as outliers and inserted one by one using normal R-tree insertion.

In [1], a new Oracle's approach for performing bulk-insertion in R-trees is presented. The characteristics of this approach are: (1) batched insertion into subtrees resulting in fast insertion times, and (2) fast reorganization of subtrees whenever there is an overlap, to ensure good quality of the final R-tree. This approach extends buffering-based techniques by not materializing the auxiliary structures and pushing the data right to the leaves; besides, it merges subtrees whenever they overlap. In general, this bulk-insertion strategy combines multiple inserts and reduces the number of tree traversals.

The basic idea presented in [2] is to attach *buffers* to the internal nodes of an R-tree (except for the root node) in pre-calculated levels and keep the total size of the buffers to fit in memory. Then, when a new data item is inserted, it is stored in the buffer until it gets full. When the buffer is full, data items in the buffer are pushed down to the buffer at the lower level. Since data items are only inserted into the leaf level, it is only when the data objects arrive at the leaf level that disk accesses occur. By using buffers, a data item is inserted as soon as it arrives without having to gather items to perform bulk operations and it is likely that disk accesses are reduced by delaying insertions using such buffers.

In [6], two new extensible buffer-based bulk-loading and bulk-insertion algorithms for the class of Space Partitioning Trees (SPTs, a class of hierarchical data structures that recursively decompose space into disjoint partitions) are presented. The authors adopt the idea of buffer-trees [2] during bulk insertions into SPTs. The main difference over [2] is that SPTs may not be balanced and hence need non trivial clustering and whenever a sufficient number of data items accumulate at the buffers at the leaf level, the algorithm clusters them to form a new part of the tree. The main idea of this algorithm is to build an in-memory tree of the target SPT. Then, data items are recursively partitioned into disk-based buffers using the in-memory tree.

In [9], the idea of the *seeded clustering* for an R-tree is used for a bulk-insertion algorithm which is performed in two steps: seeded clustering and insertion. In the *seeded clustering* step, the algorithm first builds a *seed tree* by taking a few top levels of nodes from a target R-tree (existing tree). The seed tree guides the way the new input data items are clustered. In the *insertion* step, two different methods are proposed. In the one of them, the algorithm takes each data item from a cluster and inserts it into a target R-tree, one at a time, using the standard R-tree insertion method. Although it inserts data items one by one, it reduces the construction cost dramatically because of localized insertions. In the other method, the algorithm builds an R-tree from each of the clusters and inserts them into the target R-tree one at a time in bulk.

The most representative contribution related to bulk-insertion technique for Quadtree index structures has been published in [7]. The main idea is to adapt the bulk-loading algorithm [7] to the problem of bulk-inserting into an existing PMR Quadtree index. The process of the bulk-insertion algorithm is to build a Quadtree in main-memory for the new dataset with the bulk-loading algorithm [7] and then to merge it with the existing disk-resident PMR-Quadtree. It is a merged-based algorithm, since it essentially merges a new Quadtree being built in memory with an existing disk-resident Quadtree, and writes out a new combined disk-resident Quadtree. Moreover, a transformation of this merge-based algorithm to an update-based algorithm is also proposed.

The main motivation of this work is the proposal of a new merge-based algorithm for bulk-insertion of a space-driven Quadtree variant, the xBR$^+$-tree. Note that the xBR$^+$-tree [10] (for more details, see Sect. 3.1) is unlike any other Quadtree variant, since it is a totally disk-based, height-balanced, pointer-based, multiway tree for multidimensional points and no other quadtree variant has all these characteristics.

3 The xBR$^+$-tree and the Bulk-Loading Method

In this section, we present the basics of the xBR$^+$-tree structure and an abstract description of the xBR$^+$-tree bulk-loading algorithm.

3.1 xBR$^+$-tree

The xBR$^+$-tree [10] (an extension of the xBR-tree [14]) is a hierarchical, disk-resident Quadtree-based index structure for multidimensional points (i.e. it is a totally disk-resident, height-balanced, pointer-based tree for multidimensional points). For 2d space, the space indexed is a *square* and is recursively subdivided in 4 equal subquadrants. The nodes of the tree are disk pages of two kinds: *leaves*, which store the actual multidimensional data themselves and *internal nodes*, which provide a multiway indexing mechanism.

Internal node entries in xBR$^+$-trees contain entries of the form (*Shape*, *qside*, *DBR*, *Pointer*). Each entry corresponds to a child-node pointed by *Pointer*. The region of this child-node is related to a subquadrant of the original space. *Shape* is a flag that determines if the region of the child-node is a complete or non-complete square (the area remaining, after one or more splits; explained later in this subsection). This field is heavily used in queries. *DBR* (Data Bounding Rectangle) stores the coordinates of the rectangular subregion of the child-node region that contains point data (at least two points must reside on the sides of the *DBR*), while *qside* is the side length of the subquadrant of the original space that corresponds to the child-node.

The subquadrant of the original space related to the child-node is expressed by an *Address*. This *Address* (which has a variable size) is not explicitly stored in the xBR$^+$-tree, although it is uniquely determined and can be easily calculated using *qside* and *DBR*. We depict the address only for demonstration purposes. Each *Address* represents a subquadrant that has been produced by Quadtree-like hierarchical subdivision of the current space (of the subquadrant of the original space related to the current node). It consists of a number of directional digits that make up this subdivision. The NW, NE, SW and SE subquadrants of a quadrant are distinguished by the directional digits 0, 1, 2 and 3, respectively. For 2d space, we use two directional bits each of every dimension. The lower bit represents the subdivision on horizontal (X-axis) dimension, while the higher bit represents the subdivision on vertical (Y-axis) dimension [14]. For example, the *Address* 1 represents the NE quadrant of the current space, while the *Address* 12 the SW subquadrant of the NE quadrant of the current space.

The actual region of the child-node is, in general, the subquadrant of its *Address* minus a number of smaller subquadrants, the subquadrants corresponding to the next entries of the internal node (the entries in an internal node are saved sequentially, in preorder traversal of the Quadtree that corresponds to the internal node). For example, in Fig. 1 an internal node (a root) that points to 4 internal nodes that point to 12 leaves is depicted. The region of the root is the original space, which is assumed to have a quadrangular shape with origin (0,0) on the upper left corner and side length 200. The region of the rightmost entry is the SW quadrant (2*) of the original space (the * symbol is used to denote the end of a variable size address). The region of the next (on the left) subquadrant is the NW subquadrant of the SE quadrant of the whole space. For this subquadrant, the *Address* is 30*. The flag *shape* is set at the value 'SQ' which expresses that this subquadrant is a complete square and thus, no part of its region will be found anywhere in the index, except for the child nodes of the subtree rooted at this entry. The next (on the left) entry covers the whole space of the SW quadrant of the whole space (0*). Finally, the first entry in the root node of this example, expresses the whole space minus the three descendant regions (0*, 30* and 2*), and of course it is a non-complete square area. During a search, or an insertion of a data element with specified coordinates, the appropriate leaf and its region is determined by descending the tree from the root.

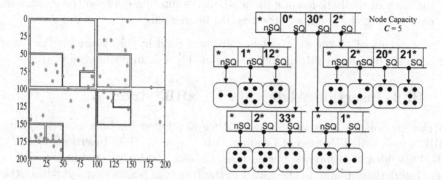

Fig. 1. A collection of 48 points, its grouping to xBR$^+$-tree nodes and its xBR$^+$-tree.

External nodes (leaves) of the xBR$^+$-tree simply contain the data elements and have a predetermined capacity C. When C is exceeded, due to an insertion in a leaf, the region of this leaf is partitioned in two subregions. The one (new) of these subregions is a subquadrant of the region of the leaf which is created by partitioning the region of the leaf according to hierarchical (Quadtree like) decomposition, as many times as needed so that the most populated subquadrant (that corresponds to this new subregion) has a cardinality that is smaller than or equal to C. The other one (old) of these subregions is the region of the leaf minus the new subregion.

3.2 Bulk-Loading Method for xBR$^+$-tree

In [11], an algorithm, called Process of Bulk Loading (*PBL*), for bulk-loading xBR$^+$-trees for large datasets residing on disk was presented, using a limited amount of main memory.

PBL consists of four phases. These phases are pipelined and each phase produces an output that is used as input for the next one.

1. During the first phase (*Transformation of input file format*), the initial dataset file is transformed to binary format and is split in two items files.
2. During the second phase (*Partitioning input data*), each of the two input items files is partitioned into items blocks of size ≤ *MemoryLimit* in a regular fashion. The resulting blocks are transferred in main memory, as input for the next phase.
3. During the third phase (*Creating the m − xBR$^+$-tree*), for each block of items, a Quadtree (a four way tree) is built top-down in main memory by splitting

this block regularly as long as the resulting regions contain more items than the capacity of xBR$^+$-tree leaves. This Quadtree is gradually transformed to an m-xBR$^+$-tree (main memory xBR$^+$-tree) in a bottom-up fashion.

4. During the last phase (*Merging of trees*), the m-xBR$^+$-tree is merged with the xBR$^+$-tree already built in secondary memory (created during the previous iteration of the bulk-loading process), discriminating between three different cases among the heights of the trees to be merged.

Improvements of all the above phases are presented in [12]. However, the main algorithmic flow and splitting into phases of [11] remain unchanged in [12].

4   Bulk-Insertion Algorithm for xBR$^+$-tree

In this section, we present the method we developed for bulk insertions into xBR$^+$-trees, called Process of Loading xBR$^+$-trees by Bulk Insertions (*PLBI*). The basic idea is as follows. For each set of points to be inserted in the xBR$^+$-tree, insert these points in the leaves of the tree (the points that fall within the area of the same leaf are handled all together), accessing the leaves from the root in depth-first mode. If a leaf overflows, then create a separate in-memory tree for the subtree rooted at the parent of this leaf and merge the in-memory tree with the rest of the tree.

The algorithm is described in more details as follows. Let's consider a set of points S to be inserted in the xBR$^+$-tree. We utilize a main memory area M of size *MemoryLimit*. If the space needed for S is larger than M, we transfer S to M in subsets that fit within M and process each such subset independently. Otherwise, we transfer to M and process the whole of S. Processing of a set of points S_M within M (in general, a subset of S) is recursive (following depth-first traversal).

- We call the recursive procedure for the xBR$^+$-tree root and S_M and make recursive calls down to the level of the parents of the leaves. The input of a recursive call is a node and a set of points which is the subset of points of S_M that fall within the region of this node.
- For each (internal) node I visited and the corresponding set of points B_I, we examine the region entries of I, from the rightmost to the leftmost, and, for each such region entry E, we determine the subset B_E of B_I that falls within E.
- If I is not a parent of leaves, for each region entry E, we apply recursively the same procedure for the child node corresponding to E and B_E.
- If I is a parent of leaves, for each region entry E, we insert B_E in the child node (leaf) corresponding to E.
- After insertions to all children of I have been completed, we examine if any of these children (leaves) has overflown.
- If none of these children has overflown, for each one of them, we update its *DBR* value and, if needed, we update *DBR* values of its ancestors (possibly, up to the root level) and the procedure returns to the previous stage of recursion.

– If any child has overflown, we create an m-xBR$^+$-tree (a main memory xBR$^+$-tree) m for I (Phase 3 of [11]) and gradually merge m with the xBR$^+$-tree, as follows.

  • We locate the leftmost non-leaf node I_m of m and replace I with I_m (this is feasible, since I and I_m both correspond to the region of the root of m).

  • We merge, one-by-one, the sub-trees that correspond to the siblings of I_m, from left to right, with the xBR$^+$-tree (Phase 4 of [11]). At this stage, processing of I has been completed.

  • Up to the root level of m, we move to the parent of the node for which processing has been completed and we merge, one-by-one, the sub-trees that correspond to the siblings of this node with the xBR$^+$-tree (Phase 4 of [11]).

When merging of m with the xBR$^+$-tree has been completed, the procedure returns to the previous stage of recursion, and if no changes in the structure of the index of the xBR$^+$-tree have been done, the procedure will be continued with the next entry E and its corresponding subset B_E. Otherwise, the procedure will be restarted from the root of the xBR$^+$-tree with the unprocessed data subset.

In Fig. 1, a collection of 48 points in a squared space with origin $(0,0)$ and side length of 200 is depicted. In the right part of this figure, the xBR$^+$-tree index for this dataset created by *PLBI* is depicted. The first 16 points were inserted in one segment using *PBL* and the rest 32 points were inserted in two equal segments (of 16 points each) using *PLBI*.

Contrary to [11] and adopting improvements of [11] that have been incorporated in [12]:

– In order to build the m-xBR$^+$-tree m, instead of building top-down a Quadtree in main memory that is transformed to m, we build m bottom-up, using an auxiliary tree T. T is a degree up-to-four tree (an incomplete Quadtree) without leaves, that holds only the information that is necessary for creating m internal nodes, making better use of the available main memory and increasing tree creation speed.

– In order to merge sub-trees of m with the xBR$^+$-tree, if the sub-tree of m under processing and the xBR$^+$-tree have equal heights, instead of creating a new root pointing to the two existing roots, without making any changes in the regions covered by these roots, we merge the roots of the two trees in a possibly overflown node. If this node is overflown, it is subsequently partitioned, in the best way possible, in two, or more nodes that are pointed by a new root that is created. If the xBR$^+$-tree is higher, we first locate in the xBR$^+$-tree the direct ancestor of the root of the m sub-tree under processing (that resides at the same level as this root) and then perform a merge between equal height subtrees. If, however, the sub-tree of m under processing is higher, we save it in secondary memory, we adjust the region of this tree to correspond to the whole space and then we apply the previous procedure of merging the roots of the two trees. Following the merge and re-partition approach, instead of leaving the regions of the original roots unchanged [11], we achieve better partitioning of space and increased query performance in the resulting tree.

Note that applying the same procedure for building the m-xBR$^+$-tree and for merging of trees as in [11] is possible. However, the alternatives [12] followed here improve performance.

5   Experimental Results

We designed and run a large set of experiments to compare *PLBI* to the Process of Loading xBR$^+$-trees by inserting items One-by-One (*PLObO*). We used real spatial datasets of North America, representing roads (NArdN with 569082 line-segments) and rail-roads (NArrN with 191558 line-segments). To create sets of 2d points, we have transformed the MBRs of line-segments from NArdN and NArrN into points by taking the center of each MBR (i.e. |NArdN| = 569082 points, |NArrN| = 191558 points). Moreover, in order to get the double amount of points from NArdN, we chose the two points with *min* and *max* coordinates of the MBR of each line-segment (i.e. we created a new dataset, |NArdND| = 1138164 points. The data of these three files were normalized in the range $[0, 1]^2$. We have also created synthetic clustered datasets of 250000, 500000 and 1000000 points, with 125 clusters in each dataset (uniformly distributed in the range $[0, 1]^2$), where for a set having N points, $N/125$ points were gathered around the center of each cluster, according to Gaussian distribution. We also used three big real datasets[1]. They represent water resources of North America (Water) consisting of 5836360 line-segments and world parks or green areas (Park) consisting of 11503925 polygons and world buildings (Build) consisting of 114736539 polygons. To create sets of points, we used the centers of the line-segment MBRs from Water and the centroids of polygons from Park and Build. The experiments were run on a Linux machine, with Intel core duo 2x2.8 GHz processor and 4 GB of RAM.

We run experiments for tree building, counting tree characteristics and creation time. We also run experiments for several single dataset queries, *Point Location Query (PLQ)*, *Window Query (WQ)*, *Distance Range Query (DRQ)*, *K Nearest Neighbor Query (KNNQ)*, *Constrained K Nearest Neighbor Query (CKNNQ)*, and for two dual dataset queries, *K Closest Pairs Query (KCPQ)* and *Disatance Join Query (DJQ)*, counting disk read accesses (I/O) and total execution time.

5.1   Experiments for Tree Building

To study tree building by *PLBI*, we split the whole (unsorted) dataset to a sequence of subsets (segments), we use the *PBL* algorithm [11] to create an xBR$^+$-tree from scratch by loading the first one of these segments as one block and, subsequently, we insert each of the rest of these segments using *PLBI*.

---

[1] Retrieved from http://spatialhadoop.cs.umn.edu/datasets.html.

The size of each *Segment (S)* is a percentage of *MemoryLimit (ML)*, which is a percentage of the cardinality of the corresponding dataset. For each of the 9 above datasets, we constructed 45 xBR$^+$-trees, using *ML* equal to 1%, 2% and 4%, *S* equal to 20%, 40%, 60%, 80% and 100% and *node size* equal to 1 KB, 4 KB and 8 KB.

In Table 1, for four indicative cases of datasets (two big and one smaller real datasets and one synthetic dataset) and *ML* values, we present the effect of creating an xBR$^+$-tree with node size equal to 4 KB by *PLBI* algorithm on the tree characteristics: tree height (H), internal nodes occupancy percentage (Iocc), leaf nodes occupancy percentage (Locc), size of the tree in disk (Size) and the total creation time of the tree (Time). For each dataset, we added a line that presents the same tree characteristics by *PLObO*.

Table 1. Tree creation characteristics, using *PLBI* and *PLObO* .

ML (%)	S (%)	H	Iocc (%)	Locc (%)	Size (MB)	Time (s)	ML (%)	S (%)	H	Iocc (%)	Locc (%)	Size (MB)	Time (s)
Dataset : Park							Dataset : NArdND						
2	20	4	64.93	65.58	685	35.29	2	20	4	63.1	66.04	67.3	2.38
2	40	4	66.15	65.58	684	33.50	2	40	4	63.85	66.04	67.3	2.02
2	60	4	66.56	65.58	684	33.84	2	60	4	64.04	66.04	67.3	1.96
2	80	4	66.89	65.58	684	35.85	2	80	4	64.43	66.04	67.3	1.94
2	100	4	67.2	65.58	684	35.03	2	100	4	64.82	66.04	67.3	1.99
–	–	4	61.93	65.31	688	107.24	–	–	4	58.11	64.3	69.2	7.74
Dataset : Build							Dataset : 1000KCN						
1	20	5	67.72	65.66	6815	462.4	4	20	4	66.1	64.43	60.6	3.47
1	40	5	68.58	65.65	6814	463.2	4	40	4	66.1	64.43	60.6	3.36
1	60	5	69.09	65.65	6813	546.7	4	60	4	66.1	64.43	60.6	3.35
1	80	5	69.36	65.65	6813	548.6	4	80	4	66.33	64.43	60.6	3.26
1	100	5	69.69	65.65	6812	534.6	4	100	4	66.1	64.43	60.6	3.29
–	–	5	61.9	65.6	6833	1378	–	–	4	63.44	64.48	60.6	7.33

Regarding the characteristics of the trees created by the two methods, we observe the following.

– Both trees have the same height.
– Internal nodes occupancy percentage of *PLBI* trees is, on the average, 5% higher than the one of *PLObO* trees.
– Leaf nodes occupancy percentage of *PLBI* trees is, on the average, 2% higher than the one of *PLObO* trees.
– Size in disk of *PLBI* trees is up to 3% less than the one of *PLObO* trees (resulting mainly from the higher leaf nodes occupancy of *PLBI* trees).

The conclusions are analogous for the rest of the trees built. Regarding the total creation time of the trees created by the two methods, *PLBI* is the big winner (on the average, *PLBI* is 50% faster). The speed improvement is maximized for large datasets. In general, the *PLBI* speed is slightly increased as the *Segment* size increases. In some cases, the opposite trend is observed, since the distribution of data may cancel the benefit of using a larger *Segment* size.

5.2 Experiments for Single Dataset Spatial Queries

For all query experiments, we used node size equal to 4K, for trees created by both algorithms (the *PLBI* trees were created using *ML* equal to 2% and *S* equal to 60%). For *PLQs*, we executed two sets of experiments for the 9 datasets. In the first set, we used as query input the original datasets (existing points). When searching for existing points the number of disk accesses in xBR$^+$-trees is equal to their height. This set of experiments is summarized in the 1st data line of Table 2. In this table, for each query, regarding disk read accesses and execution time, we present percentages of experimental cases where trees created by the two processes perform equivalently (Columns 2 and 5, respectively) and where trees created by *PLBI/PLObO* have a performance that is more than 5% better than their rivals (Columns 3 and 6/4 and 7, respectively). It is evident that, for this set of experiments, both types of trees perform almost equivalently. In the second set, we used as query input the centroids of the query windows (non-existing points). While searching for non existing points in the dataset, the disk accesses may be less than the tree-height of xBR$^+$-trees (due to *DBRs*). This set of experiments is summarized in the 2nd data line of Table 2. It is clear that trees created by *PLBI*, on the average, perform better in both metrics.

Table 2. Percentages of cases of disk accesses and execution time winners.

Query	Number of disk read accesses			Execution time		
	tie diff $\leq$ 5%	*PLBI* wins diff > 5%	*PLObO* wins diff > 5%	tie diff $\leq$ 5%	*PLBI* wins diff > 5%	*PLObO* wins diff > 5%
PLQ-existing points	100.0	0.0	0.0	33.3	66.7	0.0
PLQ-non-existing points	77.8	22.2	0.0	0.0	77.8	22.2
WQ	88.9	11.1	0.0	11.1	75.6	13.3
DRQ	86.7	13.3	0.0	13.3	75.6	11.1
KNNQ	72.2	25.0	2.8	13.9	75.0	11.1
CKNNQ	77.8	22.2	0.0	5.6	80.6	13.9
KCPQ	33.3	66.7	0.0	0.0	100.0	0.0
DJQ	50.0	50.0	0.0	6.7	93.3	0.0

For *WQs*, we executed 54 experiments (9 datasets × 6 query window sizes). Each experiments was executed for 4096 query windows (having size 1/4096 of the total space) for each dataset. All experiments are summarized in the 3rd data line of Table 2. It is clear that the trees created by *PLBI*, on the average, perform better in both metrics.

For *DRQs*, the depth-first (DF) was used (since this is the best one [11]) in 54 experiments (9 datasets × 6 sets of query circles). All experiments are summarized in the 4th data line of Table 2. It is clear that the trees created by *PLBI*, on the average, perform better in both metrics.

For *KNNQs*, the HDF algorithm was used (since this is the best one [11]) in 36 experiments (9 datasets × 4 *K*-values, using 4096 query points, in all cases). All experiments are summarized in the 5th data line of Table 2. It is clear that the trees created by *PBL*, on the average, perform better in both metrics.

Finally, for *CKNNQs*, the BF algorithm was used (since this is the best one [11]) 36 experiments (9 datasets × 4 *K*-values, using 4096 query circles, in all cases). All experiments are summarized in the 6th data line of Table 2. It is clear for this query, too, that trees created by *PLBI*, on the average, perform better in both metrics.

Overall, trees created by *PLBI*, perform better regarding both metrics, for all the single dataset queries, except for the *PLQ* for existing points, where the two trees appear almost equivalent. The explanation for the improved performance of trees created by *PBLI* is related to the structural difference between the two trees. The *PBLI* algorithm can achieve better grouping of subregions, since all data/entries are known before each node is created and this improved grouping affects positively the time spent for CPU computations during query processing.

5.3   Experiments for Dual Dataset Spatial Queries

For *KCPQs/DJQs*, the HDF algorithm was used (since this is the best one [11]) in 30 experiments (6 combinations of datasets × 5 *K*-values, in all cases). All experiments are summarized in the 7th/8th data line of Table 2. It is clear that trees created by *PLBI* perform, on the average, significantly better in both metrics. The explanation for the significantly improved performance of trees created by *PLBI* is related to the better grouping of subregions and the fact that the execution of *KCPQs/DJQs* corresponds to multiple *KNNQs/DRQs*, maximizing the benefits resulting from *PLBI*.

6   Conclusions and Future Work

In this paper, for the first time in the literature, we present an algorithm for bulk insertions into xBR$^+$-trees, using a limited amount of RAM. This algorithm was implemented and extensive experimentation was performed for comparing the characteristics, the creation time and the query performance of trees loaded by the new algorithm and trees loaded by the traditional way of inserting items one-by-one. These experiments show that, trees loaded by bulk insertions have comparable structural characteristics to traditionally loaded trees, are created in significantly less time (the bulk insertion method is the big winner of creation time performance) and perform better/significantly better in processing single/dual dataset queries.

Future work plans include:

- The development of a cost model to analytically study the performance of various operations on xBR$^+$-trees (insertion of items one-by-one, bulk insertion, bulk loading, processing of different single and dual dataset queries).
- The development of parallel bulk-insertion methods for xBR$^+$-trees, utilizing multiple CPUs/GPU cores.
- An extension of the experimental study to more real datasets (to strengthen the validity of the results in real applications) and to data of higher dimensions.
- Embedding of xBR$^+$-trees created by bulk insertion in SpatialHadoop[2] and study their performance in relation of other space partitioning strategies, already existing in this system.
- Creating variations of bulk-insertion methods for xBR$^+$-trees that will take advantage of the characteristics of SSD disks.
- Relax the constraint that an overflown node region in an xBR$^+$-tree has to be split to equal parts (examine splitting to possibly unequal rectangles, instead of equal subquadrants) and test the performance of bulk insertion, bulk loading and insertion one-by-one.

References

1. An, N., Kanth, K.V.R., Ravada, S.: Improving performance with bulk-inserts in Oracle R-trees. In: VLDB Conference, pp. 948–951 (2003)
2. Arge, L., Hinrichs, K.H., Vahrenhold, J., Vitter, J.S.: Efficient bulk operations on dynamic R-trees. Algorithmica 33(1), 104–128 (2002)
3. Chen, L., Choubey, R., Rundensteiner, E.A.: Bulk-insertions info R-trees using the small-tree-large-tree approach. In: ACM-GIS Conference, pp. 161–162 (1998)
4. Chen, L., Choubey, R., Rundensteiner, E.A.: Merging R-trees: efficient strategies for local bulk insertion. GeoInformatica 6(1), 7–34 (2002)
5. Choubey, R., Chen, L., Rundensteiner, E.A.: GBI: a generalized R-tree bulk-insertion strategy. In: Güting, R.H., Papadias, D., Lochovsky, F. (eds.) SSD 1999. LNCS, vol. 1651, pp. 91–108. Springer, Heidelberg (1999). doi:10.1007/3-540-48482-5_8
6. Ghanem, T.M., Shah, R., Mokbel, M.F., Aref, W.G., Vitter, J.S.: Bulk operations for space-partitioning trees. In: ICDE Conference, pp. 29–40 (2004)
7. Hjaltason, G.R., Samet, H.: Speeding up construction of PMR quadtree-based spatial indexes. VLDB J. 11(2), 109–137 (2002)
8. Kamel, I., Khalil, M., Kouramajian, V.: Bulk insertion in dynamic R-trees. In: SDH Conference, pp. 3B.31–3B.42 (1996)
9. Lee, T., Moon, B., Lee, S.: Bulk insertion for R-trees by seeded clustering. Data Knowl. Eng. 59(1), 86–106 (2006)
10. Roumelis, G., Vassilakopoulos, M., Loukopoulos, T., Corral, A., Manolopoulos, Y.: The xBR$^+$-tree: an efficient access method for points. In: Chen, Q., Hameurlain, A., Toumani, F., Wagner, R., Decker, H. (eds.) DEXA 2015. LNCS, vol. 9261, pp. 43–58. Springer, Cham (2015). doi:10.1007/978-3-319-22849-5_4

---

^{2} http://spatialhadoop.cs.umn.edu/.

11. Roumelis, G., Vassilakopoulos, M., Corral, A., Manolopoulos, Y.: Bulk-loading xBR⁺-tree. In: MEDI Conference, pp. 57–71 (2016)
12. Roumelis, G., Vassilakopoulos, M., Corral, A., Manolopoulos, Y.: An efficient algorithm for bulk-loading xBR⁺-trees. Comput. Stand. Interfaces (2017, to appear)
13. Roumelis, G., Vassilakopoulos, M., Corral, A.: The deletion operation in xBR-Trees. In: PCI Conference, pp. 138–143 (2012)
14. Roumelis, G., Vassilakopoulos, M., Corral, A.: Performance comparison of xBR-trees and R*-trees for single dataset spatial queries. In: Eder, J., Bielikova, M., Tjoa, A.M. (eds.) ADBIS 2011. LNCS, vol. 6909, pp. 228–242. Springer, Heidelberg (2011). doi:10.1007/978-3-642-23737-9_17
15. Roussopoulos, N., Kotidis, Y., Roussopoulos, M.: Cubetree: organization of and bulk updates on the data cube. In: SIGMOD Conference, pp. 89–99 (1997)
16. Shekhar, S., Chawla, S.: Spatial Databases: A Tour. Prentice Hall, Upper Saddle River (2003)

RkNN Query Processing in Distributed Spatial Infrastructures: A Performance Study

Francisco García-García[1], Antonio Corral[1(✉)], Luis Iribarne[1], and Michael Vassilakopoulos[2]

[1] Department of Informatics, University of Almeria, Almeria, Spain
{paco.garcia,acorral,liribarn}@ual.es
[2] Department of Electrical and Computer Engineering,
University of Thessaly, Volos, Greece
mvasilako@uth.gr

Abstract. The Reverse k-Nearest Neighbor (RkNN) problem, i.e. finding all objects in a dataset that have a given query point among their corresponding k-nearest neighbors, has received increasing attention in the past years. *RkNN* queries are of particular interest in a wide range of applications such as decision support systems, resource allocation, profile-based marketing, location-based services, etc. With the current increasing volume of spatial data, it is difficult to perform *RkNN* queries efficiently in spatial data-intensive applications, because of the limited computational capability and storage resources. In this paper, we investigate how to design and implement distributed *RkNN* query algorithms using shared-nothing spatial cloud infrastructures as SpatialHadoop and LocationSpark. SpatialHadoop is a framework that inherently supports spatial indexing on top of Hadoop to perform efficiently spatial queries. LocationSpark is a recent spatial data processing system built on top of Spark. We have evaluated the performance of the distributed *RkNN* query algorithms on both SpatialHadoop and LocationSpark with big real-world datasets. The experiments have demonstrated the efficiency and scalability of our proposal in both distributed spatial data management systems, showing the performance advantages of LocationSpark.

Keywords: Spatial data processing · RNNQ · SpatialHadoop · LocationSpark

1 Introduction

In the age of smart cities and mobile environments, there is a huge increase of the volume of available spatial data (e.g. location, routing, navigation, etc.) world-wide. Recent developments of spatial big data systems have motivated the emergence of novel technologies for processing large-scale spatial data on clusters

F. García-García, A. Corral, L. Iribarne and M. Vassilakopoulos—Work funded by the MINECO research project [TIN2013-41576-R].

© Springer International Publishing AG 2017
Y. Ouhammou et al. (Eds.): MEDI 2017, LNCS 10563, pp. 200–207, 2017.
DOI: 10.1007/978-3-319-66854-3_15

of computers in a distributed environment. These Distributed Data Management Systems (DDMSs) can be classified in disk-based [9] and in-memory-based [18]. The disk-based Distributed Spatial Data Management Systems (*DSDMSs*) are characterized by being Hadoop-based systems and the most representative ones are SpatialHadoop [4] and Hadoop-GIS [1]. On the other hand, the in-memory (*DSDMSs*) are characterized by being Spark-based systems and the most remarkable ones are Simba [15] and LocationSpark [12]. These systems allows users to work on distributed in-disk or in-memory spatial data without worrying about computation distribution and fault-tolerance.

A Reverse k-Nearest Neighbor (*RkNN*) query [8,11] returns the data objects that have the query object in the set of their k-nearest neighbors. It is the complementary problem to that of finding the k-Nearest Neighbors (kNN) of a query object. The goal of a *RkNN* query (*RkNNQ*) is to identify the *influence* of a query object on the whole dataset, and several real examples are mentioned in [8]. Although the *RkNN* problem is the complement of the k-Nearest Neighbor problem, the relationship between *kNN* and *RkNN* is not symmetric and the number of the reverse k-nearest neighbors of a query object is not known in advance. A naive solution of the *RkNN* problem requires $O(n^2)$ time, since the k-nearest neighbors of all of the n objects in the dataset have to be found [8]. Obviously, more efficient algorithms are required, and thus, the *RkNN* problem has been studied extensively in the past years for centralized environments [16]. But, with the fast increase in the scale of the big input datasets, parallel and distributed algorithms for *RkNNQ* in MapReduce [2] have been designed and implemented [6,7], and there are no *RkNNQ* implementations in Spark [17].

The most important contributions of this paper are the following:

- The design and implementation of novel algorithms in SpatialHadoop and LocationSpark to perform efficient parallel and distributed *RkNNQ* on big real-world spatial datasets.
- The execution of a set of experiments for examining the efficiency and the scalability of the new parallel and distributed *RkNNQ* algorithms. And the comparison of the performance of the two DSDMSs (SpatialHadoop and LocationSpark).

This paper is organized as follows. In Sect. 2, we present preliminary concepts related to *RkNNQ*. In Sect. 3, the parallel and distributed algorithms for processing *RkNNQ* in SpatialHadoop and LocationSpark are proposed. In Sect. 4, we present the most representative results of the experiments that we have performed, using real-world datasets, for comparing these two cloud computing frameworks. Finally, in Sect. 5, we provide the conclusions arising from our work and discuss related future work directions.

2 The Reverse k-Nearest Neighbor Query

Given a set of points, the *kNN* query (*kNNQ*) discovers the k points that are the nearest to a given query point (i.e. it reports only the top-k points from a given query point). It is one of the most important and studied spatial operations, where one spatial dataset and a distance function are involved. The formal definition of the *kNNQ* for points (the extension of this definition to other, more complex spatial objects, as line-segments, is straightforward) is the following:

Definition 1 (*k*-Nearest Neighbor query, *kNN*) [14]. *Let* $\mathbb{P} = \{p_0, p_1, \cdots, p_{n-1}\}$ *a set of points in* E^d *(d-dimensional Euclidean space), a query point* q *in* E^d, *and a number* $k \in \mathbb{N}^+$. *Then, the result of the k-Nearest Neighbor query with respect to the query point* q *is a set,* $kNN(\mathbb{P}, q, k) \subseteq \mathbb{P}$, *which contains* k *($1 \leq k \leq |\mathbb{P}|$) different points of* $\mathbb{P}$, *with the* k *smallest distances from* q:
$kNN(\mathbb{P}, q, k) = \{p \in \mathbb{P}: |p' \in \mathbb{P}: dist(p', q) < dist(p, q)| < k\}$.

For *RkNNQ*, given a set of points $\mathbb{P}$ and a query point q, a point p is called the *Reverse k Nearest Neighbor* of q, if q is one of the k closest points of p. A Reverse *k*-Nearest Neighbors (*RkNN*) query issued from point q returns all the points of $\mathbb{P}$ whose k nearest neighbors include q. Formally:

Definition 2 (Reverse *k*-Nearest Neighbor query, *RkNN*) [14]. *Let* $\mathbb{P} = \{p_0, p_1, \cdots, p_{n-1}\}$ *a set of points in* E^d, *a query point* q *in* E^d, *and a number* $k \in \mathbb{N}^+$. *Then, the result of the Reverse k-Nearest Neighbor query with respect to the query point* q *is a set,* $RkNN(\mathbb{P}, q, k) \subseteq \mathbb{P}$, *which contains all the points of* $\mathbb{P}$ *whose* k *nearest neighbors include* q:
$RkNN(\mathbb{P}, q, k) = \{p \in \mathbb{P} : q \in kNN(\mathbb{P}, p, k)\}$.

3   *RkNNQ* Algorithms in SpatialHadoop and LocationSpark

In this section, we present how *RkNNQ* can be implemented in SpatialHadoop and in LocationSpark. But in general, our parallel and distributed *RkNNQ* algorithm is based on the SFT algorithm [10] and it consists of a series of MapReduce jobs. As we can observe in Algorithm 1, the *FILTER* function aims to find a candidate set of points which are the initial results from a MapReduce-based *kNNQ* that uses the partitions from $\mathbb{P}$ that are around q [7]. The *VERIFY* function aims to examine the candidate points from the *FILTER* function using another MapReduce job and return the final set of points that are the reverse k nearest neighbours of q.

3.1   *RkNNQ* Algorithm in SpatialHadoop

From Algorithm 1, we can obtain our proposed solution for *RkNNQ* in Spatial-Hadoop which follows its general processing steps described in [5] and consists of a combination of already implemented Spatial MapReduce operations [4]. Assuming that $\mathbb{P}$ is the dataset to be processed and q is the query point, the basic idea is to have $\mathbb{P}$ partitioned by some method (e.g. grid) into b blocks or cells of points. Then, a MapReduce-based *kNNQ* is executed in order to find every possible candidate point from $\mathbb{P}$. To carry out that, we find the partition

---

Algorithm 1. General Distributed *RkNNQ* Algorithm

1: **function** FILTER($\mathbb{P}$: set of points, q: query point, k: number of points, d: dimensionality)
2:     $K \leftarrow k * d * 10$ ▷ $K = 10 \times 2 \times k$, where $d = 2$
3:     $CandidateSet \leftarrow \text{KNN}(\mathbb{P}, q, K)$
4:     **return** $CandidateSet$
5: **end function**

6: **function** VERIFY($\mathbb{P}$: set of points, q: query point, k: number of points, $CandidateSet$: set of PointAndDistance)
7:     INITIALIZE(Result)
8:     **for all** $candidate \in CandidateSet$ **do**
9:         $NumberOfPoints \leftarrow \text{RANGE}(\mathbb{P}, candidate.point, candidate.distance)$
10:        **if** $NumberOfPoints < k$ **then**
11:            INSERT($Result, candidate$)
12:        **end if**
13:     **end for**
14:     **return** $Result$
15: **end function**

---

from $\mathbb{P}$ where q is located. A first answer for the $kNN(\mathbb{P}, q, K)$ is obtained and we use the distance from the $K\text{-}th$ point to q in order to find if there are possible candidates in other partitions close to q. To ensure an exact result, the value of K must be greater than k ($K \gg k$) as proposed in [13], at a magnitude of at least $K = 10 \times d \times k$, where d is the dimensionality of the dataset being examined (e.g. for 2d points, $K = 20 \times k$). Next, a range query with a circle centered in q with that distance as radius is run to finally answer the $kNNQ$. The candidates with their distance to the query point q are written into Hadoop Distributed File System (HDFS) files in order to be the input for the next jobs. At this moment, each candidate is checked to see if it is part of the final answer. That is, it finds the number of points that are part of the range query centered on the candidate point and with radius the distance to q. If this *number* is less than k, the point is verified to be a *RkNN* of q. Finally, the results are written into HDFS files, storing only the points coordinates and the distance with q.

3.2 *RkNNQ* Algorithm in LocationSpark

The implementation in LocationSpark uses the provided *knnfilter* and *rangefilter* functions [12] and is very similar to the one implemented for SpatialHadoop. It should be noted that the most important difference when implementing *RkNNQ* in LocationSpark and SpatialHadoop is the fact that the former does not need to store intermediate results on disk, since it is an in-memory *DSDMS*.

Table 1. Configuration parameters used in the experiments.

Parameter	Values (default)
k	1, 5, (10), 15, 20, 25, 50
Number of nodes	1, 2, 4, 6, 8, 10, (12)
Type of partition	Quadtree

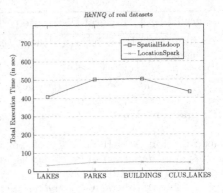

Fig. 1. *RkNNQ* execution times considering different datasets.

4   Experimentation

In this section we present the results of our experimental evaluation. We have used real 2d point datasets to test our *RkNNQ* algorithms in SpatialHadoop and LocationSpark. We have used three datasets from OpenStreetMap[1]: *BUILD-INGS* which contains 115M records of buildings, *LAKES* which contains 8.4M points of water areas, and *PARKS* which contains 10M records of parks and green areas [4]. Moreover, to experiment with the biggest real dataset (*BUILD-INGS*), we have created a new big quasi-real dataset from *LAKES* (8.4M), with a similar quantity of points. The creation process is as follows: taking one point of *LAKES*, p, we generate 15 new points gathered around p (i.e. the center of the cluster), according to a Gaussian distribution with mean $= 0.0$ and standard deviation $= 0.2$, resulting in a new quasi-real dataset, called *CLUS_LAKES*, with around 126M of points. The main performance measure that we have used in our experiments has been the total execution time (i.e. total response time). These values are the average of the execution times of the query on 10 previously obtained random points. All experiments are conducted on a cluster of 12 nodes on an OpenStack environment. Each node has 4 vCPU with 8 GB of main memory running Linux operating systems and Hadoop 2.7.1.2.3. Each node has a capacity of 3 vCores for MapReduce2/YARN use. The version of Spark used is 1.6.2. Finally, we used the latest code available in the repositories of SpatialHadoop[2] and LocationSpark[3].

Table 1 summarizes the configuration parameters used in our experiments. Default values (in parentheses) are used unless otherwise mentioned. Spatial-Hadoop needs the datasets to be partitioned and indexed before invoking the spatial operations. The times needed for that pre-processing phase are

---

[1] Available at http://spatialhadoop.cs.umn.edu/datasets.html.
[2] Available at https://github.com/aseldawy/spatialhadoop2.
[3] Available at https://github.com/merlintang/SpatialSpark.

94 s for *LAKES*, 103 s for *PARKS*, 175 s for *BUILDINGS* and 200 s for
CLUS_LAKES. We decided to exclude indexing time of SpatialHadoop (disk-
based DSDMS) for the comparison, since this is an *independent operation*. Data
are indexed and the index is stored on HDFS and for subsequent spatial queries,
data and index are already available (this can be considered as an advantage of SpatialHadoop). On the other hand, LocationSpark (in-memory-based
DSDMS) always partitions and indexes the data for every operation. The parti-
tions/indexes are not stored on any persistent file system and cannot be reused
in subsequent operations.

Our first experiment aims to measure the scalability of the distributed
RkNNQ algorithms, varying the dataset sizes. As shown in Fig. 1, the execution
times in both DSDMSs do not vary too much, showing quite stable performance.
This is due to the indexing mechanisms provided by both DSDMSs that allow
fast access to only the necessary partitions for the spatial query processing. The
smaller execution times shown by *LAKES* and *CLUS_LAKES* datasets is due
to how the points are distributed into the space and because one dataset is
built based on the other, and they show a similar behavior. From the results
with real data, we can conclude that LocationSpark is faster for all the datasets
(e.g. it is 2131 s faster for the biggest dataset, *CLUS_LAKES*) thanks to its
memory-based processing that allows to reduce execution times considerably.

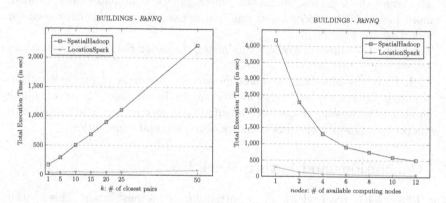

Fig. 2. *RkNNQ* cost (execution time) vs. k values (left). Query cost with respect to
the number of computing nodes (*nodes*) (right).

The second experiment studies the effect of the increasing k value for the
largest full-real dataset (*BUILDINGS*). The left chart of Fig. 2 shows that
the total execution time grows as the value of k increases. As we can see from
the results, the execution time for SpatialHadoop grows much faster than for
LocationSpark. This is because as the value of k increases, so does the number
of candidates K and for each of them a MapReduce job is done. Due to the fact
that SpatialHadoop is a disk-based DSDMS, the cost of multiple MapReduce
jobs increases the execution time by having to perform different input and output
operations for each of the candidate points (for instance, the dataset is read from

disk for each candidate). On the other hand, LocationSpark is a in-memory DSDMS, which allows to reduce the number of disk accesses since the data is already available for each candidate point and thus achieving faster and more stable results even for large k values.

The third experiment aims to measure the speedup of the $RkNNQ$ MapReduce algorithms, varying the number of computing nodes (*nodes*). The right chart of Fig. 2 shows the impact of different number of computing nodes on the performance of parallel $RkNNQ$ algorithm, for $BUILDINGS$ with the default configuration values. From this chart, it could be concluded that the performance of our approach has a direct relationship with the number of computing nodes. It could also be deduced that better performance would be obtained if more computing nodes are added. LocationSpark is still outperforming Spatial-Hadoop and it is affected to a lesser degree despite reducing the number of available computing nodes.

By analyzing the previous experimental results, we can extract several conclusions that are shown below:

- We have experimentally demonstrated the *efficiency* (in terms of total execution time) and the *scalability* (in terms of k values, sizes of datasets and number of computing *nodes*) of the proposed parallel and distributed algorithms for $RkNNQ$ in SpatialHadoop and LocationSpark.
- The larger the k values, the greater the number of candidates to be verified, more tasks will be needed and more total execution time is consumed for reporting the final result.
- The larger the number of computing *nodes*, the faster the $RkNNQ$ algorithms are.
- Both DSDMSs have similar behavior trends, in terms of execution time, although LocationSpark shows better values in all cases (if an adequate number of processing nodes with adequate memory resources are provided), thanks to its in-memory processing performance and capabilities.

5   Conclusions and Future Work

The $RkNNQ$ has received increasing attention in the past years. This spatial query has been actively studied in centralized environments, however, it has not attracted similar attention for parallel and distributed frameworks. For this reason, in this paper, we compare two of the most modern and leading DSDMSs, namely SpatialHadoop and LocationSpark. To do this, we have proposed novel algorithms in SpatialHadoop and LocationSpark, the first ones in the literature, to perform efficient parallel and distributed $RkNNQ$ algorithms on big spatial real-world datasets. The execution of a set of experiments has demonstrated that LocationSpark is the overall winner for the execution time, due to the efficiency of in-memory processing provided by Spark. However, SpatialHadoop shows interesting performance trends due to the nature of the proposed algorithm, since the use of multiple MapReduce jobs in a disk-based DSDMS needs multiple disk accesses to datasets. Our current proposal is a good foundation for the development of further improvements in which the number of candidate points could be reduced by adapting recent *RkNNQ* algorithms [16] to MapReduce methodology. Other future work might cover studying other Spark-based DSDMSs like *Simba* [15] and implement other spatial partitioning techniques [3].

References

1. Aji, A., Wang, F., Vo, H., Lee, R., Liu, Q., Zhang, X., Saltz, J.H.: Hadoop-GIS: a high performance spatial data warehousing system over MapReduce. PVLDB **6**(11), 1009–1020 (2013)
2. Dean, J., Ghemawat, S.: MapReduce: simplified data processing on large clusters. In: OSDI Conference, pp. 137–150 (2004)
3. Eldawy, A., Alarabi, L., Mokbel, M.F.: Spatial partitioning techniques in Spatial-Hadoop. PVLDB **8**(12), 1602–1613 (2015)
4. Eldawy, A., Mokbel, M.F.: SpatialHadoop: a MapReduce framework for spatial data. In: ICDE Conference, pp. 1352–1363 (2015)
5. García-García, F., Corral, A., Iribarne, L., Vassilakopoulos, M., Manolopoulos, Y.: Enhancing SpatialHadoop with closest pair queries. In: Pokorný, J., Ivanović, M., Thalheim, B., Šaloun, P. (eds.) ADBIS 2016. LNCS, vol. 9809, pp. 212–225. Springer, Cham (2016). doi:10.1007/978-3-319-44039-2_15
6. Ji, C., Hu, H., Xu, Y., Li, Y., Qu, W.: Efficient multi-dimensional spatial RkNN query processing with MapReduce. In: ChinaGrid Conference, pp. 63–68 (2013)
7. Ji, C., Qu, W., Li, Z., Xu, Y., Li, Y., Wu, J.: Scalable multi-dimensional RNN query processing. Concurr. Comput.: Pract. Exp. **27**(16), 4156–4171 (2015)
8. Korn, F., Muthukrishnan, S.: Influence sets based on reverse nearest neighbor queries. In: SIGMOD Conference, pp. 201–212 (2000)
9. Li, F., Ooi, B.C., Özsu, M.T., Wu, S.: Distributed data management using MapReduce. ACM Comput. Surv. **46**(3), 1–42 (2014)
10. Singh, A., Ferhatosmanoglu, H., Tosun, H.S.: High dimensional reverse nearest neighbor queries. In: CIKM Conference, pp. 91–98 (2003)
11. Stanoi, I., Agrawal, D., El Abbadi, A.: Reverse nearest neighbor queries for dynamic databases, pp. 44–53. In: SIGMOD Workshop on Research Issues, Data Mining and Knowledge Discovery (2000)
12. Tang, M., Yu, Y., Malluhi, Q.M., Ouzzani, M., Aref, W.G.: LocationSpark: a distributed in-memory data management system for big spatial data. PVLDB **9**(13), 1565–1568 (2016)
13. Tao, Y., Papadias, D., Lian, X.: Reverse kNN search in arbitrary dimensionality. In: VLBD Conference, pp. 744–755 (2004)
14. Wu, W., Yang, F., Chan, C.Y., Tan, K.L.: FINCH: evaluating reverse k-Nearest-Neighbor queries on location data. PVLDB **1**(1), 1056–1067 (2008)
15. Xie, D., Li, F., Yao, B., Li, G., Zhou, L., Guo, M.: Simba: efficient in-memory spatial analytics. In: SIGMOD Conference, pp. 1071–1085 (2016)
16. Yang, S., Cheema, M.A., Lin, X., Wang, W.: Reverse k nearest neighbors query processing: experiments and analysis. PVLDB **8**(5), 605–616 (2015)
17. Zaharia, M., Chowdhury, M., Das, T., Dave, A., Ma, J., McCauly, M., Franklin, M.J., Shenker, S., Stoica, I.: Resilient distributed datasets: a fault-tolerant abstraction for in-memory cluster computing. In: NSDI Conference, pp. 15–28 (2012)
18. Zhang, H., Chen, G., Ooi, B.C., Tan, K.-L., Zhang, M.: In-memory big data management and processing: a survey. TKDE **27**(7), 1920–1948 (2015)

An Evaluation of TANE Algorithm
for Functional Dependency Detection

Nikita Bobrov[1], George Chernishev[1,2(✉)], Dmitry Grigoriev[1],
and Boris Novikov[1,2]

[1] Saint Petersburg State University, St. Petersburg, Russia
nikita.v.bobrov@gmail.com, chernishev@gmail.com,
d.a.grigoriev@spbu.ru, borisnov@acm.org
[2] JetBrains Research, Prague, Czech Republic
http://www.math.spbu.ru/user/chernishev/

Abstract. Exploitation of logical schema information can allow producing better physical designs for a database. In order to exploit this information, one has to extract it from the data stored in the database. Extraction should be performed using some kind of an algorithm that provides an acceptable level of result quality. This quality has to be ensured, for example, in terms of precision.

In this paper we consider a particular type of such information: functional dependencies. One of the well-known algorithms for extraction of functional dependencies is the TANE algorithm. We propose to study its precision-related properties which are relevant for its use in our automatic physical design tool. TANE, being an approximate algorithm, returns only a fraction of existing dependencies. It is also prone to false positives. In contrast with the previous research, which measured run times and memory consumption, we aim to evaluate the quality of this algorithm.

Finally, we briefly describe the context of this study—constructing an alternative physical design tuning system that would use the output of the TANE algorithm. The system is an ordinary vertical partitioning tool, but which operates without workload knowledge, relying on data characteristics. Our plan is to employ TANE inside the functional dependency detection component. Thus, the purpose of evaluation is to study to what extent the properties of the algorithm affect our goals.

Keywords: TANE · Physical design tuning · Vertical partitioning · Logical schema information · Functional dependency · Functional dependency detection · Experimentation

1 Introduction

Functional dependency detection is a powerful tool used in many applications. Among them are data analysis, schema normalization, data cleansing,

---

This work is partially supported by Russian Foundation for Basic Research grant 16-57-48001.

© Springer International Publishing AG 2017
Y. Ouhammou et al. (Eds.): MEDI 2017, LNCS 10563, pp. 208–222, 2017.
DOI: 10.1007/978-3-319-66854-3_16

understanding the structure of unknown databases, and many more. In our paper we consider a non-traditional application of functional dependencies. We plan to construct a physical design tuner which would operate without workload knowledge. Instead it would rely on functional dependencies extracted from data.

Database tuning [1,2] aims to improve database response time, throughput and other performance metrics. Its primary difficulty is the abundance of parameters involved in the tuning process. This leads to a large number of possible alternatives and makes the search extremely difficult. To the best of our knowledge, all of the existing automatic advisors follow an approach based on workload analysis. At the first step, they obtain information regarding the prospective query set, such as queries, query frequencies, used attributes, and so on. Then, an enumeration process is run. The result is a number of candidate structures (indexes, partitions, etc.) that would improve the performance of the workload.

Our long-term goal is the development of an advisor which would operate without workload knowledge. In order to construct such a system, we propose to use logical schema information that is present in the data itself. More precisely, we propose to mine functional dependencies and use them in vertical partitioning.

In this paper we assess the viability of our approach by studying TANE [3]— popular functional dependency detection algorithm. There are a lot of studies which measure run times and memory consumption of functional dependency detection algorithms, but, to the best of our knowledge, none of them have considered the quality of the output. TANE, being an approximate algorithm, returns only a fraction of existing dependencies. Additionally, it is prone to false positives, i.e. functional dependencies which are actually absent in the original dataset. These properties may hinder successful application of this algorithm. Since a functional dependency detector is a crucial part of our advisor, it is essential to evaluate the quality of the algorithm. In this study we experimentally evaluate it in four scenarios using both synthetic and real datasets. The scenarios are specially designed to assess the suitability of the algorithm for functional dependency-assisted vertical partitioning.

The paper is structured as follows. We start by describing the context of our study—we present the physical design tuning problem and discuss our advisor in Sect. 2. Next, in Sect. 3 we present the core result of this paper—the evaluation of the TANE algorithm. Finally, in Subsect. 4 we describe physical design approaches based on external or logical schema information and survey several existing studies.

2 Physical Design Tuning Problem and the Advisor

The database tuning problem can be formulated as follows [4]. DBMS behavior can be described as a function:

$$f : C \times W \to P,$$

where C is configuration, W is workload and P is a performance metric. Configuration can be divided into the following types: hardware, software, and database configuration. In its turn, database configuration can be described by a number of general DBMS parameters like buffer size, logging and recovery strategies and so on. The notion of configuration also includes database-specific information about used physical design structures, e.g. indexes and materialized views.

Workload is the information regarding queries: their relative frequencies, arrival patterns, attributes involved and so on. Performance metric can be any metric like throughput, response time or the cost of ownership (for cloud-based systems).

Thus, the database tuning problem can be formulated as follows: for a given workload, find a configuration which optimizes (maximizes or minimizes) the given metric.

Physical design tuning problem is an essential part of the database tuning problem, which deals exclusively with physical design structures.

A typical approach to this problem is as follows:

- Construct a model which predicts the performance of the DBMS for any specified workload. This model employs workload and physical parameters;
- Run a configuration enumeration process. The configuration space is large due to the large number of possible structures and their combinations. Usually, finding an optimal set of physical design structures is an NP-hard task, so an approximate solution is sought;
- Present the solution to the user.

There are hundreds of physical design studies [5–16] which consider various physical design structures. Some surveys can be found in [1, 17–22].

All of these studies rely on the knowledge of the workload and physical parameters. The vast majority of them ignores logical schema information and other external knowledge. There is only a handful of physical design tuning studies which employ this information (see Sect. 4 for a short discussion).

In this paper we propose to use functional dependencies and other information embedded in the data to produce physical database design. Let us consider the conceptual schema of such an advisor.

The schema is presented on Fig. 1 and it consists of the following modules:

- Statistics collector. This module performs database calls and provides data samples for functional detection and various data statistics, such as cardinality of a relation;
- Adapter for functional dependency detection algorithm. Its purpose is transforming data representation into the format used by a specific functional dependency detection algorithm;
- Functional dependency detector. Functional dependencies are mined from the data by some algorithm. There are several algorithms for inference of functional dependencies from data [3, 23–27];
- Partitioning algorithm based on logical schema information. This module is the core of the system. It uses found functional dependencies and possibly other information to produce partitioning scheme;

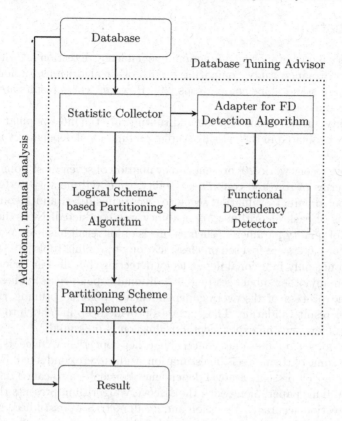

Fig. 1. Architecture

– Partitioning scheme implementer. There are several approaches to the implementation of the partitioning scheme, namely partitioning and the usage of materialized views. The latter allows to leave the queries untouched, while the former requires query rewriting. Currently, our prototype relies on the rewrite approach.

It is possible that due to the presumed low quality of found solutions manual analysis would be required.

Initially we have planned to derive partitioning scheme using some clustering algorithm. However, our first successfull attempt [28] employed attribute affinity approach [18] which we adapted for functional dependencies.

Before designing the partitioning module, we had to understand the capabilities of the existing algorithms for functional dependency detection. We have decided to consider TANE—the most popular algorithm of a such kind. In order to assess its suitability we had to evaluate its quality in terms of precision-related metrics. In the next section we present the results of our experiments.

3   Evaluation

Almost every paper proposing a functional dependency detection algorithm contained a performance study, comparing it with other algorithms. In addition to that, there are stand-alone comparisons [29]. However, these results are unsuitable for our purposes.

Scalability, memory consumption and runtime are the most popular parameters that are evaluated in the existing studies on functional dependency inference tools.

The most recent work [29] presents an evaluation of seven most popular algorithms in terms of row and column scalability, time and memory performance. In this paper different evaluation scenarios were considered and a comprehensive analysis of each algorithm's applicability was conducted. Nevertheless, no estimation of quality parameters such as precision or recall has been performed.

The other papers are focused on classification of profiling tools [30,31], which touch upon not only functional dependency detection, but also inclusion dependency and many other subclasses (e.g., conditional dependencies). These papers describe the process of discovering dependencies, possible pruning rules and methods for result validation. Those studies provide deep insights into the data profiling problem, but no experimental evaluation is presented.

If we examine similar studies concerning other dependency concepts, we may find that in some of them precision estimation studies were conducted. For example, the paper [32] presents a novel dependency concept—a so-called differential dependency. This paper, along with the discovery algorithm, presents the evaluation of detection accuracy—precision and recall metrics were studied. Although functional and differential concepts are related, we can not consider this work to be fully suitable for the context of our research.

Thus, none of the papers that surveyed tools for discovery of functional dependencies have provided an evaluation of such quality metrics.

3.1   Setting

We have decided to evaluate the algorithm using TPC-H [33]—a synthetic benchmark, and a real dataset. For the latter, we used the FRA Highway-Rail Crossing Inventory dataset [34]. The reason for such choice of the real dataset was common properties of these two datasets and their suitability for our purposes:

1. the relationship type of considered tables is the same (1:many) in both datasets;
2. the number of attributes in employed tables of both datasets is approximately the same.

Our goal is to conduct the same experiments for both real and synthetic datasets. Thus, the employed data should be as close as possible.

To conduct our experiments we join two of the tables presented in the dataset to produce the third one. In the synthetic dataset, lineorder table is the result of a join between lineitem and orders tables. The real dataset is treated similarly: PHRB table is the result of a join between the PublicHighway and ReportBase tables. You can see the description of the employed datasets in Tables 1 and 2. We have loaded this data into the PostgreSQL, an industrial DBMS. Then we used an existing implementation [35] of the TANE algorithm to mine functional dependencies from the involved tables.

Table 1. Used tables and their details (synthetic)

Table	Records	Attrs	PK	FK
Lineitem	1.8 M	16	l_orderkey, l_linenumber	l_orderkey
Orders	450 K	9	o_orderkey	o_custkey
Lineorder	1.8 M	25	l_orderkey, l_linenumber	o_custkey

Table 2. Used tables and their details (real)

Table	Records	Attrs	PK	FK
PublicHighway (PH)	427 K	17	CrossingId, ReportBaseId	ReportBaseId
ReportBase (RB)	427 K	11	ParentReportBase	ReportBaseId
PHRB	427 K	27	CrossingId, ReportBaseId	ReportBaseId

3.2   Description of Experiments

We have run the following experiments for both datasets:

– An experiment which is aimed to find out whether found dependencies persist between different algorithm invocations. In this experiment, the algorithm was run multiple times with the same parameters.
– An experiment which is aimed to find out whether the algorithm is capable of eliciting dependencies found in tables lineitem and orders in the joined table – lineorder.
– An experiment which is aimed to find out if the dependency between the primary key of one table and the corresponding attribute set would be found by the algorithm in the joined table. In this experiment the lineorder table is used.
– An experiment which is aimed to calculate the precision of the algorithm.

3.3   Experiment 1 (Persistence)

In this experiment we tried to assess the consistency of the algorithm's output. The question was "how many of the found dependencies persist between different invocations?".

We perform this experiment as follows: at first we run the algorithm n times and denote each of the results as R_j. We call an FD as a persistent one if it is contained in every R_j, $j \in [1, n]$: $FD \in R_1 \cap R_2 \cap \ldots \cap R_n$. The overall share of persistent FDs is calculated as follows:

$$Pers.FDs = \frac{sum(FD_i)}{\#FD} * 100\%,$$

where $sum(FD_i)$ denotes the number of all persistent functional dependencies and $\#FD$ is the number of all unique functional dependencies found during all algorithm runs.

In this experiment we ran 10 invocations of the algorithm with the same parameters. The output of each run was recorded and the percentage of persistent FDs was calculated.

Tables 3 and 4 show the results of this experiment. Each table contains the name of a database table, sample size, attribute number, and functional dependency information. Functional dependency information consists of two values: the number of unique functional dependencies found and the share of dependencies which persist in all invocations.

We can draw several conclusions:

- The number of mined dependencies does not vary with sample size;
- The percentage of persistent functional dependencies is about 30–40% for synthetic data and almost 100% for real data;
- The algorithm had found a significantly lesser number of functional dependencies in real data;
- The percentage of persistent functional dependencies is higher in real data even in case of a comparable number of functional dependencies (tables reportbase and orders);
- Sample size does not significantly impact the number of persistent dependencies for both datasets.

Table 3. Experiment 1. Number of persistent FDs (synthetic).

Table	Records	Attrs	FD num	Pers. FDs
Lineitem	150 K	16	17189	40.4%
Lineitem	100 K	16	15951	41.5%
Lineitem	75 K	16	15972	39.8%
Lineitem	25 K	16	14032	41.1%
Orders	150 K	9	540	32.3%
Orders	100 K	9	552	31.6%
Orders	75 K	9	555	31.7%
Orders	25 K	9	625	32.3%
Lineorder	150 K	25	99854	40.5%
Lineorder	100 K	25	87843	40.6%
Lineorder	75 K	25	95509	41.4%
Lineorder	25 K	25	76236	40.3%

Table 4. Experiment 1. Number of persistent FDs (real).

Table	Records	Attrs	FD num	Pers. FDs
PH	150 K	17	170	100.0%
PH	100 K	17	309	96.3%
PH	75 K	17	309	96.3%
PH	25 K	17	692	94.1%
RB	150 K	11	270	100.0%
RB	100 K	11	250	100.0%
RB	75 K	11	250	100.0%
RB	25 K	11	254	98.4%
PHRB	150 K	27	4181	98.9%
PHRB	100 K	27	3717	98.4%
PHRB	75 K	27	4241	98.2%
PHRB	25 K	27	4368	96.8%

Table 5. Experiment 2. The amount of new and lost dependencies (synthetic).

Table	Records	New	Lost
Lineorder+lineitem	150 K	6.9%	4.0%
Lineorder+lineitem	100 K	9.3%	5.9%
Lineorder+lineitem	75 K	11.1%	8.1%
Lineorder+lineitem	25 K	5.7%	7.1%
Lineorder+orders	150 K	12.0%	10.5%
Lineorder+orders	100 K	11.5%	12.0%
Lineorder+orders	75 K	10.9%	11.7%
Lineorder+orders	25 K	11.1%	14.2%

Table 6. Experiment 2. The amount of new and lost dependencies (real).

Tables	Records	New	Lost
PHRB+PH	150 K	17.6%	11.7%
PHRB+PH	100 K	4.6%	8.3%
PHRB+PH	75 K	4.6%	8.3%
PHRB+PH	25 K	3.5%	8.8%
PHRB+RB	150 K	12.0%	5.5%
PHRB+RB	100 K	11.4%	5.2%
PHRB+RB	75 K	11.4%	5.2%
PHRB+RB	25 K	12.0%	5.5%

3.4   Experiment 2 (New and Lost)

In this experiment we check whether the algorithm is able to find the dependencies detected in source tables (lineitem and orders; PublicHighway and ReportBase) in the joined table (lineorder; PHRB). In Tables 5 and 6 we indicate the sample size and:

- The percentage of the original dependencies which were found in the joined table (new dependencies);
- The percentage of the original dependencies which were not found in the joined table (lost dependencies).

The first column describes the experimental setup. It indicates table combinations. For example, lineorder+lineitem means that the lineitem table was used to mine dependencies and they were checked on the lineorder table.

We evaluate it as follows: at first we extract dependencies from a source table (e.g., lineitem), then we compare them with dependencies found in a joined table (lineorder). We call the dependencies that were found in lineorder for lineitem attributes "new" dependencies, and all dependencies in lineitem that no longer hold for lineorder are "lost". Thus,

$$new = \frac{|FDs(lineorder) \setminus FDs(lineitem)|}{|FDs(lineorder)|} * 100\%,$$

$$lost = \frac{|FDs(lineitem) \setminus FDs(lineorder)|}{|(FDs(lineitem)|} * 100\%.$$

We evaluate the real case in a similar manner, but using PublicHighway and ReportBase as the source tables.

Consider the following example. Suppose that T_1 is the source table and T_2 is the joined table. Let $FDs(T_1) = \{1 \to 3; 2, 4 \to 5; 5, 6, 7 \to 7; 5, 8 \to 9\}$ and $FDs(T_2) = \{1 \to 3; 2, 4 \to 5; 6, 8 \to 7; 2, 5, 9 \to 6; 3, 4, 7 \to 10\}$. For simplicity we denote attributes with numbers, and use ";" as the separator between dependencies. Since there are three dependencies in T_2, not presenting in T_1:

$new = 3/5 * 100\% = 60\%$. Similarly, there are two dependencies from T_1 not found in T_2: $lost = 2/4 * 100\% = 50\%$.

The observed results led us to the following conclusions:

- The algorithm can be considered stable, no more 15% of dependencies is lost or found;
- Sample size clearly impacts the percentage of new and lost dependencies for synthetic data;
- Again, in the real data case the number of lost dependencies is clearly lower than that in the case of synthetic data;
- The percentage of lost and new dependencies in real data is much more stable than in synthetic data;
- The number of attributes may negatively impact the stability of algorithm.

3.5 Experiment 3 (Mixed in Dependencies)

In this experiment we evaluate the ability of the algorithm to find dependencies which were "mixed in" the table. "Mixing in" happens when a dependency originating from some table is embedded into another table. The idea is the following: consider relations R_1 and R_2 which are related through primary key(R_2)–foreign key (R_1) relationships. We join these tables and keep all attributes, including the primary key attribute. This procedure will ensure that functional dependencies from the transferred primary key of R_2 to each of R_2 attributes (also transferred) still hold in the joined table. Our question is whether the functional dependency algorithm would be able to detect all such dependencies from R_2 in the resulting table. For example, in synthetic data the Attribute l_orderkey is an FK for the table order, thus the algorithm should find dependencies like $l\_orderkey \rightarrow order\_att_i$.

Consider the example presented in Table 7. Here R_3 contains the result of "mixing in" of R_2 into R_1. Thus, we can guarantee the existence of the dependencies $FK \rightarrow D$, $FK \rightarrow E$, $FK \rightarrow F$ in R_3. The idea of this experiment is to check whether TANE can detect these dependencies.

Table 7. Mixed-in example

R_1

PK	A	B	FK
1	A1	B1	FK1
2	A2	B3	FK2
3	A3	B3	FK3

R_2

FK	D	E	F
FK1	D1	E1	F1
FK2	D2	E2	F2
FK3	D3	E3	F3

R_3

PK	A	B	FK	D	E	F
1	A1	B1	FK1	D1	E1	F1
2	A2	B3	FK2	D2	E2	F2
3	A3	B3	FK3	D3	E3	F3

Tables 8 and 9 report the number of attributes which were successfully found in the joined table.

Table 8. Experiment 3. FD detection for FKs (synthetic).

Table	Records	FK attrs
Lineorder+lineitem	150 K	9/9
Lineorder+lineitem	75 K	9/9
Lineorder+lineitem	50 K	8/9
Lineorder+lineitem	25 K	8/9
Lineorder+lineitem	15 K	8/9
Lineorder+lineitem	10 K	7/9
Lineorder+orders	150 K	16/16
Lineorder+orders	75 K	16/16
Lineorder+orders	50 K	15/16
Lineorder+orders	25 K	16/16
Lineorder+orders	15 K	16/16
Lineorder+orders	10 K	16/16

Table 9. Experiment 3. FD detection for FKs (real).

Table	Records	FK attrs
PHRB+PH	150 K	11/11
PHRB+PH	75 K	11/11
PHRB+PH	50 K	11/11
PHRB+PH	25 K	11/11
PHRB+PH	15 K	11/11
PHRB+PH	10 K	10/11
PHRB+RB	150 K	17/17
PHRB+RB	75 K	17/17
PHRB+RB	50 K	17/17
PHRB+RB	25 K	17/17
PHRB+RB	15 K	17/17
PHRB+RB	10 K	17/17

We can observe that dependencies were successfully found in almost all cases. It is interesting to mention that for the orders table dependencies were found even when using very small samples (10 K). However, for the lineitem table, problems with small and medium sample sizes have arisen. Presumably, this is a result of having a small number of attributes. It is also worth mentioning that the algorithm performed much better for real data than for synthetic case.

3.6 Experiment 4 (Precision)

In this experiment we evaluate how reliable the algorithm is by evaluating how much of the found functional dependencies truly exist. We use precision [36]— a standard information retrieval metric that shows the percentage of relevant documents in the result set.

The evaluation was performed as follows: at the first step we obtained functional dependencies using the specified sample size. Then we checked them against the whole table and calculated the percentage that was held. The results are presented in Tables 10 and 11.

We can conclude the following:

- The precision is actually good, given approximate nature of the algorithm. It was about 60–80% in synthetic case. For real data it was nearing 100% in all cases;
- The number of found dependencies does not impact precision, e.g. compare ReportBase and orders tables;
- Sample size does not impact precision, except the case with the orders table. Presumably, it can be explained as a result of a low attribute number.

Unfortunately, we were unable to perform this experiment for the 150 K samples for both existing and real datasets. The reason is that even the experiment

Table 10. Experiment 4. Precision of the algorithm (synthetic).

Table	Records	Attrs	FD num	Precision
Lineitem	100 K	16	1706	76.3%
Lineitem	75 K	16	1535	71.6%
Lineitem	50 K	16	1595	74.9%
Lineitem	25 K	16	1207	75.5%
Orders	100 K	9	55	69.7%
Orders	75 K	9	56	67.8%
Orders	50 K	9	56	57.2%
Orders	25 K	9	61	57.5%
Lineorder	100 K	25	8984	86.6%
Lineorder	75 K	25	9460	85.9%
Lineorder	50 K	25	9737	83.5%
Lineorder	25 K	25	7093	80.4%

Table 11. Experiment 4. Precision of the algorithm (real).

Table	Records	Attrs	FD num	Precision
PH	100 K	17	32	96.8%
PH	75 K	17	32	96.8%
PH	50 K	17	32	96.8%
PH	25 K	17	69	94.2%
RB	100 K	11	25	100%
RB	75 K	11	25	100%
RB	50 K	11	25	100%
RB	25 K	11	24	87.5%
PHRB	100 K	27	373	100%
PHRB	75 K	27	425	100%
PHRB	50 K	27	427	99.0%
PHRB	25 K	27	437	98.3%

with a 100 K sample set took about 8 hours. Thus, we decided to experiment with 50 K records to better demonstrate the dependence of precision on sample size.

3.7   Results

The algorithm shows acceptable results in all experiments. However, the outcome of experiment 1 for synthetic data is concerning. Presumably, this may unfold into a number of complications during application of the bagging approach for similar workloads. However, this experiment for real data went perfectly. Experiments 2 and 3 have shown surprisingly good results. It is interesting to mention that the algorithm behaves comparably for both datasets in these two experiments. Experiment 4 has also provided decent precision for wide tables in synthetic experiments. For real data, precision was close to 100% in all cases. Overall, the algorithm can be deemed suitable for our purposes.

4   Related Work: Logical Schema Information and Tuning

While there are hundreds of physical design tuning studies, there is only a handful of studies which employ logical schema information. Therefore, it is essential to provide a short overview.

The notion of categorical attribute is used in the study [37]. A categorical attribute is an attribute that has a small number of possible values and which is used to identify classes of objects. It allows to produce very efficient partitioning schemes that decompose the original relation into a number of both vertical and horizontal fragments. The categorical attribute may be specified by the database administrator or taken from the system catalog. This study assumes prior knowledge of the future workload.

The reference [38] describes another approach to logical schema information usage. Here, the authors created SquashML – an XML representation for SQL database schema definitions and queries. The Prolog programming language is used to manage this knowledge, and the XQuery-like FnQuery language is used for transformations. This toolkit allows schema visualization and analysis, tuning, and refactoring. Analysis component provides detection of design flaws and anomalies like join conditions lacking FK relationships, cyclic FK references and so on. Tuning component allows index and horizontal partitioning recommendation. Index recommendation takes into account column contents (selectivity) and number of occurrences in the workload. It also uses schema information – column usages as the FK.

CRIUS [39] is a simple DBMS application based on a spreadsheet metaphor. It is aimed at inexperienced users who would like to create and maintain simple databases, such as a personal contact list. This application allows simple schema evolution by facilitating schema transformations such as column addition or column reassociation. This tool extensively relies on automatic incremental functional dependency derivation. It allows to perform duplicate handling and to address possible data entry errors.

The study [40] proposes to formalize external tuning knowledge for automatic database tuning during a permanent, changing workload. The authors propose to codify existing tuning best-practices into a form of rules. Rules describe an event-based mechanism, where an event (a problem) triggers the corresponding tuning plan. Their tool, named Autonomic Tuning Expert, allows constant tuning of databases using a feedback control loop. Unfortunately, the described tool is aimed primarily at tuning resource configuration and allocation. Physical design tuning is briefly touched and concerns index and materialized view selection. This selection is performed by invoking another well-known physical design tool – DB2 Design Advisor.

The authors of DBA Companion project [41] argue that while physical database design was deeply studied, logical database design received little attention. They emphasize the need to study logical constraints because their understanding may bring a lot of benefits.

The authors concentrate their efforts on mining functional and inclusion dependencies. Using these dependencies can provide such benefits as data integration, semantic query optimization, and logical database tuning. The authors indicate that the mined functional and inclusion dependencies can be used for logical database tuning. Moreover, database restructuring can be performed based on these dependencies.

5   Conclusions

In this paper we proposed to use logical schema information in order to produce vertical partitioning. The goal of our approach is to develop a physical design tuning system which would not require workload knowledge and which would produce reasonable partitioning. We started with a survey and described several systems which used logical schema information or external information for physical design tuning. Next, we described an architecture of such a system and discussed its modules. Then, we discussed a possible approach for the construction of such an algorithm. Finally, we conducted several experiments which evaluated the suitability of an existing functional dependency detection algorithm. The results confirmed that the TANE algorithm is an appropriate choice for constructing this kind of a system.

Acknowledgments. We would like to thank Felix Naumann for his valuable comments on the previous version of this paper. We would also like to thank anonymous reviewers for their valuable comments on this work. This work is partially supported by Russian Foundation for Basic Research grant 16-57-48001.

References

1. Bellatreche, L.: Optimization and tuning in data warehouses. In: Liu, L., Özsu, M. (eds.) Encyclopedia of Database Systems, pp. 1995–2003. Springer, New York (2009). doi:10.1007/978-0-387-39940-9_259
2. Lightstone, S.: Physical database design for relational databases. In: Liu, L., Özsu, M. (eds.) Encyclopedia of Database Systems, pp. 2108–2114. Springer, New York (2009). doi:10.1007/978-0-387-39940-9_644
3. Huhtala, Y., Kärkkäinen, J., Porkka, P., Toivonen, H.: TANE: an efficient algorithm for discovering functional and approximate dependencies. Comput. J. **42**(2), 100–111 (1999)
4. Chaudhuri, S., Weikum, G.: Self-management technology in databases. In: Liu, L., Öszu, M. (eds.) Encyclopedia of Database Systems, pp. 2550–2555. Springer, New York (2009). doi:10.1007/978-0-387-39940-9_334
5. Agrawal, S., Narasayya, V., Yang, B.: Integrating vertical and horizontal partitioning into automated physical database design. In: SIGMOD 2004, pp. 359–370 (2004)
6. Rao, J., Zhang, C., Megiddo, N., Lohman, G.: Automating physical database design in a parallel database. In: SIGMOD 2002, pp. 558–569 (2002)
7. Nehme, R., Bruno, N.: Automated partitioning design in parallel database systems. In: SIGMOD 2011, pp. 1137–1148 (2011)
8. Agrawal, S., Chu, E., Narasayya, V.: Automatic physical design tuning: workload as a sequence. In: SIGMOD 2006, pp. 683–694 (2006)
9. Alagiannis, I., Dash, D., Schnaitter, K., Ailamaki, A., Polyzotis, N.: An automated, yet interactive and portable DB designer. In: SIGMOD 2010, pp. 1183–1186 (2010)
10. Schnaitter, K., Abiteboul, S., Milo, T., Polyzotis, N.: Colt: continuous on-line tuning. In: SIGMOD 2006, pp. 793–795 (2006)
11. Hose, K., Klan, D., Marx, M., Sattler, K.U.: When is it time to rethink the aggregate configuration of your OLAP server? Proc. VLDB Endow. **1**(2), 1492–1495 (2008)
12. Bellatreche, L., Benkrid, S.: A joint design approach of partitioning and allocation in parallel data warehouses. In: Pedersen, T.B., Mohania, M.K., Tjoa, A.M. (eds.) DaWaK 2009. LNCS, vol. 5691, pp. 99–110. Springer, Heidelberg (2009). doi:10.1007/978-3-642-03730-6_9

13. Bellatreche, L., Boukhalfa, K., Abdalla, H.I.: SAGA: a combination of genetic and simulated annealing algorithms for physical data warehouse design. In: Bell, D.A., Hong, J. (eds.) BNCOD 2006. LNCS, vol. 4042, pp. 212–219. Springer, Heidelberg (2006). doi:10.1007/11788911_18

14. Bellatreche, L., Cuzzocrea, A., Benkrid, S.: $\mathcal{F\&A}$: a methodology for effectively and efficiently designing parallel relational data warehouses on heterogeneous database clusters. In: Bach Pedersen, T., Mohania, M.K., Tjoa, A.M. (eds.) DaWaK 2010. LNCS, vol. 6263, pp. 89–104. Springer, Berlin (2010). doi:10.1007/978-3-642-15105-7_8

15. Gebaly, K.E., Aboulnaga, A.: Robustness in automatic physical database design. In: EDBT 2008, pp. 145–156 (2008)

16. Zilio, D., Zuzarte, C., Lightstone, S., Ma, W., Lohman, G., Cochrane, R., Pirahesh, H., Colby, L., Gryz, J., Alton, E., Valentin, G.: Recommending materialized views and indexes with the IBM DB2 design advisor. In: ICAC 2004, pp. 180–187, May 2004

17. Chaudhuri, S., Narasayya, V.: Self-tuning database systems: a decade of progress. In: VLDB 2007, pp. 3–14. VLDB Endowment (2007)

18. Chernishev, G.: A survey of DBMS physical design approaches. SPIIRAS Proc. **24**, 222–276 (2013)

19. Quix, C., Li, X., Kensche, D., Geisler, S.: View management techniques and their application to data stream management. In: Evolving Application Domains of Data Warehousing and Mining: Trends and Solutions, pp. 83–112 (2010)

20. Mami, I., Bellahsene, Z.: A survey of view selection methods. SIGMOD Rec. **41**(1), 20–29 (2012)

21. Wah, B.: File placement on distributed computer systems. Computer **17**(1), 23–32 (1984)

22. Chernishev, G.: Towards self-management in a distributed column-store system. In: Morzy, T., Valduriez, P., Bellatreche, L. (eds.) ADBIS 2015. CCIS, vol. 539, pp. 97–107. Springer, Cham (2015). doi:10.1007/978-3-319-23201-0_12

23. Novelli, N., Cicchetti, R.: FUN: an efficient algorithm for mining functional and embedded dependencies. In: Van den Bussche, J., Vianu, V. (eds.) ICDT 2001. LNCS, vol. 1973, pp. 189–203. Springer, Heidelberg (2001). doi:10.1007/3-540-44503-X_13

24. Yao, H., Hamilton, H.J., Butz, C.J.: FD_Mine: discovering functional dependencies in a database using equivalences. In: ICDM 2002, pp. 729–732 (2002)

25. Abedjan, Z., Schulze, P., Naumann, F.: DFD: efficient functional dependency discovery. In: CIKM 2014, pp. 949–958 (2014)

26. Lopes, S., Petit, J.-M., Lakhal, L.: Efficient discovery of functional dependencies and Armstrong relations. In: Zaniolo, C., Lockemann, P.C., Scholl, M.H., Grust, T. (eds.) EDBT 2000. LNCS, vol. 1777, pp. 350–364. Springer, Heidelberg (2000). doi:10.1007/3-540-46439-5_24

27. Flach, P.A., Savnik, I.: Database dependency discovery: a machine learning approach. AI Commun. **12**(3), 139–160 (1999)

28. Bobrov, N., Chernishev, G., Novikov, B.: Workload-independent data-driven vertical partitioning. In: Kirikova, M., Nørvåg, K., Papadopoulos, G.A., Gamper, J., Wrembel, J., Darmont, J., Rizzi, S. (eds.) ADBIS 2017. CCIS, vol. 767. Springer, Cham (2017)

29. Papenbrock, T., Ehrlich, J., Marten, J., Neubert, T., Rudolph, J.P., Schönberg, M., Zwiener, J., Naumann, F.: Functional dependency discovery: an experimental evaluation of seven algorithms. Proc. VLDB Endow. **8**(10), 1082–1093 (2015)

30. Abedjan, Z., Gołab, L., Naumann, F.: Profiling relational data: a survey. VLDB J. **24**(4), 557–581 (2015)
31. Liu, J., Li, J., Liu, C., Chen, Y.: Discover dependencies from data—a review. IEEE Trans. Knowl. Data Eng. **24**(2), 251–264 (2012)
32. Song, S., Chen, L.: Differential dependencies: reasoning and discovery. ACM Trans. Database Syst. **36**(3), 16:1–16:41 (2011)
33. TPC: TPC Benchmark H. Decision Support. http://www.tpc.org/tpch
34. Federal Railroad Administration Office of Safety Analysis: FRA Highway-Rail Crossing Inventory Database. http://safetydata.fra.dot.gov/OfficeofSafety/default.aspx
35. Huhtala, Y., Kärkkäinen, J., Porkka, P., Toivonen, H.: TANE implementation. http://www.cs.helsinki.fi/research/fdk/datamining/tane/
36. Manning, C.D., Raghavan, P., Schütze, H.: Introduction to Information Retrieval. Cambridge University Press, New York (2008)
37. Papadomanolakis, S., Ailamaki, A.: Autopart: automating schema design for large scientific databases using data partitioning. In: SSDBM 2004, pp. 383–392 (2004)
38. Boehm, A.M., Seipel, D., Sickmann, A., Wetzka, M.: Squash: a tool for analyzing, tuning and refactoring relational database applications. In: Seipel, D., Hanus, M., Wolf, A. (eds.) INAP/WLP -2007. LNCS (LNAI), vol. 5437, pp. 82–98. Springer, Heidelberg (2009). doi:10.1007/978-3-642-00675-3_6
39. Qian, L., LeFevre, K., Jagadish, H.V.: CRIUS: user-friendly database design. Proc. VLDB Endow. **4**(2), 81–92 (2010)
40. Wiese, D., Rabinovitch, G., Reichert, M., Arenswald, S.: Autonomic tuning expert: a framework for best-practice oriented autonomic database tuning. In: CASCON 2008, pp. 327–341 (2008)
41. De Marchi, F., Lopes, S., Petit, J.M., Toumani, F.: Analysis of existing databases at the logical level: the DBA companion project. SIGMOD Rec. **32**(1), 47–52 (2003)

Towards an Explicitation
and a Conceptualization of Cost
Models in Database Systems

Abdelkader Ouared[(⊠)]

National High School for Computer Science (ESI), Algiers, Algeria
a_ouared@esi.dz

Abstract. In the database landscape, the mathematical cost models play a crucial role in evaluating non-functional requirements such as the query execution performance, energy consumption, monetary cost estimation. The development of a such cost model is time consuming and requires the knowledge of the whole environment of database systems. Also, cost models are scattered either in scientific papers, usually with fewer details or inside commercial and academic database management systems. Therefore, cost models become a dark entity, because they cannot be easily exploited by researchers and students for learning, analysis or reproduction purposes. In this paper, first we aim to increase the awareness about the darkness of cost models. Secondly, thanks to meta modeling techniques, we explicit the different dimensions of cost models. Persisting the cost models in a repository via a user-friendly interface is also described and stressed through several usage scenarios.

1 Introduction

Performance evaluation of database systems is crucial in many management tasks and plays a major role in database research community. Generally, this evaluation is done using cost models ($\mathcal{CM}$s), which evaluate the solutions quality without having to deploy them to real systems. $\mathcal{CM}$s are difficult to develop due to the complexity of *platform*, *database* and *query* parameters [10]. Moreover, with the evolutions of hardware and software technologies, upgrading and maintaining existed $\mathcal{CM}$s and are more challenging.

While database $\mathcal{CM}$s have become very complex the researchers demand to develop a better understanding of *dimensions* and the question arises consists of what parameters of the *dimensions* are worth to be captured in a $\mathcal{CM}$. We mean by *dimensions* in this paper, the components that impact a $\mathcal{CM}$ such as *database*, *storage device*, *operation algorithm* etc. Several works have focused on $\mathcal{CM}$s in various database architectures (e.g. [1,6,8,10,11,15,17]), the problem is that usually the more expressive the $\mathcal{CM}$ is, the most accurate is the performance analysis, but the more complex is the $\mathcal{CM}$ development.

© Springer International Publishing AG 2017
Y. Ouhammou et al. (Eds.): MEDI 2017, LNCS 10563, pp. 223–231, 2017.
DOI: 10.1007/978-3-319-66854-3_17

1.1 Problem Statement

Based on our literature review of the main conferences. There has been a lot of works that vastly explored the building and adapting database $\mathcal{CM}$s. $\mathcal{CM}$s providers enhance their $\mathcal{CM}$s due to various reasons, such as considering more parameters and also due to hardware and the new deployment platforms emerging.

$\mathcal{CM}$s can be founded in scientific papers but with a tedious task especially to understand how their developers react to changes in order to improve these $\mathcal{CM}$s. It lacks a regarding $\mathcal{CM}$ changes, comparison of the impact of parameters and workloads. That is it would be good to explicit all impact factors (*a.k.a dimensions*). By exploring the literature, we identify and categorize changes in $\mathcal{CM}$s. However, it is unclear how the $\mathcal{CM}$s evolve and how researchers react to the evolution. Since, previous works have not focused on facilitating and reusing this experience to be exploited by researchers. We conduct our study on $\mathcal{CM}$s domain from scientific papers and address the following three questions: **(i)** *Understanding:* what is the cost factors of database $\mathcal{CM}$s? **(ii)** *Modeling:* is it possible to describe relations between components of database? and if so, how should the cost functions be designed? **(iii)** *Manipulation:* how to provide an interface describing function templates CRUD pattern (Create, Retrieve-Update-Delete) for $\mathcal{CM}$s?

1.2 Paper Contribution

This research focuses on at the capitalization of $\mathcal{CM}$ domain in the light of the challenges previously mentioned and goes from implicit $\mathcal{CM}$'s information to explicit $\mathcal{CM}$ entities. Our proposal uses the paradigm of model driven engineering (MDE) to capture different dimensions of the $\mathcal{CM}$s. We provide a unified environment and can be seen as general guidelines to better explicit $\mathcal{CM}$s representation and reuse aspects. Specially we want to provide various aspects of framework. To the best of our knowledge, there is a lack of cost model development methodology covering all dimensions of databases and also a referential of cost models. This penalizes the reuse of existing models. First, we describe the approach associated with our framework. Then, we describe the main components of our architecture used in designing $\mathcal{CM}$s. Finally, we illustrate an example of utilization of the framework.

1.3 Paper Outline

Our paper is organized as follows. In Sect. 2, we introduce the $\mathcal{CM}$ advances and related works. Section 3 describes our approach. Section 4 presents some usage scenarios based supported by a developed prototype. Finally, Sect. 5 concludes the paper.

2 Cost Model Concerns

In order to make this research self-contained and straightforward, this section introduces some fundamental notions of cost models for database systems.

2.1 General Structure of $\mathcal{CM}$s

Since 1980s, a lot of cost models have been proposed [1,6,8,11,15]. Hereafter, we summarize some principles of cost models. Regularly, users manipulate different kinds of operations (such as: *join, scan, sort, etc.*), where each operation execution costs in terms of response time, size and/or energy. The cost of an operation considers the algorithm complexity, platform characteristics and various database features. Hence, a **cost model** is characterized by parameters related to the architecture layers of the database systems (for instance: operation system layer, data system layer, access method layer, buffer manager layer and storage system layer) [4]. In the rest of the paper, we use the term **context** to indicate parameters related to different layers.

Cost model is also characterized by a global **mathematical formula**, which depends on the context, such as: database size or length of instances (parameter of the data system layer), additional data structures such as indexes (parameter of access method layer), disk-layout (parameter of the storage system layer). The global math formula may be derived from a set of other basic math formulas, where every one represents a logical or a physical cost. While the **logical cost** is related to the specific properties of data processing independent of deployment layout (such as database size or workload on the database), the **physical cost** quantifies the impact of the hardware parameters such as memory size, block size [11]. Figure 1 present an example of a cost model drowned in the scientific paper discussions. Hence, to reuse an existing cost model for both producing and reproducing analysis result, generally one extracts manually the parameters and mathematical formulas from the paper.

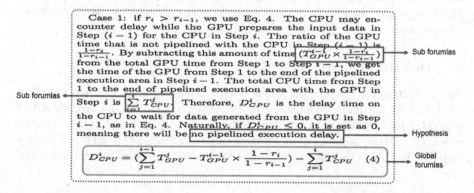

Fig. 1. Example of a cost model described in a scientific paper's discussion.

2.2 Related Works

The cost models ($\mathcal{CM}$s) in database systems are an active research topic. There has been a plethora of studies and initiatives by the research community (e.g. [1, 6,8,10,11,15,17]). While reviewing the literature of works considering the $\mathcal{CM}$s consumers are usually researchers, industrials and students for learning mode and teaching purpose. At first these $\mathcal{CM}$s were ad-hoc, with simple assumptions for evaluation costs and usually the more expressive $\mathcal{CM}$ is, the more complex is the evaluation. Traditionally, systems have relied an analytic-model based approach to estimate the physical I/O (usually disk). Manegold et al. propose a framework [11], which allows to automatically create cost functions of database operations for each layer of the memory hierarchy by combining the memory access patterns of database operations. The evolution of the database technology pushes the researchers to revisit the $\mathcal{CM}$s defined in the past by consider various aspects of a database system as database schema (relational, object-relational [8]), a cost model for query like SPARQL queries [12], storage model (column-stores, row-stores) [3], storage device (HDD and SSD) [2,17], the processing devices (CPU and GPU) (e.g. [5,7]). Also $\mathcal{CM}$s are usually driven by multiple performance metrics. Recently many works consider other metrics such as estimating the real cost of data storage [18] and energy consumption in cloud data centers [14]. The one of the main characteristics of $\mathcal{CM}$s are that they follow the evolution of database technologies [2,3]. To create a $\mathcal{CM}$ for a database architecture, people in the database community take into account several aspects (*database schema, optimization structures, queries, storage device, processing device, deployment architecture, storage model and NFR*). To the best of our knowledge, existing $\mathcal{CM}$s do not consider all layers. We claim that in order to develop a relevant $\mathcal{CM}$ all these layers have to be included.

3 Our Approach

In this section we will present steps that have been followed to get the framework. Those steps are (see Fig. 2): domain analysis, domain modeling, persistency and manipulation.

3.1 Domain Analysis

We conduct our study on cost models domain and address the first question (Sect. 1.1) by studying dimensions of the database Cost Model. We identified important impact factors that influence the database cost models: (1) Database-Schema (2) Database-Specific Parameters, (3) Workloads, (4) Hardware Parameters, (5) Database Operations, (6) Implementation Algorithms for an Operation.

3.2 Domain Modeling

In this step, we aim to answer the second question (see Sect. 1.1), we link *dimensions* whose dependencies are hierarchically modeled. The impact factors are grouped into *dimension*. This classification allows to get a well-structured overview of parameters since having a complete model of all dimensions is achievable. Actually our metamodel covers at least the most important areas that need to be considered. Moreover, users can then easily extend our parameters to additional needs. Types of dependencies considered in our framework are: *mandatory*, *optional*, *alternative*, *requires*, and *excludes* relationships. Figure 3 highlights the core elements of CM metamodel. We have chosen Ecore [16] (which is a UML-like metamodeling language) for modeling the proposed metamodel. Hereafter, we describe each component of our metamodel.

Meta-modeling the Cost Models. Figure 3 depicts the core elements of the metamodel, which its root element is `CostModel` class (i.e. the instantiating starts from this class). Every `CostModel` instance is composed of a metric (instance `Metric` class), a context (instance `Context` class) and a cost function (instance

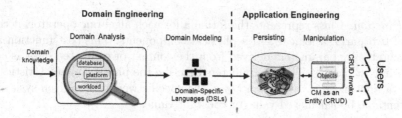

Fig. 2. Overview of our framework

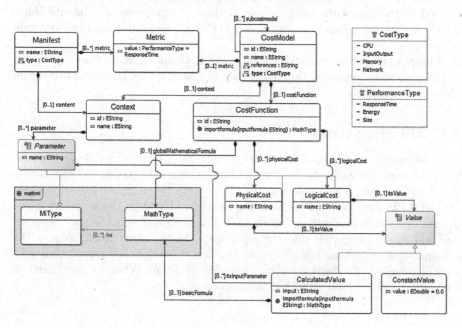

Fig. 3. Excerpt of CostModel metamodel. (Color figure online)

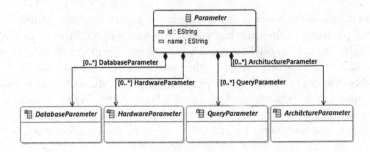

Fig. 4. Excerpt of $\mathcal{CM}$ metamodel: focus on context parameters

`CostFunction` class). It is also characterized by a name and references which indicated the scientific papers presenting the cost model. Every instance of the `CostModel` class has at least one cost type.

Cost Function. Class represents the formula for each algebraic operator, it consists of two parts: a logical and a physical components. This cost function are representable by parameters derived from the context or estimated data as cost weight in cost models. These parameters describe the physical characteristics or the data informations. In certain cases, the specific weight of a given system is representable by calculated value or constant value.

Dimension. With the given categorization, we argue that all parameters considered in the literature fall into one of these components of Context: *Hardware parameters*, *DB-Schema metamodel*, *Query parameters*, and *Architecture parameters*.

Figure 4 gives only an abstract view of the metamodel classes that correspond to the context parameters. Due to the lack of space, we are unable to present all metamodel elements.

3.3 API Manipulation

Our cost models and their dimensions are persisted by using model-based repository settings. Our objectif is to store cost models in a structured way o ease searching, uploading and downloading. To achieve this aim, we have developed an user API (Application Programming Interface) based on the proposed metamodel. The use of declarative interface offers an easy and effective way to search and add new cost models into the repository. On the other hand, it eases the manipulation of cost models files expressed in metamodel. The user can interact with all components via an interface (Add, Select, From, Where) ways is needed. The repository is based on CDO[1] infrastructure.

---

[1] http://www.eclipse.org/cdo.

4   Usage Scenarios

To stress our approach and to proof how it is useful and helpful, this section is devoted to present various usage scenarios of our framework. In parallel, technical implementations are highlighted. Figure 5 shows the architecture of our tool.

4.1   Scenario 1: A Design Tool for Instantiating and Visualization of Cost Models

We have developed a design tool allowing to create and visualize cost models conform to our design language. The design tool is based on Java EMF (Eclipse Modeling Framework) API and has been integrated as a plugin in Eclipse[2] which is an Integrated development Environment. Through the design tool, every cost model instance is saved as an XMI (XML Metadata Interchange [9]) file. We have developed a code generator which generates C-programs based on PostgreSQL API. The objective is to generate a machinable format of every cost model conforms to our metamodel.

At the end of the design, one can check the conformity of the cost model. For this, a set of structural rules have been injected in the meta-model. These rules are expressed as OCL (Object Constraint Language) [13] invariants.

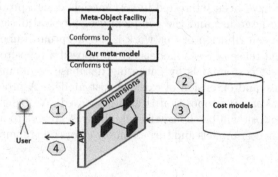

Fig. 5. Conceptual processes of our Prototype Implementation.

4.2   Scenario 2: A Catalog of Vocabulary and Concepts

The metamodel defines *dimension* and their parameters usually used as a catalog that developers of cost models should fulfill. Our framework has the main purpose of being used as a catalog of generic concepts for the cost model domain. It has been developed as an hierarchical taxonomy of vocabulary and concepts that can be utilized in development of database cost models. It relies on a semantic

---

[2] Eclipse Modeling Project. www.eclipse.org/modeling/.

vocabulary of categories and concepts that will play a key role in the database cost models. We provide a tool with a visual display format and a complete user documentation of the of each class or method in order to advise and assist the users during the construction of cost models.

4.3 Scenario 3: Searching Cost Models

This case corresponds to the scenario where a user looks for a cost model. The user can expresse its manifest. That means the user edits context. This letter can be translated to a set of accurate queries helping users to find the appropriate cost models that match the manifest.

4.4 Scenario 4: Interface for Analyzing Cost Models

Users can analyze their uploaded cost model by identifying used and unused parameters in their model. The parameters identified as unused can help users to improve the cost models. This analyze recommends the cost models stored in the repository and include the same context.

5 Conclusion

In this paper we have been interested in cost models design problem. This was motivated by the large use and the complexity of physical design applications cost models. The contribution of this work is a conceptual framework for more expressiveness and reuse of costs models. We proposed a repository enabling to persist and extract cost models by gathering database community efforts and facilitate the reuse and extension of existing cost models. A proof of feasibility and practicability of our proposition is also presented. We believe that such a persistence framework will be the key to enabling researchers to accelerate their process in building cost models and surpass many errors due to misunderstanding information.

References

1. Bausch, D., et al.: Making cost-based query optimization asymmetry-aware. In: DaMoN, pp. 24–32. ACM (2012)
2. Bellatreche, L., Bress, S., Kerkad, A., Boukorca, A., Salmi, C.: The generalized physical design problem in data warehousing environment: towards a generic cost model. In: 2013 36th International Convention on Information & Communication Technology Electronics & Microelectronics (MIPRO), pp. 1131–1137. IEEE (2013)
3. Bellatreche, L., Cheikh, S., Breß, S., Kerkad, A., Boukhorca, A., Boukhobza, J.: How to exploit the device diversity and database interaction to propose a generic cost model? In: Proceedings of the 17th International Database Engineering & Applications Symposium, pp. 142–147. ACM (2013)
4. Burns, T., et al.: Reference model for DBMS standardization. SIGMOD Rec. 15(1), 19–58 (1986)

5. Dayal, U., Kuno, H., Wiener, J.L., Wilkinson, K., Ganapathi, A., Krompass, S.: Managing operational business intelligence workloads. ACM SIGOPS Oper. Syst. Rev. **43**(1), 92–98 (2009)
6. Florescu, D., Kossmann, D.: Rethinking cost and performance of database systems. ACM Sigmod Rec. **38**(1), 43–48 (2009)
7. Fuentes-Fernández, L., Vallecillo-Moreno, A.: An introduction to UML profiles. In: UML and Model Engineering, vol. 2 (2004)
8. Gardarin, G. et al.: Calibrating the query optimizer cost model of IRO-DB, an object-oriented federated database system. In: VLDB, vol. 96, pp. 3–6 (1996)
9. O. M. Group. OMG Mof 2 XMI mapping specification. Version 2.4.1 (2011). http://www.omg.org/spec/XMI/2.4.1/. Accessed 06 March 17
10. Leis, V., et al.: How good are query optimizers, really? Proc. VLDB Endow. **9**(3), 204–215 (2015)
11. Manegold, S., Boncz, P., Kersten, M.L.: Generic database cost models for hierarchical memory systems. In: VLDB, pp. 191–202 (2002)
12. Obermeier, L.N.P., Nixon, L.: A cost model for querying distributed RDF-repositories with SPARQL. In: Proceedings of the Workshop on Advancing Reasoning on the Web: Scalability and Commonsense Tenerife, Spain (2008)
13. OMG. Object Constraint Language. OMG available specification. Version 2.0 (2006). www.omg.org/spec/OCL/2.0/. Accessed 06 Apr 16
14. Roukh, A., Bellatreche, L., Boukorca, A., Bouarar, S.: Eco-DMW: eco-design methodology for data warehouses. In: ACM DOLAP, pp. 1–10. ACM (2015)
15. Selinger, P.G., et al.: Access path selection in a relational database management system. In: ACM SIGMOD, pp. 23–34. ACM (1979)
16. Steinberg, D., Budinsky, F., et al.: EMF: eclipse modeling framework. In: Gamma, E., Nackman, L., Wiegand, J. (eds.) The Eclipse Series (2008)
17. Wu, W., Chi, Y., Zhu, S., et al.: Predicting query execution time: are optimizer cost models really unusable? In: ICDE, pp. 1081–1092. IEEE (2013)
18. Zhang, N., et al.: Towards cost-effective storage provisioning for DBMSS. Proc. VLDB Endow. **5**(4), 274–285 (2011)

Data Exploration and Exploitation

Exploiting User Feedbacks in Matrix Factorization for Recommender Systems

Haiyang Zhang[1(✉)], Nikola S. Nikolov[1,2], and Ivan Ganchev[1,3]

[1] Telecommunications Research Centre, University of Limerick, Limerick, Ireland
{Haiyang.Zhang,Nikola.Nikolov,Ivan.Ganchev}@ul.ie
[2] Department of Computer Science and Information Systems,
University of Limerick, Limerick, Ireland
[3] Department of Computer Systems, University of Plovdiv "Paisii Hilendarski",
Plovdiv, Bulgaria

Abstract. With the rapid growth of the Web, recommender systems have become essential tools to assist users to find high-quality personalized recommendations from massive information resources. Content-based filtering (CB) and collaborative filtering (CF) are the two most popular and widely used recommendation approaches. In this paper, we focus on ways of taking advantage of both approaches based only on user-item rating data. Motivated by the user profiling technique used in content-based recommendation, we propose to merge user profiles, learnt from the items viewed by the users, as a new latent variable in the latent factor model, which is one of the most popular CF-based approaches, thereby generating more accurate recommendation models. The performance of the proposed models is tested against several widely-deployed state-of-the-art recommendation methods. Experimental results, based on two popular datasets, confirm that better accuracy can be indeed achieved.

Keywords: Collaborative filtering · Recommender systems · Matrix factorization · User feedback

1 Introduction

With the rapid growth of the Web, people are inundated with massive information. Intelligent recommendation techniques have been widely used in online systems [1,2] and mobile applications [3,4] to assist users to find the information they're potentially interested in and, at the same time, help merchants to reach their valuable target users.

Collaborative filtering (CF) is one of the most popular recommendation approaches to build recommender systems, which make recommendations only based on user past behaviour [5]. The two primary approaches for CF are the neighbourhood methods, which recommend items based on the correlation between items or users, and latent factor models, which profile both users and

© Springer International Publishing AG 2017
Y. Ouhammou et al. (Eds.): MEDI 2017, LNCS 10563, pp. 235–247, 2017.
DOI: 10.1007/978-3-319-66854-3_18

items to the same latent factor space [6]. Most latent factor models used in recommender system are based on Matrix Factorization (MF). In the Netflix Prize competition, it has been experimentally demonstrated that MF models perform better than classic neighbourhood methods [5].

MF aims to learn a low-rank approximation to a rating matrix, where both users and items are characterized by vectors of latent features inferred from the rating matrix. Given a rating matrix R, by utilizing MF methods, users are represented by a set of latent features $U \in R^{m \times d}$ and items are represented by $V \in R^{n \times d}$ with: $R \approx UV^T$, where d is the number of latent features. Figure 1 illustrates how matrix factorization works.

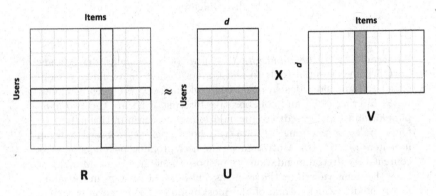

Fig. 1. Matrix factorization (MF)

The reason for MF favoured over other CF-based approaches is not only in its outstanding performance and simplicity but also in its ability to incorporate with additional information. Guo et al. [7] proposed to merge item neighbourhood with MF. Similarly, Zheng et al. [8] proposed a neighbourhood-integrated MF model using user k-nearest-neighbours. Social/trust networks have also been leveraged to regularize user features to improve the recommendation performance, as in RSTE [9] which diffuses user vectors with the interests of the user's trusted friends. SocialReg [10] leverages social network information as regularization terms in the MF objective function.

Content-based (CB) filtering is another widely deployed recommendation technique, which is based on the correlation between the representation of items and the representation of user profiles containing user preferences [11]. Therefore, user profiling is a very important stage for providing high-quality item recommendations to users in CB recommender systems. Most CB recommender systems build user profiles based on user past behaviours, which means that the user preferences are extracted from the information related to the items they liked in the past. However, in real recommendation scenarios, the only information available for analysis are the user-item ratings, which is one of the reasons why CF approaches are favoured over CB methods [12].

In this paper, taking advantage of both matrix factorization and user profiling techniques, two user feedback-based matrix factorization models, based only on user-item rating data, are proposed to improve the prediction accuracy of recommendations. Specifically, user profiles are utilized as an extended term for user feature vectors in MF. The experimental results presented further in the paper have shown that the proposed models outperform several widely used state-of-the-art recommendation approaches.

The rest of the paper is organized as follows. Section 1 introduces some related work for this study. Section 2 presents briefly several state-of-the-art matrix factorization methods. The proposed recommendation models are described in Sects. 3 and 4 presents their experimental evaluation. Finally, Sect. 5 concludes the paper and suggests future research directions.

2 Matrix Factorization: A Brief Review

Before introducing the proposed models, we first review the baseline and some state-of-the-art matrix factorization models.

2.1 Notation

In matrix factorization problem, given a rating matrix R which contains the ratings for n users to m items, the goal is to learn the low rank representations for both users and items. Notations which are utilized in the rest of this paper are listed in Table 1.

Table 1. Notations

Notation	Description
$r_{ui}, \tilde{r}_{ui}$	True rating and predicted rating for user u to item i
U, V	Low rank representations of users and items
BU, BI	User bias and item bias
$I(u)$	The set of items that user u interested in
α	Parameter to balance influence of two components
$regB$	The regularized term for the biased factor
$regU, regI$	The regularized terms for user factor and item factor

2.2 Standard Matrix Factorization

Matrix Factorization (MF) technique was first proposed for use in recommender systems in [13], named Regularized SVD. Given a rating matrix, the predicted score for user u to item i using Regularized SVD can be computed as:

$$\tilde{r}_{ui} = U_u V_i^T = \sum_{f=1}^{d} U_{u,f} V_{i,f}^T \tag{1}$$

where each row U_u in the low-rank matrix U is the feature vector representing user u, and V_i is the representation for item i.

For Regularized SVD, the model is learnt by fitting the observed ratings. The parameters in (1) are estimated by minimizing the regularized squared error on the set of observed ratings:

$$O = \sum_{(u,i)\in K} (r_{ui} - U_u V_i^T)^2 + \lambda(\|U_u\|^2 + \|V_i\|^2) \qquad (2)$$

where K is the set of the (u, i) pairs with rating observed, and $\lambda(\|U_u\|^2 + \|V_i\|^2)$ is the regularization term to avoid overfitting.

2.3 Biased Matrix Factorization

The standard MF doesn't consider user-and item bias information, which is an important factor to effect rating values [5]. For example, some users have overall higher rating behaviour and some items are more popular than others. Thus, the prediction formula involved with bias information is defined as:

$$\tilde{r}_{ui} = U_u V_i^T + \mu + BU_u + BI_i \qquad (3)$$

where μ is the overall mean rating, and parameters BU and BI represent the user bias and item bias, respectively. The lost function for Eq. (3) is as follows:

$$O = \sum_{(u,i)\in K} (r_{ui} - \tilde{r}_{ui})^2 + \lambda(\|U_u\|^2 + \|V_i\|^2 + BU_u^2 + BI_i^2) \qquad (4)$$

Since the bias-based method considers more features that contribute to the rating value, experimental results have shown its the better performance compared to the standard MF [5].

2.4 Neighbourhood-Based Matrix Factorization

MF methods are more effective at discovering the overall representation for both users and items, regardless of their strong relations with the set of their like-minded users or their closely rated items [6]. The neighbourhood methods solve the drawback of MF approaches, focusing on detecting the localized relationships, but fail to capture the global information. Methods considering both techniques have been proposed in the literature to achieve better recommendation performance. Guo et al. [7] propose a neighbourhood-based MF technique which integrates item neighborhood with MF, where the predicted score of user u of item i is defined as:

$$\tilde{r}_{ui} = \alpha U_u V_i^T + (1-\alpha) \sum_{j\in\tau(i)} w_{i,j} U_u V_j^T \qquad (5)$$

where $\tau(i)$ is the set of Top-K similar items to item i and $w_{i,j}$ is the similarity between Top-K item j and item i. The parameter α is used to balance the influence of the original item latent factor and its neighbour's latent factors.

Zheng et al. [8] proposed a similar recommendation model, but instead of considering similar items, they incorporated user neighbourhood into the MF model, with:

$$\tilde{r}_{ui} = \alpha U_u V_i^T + (1 - \alpha) \sum_{k \in \tau(u)} w_{i,j} U_k V_i^T \tag{6}$$

where $\tau(u)$ is the set of Top-K similar users for user u, and $w_{u,k}$ denotes the similarity between user u and Top-K user k.

2.5 SVD++ Model

SVD++ is a state-of-the-art recommendation model, considering both the explicit and implicit influence of user-item ratings [6], which is adopted as a key comparison method in [14]. The model is defined as:

$$\tilde{r}_{ui} = V_i^T (U_u + |I(u)|^{-\frac{1}{2}} \sum_{j \in I(u)} y_j) + \mu + BU_u + BI_i \tag{7}$$

where $I(u)$ is the set of items which user u showed implicit interest in and y_j represents the implicit influence for the unrated items by past rated items of user u. Thus, the users' feature vectors are extended with their implicit influence.

The objective function for minimization can be written similarly to (4). For each rated item r_{ui}, the paremeters are updated as [6]:

- $BU_u \leftarrow BU_u + \gamma(e_{ui} - regB \cdot BU_u)$
- $BI_i \leftarrow BI_i + \gamma(e_{ui} - regB \cdot BI_i)$
- $U_u \leftarrow U_u + \gamma(e_{ui}V_i - regU \cdot U_u)$
- $V_i \leftarrow V_i + \gamma(e_{ui}(U_u + |I(u)|^{-\frac{1}{2}} \sum_{j \in I(u)} y_j) - regI \cdot V_i)$
- $\forall j \in I(u)$
  $y_j \leftarrow y_j + \gamma(e_{ui} \cdot |I(u)|^{-\frac{1}{2}} \cdot V_i - regU \cdot y_j)$

where γ is the learning rate and $e_{ui} = r_{ui} - \tilde{r}_{ui}$. $regB$, $regU$, $regI$ are the regularized terms for the biased factor, user factor and item factor, respectively.

3 Matrix Factorization with User Feedbacks

The content-based (CB) filtering and the collaborative filtering (CF) are two primary recommendation approaches, which complement each other when dealing with the same problem but from different perspectives [7]. In CB filtering approach, user profiles are generated based on features related to the items that user consumed/viewed in the past. The predicted score is computed by matching the user profiles and item profiles. In CF methods, both users and items are represented by latent features derived from the rating matrix. By taking into consideration of both approaches, one can observe that the users can be represented with not only lantent features but also with their viewed/consumed items. In this paper, we propose a weighted combination of the mentioned user representations based on the MF model, with leveraging only the user-item rating matrix. Two unified recommendation models, respectively based on implicit feedback and explicit feedback, are introduced in this section.

Both proposed models are based on SVD++ [6], which, to the best of our knowledge, achieves the most accurate result among rating-based algorithms that merely based on rating data. Instead of importing a new low rank matrix to denote the influence of items rated by users in the past on the unrated items in SVD++, we directly leverage the low rank representation of items to model the influence of rated items in our proposed models, which makes this component more meaningful, and reduces the computational complexity in model training at the same time.

3.1 Rating Model with Implicit Feedback

As we mentioned above, users' preferences can be reflected by the items they viewed/consumed in the past. Based on this intuition, our first unified recommendation model is proposed to diffuse the user factor with the set of feature vectors of user viewed/consumed items. The predicted score in this model is given as:

$$\tilde{r}_{ui} = V_i^T(\alpha U_u + (1 - \alpha)|I(u)|^{-c} \sum_{j \in I(u)} V_j) + \mu + BU_u + BI_i \qquad (8)$$

where α is a parameter to balance the influence of the global user latent factor and its representation constructed by user's interested items and $I(u)$ denotes the set of items the user was interested in the past. c is a user specified parameter between 0 and 1. We denote this model as implicit-SVD.

The model is trained using least square errors, by minimizing the following objective function:

$$O = \sum_{(u,i) \in K} (r_{ui} - \tilde{r}_{ui})^2 + \lambda(\|U_u\|^2 + \|V_i\|^2 + BU_u^2 + BI_i^2) \qquad (9)$$

We employed the stochastic gradient descent (SGD) approach [15] to estimate the parameters in the above equation.

In the process of learning, in order to reduce the time complexity, we don't update the set of items in $I(u)$ for each rating. Details of the model learning algorithm are presented in Algorithm 1.

3.2 Rating Model with Explicit Feedback

The assumption behind the diffused user latent representation proposed in this paper is that every user's taste is not only relevant to its global information which is generated by the standard MF, but also relevant to the average representation of all items that the user was interested in before. The model, presented in Sect. 3.1 supposes that all rated items are contributed equally to the user extension term, which is not always the case. Among all rated items, items with high

---

Algorithm 1. Implicit Feedback-based Recommendation Model Learning

---

Input : R (Rating Matrix), $regB, regU, regI, \alpha, \gamma$ (learning rate), d, c,
$\quad\quad\quad\ iter \leftarrow 0$
Output: rating predictions $\tilde{r}_{ui}$
1 Initialize low-rank matrix for users (U) and items (V), and Bias factor for users
$\quad\ (BU)$ and items (BI)
2 **while** *iter < maxIter or error on validation set decrease* **do**
3 $\quad$ **while** $(u, i) \in K$ **do**
4 $\quad\quad$ $e_{ui} \leftarrow r_{ui} - \tilde{r}_{ui}$
5 $\quad\quad$ $BU_u \leftarrow BU_u + \gamma(e_{ui} - regB \cdot BU_u)$
6 $\quad\quad$ $BI_i \leftarrow BI_i + \gamma(e_{ui} - regB \cdot BI_i)$
7 $\quad\quad$ $U_u \leftarrow U_u + \gamma(e_{ui}V_i - regU \cdot U_u)$
8 $\quad\quad$ $V_i \leftarrow V_i + \gamma(e_{ui}(\alpha U_u + (1 - \alpha)|I(u)|^{-c}\sum_{j \in I(u)} V_j) - regI \cdot V_i)$
9 $\quad$ **end**
10 $\quad$ $iter \leftarrow iter + 1$
11 **end**
12 $\tilde{r}_{ui} \leftarrow V_i^T(\alpha U_u + (1 - \alpha)|I(u)|^{-c}\sum_{j \in I(u)} V_j) + \mu + BU_u + BI_i$

---

rating scores should have higher importance. In this section, a more realistic model is proposed that treats all rated items differently based on their ratings. The predict model is represented as:

$$\tilde{r}_{ui} = V_i^T(\alpha U_u + (1 - \alpha)\frac{\sum_{j \in I(u)} r_{uj}V_j}{\sum_{j \in I(u)} r_{uj}}) + \mu + BU_u + BI_i \tag{10}$$

We denote this model as explicit-SVD. The objective function for this model is represented similarly to (9). Details of the model learning are presented in Algorithm 2.

3.3 Complexity Analysis

Compared with the SVD++ model, the two models proposed above utilize a simpler user factor, avoiding the use of an additional matrix indicating the implicit feedback influence in SVD++, which obviously improves the efficiency of the model learning process. The training time is primary taken by the computation of the objective function and its gradient respect with different features. The computational complexity for the objective function O is $O(td|R|)$, where t and d denote the number of iterations and the dimensionality of the low-rank matrixes and $|R|$ is the number of observed ratings. The costs of computing the gradients for BU, BI, U and V are $O(t|R|), O(t|R|), O(td|R|)$ and $O(td|R|)$, respectively. Thus, the complexity of both proposed training algorithms is $O(td|R|)$. Table 2 shows a comparison of computational complexity of the offline training and online recommendation stages for selected recommendation algorithms where k is the average number of rated items by each user.

Algorithm 2. Explicit Feedback-based Recommendation Model Learning

---

   Input : R (Rating Matrix), $regB, regU, regI, \alpha, \gamma$ (*learning rate*), d
        $iter \leftarrow 0$
   Output: rating predictions $\tilde{r}_{ui}$
1 Initialize low-rank matrix for users (U) and items (V), and Bias factor for users
    (BU) and items (BI)
2 while $iter < maxIter$ or error on validation set decrease **do**
3   **while** $(u, i) \in K$ **do**
4 $e_{ui} = r_{ui} - \tilde{r}_{ui}$
5 $BU_u \leftarrow BU_u + \gamma(e_{ui} - regB \cdot BU_u)$
6 $BI_i \leftarrow BI_i + \gamma(e_{ui} - regB \cdot BI_i)$
7 $U_u \leftarrow U_u + \gamma(e_{ui}V_i - regU \cdot U_u)$
8 $V_i \leftarrow V_i + \gamma(e_{ui}(\alpha U_u + (1 - \alpha)\frac{\sum_{j \in I(u)} r_{uj} V_j}{\sum_{j \in I(u)} r_{uj}}) - regI \cdot V_i)$
9   **end**
10 $iter \leftarrow iter + 1$
11 end
12 $\tilde{r}_{ui} = V_i^T(\alpha U_u + (1 - \alpha)\frac{\sum_{j \in I(u)} r_{uj} V_j}{\sum_{j \in I(u)} r_{uj}}) + \mu + BU_u + BI_i$

Table 2. Computational complexity on selected recommendation algorithms comparison

Algorithms	Offline	Online
SVD++	$O(td|R|k)$	$O(kd)$
Implicit-SVD	$O(td|R|)$	$O(kd)$
Explicit-SVD	$O(td|R|)$	$O(kd)$

4 Experimets

4.1 Experiment Setup

To examine the effectiveness of the proposed recommendation models, two datasets were chosen for empirical studies. The first one is the FilmTrust dataset [16], which contains 35497 ratings provided by 1508 unique users over 2071 movies. Each movie is rated using a discrete scale from 0.5 to 4.0, with a step of 0.5. The second dataset used is the popular Movielens-100k dataset[1], which consists of 100,000 ratings (on a scale from 1 to 5) provided by 943 users on 1682 movies.

For both datasets, we use the K-fold cross validation technique [17] for learning and testing, with K = 5. Specifically, in each iteration, we randomly split the dataset into 5 folds, and 4 folds are used as a training set and the remaining one as a test set. Five iterations have been conducted in order make sure every fold was tested.

---

[1] http://grouplens.org/datasets/movielens/100k/.

4.2 Evaluation Metrics and Comparative Approaches

We adopt two widely used metrics, the mean absolute error (MAE) [15] and the root mean square error (RMSE) [16], to evaluate the predictive accuracy of our proposed methods in comparison with several widely-deployed state-of-the-art recommendation approaches.

Given a set of predictions $\{p_1, p_1, \ldots p_N\}$, and their corresponding real ratings $\{r_1, r_1, \ldots r_N\}$, the MAE is calculated as follows:

$$MAE = \frac{1}{N} \sum_{i=1}^{N} |r_i - p_i| \tag{11}$$

where N denotes the number of tested ratings. RMSE is based on the accuracy and measures the distance between predicted scores and actual scores, but puts more emphasis on large errors compared with MAE. The RMSE is defined as:

$$RMSE = \sqrt{\frac{1}{N} \sum_{i=1}^{N} (r_i - p_i)^2} \tag{12}$$

From the two definitions above, it is clear that the smaller MAE/RMSE value means a better performance of the corresponding method.

To demonstrate the effectiveness of the proposed models, we evaluated and compared them with the following recommendation approaches:

- UserMean: Making predictions for the active user by his/her average ratings.
- ItemMean: Predicting the missing ratings for items by employing the mean value of every item directly.
- Non-negative MF (NMF): Restricting the latent features with non-negative values in the parameter updating process [20].
- RegSVD: The basic MF technique aiming to learn a low-rank approximation to the original rating matrix with point-wise regression optimization approach [18].
- BiasedMF: Extending the baseline MF approach by adding user- and item biases [5].
- SVD++: Considering both explicit and implicit user influence of ratings to make predictions [6].

4.3 Experimental Result

Validation of Parameter Influence. The parameter α controls the percentage of influence for the user feature vectors by the users themselves and their viewed/consumed items. We explore the impact of α for the proposed models by adjusting its value from 0 to 1. When $\alpha = 1$, it indicates that the user feature vectors are only influence by users themselves, which is equal to BiasedMF [5]. When $\alpha = 0$, it means that the user feature vectors are only influenced by user viewed/consumed items. Figure 2 shows the impact (MAE and RMSE value) of parameter α on the example of using the FilmTrust dataset. We can see that both proposed models achieve optimal MAE values at $\alpha = 0.6$. For RMSE, implicit-SVD gets the best RMSE value at $\alpha = 0.6$, where explicit-SVD at $\alpha = 0.7$. This indicates that the consideration of user's past interest in items for the user feature vector is a valuable approach for the proposed models. Generally, for both MAE and RMSE, explicit-SVD performs better than implicit-SVD when $\alpha < 0.6$, and with α increasing, implicit-SVD exhibits better performance.

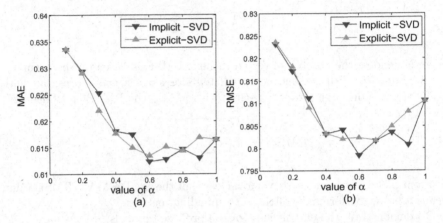

Fig. 2. The impact of parameter (FilmTrust dataset) on: (a) MAE (b) RMSE

Performance Comparison with Other Models. The experimental results for the proposed recommendation models and several popular recommendation models, based only on user-item ratings, are presented in Table 3. The learning rate equals 0.05 and α equals 0.6 for both proposed models on both datasets. The following points could be observed.

Table 3. Performance comparison using the FilmTrust and Movielens datasets. ($iter = 100$, $lrate = 0.05$, $regB = regU = regI = 0.1$, $c = 0.8$).

Film-Trust	Metrics	User-Mean	Item-Mean	NMF	Reg-SVD	Biased MF	SVD++	Implicit-SVD	Explicit-SVD
$d = 5$	MAE	0.6363	0.7275	0.6927	0.6665	0.6189	0.6162	**0.6156**	0.6162
	RMSE	0.8243	0.9291	0.9355	0.8661	0.8097	0.8033	**0.8025**	0.8038
$d = 10$	MAE	0.6363	0.7275	0.7077	0.6515	0.6165	0.6161	**0.6127**	0.6134
	RMSE	0.8243	0.9291	0.9523	0.8412	0.8106	0.8060	**0.8017**	0.8023
Movie-lens	Metrics	User-Mean	Item-Mean	NMF	Reg-SVD	Biased MF	SVD++	Implicit-SVD	Explicit-SVD
$d = 5$	MAE	0.8355	0.8172	0.7622	0.7289	0.7195	0.7193	0.7188	**0.7177**
	RMSE	1.0423	1.0243	0.9815	0.9206	0.9136	0.9141	**0.9048**	0.9101
$d = 10$	MAE	0.8355	0.8172	0.7903	0.7288	0.7207	0.7194	0.7194	**0.7177**
	RMSE	1.0423	1.0243	1.0217	0.9206	0.9159	0.9142	**0.9031**	0.9080

First, the recommendation models which consider user and item biases (BiasedMF, SVD++, Implicit -SVD, Explicit-SVD) get overall outstanding better performance than other models.

Second, SVD++ performs the best among all existing methods, which make the recommenddations merely based on rating matrix.

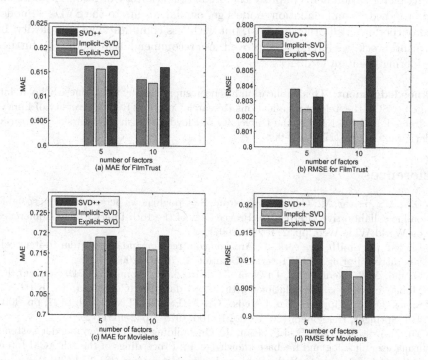

Fig. 3. Recommendation accuracy comparison between SVD++ and proposed methods

Third, the proposed recommendation models get equal or better (in majority of cases) performance than SVD++ in terms of both MAE and RMSE on both datasets (Fig. 3).

Fourth, among the two proposed recommendation models, implicit-SVD is overall more accate than explicit-SVD. Explicit-SVD only performs slightly better than or equal to implicit-SVD on the Movielens dataset on MAE metric. This indicates that the more accurate presentation of user features (explicit-based model) does not always result in more accurate recommendations/predictions than the average-based presentation of user features (implicit-based model).

5   Conclusion

Due to user privacy issue, in most cases, the only available information for analysis in recommender system is the user-item rating data. This paper has proposed a novel user feedback-based matrix factorization approach, which considers both the rating matrix from a global perspective and the user feedbacks from a localized persperctive. Two recommendation models, based respectively on user implicit feedback and explicit feedback have been proposed. According to the experimental results and analysis, the consideration of user feedbacks in the matrix factorization helps improve the prediction accuracy of recommendations. The proposed recommendation models get similar results to the SVD++ model (and outperforms all other models), but with less computational complexity. In the future work, we intend to improve these recommendation models by further considering the item feedbacks.

Acknowledgement. This publication has been supported by the Chinese Scholarship Council (CSC), the Telecommunications Research Centre (TRC), University of Limerick, Ireland, and the NPD of the University of Plovdiv "Paisii Hilendarski", Bulgaria, under Grant No. ФП17-ФМИ-008.

References

1. Das, A.S., Datar, M., Garg, A., Rajaram, S.: Google news personalization: scalable online collaborative filtering. In: Proceedings of the 16th International Conference on World Wide Web, pp. 271–280 (2007)
2. Linden, G., Smith, B., York, J.: Amazon.com recommendations: item-to-item collaborative filtering. IEEE Internet Comput. **7**, 76–80 (2003)
3. Ostuni, V.C., Gentile, G., Di Noia, T., Mirizzi, R., Romito, D., Di Sciascio, E.: Mobile movie recommendations with linked data. In: Cuzzocrea, A., Kittl, C., Simos, D.E., Weippl, E., Xu, L. (eds.) CD-ARES 2013. LNCS, vol. 8127, pp. 400–415. Springer, Heidelberg (2013). doi:10.1007/978-3-642-40511-2_29
4. Yu, X., Ma, H., Hsu, B.-J.P., Han, J.: On building entity recommender systems using user click log and freebase knowledge. In: Proceedings of the 7th ACM International Conference on Web search and Data Mining, pp. 263–272 (2014)
5. Koren, Y., Bell, R., Volinsky, C.: Matrix factorization techniques for recommender systems. Computer **42** (2009)
6. Koren, Y.: Factorization meets the neighborhood: a multifaceted collaborative filtering model. In: Proceedings of the 14th ACM SIGKDD International Conference on Knowledge Discovery and Data Mining, pp. 426–434 (2008)
7. Guo, M.-J., Sun, J.-G., Meng, X.-F.: A neighborhood-based matrix factorization technique for recommendation. Ann. Data Sci. **2**, 301–316 (2015)
8. Zheng, Z., Ma, H., Lyu, M.R., King, I.: Collaborative web service QoS prediction via neighborhood integrated matrix factorization. IEEE Trans. Serv. Comput. **6**, 289–299 (2013)
9. Ma, H., King, I., Lyu, M.R.: Learning to recommend with explicit and implicit social relations. ACM Trans. Intell. Syst. Technol. (TIST) **2**, 29 (2011)
10. Ma, H., Zhou, D., Liu, C., Lyu, M.R., King, I.: Recommender systems with social regularization. In: Proceedings of the Fourth ACM International Conference on Web Search and Data Mining, pp. 287–296 (2011)
11. Lops, P., De Gemmis, M., Semeraro, G.: Content-based recommender systems: state of the art and trends. In: Ricci, F., Rokach, L., Shapira, B., Kantor, P. (eds.) Recommender Systems Handbook, pp. 73–105. Springer, Cham (2011). doi:10. 1007/978-0-387-85820-3_3

12. Ronen, R., Koenigstein, N., Ziklik, E., Nice, N.: Selecting content-based features for collaborative filtering recommenders. In: Proceedings of the 7th ACM Conference on Recommender Systems, pp. 407–410 (2013)
13. Funk, S.: Try This At Home. http://sifter.org/simon/journal/20061211.html
14. Guo, G., Zhang, J., Yorke-Smith, N.: A novel recommendation model regularized with user trust and item ratings. IEEE Trans. Knowl. Data Eng. 28, 1607–1620 (2016)
15. Zinkevich, M., Weimer, M., Smola, A.J., Li, L.: Parallelized Stochastic Gradient Descent. In: NIPS, p. 4 (2010)
16. Golbeck, J.: FilmTrust: movie recommendations from semantic web-based social networks. In: Consumer Communications and Networking Conference, vol. 2, pp. 1314–1315 (2006)
17. Kohavi, R.: A study of cross-validation and bootstrap for accuracy estimation and model selection. In: International Joint Conference on Artificial Intelligence, vol. 14, pp. 1137–1145 (1995)
18. Herlocker, J.L., Konstan, J.A., Terveen, L.G., Riedl, J.T.: Evaluating collaborative filtering recommender systems. ACM Trans. Inf. Syst. (TOIS) 22, 5–53 (2004)
19. Chai, T., Draxler, R.R.: Root mean square error (RMSE) or mean absolute error (MAE)?–arguments against avoiding RMSE in the literature. Geoscientific Model Dev. 7, 1247–1250 (2014)
20. Lee, D.D., Seung, H.S.: Algorithms for non-negative matrix factorization. In: Advances in Neural Information Processing Systems, pp. 556–562 (2001)
21. Paterek, A.: Improving regularized singular value decomposition for collaborative filtering. In: Proceedings of KDD Cup and Workshop, pp. 5–8 (2007)

A Feature Selection Method Based on Feature Correlation Networks

Miloš Savić[1]([✉]), Vladimir Kurbalija[1], Mirjana Ivanović[1], and Zoran Bosnić[2]

[1] Department of Mathematics and Informatics, Faculty of Sciences,
University of Novi Sad, Novi Sad, Serbia
`{svc,kurba,mira}@dmi.uns.ac.rs`
[2] Faculty of Computer and Information Science, Univeristy of Ljubljana,
Ljubljana, Slovenia
`zoran.bosnic@fri.uni-lj.si`

Abstract. Feature selection is an important data preprocessing step in data mining and machine learning tasks, especially in the case of high dimensional data. In this paper we present a novel feature selection method based on complex weighted networks describing the strongest correlations among features. The method relies on community detection techniques to identify cohesive groups of features. A subset of features exhibiting a strong association with the class feature is selected from each identified community of features taking into account the size of and connections within the community. The proposed method is evaluated on a high dimensional dataset containing signaling protein features related to the diagnosis of Alzheimer's disease. We compared the performance of seven widely used classifiers that were trained without feature selection, with correlation-based feature selection by a state-of-the-art method provided by the WEKA tool, and with feature selection by four variants of our method determined by four different community detection techniques. The results of the evaluation indicate that our method improves the classification accuracy of several classification models while drastically reducing the dimensionality of the dataset. Additionally, one variant of our method outperforms the correlation-based feature selection method implemented in WEKA.

Keywords: Feature selection · Feature correlation networks · Community detection · Alzheimer's disease

1 Introduction

The feature selection problem has been studied by the data mining and machine learning researchers for many years. The main aim of feature selection is to reduce the dimensionality of data such that the most significant aspects of the data are represented by selected features. Consequently, feature selection has become an important data preprocessing step in data mining and machine learning tasks due to the rise of high dimensional data in many application domains.

© Springer International Publishing AG 2017
Y. Ouhammou et al. (Eds.): MEDI 2017, LNCS 10563, pp. 248–261, 2017.
DOI: 10.1007/978-3-319-66854-3_19

Feature selection usually leads to better machine learning models in terms of prediction accuracy, lower training time and model comprehensibility [29]. The two most dominant types of feature selection approaches are filter and wrapper methods [9, 15]. Wrapper methods rely on performance of some prespecified classifier to evaluate the quality of selected features. In contrast to wrapper methods, filter methods are independent of learning algorithms. Those methods usually rely on some efficiently computable measure for scoring features considering their redundancy, dependency and discriminative power.

In this paper we present a novel graph-based approach to feature selection. Our feature selection approach belongs to the class of filter-based methods. The main idea of the proposed approach is to select relevant features considering community structure of *feature correlation networks*. A feature correlation network is a weighted graph where nodes correspond to features and links represent their strongest correlations. Feature correlation networks used in our feature selection method are conceptually similar to weighted correlation networks used in the analysis of genomic datasets [11] with one important difference: a class variable (a special feature denoting example classes) is not included as a node in the feature correlation network, but to each node in the feature correlation network is associated a number which specifies the strength of association between the corresponding feature and the class variable.

A *community* (cluster, module or cohesive group) within a weighted network is a subset of nodes such that the weight of links among them is significantly higher than with the rest of the network [17]. We say that a network has a community structure if the set of nodes can be partitioned into communities. The existence of communities is a typical feature of complex networks in various domains [2, 16]. Various community detection techniques enable automatic identification of communities in complex networks [7]. Uncovering communities helps to understand the structure of complex networks on a higher level of abstraction by constructing and analyzing their coarse-grained descriptions (networks of communities). Our approach to feature selection relies on community detection techniques to identify communities of features such that correlations within a community are stronger than correlations between features belonging to different communities. Then, one or more features strongly associated to the class variable is selected to represent each of identified communities taking into account the number of nodes and connections within communities.

The paper is structured as follows. Related work is presented in Sect. 2. The proposed method for feature selection is described in Sect. 3. The evaluation of the method is given in Sect. 4. The last section concludes the paper and gives directions for possible future work.

2   Related Work

Feature selection is a common data mining preprocessing step, which aims at reducing the dimensionality of the original dataset. Adequate selection of features has numerous advantages [24] like: simplification of learning models, improving the performance of algorithms, data reduction (avoidance of curse of dimensionality), improved generalization by reducing overfitting etc.

Wrapper-based feature selection methods estimate usefulness of features using the selected learning algorithm. These methods usually give better results than filter methods since they are adapting their result to a chosen learning algorithm. However, since a learning algorithm is employed to evaluate each subset of features, wrapper methods are very time consuming and almost unusable for high dimensional data. Furthermore, since the feature selection process is tightly interconnected with a learning algorithm, wrappers are less general than filters and have the increased risk of overfitting. On the other hand, filter methods are independent of learning algorithm. They are based only on general features like the correlation with the variable to predict. These methods are generally many times faster than wrappers and robust to overfitting [10]. Recently, some embedded methods are introduced [14] which try combine the positive characteristics of both previous methods.

Relying on the characteristics of data, filter models evaluate features without utilizing classification algorithms. Usually, a filter algorithm has two steps: it ranks features based on certain criteria and it selects the features with highest rankings [6]. Considering the first step, a number of performance criteria have been proposed for filter-based feature selection. Correlation based Feature Selection (CFS) is a simple filter algorithm that ranks features according to a feature-class correlation [10]. The fast correlated-based filter (FCBF) method [29] is based on symmetrical uncertainty, which is defined as the ratio between the information gain and the entropy of two features. The INTERACT algorithm [31] uses the same goodness measure as FCBF filter, but it also includes the consistency contribution as an indicator about how significantly the elimination of particular feature will affect accuracy. The original RELIEF [12] and extended ReliefF [22] algorithms estimate the quality of attributes according to how well their values distinguish between instances that are near to each other but belonging to different classes.

Recently, several approaches proposed feature clustering in order to avoid selection of redundant features [3,13,26]. The authors in [25] proposed Fast clustering-bAsed feature Selection algoriThm (FAST). Here, the features are divided into clusters by using graph-theoretic clustering methods and the final subset of features is selected by choosing the most representative feature that is strongly related to target classes from each cluster. Similarly, the approach in [30] proposed hyper-graph clustering to extract maximally coherent feature groups from a set of objects. Furthermore, this approach neglects the assumption that the optimal feature subset is formed by features that only exhibit pairwise interactions. Instead of that, they are using multidimensional interaction information which includes third or higher order dependencies feature combinations in final selection.

Compared to existing graph-based and clustering-based feature selection methods, our approach leans on community detection techniques to cluster graphs that describe the strongest correlations among features. Additionally, the approach takes into account the size of identified communities. In contrast to traditional graph partitioning and data clustering techniques, a majority of community detection techniques are not computationally demanding and they do not require to specify the number of clusters in advance [7].

3 FSFCN: Feature Selection Based on Feature Correlation Networks

The method for feature selection proposed in this paper, denoted by FSFCN, is based on the notion of feature correlation networks. A feature correlation network describes correlations between features in a dataset that are equal or higher than a specified threshold. To formally define feature correlation networks, we will assume that a dataset is composed of data instances having numeric features and a categorical class variable. The below stated definition of feature correlation networks can be adapted in a straightforward manner for other types of datasets (categorical features, a mix of categorical and numeric features, continuous target variable) by taking appropriate correlation measures.

Definition 1 (Feature Correlation Network). Let D be a dataset composed of data instances described by k real-valued features $f_1, f_2, \ldots, f_k \in \mathbb{R}$ and a categorical class variable c. Let $C_f : \mathbb{R} \times \mathbb{R} \rightarrow [-1, 1]$ denote a correlation measure applicable to features (e.g. the Pearson or Spearman correlation coefficient) and let C_c be a correlation measure applicable to a feature and the class variable (e.g. the mutual information, the Goodman-Kruskal index, etc.). The feature correlation network corresponding to D is an undirected, weighted, attributed graph $G = (V, E)$ with the following properties:

- The set of **nodes** V corresponds to the set of features ($f_i \in V$ for each i in $[1 .. k]$).
- Two features f_i and f_j, $i \neq j$, are connected by an **edge** $e_{i,j}$ in G, $e_{i,j} \in E$, if $|C_f(f_i, f_j)| \geq T$, where T is previously given threshold indicating a significant correlation between features. The weight of $e_{i,j}$ is equal to $|C_f(f_i, f_j)|$.
- Each node in the network has a real-valued **attribute** reflecting its association with the class variable which is measured by C_c.

The features in D can be ranked according to the C_c measure and highly ranked features can be considered as the most relevant for training a classifier.

Definition 2 (Subset of Relevant Features). A subset F_r of the set of features F is called *relevant* if $(\forall f \in F_r) \, C_c(f) \geq R$ where R denotes a threshold indicating a significant association between a feature and the class variable.

Definition 3 (Pruned Feature Correlation Network). A pruned feature correlation network is a feature correlation network constructed from a subset of relevant features.

Our implementation of the FSFCN method for datasets with real-valued features and categorical class variables uses pruned feature correlation networks which are constructed without explicitly stating the threshold T. This means that the algorithm for constructing pruned correlation networks has only one parameter R separating relevant from irrelevant features. Additionally, the algorithm uses the Spearman correlation coefficient to determine correlations among relevant features (the C_f measure), while correlations between relevant features and the class variable are quantified by their mutual information (the C_c measure). The mutual information between a real-valued feature f and the categorical class variable c, denoted by $I(f, c)$, can be approximated by

$$I(f, c) \approx \sum_{y \in c} \sum_{x \in f'} p(x, y) \log \left(\frac{p(x, y)}{p(x)p(y)} \right),$$

where f' is the set of discrete values obtained by a discretization of f, $p(x, y)$ is the joint probability distribution function of f' and c, and $p(x)$ and $p(y)$ are the marginal probability distribution functions of f' and c, respectively. $I(f, c)$ equal to 0 means that f and c are totally unrelated. A larger value of $I(f, c)$ implies a stronger association between f and c.

The algorithm for constructing pruned correlation network consists of the following steps (see Algorithm 1):

1. The subset of relevant features F_r is determined using the mutual information measure. Then, the nodes of the network are created such that each node corresponds to one feature from F_r.
2. For each pair of relevant features f_i and f_j, the algorithm forms a list L, where elements are tuples in the form (f_i, f_j, S_{ij}), where S_{ij} denotes the value of the Spearman correlation coefficient between features f_i and f_j.
3. L is sorted by the third component (S_{ij}) in decreasing order, i.e. the first element of the sorted list is the pair of features exhibiting the highest correlation, while the last element is the pair of features with the lowest correlation.
4. In the last step, the algorithm forms the links of the network by iterating through the sorted list L beginning from the first element. Let $e_k = (f_i, f_j, S_{ij})$ denotes the element processed in the k-th iteration. The algorithm forms a link l_{ij} connecting f_i and f_j with weight S_{ij}. If the addition of l_{ij} results in a connected graph (i.e., a graph that has exactly one connected component or, equivalently, a graph in which there is path between each pair of nodes) then the algorithm stops, otherwise it goes to the next element in the sorted list and repeats the same procedure. In other words, the algorithm iteratively builds the network by connecting features having the highest correlation until the network becomes a connected graph. Consequently, the weight of the last added link determines the value of the threshold T.

The basic idea of the FSFCN method is to cluster a pruned feature correlation network in order to obtain cohesive groups of relevant features such that correlations between features within a group are stronger than correlations between

---

Algorithm 1. Construction of pruned feature correlation networks

---

input : D, R

D – a dataset of instances with real-valued features $F = \{f_1, f_2, \ldots, f_k\}$ and a categorical class variable c

R – the threshold separating relevant from irrelevant features

output: $G = (V, E)$ – the pruned feature correlation network of D

// determine relevant features and form nodes in G
$F_r :=$ empty set of relevant features
foreach $f \in F$ **do**
    $m :=$ the value of the mutual information of f and c
    if $m \geq R$ **then**
       | $F_r := F_r \cup \{f\}$
    end
end
$V := F_r$

// compute the Spearman correlation for each pair of relevant features
$L :=$ empty list of tuples (f_i, f_j, S_{ij})
foreach $(f_i, f_j) \in F_r \times F_r, i \neq j$ **do**
    $s :=$ the value of the Spearman correlation for f_i and f_j
    $L := L + (f_i, f_j, s)$
end
$L :=$ sort L in non-increasing order of the Spearman correlation

// form links
$i := 1, cont := \top$
while $cont$ **do**
    $s :=$ the first component of $L[i]$
    $d :=$ the second component of $L[i]$
    $E := E \cup \{\{s, d\}\}$
    $i := i + 1$
    $cont := G$ is not a connected graph
end

---

features belonging to different groups. The FSFCN method leans on community detection techniques to identify clusters in feature correlation networks. The development of community detection techniques started with Newman and Girvan [18] who introduced a measure called modularity to estimate the quality of a partition of a network into communities. The main idea behind the modularity measure is that a subgraph can be considered a community if the actual number of links connecting nodes within the subgraph is significantly higher than the expected number of links with respect to some null random graph model. In the case of weighted networks, modularity accumulates differences between the total weight of links within a community and the mathematical expectation of the previous quantity with respect to a random network having the same degree and link weight distribution [17].

Definition 4 (Modularity). For weighted networks modularity Q is defined as

$$Q = \sum_{c=1}^{n_c} \left[\frac{W_c}{W} - \left(\frac{S_c}{2W} \right)^2 \right],$$

where n_c is the number of communities in the network, W_c is the sum of weights of intra-community links in c, S_c is the total weight of links incident to nodes in c, and W is the total weight of links in the network.

Four widely used community detection algorithms provided by the iGraph library [5] are employed to detect non-overlapping communities in feature correlation networks:

1. The Greedy Modularity Optimization (GMO) algorithm [4]. This algorithm relies on a greedy hierarchical agglomeration strategy to maximize modularity. The algorithm starts with the partitioning in which each node is assigned to a singleton cluster. In each iteration of the algorithm, the variation of modularity obtained by merging any two communities is computed. The merge operation that maximally increases (or minimally decreases) modularity is chosen and the merge of corresponding clusters is performed.
2. The Louvain algorithm [1]. This method is an improvement of the previous method. The algorithm uses a greedy multi-resolution strategy to maximize modularity starting from the partition in which all nodes are put in different communities. When modularity is optimized locally by moving nodes to neighboring clusters, the algorithm creates a network of communities and then repeats the same procedure on that network until a maximum of modularity is obtained.
3. The Walktrap algorithm [19]. This algorithm relies on a node distance measure reflecting probability that a random walker moves from one node to another node in exactly k steps (k is the only parameter of the algorithm having default value $k = 4$). The clustering dendrogram is constructed by Ward's agglomerative clustering technique and the partition which maximizes modularity is taken as the output of the algorithm.
4. The Infomap algorithm [23]. This method reveals communities by optimally compressing descriptions of information flows on the network. The algorithm uses a greedy strategy to minimize the map equation which reflects the expected description length of a random walk on a partitioned network.

Each of used community detection algorithms defines one concrete implementation instance (i.e. one variant) of the FSFCN method.

The final step in the FSFCN method is the selection of features according to obtained community partitions in pruned feature correlation networks. The main idea is to select one or more features within each community such that:

1. selected features have a strong association with the class variable, and
2. any two selected features belonging to the same community are not directly connected.

Algorithm 2. The FSFCN algorithm

---

input : D, R, CDA

    D – a dataset of instances with real-valued features $F = \{f_1, f_2, \ldots, f_k\}$ and a categorical class variable c

    R – the threshold separating relevant from irrelevant features

    CDA – a community detection algorithm

output: S – the set of selected features

// form the pruned feature correlation network corresponding to D
$G := \text{Algorithm1}(D, R)$

$C :=$ the set of clusters in G obtained by CDA

$S :=$ empty set
foreach $c \in C$ **do**
    $(V_q, E_q) :=$ subgraph of G induced by nodes in c
    while $V_q \neq empty\ set$ **do**
        // determine feature having the highest mutual information
        // with the class variable
        $f := \text{argmax}_{x \in V_q}\ C_c(x)$

        // remove f and its neighbors from (V_q, E_q)
        $V_r := \{a \in V_q : \{f, a\} \in E_q\} \cup \{f\}$
        $E_r := \{\{a, b\} \in E_q : a \in V_r \vee b \in V_r\}$
        $V_q := V_q \setminus V_r$
        $E_q := E_q \setminus E_r$

        // add f to the set of selected features
        $S := S \cup \{f\}$
    end
end

The procedure for forming the set of selected features is described in Algorithm 2.

After the pruned correlation network is constructed and clustered, the FSFCN method forms subgraphs of the network corresponding to identified communities where one subgraph is induced by nodes belonging to one community. For each of community subgraphs the following operations are performed:

1. A feature having the highest association with the class variable is identified and put in the set of selected features. Then, it is removed from the community subgraph together with its neighbors.
2. The previous step is repeated while the community subgraph is not empty.

In other words, for each of identified communities the FSFCN method selects one or more features which represent the whole community. The method also takes into account the size of communities – for larger communities a higher number of features is selected. Also, when a feature is added to the set of selected features its neighbors are removed from the community subgraph which implies that the set of selected features will not contain features having a high mutual correlation (otherwise, such two features would be directly connected in the community subgraph).

4   Experiments and Results

The experimental evaluation of the FSFCN feature selection method was performed on a dataset with 120 plasma signaling protein features related to the diagnosis of Alzheimer's disease [21]. The class variable indicates whether a patient was diagnosed with Alzheimer's or not. The total number of instances in the dataset is equal to 176 where 64 data instances correspond to patients diagnosed with Alzheimer's.

We performed feature selection using 4 variants of the FSFCN method. Each of those variants relies on a different community detection technique to cluster pruned feature correlation networks obtained at the threshold R equal to 0.05. The variants of the method are denoted by:

1. FG – the FSFCN method with the Fast greedy modularity optimization community detection algorithm,
2. LV – the FSFCN method with the Louvain algorithm,
3. WT – the FSFCN method with the Walktrap algorithm, and
4. IM – the FSFCN method with the Infomap algorithm.

Using the WEKA machine learning workbench [8,28] we trained 7 different classifiers on datasets containing features selected by different variants of the FSFCN method. The examined classification models are denoted by:

1. RF – the random forest classifier,
2. J48 – the C4.5 decision tree classifier,
3. LMT – the logistic model tree classifier,
4. JRIP – the RIPPER rule induction classifier,
5. LOGR – the logistic regression classifier,
6. SMO – the Support Vector Machine classifier, and
7. NB – the Naive Bayes classifier.

The classifiers were trained and evaluated using the 10-fold cross-validation procedure with the default WEKA values for the parameters of classification algorithms. We used the classification accuracy measure (the fraction of correctly classified data instances) to compare the performance of classifiers. The classification accuracy of classifiers trained after feature selection by different variants of the FSFCN method was also compared to the accuracy of the same classifiers trained on the full dataset (the original dataset without any feature selection) and the dataset containing features selected by the CFS method [10] provided by WEKA.

The pruned feature correlation network of the dataset contains 35 nodes which means that 35 out of 120 features exhibit significant association with the class variable in terms of mutual information. Those 35 nodes representing relevant features are connected by 161 links which implies that a randomly selected relevant feature has a significant correlation with 9.2 other relevant features on average. The maximal and the minimal absolute value of link weights are 0.72 and 0.32, respectively, which means that there are moderate to strong Spearman correlations among relevant features.

The results of community detection on the pruned feature correlation network are summarized in Table 1. To compare obtained community partitions we computed the Rand index [20] for each pair of them. The FG and LV methods identified exactly the same communities: the Rand index for the community partitions obtained by FG and LV is equal to 1. The WT method identified a partition with a higher number of communities and a lower value of modularity compared to FG/LV. The Rand index between partitions obtained by WT and FG/LV is equal to 0.79 which indicates that those two partitions are highly similar. Finally, it can be seen that the IM method failed to identify communities in the network, i.e. this method identified one community encompassing all nodes in the network. Consequently, the features selected by this method can be seen as features selected from the pruned correlation network without the clustering step.

Table 1. The results of community detection on the pruned feature correlation network. NC – the number of identified communities, Q – the value of the modularity measure, S – the vector giving the size of identified communities.

Method	NC	Q	S
FG	4	0.275	(14, 8, 7, 6)
LV	4	0.275	(14, 8, 7, 6)
WT	7	0.218	(13, 8, 5, 5, 2, 1, 1)
IM	1	0	(35)

The features selected by different variants of the FSFCN method are shown in Table 2. FS and LV selected the same features since community partitions obtained by the corresponding community detection algorithms are equal. It can be observed that each of the FSFCN variants drastically reduced the dimensionality of the dataset – the number of selected features varies from 7 to 12. On the other hand, the CFS method implemented in WEKA selected 25 features.

The accuracy of trained classifiers are shown in Table 3. It can be observed that classifiers trained without feature selection tend to exhibit the worst performance. The classifiers trained on the dataset containing features selected by the WEKA CFS method are always better than the classifiers trained on the full dataset. On the other hand, the classifiers trained on the datasets containing features selected by FG/LV and WT show a better performance compared to the classifiers trained on the full dataset except in one case. Namely, the accuracy of the LMT classifier trained on the full dataset is equal to the accuracy of

Table 2. The features selected by four different variants of the FSFCN method. Feature ranks are determined according to the mutual information with the class variable.

FG/LV	Rank	WT	Rank	IM	Rank
IL-1a	1	IL-1a	1	IL-1a	1
IL-8	2	TNF-a	3	PDGF-BB	7
TNF-a	3	GCSF	6	sTNF RI	12
PDGF-BB	7	PDGF-BB	7	Eotaxin	15
sTNF RI	12	sTNF RI	12	MCP-2	17
VEGF-B	14	Eotaxin	15	IGFBP-2	23
Eotaxin	15	SCF	16	TPO	31
MIP-1d	19	MIP-1d	19		
IGFBP-2	23	CTACK	22		
		IGFBP-2	23		
		BTC	30		
		TPO	31		

the same classifier trained after feature selection based on the FG/LV and WT methods. Consequently, we can say feature selection based on properly clustered feature correlation networks does not decrease the performance of all examined classifiers while drastically reducing the dimensionality of the dataset.

Table 3. The classification accuracy of examined classifiers. The column FULL corresponds to classifiers trained without feature selection, while the column WEKA-CFS corresponds to classifiers trained on the dataset containing features selected by the CFS feature selection method implemented in WEKA. One star indicates the worst performance, while two stars indicate the best performance.

	FULL	WEKA-CFS	FG/LV	WT	IM
RF	0.82	0.85**	0.82	0.85**	0.79*
J48	0.74*	0.77	0.77	0.81**	0.74*
LMT	0.84	0.85**	0.84	0.84	0.83*
JRIP	0.72*	0.81**	0.79	0.78	0.75
LOGR	0.73*	0.81	0.85**	0.85**	0.84
SMO	0.82*	0.83	0.84	0.86**	0.85
NB	0.78*	0.84	0.88**	0.88**	0.84

The next important result that can be observed in Table 3 is that the IM variant of the FSFCN method exhibits the worst performance compared to other three FSFCN variants. The IM variant is actually equivalent to the FSFCN method without clustering since IM identified exactly one cluster encompassing features in the network. Therefore, we can conclude that clustering of feature correlation networks enables a better selection of relevant features.

The best performing classifier trained without feature selection is LMT achieving accuracy of 0.84, the best classifier trained after the WEKA CFS feature selection are RF and LMT achieving accuracy of 0.85. On the other hand, the classifier with the highest accuracy is NB trained after features are selected by three different variants of the FSFCN method. Finally, the classifiers trained after the WT variant of the FSFCN method tend to exhibit the best overall performance. It can be observed that this feature selection method outperforms other feature selection methods in case of 5 out of 7 classifiers. It is also important to emphasize that this variant of the FSFCN method drastically improves the performance the J48, LOGR and NB in comparison with the classifiers trained on the full dataset.

5 Conclusions and Future Work

In this paper we presented a novel method for feature selection based on feature correlation networks. Feature correlation networks are weighted graphs showing the strongest correlations between features. The main idea of the approach is to cluster feature correlation networks using community detection techniques in order to identify groups of features such that correlations between features within a group tend to be stronger than correlations between features belonging to different groups. Then, one or more features representing each group is selected considering their correlations with the class variable, the size of groups and connections within them.

The experimental evaluation of four variants of the method, each of them relying on a different community detection technique, was conducted on a highly dimensional dataset (120 features) related to the diagnosis of Alzheimer's disease. More specifically, we compared the accuracy of 7 different classifiers trained without feature selection, with feature selection by the CFS method implemented in WEKA, and with feature selection performed by the variants of our method. The obtained results show that the variant of our method which employs the Walktrap community detection algorithm exhibits the best overall performance compared to the alternatives. Additionally, our results indicate that clustering of feature correlation networks is a necessary step to obtain relevant sets of features for classification purposes.

The main task in our future work will be to perform a more comprehensive evaluation of our approach considering high dimensional datasets from various domains. The evaluation will also include a statistically robust comparison with other representative graph-based and clustering-based feature selection methods. It is also possible to experiment with additional variants of the method taking into account other correlation measures and community detection algorithms (including also detection of overlapping communities [27]). Finally, in this paper we focused on feature selection in the context of classification. In our future work we will also focus on adaptations of the method for clustering problems. Currently, the selection of features representing feature clusters is guided by the mutual information between a feature and the class variable. We plan to examine different network centrality measures instead of the mutual information in order to be able to apply the method on uncategorized data and investigate its performance in this setting.

Acknowledgments. This work is supported by the bilateral project "Intelligent computer techniques for improving medical detection, analysis and explanation of human cognition and behavior disorders" between the Ministry of Education, Science and Technological Development of the Republic of Serbia and the Slovenian Research Agency. M. Savić, V. Kurbalija and M. Ivanović also thank the Ministry of Education, Science and Technological Development of the Republic of Serbia for additional support through project no. OI174023, "Intelligent techniques and their integration into wide-spectrum decision support."

References

1. Blondel, V.D., Guillaume, J.L., Lambiotte, R., Lefebvre, E.: Fast unfolding of communities in large networks. J. Stat. Mech: Theory Exp. **2008**(10), P10008 (2008)
2. Boccaletti, S., Latora, V., Moreno, Y., Chavez, M., Hwang, D.U.: Complex networks: structure and dynamics. Phys. Rep. **424**(4–5), 175–308 (2006)
3. Butterworth, R., Piatetsky-Shapiro, G., Simovici, D.A.: On feature selection through clustering. In: Proceedings of the Fifth IEEE International Conference on Data Mining ICDM 2005, Washington, DC, pp. 581–584. IEEE Computer Society (2005)
4. Clauset, A., Newman, M.E.J., Moore, C.: Finding community structure in very large networks. Phys. Rev. E **70**, 066111 (2004)
5. Csardi, G., Nepusz, T.: The igraph software package for complex network research. InterJournal **Complex Systems**, 1695 (2006). http://igraph.org
6. Duch, W.: Filter methods. In: Guyon, I., Nikravesh, M., Gunn, S., Zadeh, L.A. (eds.) Feature Extraction. STUDFUZZ, vol. 207, pp. 89–117. Springer, Heidelberg (2006). doi:10.1007/978-3-540-35488-8_4
7. Fortunato, S.: Community detection in graphs. Phys. Rep. **486**(3–5), 75–174 (2010)
8. Frank, E., Hall, M., Holmes, G., Kirkby, R., Pfahringer, B., Witten, I.H., Trigg, L.: Weka-A machine learning workbench for data mining. In: Maimon, O., Rokach, L. (eds.) Data Mining and Knowledge Discovery Handbook, pp. 1269–1277. Springer, Heidelberg (2010). doi:10.1007/978-0-387-09823-4_66
9. Guyon, I., Elisseeff, A.: An introduction to variable and feature selection. J. Mach. Learn. Res. **3**, 1157–1182 (2003)
10. Hall, M.A.: Correlation-based feature subset selection for machine learning. Ph.D. thesis, University of Waikato, Hamilton, New Zealand (1998)
11. Horvath, S.: Correlation and gene co-expression networks. In: Horvath, S. (ed.) Weighted Network Analysis, pp. 91–121. Springer, Heidelberg (2011). doi:10.1007/978-1-4419-8819-5_5
12. Kononenko, I.: Estimating attributes: analysis and extensions of RELIEF. In: Bergadano, F., De Raedt, L. (eds.) ECML 1994. LNCS, vol. 784, pp. 171–182. Springer, Heidelberg (1994). doi:10.1007/3-540-57868-4_57
13. Krier, C., François, D., Rossi, F., Verleysen, M.: Feature clustering and mutual information for the selection of variables in spectral data. In: Proceedings of European Symposium on Artificial Neural Networks Advances in Computational Intelligence and Learning, pp. 157–162 (2007)

14. Lal, T.N., Chapelle, O., Weston, J., Elisseeff, A.: Embedded methods. In: Guyon, I., Nikravesh, M., Gunn, S., Zadeh, L.A. (eds.) Feature Extraction. STUDFUZZ, vol. 207, pp. 137–165. Springer, Heidelberg (2006). doi:10.1007/978-3-540-35488-8_6

15. Li, J., Cheng, K., Wang, S., Morstatter, F., Trevino, R.P., Tang, J., Liu, H.: Feature selection: a data perspective. arXiv preprint (2016). arXiv:1601.07996

16. Newman, M.E.J.: The structure and function of complex networks. SIAM Rev. **45**(2), 167–256 (2003)

17. Newman, M.E.J.: Analysis of weighted networks. Phys. Rev. E **70**, 056131 (2004)

18. Newman, M.E.J., Girvan, M.: Finding and evaluating community structure in networks. Phys. Rev. E **69**, 026113 (2004)

19. Pons, P., Latapy, M.: Computing communities in large networks using random walks. J. Graph Algorithms Appl. **10**(2), 191–218 (2006)

20. Rand, W.M.: Objective criteria for the evaluation of clustering methods. J. Am. Stat. Assoc. **66**(336), 846–850 (1971)

21. Ray, S., Britschgi, M., Herbert, C., Takeda-Uchimura, Y., Boxer, A., Blennow, K., Friedman, L., Galasko, D., Jutel, M., Karydas, A., Kaye, J., Leszek, J., Miller, B., Minthon, L., Quinn, J., Rabinovici, G., Robinson, W., Sabbagh, M., So, Y., Sparks, D., Tabaton, M., Tinklenberg, J., Yesavage, J., Tibshirani, R., Wyss-Coray, T.: Classification and prediction of clinical Alzheimer's diagnosis based on plasma signaling proteins. Nat. Med. **13**(11), 1359–1362 (2007)

22. Robnik-Šikonja, M., Kononenko, I.: Theoretical and empirical analysis of relieff and rrelieff. Mach. Learn. **53**(1), 23–69 (2003)

23. Rosvall, M., Bergstrom, C.T.: Maps of information flow reveal community structure in complex networks. Proc. Nat. Acad. Sci. USA **105**(4), 1118–1123 (2007)

24. Sánchez-Maroño, N., Alonso-Betanzos, A., Tombilla-Sanromán, M.: Filter methods for feature selection – a comparative study. In: Yin, H., Tino, P., Corchado, E., Byrne, W., Yao, X. (eds.) IDEAL 2007. LNCS, vol. 4881, pp. 178–187. Springer, Heidelberg (2007). doi:10.1007/978-3-540-77226-2_19

25. Song, Q., Ni, J., Wang, G.: A fast clustering-based feature subset selection algorithm for high-dimensional data. IEEE Trans. Knowl. Data Eng. **25**(1), 1–14 (2013)

26. Van Dijck, G., Van Hulle, M.M.: Speeding up the wrapper feature subset selection in regression by mutual information relevance and redundancy analysis. In: Kollias, S.D., Stafylopatis, A., Duch, W., Oja, E. (eds.) ICANN 2006. LNCS, vol. 4131, pp. 31–40. Springer, Heidelberg (2006). doi:10.1007/11840817_4

27. Wang, M., Yang, S., Wu, L.: Improved community mining method based on LFM and EAGLE. Comput. Sci. Inf. Syst. **13**(2), 515–530 (2016)

28. Witten, I.H., Frank, E.: Data Mining: Practical Machine Learning Tools and Techniques, 2nd edn. Morgan Kaufmann Publishers Inc., San Francisco (2005). (Morgan Kaufmann Series in Data Management Systems)

29. Yu, L., Liu, H.: Feature selection for high-dimensional data: a fast correlation-based filter solution. In: Fawcett, T., Mishra, N. (eds.) Proceedings of the 20th International Conference on Machine Learning (ICML-03), pp. 856–863 (2003)

30. Zhang, Z., Hancock, E.R.: A graph-based approach to feature selection. In: Jiang, X., Ferrer, M., Torsello, A. (eds.) GbRPR 2011. LNCS, vol. 6658, pp. 205–214. Springer, Heidelberg (2011). doi:10.1007/978-3-642-20844-7_21

31. Zhao, Z., Liu, H.: Searching for interacting features. In: Proceedings of the 20th International Joint Conference on Artifical Intelligence IJCAI 2007, pp. 1156–1161. Morgan Kaufmann Publishers Inc., San Francisco (2007)

Collecting and Processing Arabic Facebook Comments for Sentiment Analysis

Abdeljalil Elouardighi[1,2(✉)], Mohcine Maghfour[1], and Hafdalla Hammia[1]

[1] LM2CE Laboratory, FSJES, Hassan 1st University, Settat, Morocco
abdeljalil.elouardighi@uhp.ac.ma, maghfour.mohcin@gmail.com,
hhammia@gmail.com
[2] LRIT Laboratory, FSR, Mohammed V University, Rabat, Morocco

Abstract. Social networks platforms such as Facebook are becoming one of the most powerful sources for information. The produced and shared data are important in volume, in velocity and in variety. Processing these data in the raw state to extract useful information can be a very difficult task and a big challenge. Furthermore, the Arabic language under its modern standard or dialectal shape is one of the languages producing an important quantity of data in social networks and the least analyzed. The characteristics and the specificity of the Arabic language present a big challenge for sentiment analysis, especially if this analysis is performed on Arabic Facebook comments. In this paper, we present a methodology that we have elaborated, for collecting and preprocessing Facebook comments written in Modern Standard Arabic (MSA) or in Moroccan Dialectal Arabic (MDA) for Sentiment Analysis (SA) using supervised classification methods. In this methodology, we have detailed the processing applied to the comments' text as well as various schemes of features' construction (words or groups of words) useful for supervised sentiments' classification. This methodology was tested on comments written in MSA or in MDA collected from Facebook for the sentiment analysis on a political phenomenon. The experiments' results obtained are promising and this encourages us to continue working on this topic.

Keywords: Natural Language Processing · Sentiment analysis · Supervised classification · Modern standard Arabic · Moroccan Dialectal Arabic · Facebook comments

1 Introduction

With the transition of the Internet communication on discussion forums, blog and social networks such as Facebook and Twitter, there are new opportunities for improving the exploration of information via SA. In the social media, people share their experiences, their opinions or just talk more or less about all that concerns them online. The increasing expansion of the contents and services of social media provide an enormous collection of textual resources and present an excellent opportunity to understand the public's sentiment by analyzing its data.

© Springer International Publishing AG 2017
Y. Ouhammou et al. (Eds.): MEDI 2017, LNCS 10563, pp. 262–274, 2017.
DOI: 10.1007/978-3-319-66854-3_20

SA or Opinion Mining is a domain of study, which tries to analyze the opinions, the sentiments, the attitudes and peoples' emotions on entities such as products, services organizations and so on. Data in social networks are unstructured, informal and evolving rapidly. Their volume, their variety and their velocity, can be a challenge for the analysis' methods that are based on traditional techniques. Messages and comments shared in the social networks, on a subject, an event or a phenomenon etc, are the most important information sources, which can be extracted and exploited for the SA [1].

Collecting and processing these raw data to extract useful information can be a big challenge. Many studies have been carried out for SA by exploiting messages shared in the social networks and written in English or in French etc. However, a few studies have been conducted for SA based on Arabic language. The structure and the specificity of the Arabic language require a processing step, which can be a very difficult task and a serious challenge.

In this paper, we propose a methodology for collecting and pre-processing of comments written in MSA or in MDA. This methodology was exploited to collect Arabic comments from the Facebook network for the SA about the Moroccan's legislatives elections, which took place on October 7, 2016. The experiments' results obtained are promising and this encourages us to continue working on this topic.

The rest of this article is structured as follows: in Sect. 2, we present a state of art on the SA exploiting the social networks. Section 3, describes our methodology for collecting and processing Facebook's comments written in MSA or in MDA for SA using supervised classifications' methods. The application of this methodology for the SA is detailed in Sect. 4. In Sect. 5, we present our experimental results. We conclude this work by a conclusion and perspectives that can follow up these works.

2   Related Work

Researchers had proposed many different approaches in the field of SA. In this context, there are, generally, two main methods: the first uses supervised learning techniques, and the other uses unsupervised techniques. Pang and Lee [2] used machine-learning techniques for sentiment classification. They employed three classifiers (Naive Bayes, Maximum Entropy classification, Support Vector machines) with the Internet Movie Database (IMDB).

Dave et al. [3] attracted attention on information retrieval techniques for feature extraction and scoring in the sentiment classification task.

Pablos et al. [4] proposed a simple and unsupervised method to bootstrap and rank a list of domain aspect terms using a set of unlabeled domain texts. They used a double-propagation approach, and they model the obtained terms and their relations as a graph.

Several studies concerning Arabic sentiment analysis were led using various methodologies and approaches depending on specificities of the Arabic language according to its forms: modern standard or dialectal.

Abdul-Mageed et al. presented a manually annotated corpus, developed from modern standard Arabic with a new polarity lexicon [5]. They adopted two steps for the classification approach. First, they constructed a binary classifier to sort subjective cases. For the second stage, they applied the binary classification to distinguish the positive cases from the negative ones.

Moreover, Diab et al. [6], describe new resources and processing tools for Dialectal Arabic (DA) Blogs. They present a morphological analyzer/generator, MAGEAD, which can handle both MSA and DA, but requires some further pre-processing steps, including manual lemmatization of DA words.

In [7], Nabil et al., present ASTD (Arabic Sentiment Tweets Dataset) an Arabic social sentiment analysis dataset collected from Twitter. It consists of 10 000 tweets which are classified as objective, subjective positive, subjective negative, and subjective mixed. They investigated the properties and the statistics of the dataset and performed two set of benchmark experiments.

Shoukry and Rafea [8] conducted a sentence level sentiment analysis on tweets (1 000 tweets) written in MSA and Egyptian dialects, their adopted supervised classification was based on two classifiers: SVM and NB, as result, they registered a maximum accuracy score of 72.6% that was obtained through SVM classifier after executing preprocessing steps.

Duwairi et al. [9] collected a twitter dataset (+25 000 tweet) including MSA and Arabic dialectal text (Arabizi), their approach consist of verifying the adopted preprocessing steps on sentiment classification, by developing three classifiers K Nearest Neighbor (KNN), Support Vector Machines (SVM) and Naive Bayes(NB), their results shows maximal accuracy of 76.78% obtained with Naive Bayes classifier.

Abdul-Mageed et al. [10], proposed the SAMAR system that perform subjectivity and sentiment analysis for Arabic social media where they used different multi-domain datasets collected from Wikipedia Talk Pages, Twitter, and Arabic forums.

Furthermore, Abdul-Mageed and Diab [11], proposed SANA, a large-scale, multi-domain, and multi-genre Arabic sentiment lexicon. The lexicon automatically extends two manually collected lexicons HUDA (4 905 entries) and SIFFAT (3 355 entries).

Refaee and Rieser [12], presented a manually annotated Arabic social corpus of 8 868 Tweets and they discussed the method of collecting and annotating the corpus.

Ibrahim et al. [13], built a manual corpus of 1 000 tweets and 1 000 micro blogs and used it for sentiment analysis task.

Although the SA in social networks was focused on tweets of Twitter. The possibility of classifying sentiments from Facebook status messages is promising due to their nature [14].

Facebook status messages are more succinct than tweets, and are easier to classify than tweets because their ability to contain more characters allows for better writing and a more accurate portrayal of emotions. However, few works that focuses exclusively on SA of Facebook status messages.

This work aims to analyze Facebook comments posted in MSA or in MDA, by proposing a methodology of collecting and preprocessing these comments in order to conduct SA by applying supervised classification methods.

3   Methodology for Collecting and Processing Arabic Facebook Comments for SA

3.1   Characteristics of Arabic Facebook Comments

SA of published Arabic texts, in social networks like Facebook, presents several difficulties and challenges. The shared comments contain most of time unstructured texts that is full of irregularities, what imposes of advantage the execution of diverse tasks of cleaning and preprocessing. One of the particularities of the textual publications in the social networks is the non-compliance with the linguistic rules in a voluntary or involuntary manner. In fact, spelling errors are very frequent, the sentences structures are less respected and the writing style is less formal. In general, the Arabic language used in Facebook, takes the form of the Modern Standard Arabic (MSA) or Dialectal Arabic (DA) [9]. Furthermore, unlike other languages, like English, the Arabic language has more complex particularities, especially with its richer vocabulary and its more compact aspect. For example, the word "فأسقيناكموه" consists of a sentence that is condensed into a single entity: "and we gave it to you to drink". Diacritics (vowels) are also one of the important characteristics of the Arabic language, since they can radically change the meaning of words. For example, the word "ركب" with different diacritics involve different meanings: "رَكِبَ" (to ride), "رَكَّبَ" (to form), "رُكِّبَ" (is formed), "رَكَّبَ" (level), "رُكَبْ" (knees). In this work, we hadn't handled this situation because in all the comments which we had collected, diacritics weren't used.

The morphological complexity of the Arabic language and the dialectal variety require advanced preprocessing, especially with the lack of published works and specific tools for preprocessing the Arabic texts [15].

3.2   Proposed Methodology

The Fig. 1 presents a methodology that we have developed, for collecting and processing Facebook's comments written in MSA or in MDA for SA by using supervised classification methods.

3.3   Data Collection Step

The collection of data from Facebook was carried out via the Application Programming Interface: "Facebook Graph API", through which it was possible to collect comments shared publicly by Facebook users. In this regard, a task of data sources targeting must be conducted beforehand according to the analysis objectives.

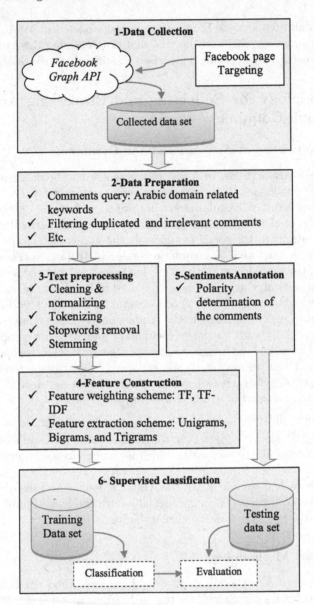

Fig. 1. Proposed methodology

3.4   Data Preparation Step

The collected comments can be irrelevant of the studied phenomenon even for a single source. Thus, in order to extract the targeted comments; an interrogation task is conducted at the level of the collected data set, based on relative keywords of the studied subject. As in Twitter, Facebook comments may be copied and republished (100 % identical). Furthermore, they do not contain only sentences or words, but also URL (http://www...), hashtag sand signs (# $% =), punctuations etc. This requires, at this stage, a filtering and cleaning step.

3.5 Text Processing Step

Cleaning and Normalizing the Text. The comments published in Facebook in dialectal or standard Arabic contain often several irregularities and anomalies, which can be voluntary, such as the repetition of certain letters in some words as in: "ماشي معقوووووول هههههه" (not reasonable hahahahahaha), or involuntary, such as spelling mistakes or the incorrect use of a letter in place of another. By way of illustration, the incorrect use of these letters «د» and «ذ», «ت» and «ث», «ض» and «ظ», in some words will lead to an incorrect sentence, here: "المواطنون تحت ضلال المنتخبين" (Citizens are under the misguidance of the elected) is actually a misspelled sentence. Its correct writing is "المواطنون تحت ظلال المنتخبين" (Citizens are under the care of the elected). So we were brought to normalize the text to supply a unified shape of a letter in a word, for example: "الأخر"; "الآخر"; "لاخر" are unified in : "الاخر" (the last). Moreover we have removed the letters that are repeated several times taking into consideration the special status of some letters like "ي" or «ه» and keep these letters twice if they was duplicated: here "ماشي معقوووووول هههههه" becomes: "ماشي معقول هه" (not reasonable haha).

Tokenization. The extraction of words requires a prior step through which the comment's text is divided into tokens. In other languages like English or French, a token, in most cases, is composed of a single word. However, the tokenization of an Arabic text results in several cases to tokens that are more complex. If we consider the token "كتبناه" , it's equivalent to a sentence in English: (we wrote it), this is the result of the compact morphology of the Arabic language. We will present in the next paragraph, the stemming technique that simplifies this complexity.

Stopwords Removal. Among the obtained tokens, there is some words that are not significant, irrelevant or do not bring information [16]. Of this fact, we have developed several lists of stopwords that we have eliminated from the formed corpus. We distinguish logical prepositions and connectors from MSA and those of the MDA, stopwords referring to the places like names of cities and countries, stopwords referring to names of organizations and people, etc. We note that we have preserved certain prepositions as that relative to the negation: (... "ماشي" ; "ما"; "لا"; "ليس").

Stemming. Extracting words from the corpus involve preprocessing at the level of the tokens to unify the varieties of a word. Information retrieval (IR) state two important types of stemmer for the Arabic language. The first is the root stemmer; it's an aggressive stemmer that reduces the word to its basic root [17].

This type of stemmer is more efficient in reducing dimensions for classifying text, but it leads to a unification of words that are completely different. On the other hand the light stemmer eliminates only the most common prefixes and suffixes of a token [18]. It reduces less the dimension of the features, but it preserves more the meaning of the words [19]. In this work we have applied a light stemmer to the Arabic comments collected from Facebook. We were inspired by the works of Larkey et al., concerning their light10 Stemmer [20], to implement a stemmer that treats both MSA and MDA. For example, the words: "سياسي", "السياسيات", "السياسة", "السياسة", are varieties of the word «سياسة» , that our stemmer unifies in only one stem "سياس" .

3.6   Features Construction Step

Features construction is an important step in SA because it establishes the transition of unstructured data (text) towards the structured data (Features*Observations). In this work, we have adopted two types of schemes for features construction; the first one is the n-grams extraction scheme [21], while the second is the features weighting schemes TF (Term Frequency) and TF-IDF (Term FrequencyInverse Document Frequency) [22].

3.7   Sentiment Annotation Step

Labeling sentiment that are embedded in Facebook's comments is a difficult task, because, on the one hand, these publications do not generally have indicators on the polarity of opinions as in the case of movie or product that have an evaluation system allowing to deduct the polarity of the sentiment (stars **** or a score). On the other hand, the opinions expressed in these comments concern not only the topic of interest but also they concern other entities related to this topic [21]. Complexity of sentiments annotation becomes more accentuated with the analysis of an Arabic text, because of the lack of sentiment lexicon for the Moroccan dialectal language that has imposed on us for the moment to use a human annotation.

3.8   Supervised Classification Step

The comments annotation and features construction are followed by supervised classification step. In this step, the constructed data set is divided into a learning subset for the developing the classification models and testing subset for the evaluation of their performance.

4   SA Using Facebook Comments Published in MSA or MDA

In this section, we aim to experiment our methodology for collecting and pre-processing Facebook comments written in MSA or in MDA, about the Moroccan's legislatives elections, which took place on October 7, 2016. We specify that our main objective is not to analyze these elections in order to draw conclusions but mainly to test our methodology, which can be applied for the SA using Facebook's comments published in MSA or in MDA in touch with a subject or a given phenomenon. Therefore, we have targeted Moroccan online newspapers, which publish comments in Arabic language (modern or dialectal).

Two major criteria have been set for this purpose, firstly the number of visits to the online website of the newspaper according to the Alexa websites ranking [23]. The second criterion is the number of subscribers to Facebook page. Therefore, only newspapers with a Facebook page that exceeds one million subscribers are retained. This process has targeted political comments published for a period of 70 days, which coincides with the period the Moroccan legislative elections. The data preparation step allowed us to select a dataset of 10 254 comments. In order to enable reproducibility of our findings or for free uses in other similar works, we have published our dataset in [24].

Text pre-processing is a very important step toward the features construction. This stage has a major impact on the classification models performance. It determines the words or group of words to be integrated as features or those to be removed from the data set. We present in the following table (Table 1) an example of executing preprocessing tasks on a comment.

Table 1. Example of executing the processing tasks on a comment

Task	Result
Original text	الكلام الي كي يقولو هاذ السياسي ماشي معقووووول ! هههههه #السياسة ـ المغربية (*The statement that this politician says is unreasonable! hahahahaha #moroccan_politics*)
Cleaning	الكلام الي كي يقولو هاذ السياسي ماشي معقووووول هههههه السياسة المغربية
Normalizing	الكلام الي كي يقولو هاد السياسي ماشي معقول هه السياسة المغربية
Tokenization	'الكلام', 'الي', 'كي', 'يقولو', 'هاد', 'السياسي', 'ماشي', 'معقول', 'هه', 'السياسة', 'المغربية'
Stop words removal	'الكلام', 'يقولو', 'السياسي', 'ماشي', 'معقول', 'هه', 'السياسة', 'المغربية'
Stemming	'كلام', 'قول', 'سياس', 'ماش', 'معقول', 'هه', 'سياس', 'مغرب'

The preprocessing step allowed us to extract from the 10 254 comments, 1 526 words (unigrams). Pang and Lee [22] have emphasized that the performance of classification models is influenced by the specificities of the studied data set, such as language, topic, text length, etc. For this reason, we have tested several configurations, combining the weights of the features (TF and TF-IDF) with the n-grams configurations for feature extraction in order to find out the best classification models using three algorithms. In the end, eight experiments were performed (Table 2).

Table 2. Configuration tests table

Test	Configuration
Test 1	Unigrams / TF
Test 2	Unigrams / TF-IDF
Test 3	Bigrams / TF
Test 4	Bigrams / TF-IDF
Test 5	Trigrams / TF
Test 6	Trigrams / TF-IDF
Test 7	Unigrams + Bigrams / TF
Test 8	Unigrams + Bigrams / TF-IDF

SA methods using supervised learning imply prior determination of the polarity of opinions expressed in the text. The annotation task allows a labeling of dissimilar polarity between the text and the entities contained in it [19]. Labeling sentiments of our data set is achieved through crowdsourcing [9], since this task was assigned to a group of judges to define the polarity of the comments, positive or negative. In the end, 6 581 comments were labeled as negative and 3 673 are annotated positive. The following table (Table 3) represents an example of annotated comments.

Table 3. Example of annotated comments

Comment	English translation	Sentiment	Language
راحة البرلمانين مجانية والتعليم ؟ الشعب=... تحشمت نقولها ولو البرلمانين ماتحشموش ملي قالوها	The parliamentarians luxury is free and the education?...the people=...I am ashamed to say it even if the parliamentarians are not ashamed when they said that	Negative	MSA & MDA
مال الدولة حرام على البسطاء وحلال على الاغنياء	The states money is illegitimate for the poor people and legitimate for rich ones	Negative	MSA
راه أحسن رئيس حكومة داز في المغرب من الإستقلال	He's the best president of the government of Morocco since independence	Positive	MDA

For the classification stage, the constructed data sets (for the eight configurations) were randomly split into the learning subset with 75% of the observations, in which we applied 10 folds cross-validation and the testing subset with the remaining 25%, in order to test the developed models performance. For classifying Facebook comments, we have applied three supervised classification algorithms: Decision Trees (Dtrees), Random Forests and Support Vectors Machines (SVM) using R software. To evaluate the performances of our three models developed, we have used the Accuracy and F-score measurements [25].

5   Experimental Results

The results reported in Tables 4 and 5 present successively the accuracy and the Fscore obtained by applying our three classifiers for the various weighting / extraction configurations. These results show, in terms of performance, that the best-developed models are those obtained with the SVM classifier regardless of the weighting / extraction configuration. Yet the best performance is obtained with the unigrams and bigrams configuration combined with a TF-IDF weighting. Moreover, the performance of unigrams exceeds that of bigrams and trigrams. We assume that two elements participate in this result. First, the extraction scheme itself, since in the case of bigrams and trigrams, appearance frequency of two or three same token, with the same order decreases in the documents' corpus. The second element resides in the specificities of the language of Facebook comments; in fact, the Arabic language is characterized by a great richness of its vocabulary, which leads to express the same meaning in much diversified ways, although the use of the Moroccan dialect increases this diversity.

Table 4. Experiment results: accuracy

Configuration	Dtrees	Random Forest	SVM
1-unigrams/TF	0.74	0.76	0.78
2-unigrams/TF-IDF	0.75	0.77	0.80
3-bigrams/TF	0.70	0.71	0.71
4-bigrams/TF-IDF	0.70	0.71	0.72
5-trigrams/TF	0.66	0.68	0.68
6-trigrams/TF-IDF	0.66	0.67	0.68
7-unigrams + bigrams/TF	0.75	0.77	0.78
8-unigrams + bigrams/TF-IDF	0.74	0.77	0.81

Other Sentiment analysis works based on both standard and dialectal Arabic shows more or less similarities to our study in term of results. In [8], authors found that SVM is resulting the best accuracy for classifying tweet opinions with a score of 72.6%. Otherwise, in [9], the best performance of sentiment classification was accomplished with Naive Bayes by 76.78%, that outperformed both SVM and KNN (K Nearest Neighbor).

Table 5. Experiment results: Fscore

Configuration	Dtrees	Random Forest	SVM
1-unigrams/TF	0.82	0.82	0.84
2-unigrams/TF-IDF	0.82	0.83	0.85
3-bigrams/TF	0.81	0.80	0.81
4-bigrams/TF-IDF	0.80	0.80	0.81
5-trigrams/TF	0.79	0.80	0.80
6-trigrams/TF-IDF	0.79	0.79	0.80
7-unigrams + bigrams/TF	0.82	0.83	0.84
8-unigrams + bigrams/TF-IDF	0.82	0.83	0.86

6   Conclusion

This work is focused on the SA for Facebook's comments written and shared in MSA or in MDA. At first, we have developed a methodology for collecting, preprocessing Facebook comments to perform supervised classification of sentiments, and then we have tested this methodology on comments concerning the last Moroccan legislative elections (2016). 10 254 comments have been collected and prepared. Many tasks of preprocessing were applied to the collected comments' texts before the stage of classification, like cleaning, normalization, tokenization, stopwords removal and stemming. 1 526 words were extracted from 10 254 comments. The 10 254 comments were annotated through the Crowdsourcing. 6 581 were annotated negative, 3 673 were annotated positive. Several combinations of (n-grams) and (TF / TF-IDF) for features extraction (words or words groups) were conducted which guarantee the most high-performance of the developed classification models. For the supervised classification task, we have applied three algorithms: Decision Trees, Random Forests and SVM. To measure the performances of the developed models we have used the Accuracy and the F-score measures. The results obtained are promising and this encourages us to continue working on this topic.

Our main contributions in this work can be summarized as follows:

- Describing the properties of MSA and MDA and their challenges for the SA;
- Presenting a set of pre-processing techniques of Facebook comments written in MSA or in MDA for SA;
- Constructing and selecting features (words or groups of words) from Facebook comments written in MSA or MDA which allows us to obtain the best sentiment classification model.

In a future work, we intend to bring necessary improvements for sentiments annotation by developing methods of automatic annotation based on a lexicon. To improve significantly the performances of sentiment classification's models, a stage of dimensionality reduction will be necessary before the processes of features extraction and construction.

There are other ways that our work can and will be improved. The size of the dataset is rather small and if we want to make solid conclusions, we shall certainly need big datasets. This will require us the implementation of SA tools that based on machine learning algorithms alongside with Natural Language Processing techniques over an open-source distributed database management system that can run in parallel and distributed manner [26,27]. In order to accomplish that we propose a system architecture scheme such as Apache Spark an open-source framework for programming with Big Data [28–30].

References

1. Abdulla, N., Ahmed, N., Shehab, M., Al-Ayyoub, M.: Arabic sentiment analysis: lexicon-based and corpus-based. In: 2013 IEEE Jordan Conference on Applied Electrical Engineering and Computing Technologies (AEECT) (2013)
2. Pang, B., Lee, L.: A sentimental education. In: Proceedings of the 42nd Annual Meeting on Association for Computational Linguistics - ACL 2004 (2004)
3. Dave, K., Lawrence, S., Pennock, D.: Mining the peanut gallery. In: Proceedings of the Twelfth International Conference on World Wide Web - WWW 2003 (2003)
4. Pablos, A., Cuadros, M., German, R., Gaines, S.: Unsupervised acquisition of domain aspect terms for aspect based opinion mining. Procesamiento del Lenguaje Nat. **53**, 121–128 (2014)
5. Abdul-Mageed, M., Diab, M., Korayem, M.: Subjectivity and sentiment analysis of modern standard Arabic. In: Proceedings of the 49th Annual Meeting of the Association for Computational Linguistics: Human Language Technologies: Short Papers, vol. 2, pp. 587–591 (2011)
6. Diab, M., Habash, N., Rambow, O., Altantawy, M., Benajiba, Y.: COLABA: Arabic dialect annotation and processing. In: Lrec Workshop on Semitic Language Processing, pp. 66–74 (2010)
7. Nabil, M., Aly, M., Atiya, A.: ASTD: Arabic sentiment tweets dataset. In: EMNLP, pp. 2515–2519 (2015)
8. Shoukry, A., Rafea, A.: Sentence-level Arabic sentiment analysis. In: 2012 International Conference on Collaboration Technologies and Systems (CTS), pp. 546–550 (2012)
9. Duwairi, R., Marji, R., Sha'ban, N., Rushaidat, S.: Sentiment analysis in Arabic tweets. In: 2014 5th International Conference on Information and Communication Systems (ICICS) (2014)
10. Abdul-Mageed, M., Diab, M., Kbler, S.: SAMAR: subjectivity and sentiment analysis for Arabic social media. Comput. Speech Lang. **28**, 20–37 (2014)
11. Abdul-Mageed, M., Diab, M.: SANA: a large scale multi-genre, multi-dialect lexicon for Arabic subjectivity and sentiment analysis. In: LREC, pp. 1162–1169 (2014)
12. Refaee, E., Rieser, V.: An Arabic Twitter corpus for subjectivity and sentiment analysis. In: LREC, pp. 2268–2273 (2014)
13. West, D., Ford, J., Ibrahim, E.: Strategic Marketing. Oxford University Press, Oxford (2015)
14. Ahkter, J., Soria, S.: Sentiment analysis: Facebook status messages. Unpublished Master's thesis, Stanford, CA (2010)
15. Assiri, A., Emam, A., Aldossari, H.: Arabic sentiment analysis: a survey. Int. J. Adv. Comput. Sci. Appl. **6**, 75–85 (2015)

16. Duwairi, R., Qarqaz, I.: Arabic sentiment analysis using supervised classification. In: 2014 International Conference on Future Internet of Things and Cloud (2014)

17. Duwairi, R., Al-Refai, M., Khasawneh, N.: Stemming versus light stemming as feature selection techniques for Arabic text categorization. In: 2007 Innovations in Information Technologies (IIT) (2007)

18. Al-Anzi, F., AbuZeina, D.: Stemming impact on Arabic text categorization performance: a survey. In: 2015 5th International Conference on Information and Communication Technology and Accessibility (ICTA) (2015)

19. Saif, H., Fernandez, M., He, Y., Alani, H.: Evaluation datasets for twitter sentiment analysis: a survey and a new dataset, the STS-gold (2013)

20. Larkey, L.S., Ballesteros, L., Connell, M.E.: Light stemming for Arabic information retrieval. In: Soudi, A., Bosch, A., Neumann, G. (eds.) Arabic Computational Morphology. Text, Speech and Language Technology, vol. 38, pp. 221–243. Springer, Dordrecht (2007). doi:10.1007/978-1-4020-6046-5_12

21. Liu, B.: Sentiment analysis and opinion mining. Synth. Lect. Hum. Lang. Technol. **5**, 1–167 (2012)

22. Pang, B., Lee, L.: Opinion mining and sentiment analysis. Found. Trends Inf. Retr. **2**, 1–135 (2008)

23. Alexa website. http://www.alexa.com/topsites/countries/MA. Accessed 20 Sep 2016

24. ElecMorocco2016 dataset. https://github.com/sentiprojects/ElecMorocco2016. Accessed 27 Jun 2017

25. Sebastiani, F.: Machine learning in automated text categorization. ACM Comput. Surv. **34**, 1–47 (2002)

26. Kanavos, A., Nodarakis, N., Sioutas, S., Tsakalidis, A., Tsolis, D., Tzimas, G.: Large scale implementations for twitter sentiment classification. Algorithms **10**, 33 (2017)

27. Nodarakis, N., Pitoura, E., Sioutas, S., Tsakalidis, A., Tsoumakos, D., Tzimas, G.: kdANN+: a rapid AkNN classifier for big data. In: Hameurlain, A., Küng, J., Wagner, R., Decker, H., Lhotska, L., Link, S. (eds.) Transactions on Large-Scale Data- and Knowledge-Centered Systems XXIV. LNCS, vol. 9510, pp. 139–168. Springer, Heidelberg (2016). doi:10.1007/978-3-662-49214-7_5

28. Nodarakis, N., Sioutas, S., Tsakalidis, A., Tzimas, G.: MR-SAT: a MapReduce algorithm for big data sentiment analysis on Twitter. In: Proceedings of the 12th International Conference on Web Information Systems and Technologies (2016)

29. Nodarakis, N., Sioutas, S., Tsakalidis, A., Tzimas, G.: Large scale sentiment analysis on twitter with spark. In: EDBT/ICDT Workshops (2016)

30. Sioutas, S., Mylonas, P., Panaretos, A., Gerolymatos, P., Vogiatzis, D., Karavaras, E., Spitieris, T., Kanavos, A.: Survey of machine learning algorithms on spark over DIIT-based structures. In: Sellis, T., Oikonomou, K. (eds.) ALGO-CLOUD 2016. LNCS, vol. 10230, pp. 146–156. Springer, Cham (2017). doi:10.1007/978-3-319-57045-7_9

Modeling Heterogeneity and Behavior

Conceptual Modelling of Hybrid Systems
Structure and Behaviour

Andreea Buga[1], Atif Mashkoor[2], Sorana Tania Nemeş[1],
Klaus-Dieter Schewe[2(✉)], and Pornpan Songprasop[1]

[1] Johannes Kepler University Linz, Linz, Austria
{a.buga,t.nemes}@cdcc.faw.jku.at, pornpansongprasop@gmail.com
[2] Software Competence Center Hagenberg, Hagenberg im Mühlkreis, Austria
atif.mashkoor@scch.at, kd.schewe@gmail.com

Abstract. Complex systems comprising hardware, software, facilities and personnel are gaining more and more importance. Such systems are hybrid, as some components are characterised by continuous behaviour, whereas the behaviour of others is discrete. In this paper we present a concise conceptual model that is capable to capture structure and behaviour of such systems. We show that structural modelling can be based on well-known concepts of the entity-relationship model requiring only some extensions to constraints. We further show that behavioural modelling requires only a careful separation of synchronous and asynchronous interaction and high-level means for the integration of continuous functions. We show that all these concepts can be captured by defining a semantics in hybrid Event-B. The paper illustrates the modelling method by a sophisticated industrial example of a hemodialysis machine.

1 Introduction

Hybrid dynamic systems, i.e. systems integrating components characterised by continuous behaviour as well as components with discrete behaviour [14], are gaining more and more importance. They capture the essentials of systems subsumed under the current buzz around "cyber-physical systems" or the "internet of things". Despite the importance of such systems surprisingly little research is dedicated to their conceptual modelling.

A typical example of such a hybrid system is a hemodialysis machine (as illustrated schematically in Fig. 1), which is used as an artificial filtration system, in lieu of kidneys, that extra-corporally purifies the blood by removing impurities and unwanted fluids. In this paper we will use the hemodialysis machine case study [11] to illustrate our ideas. A typical hemodialysis procedure is performed in the following fashion:

1. Two needles are inserted into a patient's arm, one to take out the blood and the other to put the blood back. A specific amount of blood (approximately five percent of the patient's blood) is taken outside the body at a given time.

© Springer International Publishing AG 2017
Y. Ouhammou et al. (Eds.): MEDI 2017, LNCS 10563, pp. 277–290, 2017.
DOI: 10.1007/978-3-319-66854-3_21

2. The blood is taken through the arterial access of the patient's arm. The blood then travels through a thin tube that takes the blood to the dialyzer. A dialyzer is comprised of many fine hollow fibres which are made of a semi-permeable membrane.
3. As the blood flows through these fibres, the dialysate (a chemical substance) flows around them, removing impurities and excess water and adjusting the chemical balance of the blood.
4. After being cleansed and treated, the blood is returned to the patient's arm through the venous access.

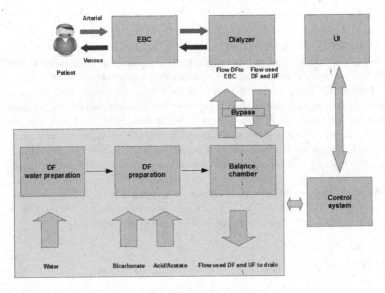

Fig. 1. Schematic view of a hemodialysis machine [11]

The state of the art in systems engineering is dominated by SysML, the OMG Systems Modeling Language (OMG SysML™) [13], and support tools such as PTC Integrity Modeller [15], Magic Draw [10], Enterprise Architect [8] and others. SysML has been adapted from the commonly known Universal Modelling Language (UML), thus provides graphical notations on a high level of abstraction that permit to describe structure and behaviour of components. As a derivative of UML it inherits some of the known deficiencies, in particular the striking lack of formal semantics, the lack of guidelines how to use the language, and the integration into a development methodology, by means of which high-level constructs can be reified into system implementations [18].

Concerning formal semantics translations of behavioural diagrams to Abstract State Machines (ASMs) [6] have been developed in [16,20], but these can be merely understood as formalisations of the corresponding UML diagrams, in particular sequence, activity and statechart diagrams with almost no consideration of the true extensions concerning the integrated continuous parts. The work in [19] exploits the well-known elegant possibility to capture UML class diagrams in the higher-order entity relationship model (HERM) [22] and shows that other structural diagrams either give rise to data types associated with attributes or define integrity constraints.

Alternative approches are grounded in using slightly extended rigorous methods such as (hybrid) ASMs [4], (hybrid) Event-B [1,2,21] or TLA$^+$ [9] to capture hybrid dynamic systems and to enable rigorous refinement towards implementation.

In this paper we continue our research in [7], where we developed a conceptual model for hybrid dynamic systems based on HERM for structural modelling and constraints, and on concurrent hybrid ASMs for behavioural modelling. In Sect. 2 we present our structural approach, which is based on meromorphic part-of-relationships. We integrate continuous functions as values associated with attributes, which is in strict analogy to the hybrid extensions to Event-B and ASMs. We emphasise the importance of flow dependencies, and integrate differential equations in parametric constraints. The constraints in the specification are related to safety-critical issues [12]. In Sect. 3 we present our approach to behavioural modelling. While flow dependencies imply synchronous behaviour, we support general asynchronous behaviour exploiting the behavioural theory of concurrent systems [5]. However, different from our previous work we formalise the semantics using multiple Event-B machines with common contexts thus showing that the behavioural model is not only supported by ASMs. The section contains a brief description of formal semantics using Event-B. We conclude with a brief summary and outlook in Sect. 4.

2   Structural Constructs

The structural building blocks of our conceptual model are block types and clusters of different order $n \geq 0$, which we derive from HERM. The attributes in bocks are further associated with data types. Various types of constraints are defined to capture structural semantics of the blocks.

2.1   Blocks, Clusters and Structures

A *block type* B of order $n \geq 0$ consists of a set $\{r_1 : B_1, \ldots, r_k : B_k\}$ of pairwise different (labelled) *components* and a set $\{A_1, \ldots, A_\ell\}$ of *attributes*. The labels $r_i \in \mathcal{L}$ are taken from a set $\mathcal{L}$ of labels, also called *roles*. Each component B_i is a block type or a cluster of order $n_i < n$, and for at least one component the order must be exactly $n - 1$. Each attribute A_i is associated with a *data type* type(A_i).

A *cluster* C of order $n \geq 0$ consists of a labelled set $\{c_1 : B_1, \ldots, c_m : B_m\}$ with pairwise different labels $c_i \in \mathcal{L}$, where each component B_i is a block type of order $n_i \leq n$, and for at least one component the order must be exactly n.

Each block type defines its parts and describing properties. The intended semantics is easily explained. A block type gives rise to a relation, and each cluster to a disjoint (labelled) union of relations. More precisely, if B is a block type, then a B-tuple is a record $(id : i, r_1 : i_1, \ldots, r_k : i_k, A_1 : v_1, \ldots, A_\ell : v_\ell)$ of arity $k + \ell + 1$ (k is the number of components, ℓ the number of attributes), where $i, i_1, \ldots, i_k$ are identifiers taken from some not further specified set ID of identifiers, and each v_i is a value of type $\mathrm{type}(A_i)$.

A *structure* St associates a set $\mathcal{B}$ of B-tuples with each block type B, and the labelled disjoint union $\mathcal{C} = \bigcup_{i=1}^m \{(c_i, t_i) \mid t_i \in \mathcal{B}_i\}$ with each cluster B. The structure St is *well-defined* iff all identifiers associated to tuples are pairwise different, and whenever $r_j : i_j$ appears in a B-tuple in $\mathcal{B}$, then there exists an B_j-tuple in $\mathcal{B}_j$ with identifier i_j. We only consider well-defined structures in this paper.

As usual for schemata, these can be easily represented by diagrams, i.e. labelled graphs. If $\mathcal{S}$ is a *schema*, i.e. a well-defined set $\{B_1, \ldots, B_n\}$ of block types and clusters, then we define a directed graph (V, E), the *diagram* representing $\mathcal{S}$. Each block type B defines a vertex labelled by B (usually represented by a rectangle), each cluster C defines a vertex labelled by C (usually represented by a rectangle adorned with the $\oplus$ symbol), and each attribute A of a block type B defines a vertex labelled by A and optionally also by the associated type $\mathrm{type}(A)$. Each component block B' defines an edge (usually represented by an arrow pointing to the component) labelled by the role $r \in \mathcal{L}$. Components of a cluster C define edges labelled by $c \in \mathcal{L}$ (usually represented by arrows from the components B_i to C). Attributes A define edges from a block type B to A. If the component of a block indicates a subpart, the arrow is often replaced by a line decorated with a filled diamond.

2.2   Data Types

Data types are crucial in our model, so let b stand for an arbitrary *base type* such as INT, $BOOL$, $REAL$, etc. We do not impose restrictions on these base types, but we request that $BOOL$ and $REAL$ are always in the given collection of base types. Then $\hat{b}$ denotes an extension of the base type b by the value *undef*, which is necessary for partial functions. For the base types we assume a predefined set of operators such as the Boolean operators $\neg$, $\wedge$ and $\vee$ (and any shortcut), addition $+$, multiplication $\cdot$, etc. for integers and reals, etc. Then *data types* t are defined by the following abstract syntax:

$$t = b \mid \hat{b} \mid (a_1 : t_1, \ldots, a_n : t_n) \mid \{t\} \mid \langle t \rangle \mid [t] \mid (a_1 : t_1) \uplus \cdots \uplus (a_n : t_n) \mid t \to t'$$

As usual $(a_1 : t_1, \ldots, a_n : t_n)$ denotes a record type constructor with component types $t_1, \ldots, t_n$ with labels $a_1, \ldots, a_n$, $\{t\}$ denotes a constructor for finite sets with elements of type t, $\langle t \rangle$ denotes a constructor for finite multisets with elements of type t, $[t]$ denotes a constructor for finite lists with elements of type t, $(a_1 : t_1) \uplus \cdots \uplus (a_n : t_n)$ denotes a constructor for disjoint unions of component types $t_1, \ldots, t_n$ with labels $a_1, \ldots, a_n$, and $t \to t'$ denotes a constructor for the type of *continuous functions* defined on values of type t and resulting in values of type t'. Here we use the usual topology for the reals and product topologies, whenever this is applicable, as e.g. for the case of record types. In all other cases the topology is the discrete topology. For all constructed types we permit subtyping in the usual way [22].

For all constructed types we also use the usual operators such as projections for records, structural recursion for sets, multisets and lists, selection for union types, and concatenation, restriction, etc. for function types. Such operators are defined in detail in [17]. In addition, we require a derivation operator $\mathcal{D}_t = \frac{\partial}{\partial t}$ that is defined for (partial) functions with domain $REAL$. Naturally, $\mathcal{D}_t(f)$ is also a partial function with domain $REAL$, and $\mathcal{D}_t(f)(x)$ is the derivative of f at the point x (sometimes also denoted as $f'(x)$), provided this exists. Thus, $\mathcal{D}_t$ is actually a functional.

2.3   Components and Data Types in a Hemodialysis Machine

As shown in Fig. 2 with further details in Fig. 3, a typical hemodialysis machine is composed of several components[1] Full details are described in [19]. The most important component is the Extracorporeal Blood Circuit (EBC). EBC further contains an arterial blood pump (to pump the blood from the body), arterial and venous pressure transducers (to maintain the blood pressure), a heparin pump (to avoid blood coagulations), a safety air detector (an ultrasonic device that prevents entry of air bubbles into the returning needle), and two (venous and arterial) blood chambers. In our model the definition of the block type HEMODIALYSIS_MACHINE takes the form

$$(\{\text{ui} : \text{USER\_INTERFACE}, \text{cs} : \text{CONTROL\_SYSTEM}, \text{dial} : \text{DIALYSER},$$
$$\text{ebc} : \text{EXTRA-CORPORAL\_BLOD-CIRCUIT}, \text{df} : \text{DF\_SUBSYSTEM},$$
$$\text{art} : \text{ARTERIAL\_CONNECTOR}, \text{ven} : \text{VENOUS\_CONNECTOR}\},$$
$$\{\text{Acetat}, \text{Acid}, \text{Bad\_Blood}, \text{Bicarbonate}, \text{Water}, \text{DF\_Used}, \text{Good\_Blood}\}).$$

Another important component is the dialyzer. It comes in a cylindrical shape and is made of a semipermeable membrane configured as hollow fibers that separates blood from dialysate. The balance chamber of the dialyzer, which contains two chambers (one for blood and one for dialysate), allows each to be filled from one side while an identical volume is emptied to the other side. The outlet fluid volume is equal to the input fluid volume. Each membrane has a magnetic sensor for monitoring purposes. In our model the definition of the block type DIALYSER takes the form

$$(\emptyset, \{\text{Bad\_Blood}, \text{DF}, \text{DF\_Used}, \text{Good\_Blood}\}).$$

In these block types the attributes Bad_Blood and Good_Blood are used to quantify the blood flow in ml/minute, so we use $Volume = REAL \rightarrow REAL$

---

[1] The pictures were produced by the SysML tool Enterprise Architect [8].

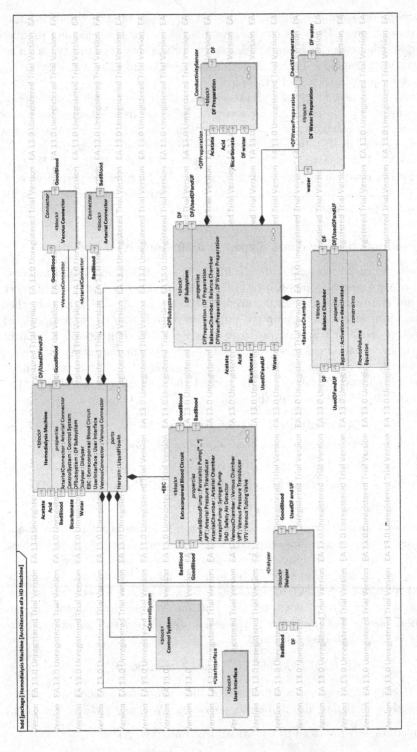

Fig. 2. Components of the hemodialysis machine

as associated data type, the domain representing time and the co-domain blood volume. In fact, the blood flow over a time interval $[a, b]$ is determined by the integrals $\int_a^b \text{Bad\_Blood}(t)dt$ or $\int_a^b \text{Good\_Blood}(t)dt$, respectively, of these functions. Analogously, the data type associated with DF and DF_Used is also *Volume*.

Following the convention to fix an identifier, i.e. to consider only a single instance of a hemodialysis machine, we obtain the following Event-B variables, all of which are pliant:

Pliant

Acetat, Acid, Bad_Blood,

Bicarbonate, Water, DF_Used, Good_Blood

Furthermore, the typing constraints give rise to the invariants:

$$\text{Bad\_Blood} \in \textit{Volume} \qquad \text{Good\_Blood} \in \textit{Volume}$$
$$\text{DF} \in \textit{Volume} \qquad \text{DF\_Used} \in \textit{Volume}$$

Arterial and venous connectors are physical connectors with tubes used for blood transportation between the patient and the machine. The control system controls the overall functioning of the machine, monitors the process for safety purposes and triggers alarms when necessary. User Interface (UI) is used for human-machine interaction. Through the tactile screen, the caregiver can monitor and administer the dialysis process such as the dialysis time, the UF volume, the heparin pump flow, and various other dialysis parameters. Overall, the block type DF_SUBSYSTEM takes the form

$$(\{\text{balc} : \text{BALANCE\_CHAMBER}, \text{dfwp} : \text{DF\_WATER-PREPARATION},$$
$$\text{dfp} : \text{DF\_PREPARATION}\},$$
$$\{\text{Acetat}, \text{Acid}, \text{Bad\_Blood}, \text{Bicarbonate}, \text{Water}, \text{DF\_Used}, \text{DF}\}).$$

As before the associated data type for the attributes is *Volume* as defined above, so over each time interval the concentration of the various chemicals in the dialyser liquid can be easily computed.

The Dialyzing Fluid (DF) preparation component is responsible for concentrate preparation that consists of mixing the heated and degassed water with bicarbonate concentrate and acid concentrate. The accuracy of the DF concentration is controlled by the conductivity sensors. The DF water preparation component is responsible for degassing and heating the purified water, coming from the reverse osmosis system, to a predetermined temperature. The temperature is set by the user (usually $37\,^\circ\text{C}$), before the concentrate is prepared. The degassing chamber and the heater assembly are integral part of the system.

2.4 Flow Dependencies

A *path* is a sequence $\wp = B_1, \ldots, B_k$ of block types or clusters such that B_{i+1} appears as a component of B_i for all $i = 0, \ldots, k - 1$. If we replace a component $r_{i+1} : B_{i+1}$ in B_i by $r_{i+1,j} : B_j'$ for all components $r_j' : B_j'$ of B_{i+1} and add all attributes of B_{i+1} to those of B_i, we obtain an expanded block type $B_{i,i+1}$. Doing this for all components in a path defines an expanded block type B_φ.

With respect to attributes that are bound to types of continuous functions we introduce *flow dependencies* and *parametric constraints*. The former ones indicate that a value from one component may flow into another component. In order to capture such dependencies in our conceptual model we permit some of the attributes of a block type to be declared as *ports*. These can be *in*-ports, *out*-ports and *in-out*-ports. A *flow dependency* links an out-port of one block type with an in-port of another one, or two in-out-ports. It indicates that at any time the value associated with the connected attributes are equal. That is, flow dependencies are technically just specific path dependencies. They are particularly relevant, if the associated data type, which must be the same for both ports, is $\mathbb{R} \to t$. By means of a flow dependency a synchronisation of the values in a structure will be enforced. This will become relevant in the behavioural part of our model.

Among these components, we have several flow dependencies. In Dialyzer, we have BadBlood and DF as in-ports and GoodBlood and Used DF and UF as out-ports. In Balance Chamber, we have DF and Used DF and UF as in-ports and the same as out-ports. In DF Water Preparation, we have Water as in-port and DF Water as out-port. In DF Preparation, we have Acid, Acetate, Bicarbonate and DF Water as in-port and DF as out-port. In DF Subsystem, we have Acid, Acetate, Bicarbonate, Water and Used DF and UF as input and DF and Used DF and UF as out-port. In EBC, we have BadBlood and GoodBlood both as in-port as well as out-port. In the Venous Connector component, GoodBlood acts both as in-port as well as out-port. In Arterial Connector, BadBlood performs the same role. In the overall Hemodialysis Machine, Acid, Acetate, Bicarbonate, Water and BadBlood are in-port and DF, Used DF and UF and GoodBlood are out-ports. Full details of flow dependencies are contained in [19].

2.5 Parametric Constraints

A *parametric constraint* is given by an equation or inequality with n variables $x_1, \ldots, x_n$, each of which is linked to an attribute in some block type. This may involve the derivation functionals $\mathcal{D}_t$, by means of which differential equations, in particular solutions to initial value problems, can be requested as constraints. Same as the flow dependencies a synchronisation of the values in a structure will be enforced.

For the proper functioning of the machine several parametric constraints must be satisfied. The following list contains a small selection of such constraints:

- When running the EBC with a 8/12 mm pump segment, the machine shall be able to perform a blood flow in the range of 30...600 ml/min with a tolerance of 10% (Arterial Pressure $= -200$ to $+400$ mmHg) and of 25% (Arterial Pressure $= -300$ to -200 mmHg). That is, we require

$$0.9 \; bf \leq \frac{60}{b-a} \int_a^b f_{\text{blood}}(t) \, dt \leq 1.1 \; bf,$$

where $a \leq b$ are any points in time, f_{blood} is one of the functions associated with Bad_Blood or Good_Blood, and bf is the value in $[30, 600]$ set for the blood flow.

- During the therapy, if the blood pump is running and if the Venous Pressure (VP) is lower than the VP lower alarm limit minus 10 mmHg (VPAbsoluteMin -10 mmHg) for more than 5 s then the control system shall stop the blood pump and execute an alarm signal. According to Fig. 3 Venous_Pressure is an attribute of the block type VENOUS_PRESSURE_TRANSDUCER, which itself is a component of the cluster PRESSURE_TRANSDUCER. The associated data type is $Pressure = REAL \rightarrow REAL$, again indicating the dependency of the pressure on time. Then the requirement can be formalised as follows:

$$\forall a, b. b - a \geq 5 \Rightarrow \exists t. a \leq t \leq b \wedge \text{Venous\_Pressure}(t) > \text{Min\_Pressure} - 10.$$

- The common dependency between volume and pressure defines a parametric constraint between Venous_Pressure and Good_Blood:

$$\mathcal{D}_t \text{ Venous\_Pressure}(t) = \frac{- const}{\text{Good\_Blood}(t)^2} \mathcal{D}_t \text{ Good\_Blood}(t).$$

- During the therapy, the control system shall monitor the blood flow in the EBC and if no flow is detected for more than 120 s, then the control system shall stop the blood pump and execute an alarm signal. This involves the parametric constraint

$$b - a \geq 120 \Rightarrow \int_a^b f_{\text{blood}}(t) \, dt > 0.$$

- The liquids flowing in and out of the dialyser must have the same volume, i.e.

$$\forall t. \text{ Bad\_Blood}(t) + \text{DF}(t) = \text{Good\_Blood}(t) + \text{DF\_Used}(t).$$

3   Behavioural Constructs and Formal Semantics

For the semantics of the structural part we exploit Event-B, more precisely multiple Event-B machines with a single context. The context captures the data type definitions from the structural model. As each data type defines a set of values, the context specifies these sets explicitly.

3.1   Event-B Semantics

Then each machine defines variables and invariants. Let $\mathcal{St}$ be a well-defined structure. In general, if B is a block and $i \in ID$ is an identifier, then $B(i)$ denotes the B-tuple in the structure with identifier i. Then $B(i).r_j$ (for $j = 1, \ldots, k$) and

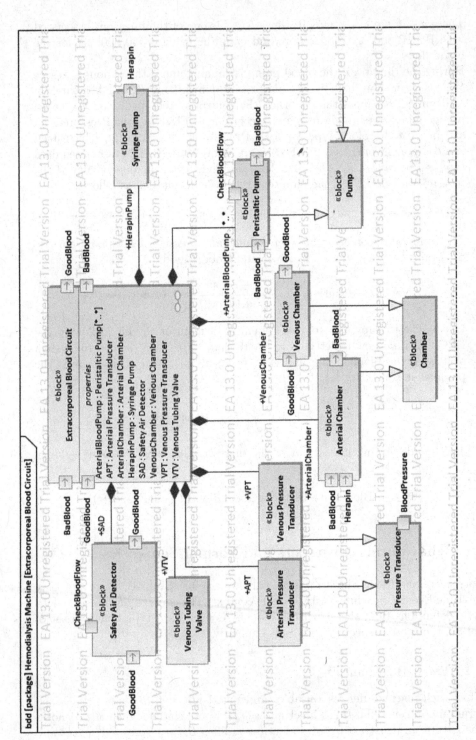

Fig. 3. Components of the extra-corporal blood circuit in a hemodialysis machine

$B(i).A_j$ (for $j = 1, \ldots, \ell$), are used to denote the value of the corresponding component, i.e. $B(i).r_j \in ID$, or attribute, i.e. $B(i).A_j \in \text{type}(A_i)$, respectively. As identifiers are of minor importance (except for referencing and unique identification), we also use the notation $B(i)!r_j$ (for $j = 1, \ldots, k$) for the B_j-tuple with identifier $B(i).r_j$. In doing so, we can further use paths $\wp = B_0, \ldots, B_n$ with $B_0 = B$ and let $B(i).\wp$ denote the B_n-tuple that is reached from $B(i)$ through this path.

Pragmatically, there is usually a *root* block type B_r, from which all attributes of all components can be reached by some path. If we fix an identifier $i \in ID$, then any attribute in any component can be denoted by some expression $B_r(i).\wp.A_j$. Instead of this lengthy notation we permit shortcuts: if the attribute name A_j is unique and there is only one path $\wp$ from B_r to it, then we simply use A_j, otherwise use a shortcut name $\wp'$ for $B_r(i).\wp$ and write $\wp'\_A_j$.

In this way we determine the set of variables used in the Event-B machines. A variable is pliant, if its type involves the continuous function type constructor; otherwise it is mode. Which variables obtained this way occur together in a single machine is determined by the constraints. If updating one variable implies that another one must be updated simultaneously, they must appear jointly in a machine. In particular, joint occurrences of variables in a single machine are implied by flow dependencies.

Each dependency defines an invariant that is placed into any machine affecting the variables involved.

For the behavioural part of our conceptual model we directly exploit Event-B, i.e. in addition to variables and invariants, each machine defines events including an initialisation event. Each event specifies a condition, under which it is fired, and a set of parallel updates of the variables. Whenever the condition of an event is satisfied, the updates are executed. When conditions of several events are simultaneously satisfied, the events are executed in parallel in a synchronous way, which defines the successor state with respect to the single machine. Shared variables may at the same time be updated by the environment, i.e. the other machines in the system.

For the interaction of these machines we adopt the asynchronous combination of runs defined in [5]. According to this theory a concurrent system comprises a set of autonomous machines that are linked via shared memory. The interaction of the machines is defined as follows: In a concurrent run started in some initial state S_0 each interaction state S_n ($n \geq 0$), where some finite set M_n of machines interact with each other, yields a next state S_{n+1} by the moves of all machines $m \in M_n$ that simultaneously complete the execution of their current events they had started in some preceding state S_j ($j \leq n$ depending on m).

While the variables of the machines are linked to the attributes of the components in the structural model, these two notions have to separated carefully. As machines interact asynchronously, whereas flow dependencies enforce synchronous behaviour, the variables associated with each Event-B machine correspond to views. A *view schema* S_v is another schema that results from S by omitting block types or clusters B_i, omitting components or attributes of a block type B_i, and replacing any attribute A_j of a block type B_i by a subattribute.

3.2   Events in a Hemodialysis Machine

Let us look at a few events associated with the control of the venous return flow pressure, which is monitored by an automatically set limits window. The limits window is set 10 s after the last activation of the BP and is identified by markings on the bar showing the venous return flow pressure. Thus we first require an event to activate the blood pump:

EVENT *activiate_blood_pump*
WHEN activate_bp = on
THEN bp_status := on
    bp_timing := $\max(0, \mathbf{I}f.\mathcal{D}_t f(t) = -1 \wedge f(now = 10)$

The width and thresholds of the limits window are set in the hemodialysis machine. The venous lower limit value is automatically adjusted during treatment. This means that the distance between the lower limit and the actual pressure decreases. This compensates for the hematocrit increase generally caused by the added UF. The adjustment is carried out every 5 min and adds up to 2.5 mmHg at a time. So we need an event to adjust the pressure limit:

EVENT *adjust_pressure_limit*
WHEN bp_status = on $\wedge$ vp_timing($now = 0$
THEN vp_limit := vp_limit + 2.5
    vp_timing := $\max(0, \mathbf{I}f.\mathcal{D}_t f(t) = -1 \wedge f(now = 300)$

The minimum distance of 22.5 mmHg is, however, always maintained. The venous lower pressure limit during hemodialysis is checked. An optimal interval is approximately 35 mmHg between the lower pressure limit and the current value. By changing the speed of the blood pump for a brief period, it is possible to reposition the limits window. So we define events for increasing the pressure and accelerating the blood pump:

EVENT *increase_pressure*
WHEN Venous_Pressure(now) $-$ vp_limit ≤ 22.5
THEN accelerate_bp := on
EVENT *accelerate_blood_pump*
WHEN bp_status = on $\wedge$ accelerate_bp = on
THEN bp_speed := bp_speed + $const_1$
    accelerate_bp := accelerating
    Bad_Blood := $\mathbf{I}f.f(t) = $ Bad_Blood$(t) + const_2$
    Venous_Pressure := $\mathbf{I}f.f(t) = \dfrac{-const}{\text{Good\_Blood}(t)^2} \mathcal{D}_t \text{Good\_Blood}(t))$

Furthermore, the request that the blood pump is only accelerated for a brief period of time has to be taken care of by another event

EVENT *stop_accelerating_blood_pump*
   WHEN accelerate_bp = accelerating $\wedge$
        Venous_Pressure(now) $-$ vp_limit $\geq$ 35
   THEN bp_speed := bp_speed - $const_1$
        accelerate_bp := off

4 Conclusion

In this paper we presented the core of a conceptual model for hybrid dynamic systems and exemplified its practical usage on a complex application case study concerning a hemodialysis machine [11]. The conceptual model comprises a structural and a behavioural part. The former one is grounded in HERM [22] and emphasises part-of-relationships among components and descriptive attributes associated with complex data types, in particular capturing continuous functions. Furthermore, complex parametric constraints allow us to capture continuous behaviour by integrating differential equations.

The behavioural part in grounded in hybrid Event-B [1,2] and emphasises multiple asynchronous machines with common contexts and shared variables. It obeys restrictions arising from flow dependencies in the structural part which imply synchronised behaviour. Therefore, individual machines with a synchronous behaviour are associated with views on the structural model, which provides guidelines how to use the modelling language.

As Event-B supports rigorous refinement, our model does not only provide a method for high-level modelling with formal semantics, it also supports targeted systems development. Concerning the continuous extensions it will be necessary to integrate retrenchment [3]. The next step of the research will consist of taking the application case study further towards refinement and retrenchment.

References

1. Banach, R., Butler, M.J., Qin, S., Verma, N., Zhu, H.: Core hybrid Event-B I: single hybrid Event-B machines. Sci. Comput. Program. **105**, 92–123 (2015)
2. Banach, R., Butler, M.J., Qin, S., Zhu, H.: Core hybrid Event-B II: multiple cooperating hybrid Event-B machines. Sci. Comput. Program. **139**, 1–35 (2017)
3. Banach, R., Jeske, C.: Retrenchment and refinement interworking: the tower theorems. Math. Struct. Comput. Sci. **25**(1), 135–202 (2015)
4. Banach, R., Zhu, H., Su, W., Huang, R.: Continuous KAOS, ASM, and formal control system design across the continuous/discrete modeling interface: a simple train stopping application. Form. Asp. Comput. **26**(2), 319–366 (2014)
5. Börger, E., Schewe, K.D.: Concurrent abstract state machines. Acta Inform. **53**(5), 469–492 (2016). https://link.springer.com/article/10.1007/s00236-015-0249-7
6. Börger, E., Stärk, R.: Abstract State Machines. Springer, Heidelberg (2003)
7. Buga, A., Nemeş, S.T., Schewe, K.D., Songprasop, P.: A conceptual model for systems engineering and its formal foundation. In: Kiyoki, Y., Thalheim, B. (eds.) Proceedings of the 27th International Conference on Information Modelling and Knowledge Bases (EJC 2017) (2017, to appear)

8. Enterprise Architect - UML design tools and UML case tools for software development (2016). http://www.sparxsystems.com.au/products/ea/index.html
9. Lamport, L.: Hybrid systems in TLA$^+$. In: Grossman, R.L., Nerode, A., Ravn, A.P., Rischel, H. (eds.) HS 1991-1992. LNCS, vol. 736, pp. 77–102. Springer, Heidelberg (1993). doi:10.1007/3-540-57318-6_25
10. Magicdraw (2016). http://www.nomagic.com/products/magicdraw.html
11. Mashkoor, A.: The hemodialysis machine case study. In: Butler, M., Schewe, K.-D., Mashkoor, A., Biro, M. (eds.) ABZ 2016. LNCS, vol. 9675, pp. 329–343. Springer, Cham (2016). doi:10.1007/978-3-319-33600-8_29
12. Mashkoor, A., Biro, M.: Towards the trustworthy development of active medical devices: a hemodialysis case study. IEEE Embed. Syst. Lett. **8**(1), 14–17 (2016)
13. OMG Systems Modeling Language (OMG SysML), Version 1.4, OMG document number formal/2015-06-03(2015) (2015). http://www.omg.org/spec/SysML/1.4/
14. Platzer, A.: Analog and hybrid computation: dynamical systems and programming languages. Bull. EATCS **114**, 152–199 (2014)
15. PTC Integrity Modeler (2016). http://www.ptc.com/model-based-systems-engineering/integrity-modeler
16. Sarstedt, S.: Semantic foundation and tool support for model-driven development with UML 2 activity diagrams. Ph.D. thesis, Universität Ulm (2006)
17. Schewe, K.D.: On the unification of query algebras and their extension to rational tree structures. In: Orlowska, M.E., Roddick, J.F. (eds.) Twelfth Australasian Database Conference (ADC2001), Bond University, Queensland, Australia, 29 January 1 February 2001, pp. 52–59. IEEE Computer Society (2001)
18. Schewe, K.D.: UML: a modern dinosaur? A critical analysis of the unified modelling language. In: Jaakkola, H., Kangassalo, H., Kawaguchi, E. (eds.) Information Modelling and Knowledge Bases XII, Frontiers in Articial Intelligence and Applications, vol. 67, pp. 185–202. IOS Press (2001)
19. Songprasop, P.: Structural modelling in systems engineering. Master's thesis, Johannes-Kepler-University Linz (2017)
20. Stan-Ober, I.: Harmonisation des languages de modelisation avec des extensions orientées-object et une Sémantique Exécutable. Ph.D. thesis, Institut National Polytechnique de Toulouse (2001)
21. Su, W., Abrial, J.R., Zhu, H.: Formalizing hybrid systems with Event-B and the Rodin platform. Sci. Comput. Program. **94**, 164–202 (2014)
22. Thalheim, B.: Entity-Relationship Modeling - Foundations of Database Technology. Springer, Heidelberg (2000)

Mastering Heterogeneous Behavioural Models

J. Christian Attiogbé[(✉)]

LS2N - UMR CNRS 6004 - University of Nantes, Nantes, France
Christian.Attiogbe@univ-nantes.fr

Abstract. Heterogeneity is one important feature of complex systems, leading to the complexity of their construction and analysis. Moving the heterogeneity at model level helps in mastering the difficulty of composing heterogeneous models which constitute a large system. We propose a method made of an algebra and structure morphisms to deal with the interaction of behavioural models, provided that they are compatible. We prove that heterogeneous models can interact in a safe way, and therefore complex heterogeneous systems can be built and analysed incrementally. The Uppaal tool is targeted for experimentations.

Keywords: Behavioural models · Heterogeneous systems · Interaction

1 Introduction

Mastering the composition of heterogeneous models contributes to settle the challenge of building and analyzing large systems. Models are used at different abstraction levels and for different purposes. Data models capture the structure of manipulated data, behavioural models often based on transition systems or event systems help to predict and reason about the behaviour of the software to be built. Other models such as timed models, security models, functional models are required according to the needs. A combination of these models is often necessary. In this article we focus on behavioural models used to capture the evolution and the interaction between processes of a more general heterogeneous system which can combine various components. An example of an heterogeneous system is an assembly of pieces of software and hardware communicating with a distributed architecture (using smart objects, sensors, actuators, mechanical parts driven by software). This kind of systems is spreading more and more. However mastering their design, proving their correctness and maintaining these systems are a challenge of first importance for the security of services and software, and especially for reducing time to market of smart objects.

There are several works and proposals related to heterogeneous issues; they embrace different abstraction levels and adopt various policies. There are a body of work around Interface Theories [7]. SysML [6] adresses system engineering at modeling levels. SystemC [4] adopts a rather low abstraction level by composing software or hardware modules which are classes containing processes modelling functionalities. The core of SystemC consists of an event-driven simulator working as a scheduler. The Ptolemy project [5,9] proposes one of the most advanced

© Springer International Publishing AG 2017
Y. Ouhammou et al. (Eds.): MEDI 2017, LNCS 10563, pp. 291–299, 2017.
DOI: 10.1007/978-3-319-66854-3_22

framework, Ptolemy II [17] with which we share some concerns. But these are general purpose and heavy weight approaches which, from our point of view, constraint a lot the used components; they build a kind of a scheduler of the whole composition of components. Unlike approaches with strong coupling of formalisms inside a main one, we target a specific framework with a weak coupling of components described with different formalisms. We address systems with evolving adhoc structures, for small aperture net of components. The components can the be composed (plugged) or unplugged at any time.

This work is motivated by the necessity of light methods and tools to face the construction and the analysis of heterogeneous systems. The difficulties of heterogeneity arise not only at language level (data, property or behavioural), but also at the semantic level.

We propose a method supported by a tool (aZiZa), to make it easier the composition and the interaction between heterogeneous behavioural models. The main idea is that one can easily compose models described with different formalisms but having the same compatibility domain. Currently we focus on behavioural models.

The article is organized as follows. Section 2 introduces the materials we have used. Section 3 is devoted to the proposed method, an algebra to structure the composition of models. Section 4 reports on experimentations and evaluation supported by the developed tool. Section 5 concludes the article.

2   Materials: Models Compatibility and Composition

Heterogeneity is concerned with description formalisms and semantic models; but we focus on semantic models which we consider as *compatibility domains*. Several categories of compatibility domains can be considered, for instance labelled transition systems, event-based models, predicate transformer *á la Dijkstra*.

Compatible Models. Two models M_1 and M_2 (or more) are said *compatible* or not, with regard to at least three compatibility levels: syntactic compatibility, semantic compatibility and formal-reasoning compatibility. Transition Systems [2], Mealy Machines [16], with their various extensions, are widely used to handle complex dynamic systems and are at the heart of many methods analysis and verification tools. The underlying theories are well studied and, in the current state of the art a lot of effective systems are *compiled* into labelled transition systems (LTS). Process Algebra (such as CCS [14], CSP [15], LOTOS [12], π-calculus [13]) built on top of transition systems are recognized as powerful behavioural description models; they are also representative of many behavioural languages, hence their use as composition and interoperability basis.

Definition 1. *(Compatibility Domain) A Compatibility Domain is defined as a category of models characteristics in such a way that, any two models considered within this domain, are comparable w.r.t. the considered characteristics. It is a model integration basis.*

Examples of *semantic compatibility domains* are: logics, labelled transition systems, trace semantics, temporal logics, weakest preconditions, Kripke model.

Proposition 1. *Within a compatibility domain, it is always possible to translate objects semantics (from one formalism and paradigm) into the domain, to compose or integrate them, to reason within the basis, and to possibly translate results in target formalisms.*

Semantic Models and Semantic Embedding. A direct application of the notion of compatibility is the construction of semantic bridges between models or the semantic embedding of one model into another one. We choose the LTS as a reference behavioural model, because it is widely used and equipped with various tools.

If two models M_1 and M_2 are in a compatible semantic domain (LTS in our case), it exists structure morphisms[1] ζ_1 and ζ_2 with related meaning matching such that $\zeta_1(M_1) = LTS_1$ and $\zeta_2(M_2) = LTS_2$. Accordingly, we are about to define some operators Φ which arguments are different but compatible behavioural models; these operators form an algebra that leads the interaction of behavioural models. The idea is that $\Phi(M_i, M_j)$ is semantically unfolded as $\phi(\zeta_i(M_j), \zeta_j(M_j))$ where ϕ is the domain-compatible equivalent of Φ.

If we consider a behavioural model M as a term of a given algebra $\mathcal{A}$, a sketch of the semantic embedding of models is as follows: we consider $\mathcal{A}_i$ as the source algebra to describe various but compatible models, then it exists a compatible domain denoted here by $(\mathcal{S}, L, \rightarrow)$, a LTS with the set of state, the set of labels and the transition relation.

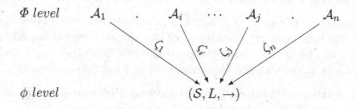

It follows that when models are compatible, a semantic bridge can be used to relate them via the semantic structure induced by the compatibility domain (for instance their LTS). Consequently, a multilevel bridge can also be gradually built between compatibility domains to link two or more models.

3   Interaction of Hererogeneous Models: An Algebra

Interaction between behavioural models, whatever their description formalisms, is viewed as exchanges through common communicating channels. Typically the

---

[1] like a function on elements, a structure morphism relates mathematical objects or structures.

interaction is denoted by a flow of emission and reception statements. Process algebra models, as a compatibility domain, capture very well these interactions, where the unit of specifications is a *process* expressing an elementary sequential behaviour; more complex behaviours are expressed with the composition (sequential, parallel, etc.) of other processes, elementary or not.

Handling the heterogeneity is as simpler as if the LTS is the known user manual of each component. On the one hand, we extract the LTS from given components to compose them; on the other hand the LTS can be given by the component providers. Besides, an implementation can be built from a LTS used to tune a composition. We define a set of operators that impact the behaviour of composition:

- a process composition can be restructured through the renaming of channels;
- process communications can be broken through the modification of channels;
- the structure of a complete net of processes can evolve through channel restructuring, etc.

3.1   The Core Operators for Model Interaction

We are about to elaborate an algebra $\mathcal{A}$ to structure and analyse the composition of heterogeneous processes. The operators of the algebra are related to the two levels (Φ level and ϕ level) considered in Sect. 2, while the structure set of the algebra is the set of processes $\mathcal{P}$ to be composed. Our target is an algebra $\mathcal{A} = \langle \mathcal{P}, O_\Phi, O_\phi \rangle$; therefore we introduce these sets of operators. In the following, a *process* is denoted by the term:

Process procName [channel parameters](other parameters) {body}

where we consider its name, its channels and parameters, and a body. The body is an LTS which describes the behaviour of the process. Several named instances of a process can be defined using the process name as a type.

A *system* is made with the composition of at least two processes.

compose: *Abstract Parallel Composition of Processes.* Let P_1 and P_2 be two processes which use a shared communication channel nc.

Process Proc[nc]() P1;   Process Proc[nc]() P2.

The expression $S = \text{compose}(P_1, P_2)$ is the system made of the parallel composition of the processes P_1 and P_2 which interact via their common nc channel. Note that a channel can be hidden in a process by the renaming of the channel. The arity of the compose operator is not a strong constraint; a set of n processes can be composed either with the binary composition
$$\text{compose}(\dots (\text{compose}(\text{compose}(P_1, P_2), P_3), \cdots), P_n)$$
or directly with the list of processes as arguments: $\text{compose}(P_1, P_2, \cdots, P_n)$.

The compose operator is an instance of the Φ operator. Typically, the embedding functions ζ_i compute the transition systems from the processes used as arguments of compose; then ϕ is the synchronous product [15] of the resulting transition systems. A component process of a system built by the compose operator may be **selected** with the projection operator denoted by ↑. Consequently an operation α can be applied to a process inside a composition by selecting it as follows: $\alpha(\mathsf{compose}(P_1, P_2, \cdots, P_n) \uparrow P_3)$.

rename: *Renaming a Channel in a Process.* The expression $(P$ rename c as $nc)$ denotes a process P where the channel c is renamed as nc.

Let P_3 be a process using nc as a channel: Process Proc[nc]() P3. The expression $S = \mathsf{compose}(P_1, P_2$ rename nc as $c, P_3)$ results in a system where only P_1 and P_3 interact through nc. The behaviour of P_2 does not impact the behaviour of S since P_2 uses a local channel, thus the behaviour of P_2 is ignored in S.

replace: *Substitution of Processes.* Within a system, a given process is substituted by a given new one. The replace operator needs three arguments: a system S, a process oP already in S, a new process nP not in S. The process oP should share its channels with S. The process nP should have the same shared channels (for the substitution) but it can have more channels. The effect of the replacement is based on the shared channels; the shared channel oP is cut and replaced by the common channel in nP. The expression $sys = \mathsf{replace}(Sys, oP, nP)$ modifies Sys by replacing inside it, the behaviour of oP by the new behaviour expressed by nP.

Formally the channels shared by Sys and oP are renamed in oP with a new name unused in Sys and nP. Then Sys is composed with nP. Consequently if nc is the channel shared by the three processes, c a fresh channel, then we have:

$$\mathsf{replace}(Sys, oldP, newP) = \mathsf{compose}(Sys, (Sys \uparrow oP) \text{ rename } nc \text{ as } c, nP)$$

remove: *Removing a Process from a Composition.* A given process can be removed from a system. The remove operator (symbolically denoted by ↓) requires two arguments: a system S made at least with two processes, a process P already part of S. The process P will be removed from S; this is symbolically denoted by $S \downarrow P$. For instance the expression $sys = \mathsf{remove}(\mathsf{compose}(P_1, P_2, P_3), P_2)$ results in a system composed of the processes P_1 and P_3.

extractChan: *Listing the Channels of a Process.* This operator, when applied to a process, gives the list of channels used inside the process. The channels of processes can then be compared, reused, renamed, hidden.

These operators make our target algebra and practically a core language: $\langle \mathcal{P}, \{\mathsf{compose}, \mathsf{replace}, \mathsf{select}, \mathsf{remove}\}, \{\mathsf{rename}, \mathsf{extractChan}\}\rangle$. It is enough expressive, to describe the composition and the interaction between behavioural models as illustrated in the next section.

Semantics of Interaction. As far as the interaction between the behavioural models is considered, each process evolves according to the channels it uses. Interaction is based on communication via shared channels using emission and reception mechanisms (message passing). Synchronous channels involve handshake communications. A reception takes place when a process applies the appropriate reception primitive relatively to a channel and, there is a (abstract) data sent on the addressed channel by the emission primitive applied by another process. In the case of asynchronous channel, if there is nothing on the channel, the attempt of reception is aborted.

3.2 Illustration: A Heterogeneous Control System

We consider the interaction between a net of processes modelling a control system equipped with sensors, actuators and controlers, from various vendors.

Let a process controller C_1 interacting by reading a channel ic and writing on a control channel cc. Let a process Sensor S_1 interacting by sending data on the same channel ic. At the modelling level, we could simply write compose(C_1, S_1) so that C_1 and S_1 interact via ic. Considering A_1 as the actuator process interacting by reading the channel cc, then the description $sys =$ compose(compose(C_1, S_1), A_1) builds a new system where the three processes interact together through the channels ic and cc. The controler C_1 may send orders to the actuator A_1 depending on data read from S_1. Now, we define two actuator processes A_2 and A_3 and a hub of actuators HA which sends its data to A_1, A_2 and A_3:

Actuator A2; Actuator A3; HA = compose((A1 rename cc as sc), A2, A3)

The behaviour expressed by replace($sys, A_1, (HA$ rename sc as cc)) results in a new system where the controler C_1 is not anymore directly connected to A_1 but to HA via the channel cc, a renaming of the previous sc channel of HA. In the same way we can easily add new sensors S_2, S_3 into an existing pool of sensors with the compose operator: compose(sys, S_2, S_3). The three sensors will write on the channel ic.

3.3 Extending the Core Operators

Consider that we have a system made of sensors, actuators, controlers and many other smart devices, making an adhoc network of communicating processes. We would like to plug a new device in the system; for instance a new plugged sensor detects the existing controlers and sends data to them, or a new plugged actuator joins the system and becomes ready to interact with the existing processes which send orders to the actuators. The system builder may evaluate the forthcoming system, decide if some components or operations are correct before performing them on the real system. This is profitable if the used models and operations on models are trustworthy. Consequently we would like to easily check the consistency of the new composition of processes prior to implementing it. For instance,

check($compose(sys, newSensor)$)
check($replace(sys, oldProcess, newProcess)$)

These scenario motivate the need to define the check operator which is not a process composition operator but an analysis one. Typically this kind of operators should implement at least the interaction compatibility, the absence of deadlock, liveness property. In the current stage of the work we reuse for this purpose, the existing tools of process algebra: UPPAAL [3] which has its own graphical input description formalism, SPIN [10] which has the Promela language as input process description language and CADP [8] which uses Lotos as input process description language.

4   Experimentations and Evaluation

We used the proposed operators to experiment with case studies, see for instance[2] for a detailed version of a case study of a distributed control system where various processes cooperate to control objects evolving within a given area.

The system consists of a set of robots which supervise a geographically widespread area and take actions with respect to events in the area: intruders or found unusual objects. Sub-components of the system are responsible of patrolling in different parts of the area and looking for preassigned objects; in case of detection of such objects a signal is sent to a supervisor. Other sub-components follow a specific object or a detected intruder and communicate its location to the supervisor. Several compatible processes initially described using DOT, Uppaal, promela were composed using our algebra. Several ζ_i morphisms were used to embed the described process models into LTS. The DOT formalism have been intensively used. The LTS are then embeded into Uppaal. For the current experiments the Uppaal tool have been used for the composition and the formal analysis of the composed system. We have been able to perform deadlock analysis and state reachability on the composed system.

Tool Support. To experiment with examples, we have developed the main modules of a prototype tool called aZiZa (see footnote 2), to support our method proposal. This is necessary to experiment and validate the proposed concepts and to improve the global composition method.

5   Conclusion

We have shown that under the hypothesis of semantic domain compatibility, the composition of heterogeneous behavioural models can be overcomed. We have used labelled transition systems as common semantics domain to found our method of composition. The method is based on an algebra of operators that focus on the manipulation of channels as the communication mechanism between the composed models. We have equipped the method with a tool in order to experiment with case studies that serve as a mean of assessment of the proposal.

---

[2] http://aziza.ls2n.fr.

One representative of the related works is Ptolemy II [11,17]. Ptolemy achieves the interaction between different actor-oriented models using an abstract semantics (namely the actor semantics). It also enables the use of finite state machines in place of actor-oriented models, but the interaction works rather as a global scheduler, controling a sequential execution flow of the FSM considered each as a global state linked via a port to another one. Moreover Ptolemy II is a general purpose heavy weight composition framework. Unlikely we target a specific, flexible and extensible framework dedicated to the composition and analysis of behavioural models dedicated to the growing small aperture nets of processes.

Yet we have considered some experiments where components deal locally with time constraints but dealing with time constraints at the global level is a challenge. As future work, we have planned experimentations with the CADP framework and especially its exp.open composition tool. We plan some improvements among which the propagation of global properties inside local components and vice versa. For this purpose we are investigating the Property Specification Language [1], an IEEE standard, as a pivotal for property passing through the components and through the various tools.

References

1. IEC 62531 Ed. 1 (2007–2011) (IEEE Std 1850–2005): Standard for Property Specification Language (PSL). IEC 62531:2007 (E), pp. 1–152, December 2007
2. Arnold, A.: Verification and comparison of transition systems. In: Gaudel, M.-C., Jouannaud, J.-P. (eds.) CAAP 1993. LNCS, vol. 668, pp. 121–135. Springer, Heidelberg (1993). doi:10.1007/3-540-56610-4_60
3. Behrmann, G., David, A., Larsen, K.G.: A tutorial on UPPAAL. In: Bernardo, M., Corradini, F. (eds.) SFM-RT 2004. LNCS, vol. 3185, pp. 200–236. Springer, Heidelberg (2004). doi:10.1007/978-3-540-30080-9_7
4. Black, D.C., Donovan, J., Keist, A., Bunton, B. (eds.): SystemC: From the Ground Up, 2nd edn. Springer, Heidelberg (2010)
5. Eker, J., Janneck, J.W., Lee, E.A., Liu, J., Liu, X., Ludvig, J., Neuendorffer, S., Sachs, S., Xiong, Y.: Taming heterogeneity - the ptolemy approach. Proc. IEEE 91(1), 127–144 (2003)
6. Friedenthal, S., Moore, A., Steiner, R.: A Practical Guide to SysML. The MK/OMG Press, Morgan Kaufmann, Boston (2015)
7. de Alfaro, L., Henzinger, T.A.: Interface theories for component-based design. In: Henzinger, T.A., Kirsch, C.M. (eds.) EMSOFT 2001. LNCS, vol. 2211, pp. 148–165. Springer, Heidelberg (2001). doi:10.1007/3-540-45449-7_11
8. Garavel, H., Lang, F., Mateescu, R., Serwe, W.: CADP 2011: a toolbox for the construction and analysis of distributed processes. STTT 15(2), 89–107 (2013)
9. Goderis, A., Brooks, C.X., Altintas, I., Lee, E.A., Goble, C.A.: Heterogeneous composition of models of computation. Future Gener. Comp. Syst. 25(5), 552–560 (2009)
10. Holzmann, G.J.: The spin model checker. IEEE Trans. Softw. Eng. 23(5), 279–295 (1997)

11. Lee, E.A.: Disciplined heterogeneous modeling. In: Petriu, D.C., Rouquette, N., Haugen, Ø. (eds.) MODELS 2010. LNCS, vol. 6395, pp. 273–287. Springer, Heidelberg (2010). doi:10.1007/978-3-642-16129-2_20

12. LOTOS: a formal description technique based on the temporal ordering of observational behaviour. International Standard 8807, IOS - OSI, Geneva (1988)

13. Milner, R., Parrow, J., Walker, D.: A calculus of mobile processes. J. Inf. Comput. **100**, 1–40 (1992)

14. Milner, R.: Communication and Concurrency. Prentice-Hall, Upper Saddle River (1989)

15. Roscoe, A.W., Davies, J.: CSP (communicating sequential processes). In: Padua, D.A. (ed.) Encyclopedia of Parallel Computing. Springer, Heidelberg (2011). doi:10.1007/978-0-387-09766-4_186

16. Roth, C.H., Kinney, L.L.: Fundamentals of Logic Design. Thomson, Luton (2004)

17. Tripakis, S., Stergiou, C., Shaver, C., Lee, E.A.: A modular formal semantics for ptolemy. Math. Struct. Comput. Sci. **23**(4), 834–881 (2013)

Intelligent Detection Without Modeling of Behavior Unusual by Fuzzy Logic

Hocine Chebi[1(✉)], Dalila Acheli[2], and Mohamed Kesraoui[1]

[1] Faculty of Hydrocarbons and Chemistry,
University M'hamed Bougara Boumerdès, Boumerdès, Algeria
chebi.hocine@yahoo.fr, mkesraoui@umbb.dz
[2] Laboratoire d'Automatique Appliqué, Faculty of Engineering,
University M'hamed Bougara Boumerdès,
Avenue de l'Indépendance, 35000 Boumerdès, Algeria
dacheli2000@yahoo.fr

Abstract. This work falls within the framework of the video surveillance research axis. It involves a link between automatic processing and problems related to video surveillance. The job is to analyze video streams coming from a network of surveillance cameras, deployed in an area of interest in order to detect abnormal behavior. Our approach in this paper is based on the new application and the use of fuzzy logic with an aim of avoided the modeling of abnormal crowd behavior. By introducing the notion of degree in the verification of a condition, thus allowing a condition to be in another state rather than true or false, fuzzy logic confers a very appreciable flexibility on the reasoning that uses it, taking into account inaccuracies and uncertainties. One of the work interests performed in formalized human reasoning is that the rules are spelled out in a natural language. Detecting these behaviors will increase the response speed of security services to perform accurate analysis and detection of abnormal events. We then present a comparative table followed by a study on the effects of using another technique. Despite the complexity of the sequences, our approach provides highly relevant results including in the detection areas of several crowd behaviors.

Keywords: Abnormal detection · Crowd behavior · Classification · Segmentation · Tracking · Fuzzy logic · Events

1 Introduction

The computer vision field (also called artificial vision, digital vision or cognitive vision) aims at reproducing on a computer the capacities of analysis and interpretation proper to human vision. The general objective is to design models and systems capable of representing and interpreting the visual content of a scene. Computer vision is an exciting topic in artificial intelligence research. Although considerable progress has been made in the resolution of certain problems such as automatic video surveillance, the latter treats the framework of analysis of the behavior of people present in the scene making it possible to predict incidents and to detect certain events. It also provides information that explains the activity of these individuals and their interests. Therefore, the analysis of human behavior using video is rich field in various experiments [1–4];

© Springer International Publishing AG 2017
Y. Ouhammou et al. (Eds.): MEDI 2017, LNCS 10563, pp. 300–307, 2017.
DOI: 10.1007/978-3-319-66854-3_23

we use the term computer vision behavior to denote the physical and apparent behavior produced as a result of movement, without psychological or cognitive interpretation. The analysis of human behavior is very useful in a large number of applications. We are interested in our work with crowd behavior, the automatic study of crowd behavior makes it possible to develop crowd management strategies, especially for popular events or events frequented by a large number of people (example: sports meetings, Large concerts, public events, etc.). The study of the crowds makes it possible to anticipate certain abnormal behaviors in order to avoid accidents caused by disorganized movement of the crowds. Although anomalous crowd detection has received some attention in recent years, most research however, has focused on identifying and tracking abnormal behaviors (such as suspicious events, irregular behavior, uncommon behavior, unusual activity, abnormal behavior, anomaly, etc.) of a single person or a few moving objects in a crowd. The Approaches used for the analysis of crowd behavior in video sequences generally comprises of four essential stages: detection of movement, segmentation, classification, and tracking [1, 5–11].

Whereas the temporal derivative quantifies the variation of the aspect of each pixel considered individually in the movement detection case, the optical flow is modeled by a vector field in two dimensions representing the projection on the image plane of the real movement observed (in 3D). Accordingly many methods [12–14] were proposed since the precursory article of Horn and [15] with an aim of improving the implementation of the latter. In [16], nine algorithms are studied and compared according to criteria of precision and density of the obtained vector field, but no mention is made of algorithmic complexity. The work of [17] makes it possible to fill this gap by measuring the reports/ratios (precision)/(calculations team) of these methods. The segmentation is the stage which consists of cutting out the image in a successive way by considering the apparent movement dominating the zones not labeled then by detecting the zones not conforming to this model of movement [18]. The principle of this method rests on the taking into account of a total image in which the dominant movement and the zones in conformity with this movement forming a first area of the partition are estimated. This process of estimate and detection is reiterated on the non-conforming zones until all pixels are classified [19, 20]. The method of training for a phase of classification generates a function which corresponds to an image received in a specific labeled entry. There are several methods of training in literature, such as decision trees [21], neural networks [22], fuzzy logic, AdaBoost (Adaptive Boosting) [23], or machines with vectors of support (MVS) [24].

The main contribution in this article is the proposed intermediate level visual characteristic, and thus the use of fuzzy logic in the case of abnormal behavior in a crowd scene. The major advantage of this method is that it doesn't need to be modeled [25], because it consists of detecting the movement by mathematical calculation in any point of the image, which is a function of the intensity or the color of all the pixels and which is supposed to reflect the importance of the visible movement in the scene. By introducing the notion of degree in the verification of a condition, thus allowing a condition to be in another state of crowd behavior other than true or false, fuzzy logic confers a very appreciable flexibility to the reasoning that uses it. This makes it possible to take into account inaccuracies and uncertainties in the case of detection of crowd behavior. Speed is considered a characteristic of images and fuzzy rules explore the modeling of normal and abnormal behaviors. The remainder of the paper is organized as follows. In Sect. 2, this paper represents the proposed global approach to crowd behavior detection. In Sect. 3, experiment results on real world video scenes are presented. Finally, the conclusion and potential extensions of this work are described in Sect. 4.

2 Application of Fuzzy Logic

Classical logic is a part of mathematics relatively well known to the public. It is on its principle that computers and most digital machines work. In classical logic, decisions are binary: either true or false. It is on this point that fuzzy logic will be distinguished from classical logic. In fuzzy logic, a decision can be both true and false at the same time, with a certain degree of belonging to each of these two beliefs. In our work we use fuzzy logic as a method of automatic classification of crowd behavior. For example, consider these two rules of inferences:

- If the speed magnitude is low, then behavior is normal;
- If the speed magnitude is high then behavior is abnormal.

In classical logic, an object can only be near or far. If the distance of behavior is low, then this one will be normal. In fuzzy logic, however, the object will be both normal and abnormal at the same time. Here, the object that is low will, for example, be 60% normal and 40% abnormal. One realizes that in fuzzy logic, a fact no longer has a strict belonging to a belief, but a "fuzzy" belonging.

3 Experimental Results

In this section, we propose the evaluation of the simulation results according to synthetic data by videos. The videos are mainly gathered from the whole of UMN data [26] and the whole of data PETS2009 [27], which were largely widespread for the performance evaluation [28], the results will be detailed in the nearest sections.

3.1 Evaluation of Behavior Analysis with Fuzzy Logic in UMN Dataset

We can easily detect visual reinforcements like abnormal ones using the automatic architecture of classification. In particular, the advantage of the method suggested is obvious in outdoor and indoor scenes, the detection of normal and abnormal behavior in the various scenes is made in an automatic way one using fuzzy logic. The sufficient results of the comparison between the social force method [2] and the method of the acceleration feature; the method suggested carries out a stable detection of behavior. Results more representative of comparison for scenarios is shown in Fig. 1. We can see that the execution of the method proposed is more precise and stable in almost all the scenarios. Fuzzy logic thus makes it possible to control complex systems that can not necessarily be modulated in an "intuitive" way. However, this method has various disadvantages. First, expressing one's knowledge in the form of natural language (and therefore qualitative) rules does not prove that the system will behave optimally.

This method cannot guarantee that the behavior is precise or optimal, or even guarantee that the rules entered by the programmer are not contradictory.

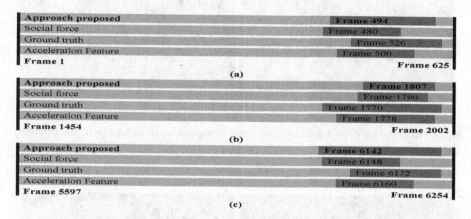

Fig. 1. Crowd escapes behavior detection for several scenarios in the UMN dataset. Our performance is compared with the social force method, ground truth and acceleration feature. (a) Result of the scenario UMN 1. (b) Result of the scenario UMN 3. (c) Result of the scenario UMN 9.

3.2   Evaluation of Dangerous Situations with Dataset BMVA

The results of the approach are represented in Figs. 2, 3 and 4. In our work we suppose that the number of people in an occulted group is not limited. The obtained results are encouraging when the automatic detection of anomalies is close to the real time measurement. The approach suggested shows a great robustness against false alarm detection since the automatic detection of anomaly occurs after the real release of the anomaly. Our approach presents some advantages as it presents a positive contribution to the detection of movement in a complex environment. However, it requires the estimation of temporal time for each image bloc and at every moment of the video sequence which makes it very greedy in computing power consumption. To show the effectiveness of the method we simulated Fig. 6 which shows satisfactory results in other behaviors.

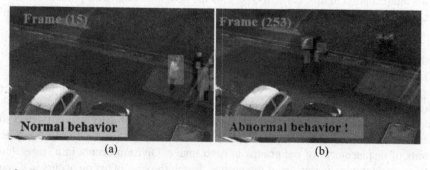

Fig. 2. Example 1 of event detected by fuzzy logic in dangerous situations (a- normal behavior, and b- abnormal behavior).

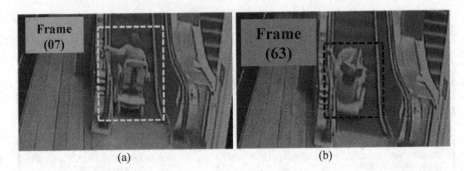

(a)   (b)

Fig. 3. Example 2 of event detected by fuzzy logic in situation in an escalator (a- normal behavior, and b- abnormal behavior).

(a)   (b)

Fig. 4. Detection of behavior by fuzzy logic in dataset BMVA, (a) normal behavior, (b) abnormal behavior.

3.3 Evaluation Behavior Fusion and Division on the PETS2009 Dataset and UMN Dataset

The proposed approach is based on computing the magnitude of the motion vector which presents the optical flow in the Cartesian frame. The point $P(x, y)$ is the position of his interest point at time t where $Q(x, y)$ is the position of the same point at $t + 1$. We use the Euclidean distance to compute the distance travelled by the interest point :

$$M_i = \sqrt[2]{\left(Q_{xi} - P_{xi}\right)^2 + \left(Q_{yi} - P_{yi}\right)^2}.$$ This method is very useful when confronted with systems that are impossible, or difficult to model. Similarly, this method is very advantageous if one possesses a good level of human expertise. Indeed, it is necessary to provide to the fuzzy system a whole set of rules expressed in natural language to allow reasoning and draw conclusions. The greater the human expertise of a system, the greater the ability to add inference rules to the system of detection. To detect the events of fusion and division we calculate the circular variance relating to the orientations of displacement of the groups in each image. Division occurs in a larger zone with a considerable divergence of the groups. But in the case of fusion occurs in a zone restricted for a short length of time. The results evolution is represented in Fig. 5.

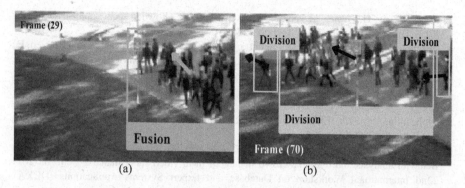

Fig. 5. Representation of the events, (a) fusion (b) division.

Fig. 6. Detection of behavior by fuzzy logic, (a) normal behavior, (b) abnormal behavior.

4   Conclusion

In conclusion, it can be said that fuzzy logic has the advantage of being intuitive and able to operate a large number of different systems with strong human expertise. Nevertheless, one should bear in mind that in fuzzy logic it is impossible to predict detection performance. If the settings are fine, the performance will be fine, but if there is a lack of precision in the settings, the performance will be imperfect also. In spite of this inconvenience we can say that the results show that our system proves to be very robust and precise for the sets of videos used in this application. Ultimately in the future, we want to implement the application on a real-time map and to use a hybrid method to fuzzy logic.

References

1. Chebi, H., Acheli, D., Kesraoui, M.: Dynamic detection of abnormalities in video analysis of crowd behavior with DBSCAN and neural networks. Adv. Sci. Technol. Eng. Syst. J. 1(5), 56–63 (2016)
2. Chen, C., Shao, Y., Bi, X.: Detection of anomalous crowd behavior based on the acceleration feature. IEEE Sens. J. 15(12), 7252–7261 (2015)

3. Li, T., Chang, H., Wang, M., Ni, B., Hong, R., Yan, S.: Crowded scene analysis: a survey. IEEE Trans. Circ. Syst. Video Technol. **25**(3), 367–386 (2015)

4. Burghouts, G.J., den Hollander, R., Schutte, K., Marck, J.W., Landsmeer, S., den Breejen, E.: Increasing the security at vital infrastructures: automated detection of deviant behaviors. In: International Society for Optics and Photonics SPIE Defense, Security, and Sensing, pp. 80190C–80190C, May 2011

5. Ko, T.: A survey on behavior analysis in video surveillance for homeland security applications. In: 37th IEEE Applied Imagery Pattern Recognition Workshop, AIPR 2008, pp. 1–8, 15–17 October 2008

6. Szczodrak, M., Kotus, J., Kopaczewski, K., Lopatka, K., Czyzewski, A., Krawczyk, H.: Behavior analysis and dynamic crowd management in video surveillance system. In: 2011 22nd International Workshop on Database and Expert Systems Applications (DEXA), pp. 371–375, 29 August–2 September 2011

7. El Maadi, A., Djouadi, M.S.: Suspicious motion patterns detection and tracking in crowded scenes. In: 2013 IEEE International Symposium on Safety, Security, and Rescue Robotics (SSRR), pp. 1–6, 21–26 October 2013

8. Li, J., Wang, G.: A shadow detection method based on improved Gaussian mixture model. In: 2013 IEEE 4th International Conference on Electronics Information and Emergency Communication (ICEIEC), pp. 62–65, IEEE. November 2013

9. Qian, H., Wu, X., Ou, Y., Xu, Y.: Hybrid algorithm for segmentation and tracking in surveillance. In: IEEE International Conference on Robotics and Biomimetics, ROBIO 2008, pp. 395–400. IEEE, February 2009

10. Ali, S., Shah, M.: A lagrangian particle dynamics approach for crowd flow segmentation and stability analysis. In: IEEE Conference on Computer Vision and Pattern Recognition, CVPR 2007, pp. 1–6, 17–22 June 2007

11. Shi, J., Tomasi, C.: Good features to track. In: IEEE Computer Society Conference on Computer Vision and Pattern Recognition, Proceedings CVPR 1994, pp. 593–600, 21–23 June 1994

12. Atcheson, B., Heidrich, W., Ihrke, I.: An evaluation of optical flow algorithms for background oriented schlieren imaging. Exp. Fluids **46**(3), 467–476 (2009)

13. Burt, P.J., Adelson, E.H.: The laplacian pyramid as a compact image code. IEEE Trans. Commun. **31**(4), 532–540 (1983)

14. Horn, B.K., Schunck, B.G.: Determining optical flow. In: 1981 Technical Symposium East, International Society for Optics and Photonics (1981)

15. Barron, J.L., David, J.F., Steven, S.B.: Performance of optical flow techniques. Int. J. Comput. Vis. **12**(1), 43–77 (1994)

16. Liu, H., Hong, T.H., Herman, M., Camus, T., Chellappa, R.: Accuracy vs efficiency trade-offs in optical flow algorithms. Comput. Vis. Image Underst. **72**(3), 271–286 (1998)

17. Demonceaux, C.: Etude du mouvement dans les séquences d'images par analyse d'ondelettes et modélisation markovienne hiérarchique. Application à la détection d'obstacles dans un milieu routier. Diss. Université de Picardie Jules Verne (2004)

18. Irani, M., Rousso, B., Peleg, S.: Detecting and tracking multiple moving objects using temporal integration. In: Proceedings of European Conference on Computer Vision, Santa Margherita Ligure, Italy, pp. 282–287, May 1992

19. Ayer, S., Schroeter, P., Bigun, J.: Segmentation of moving objects by robust motion parameter estimation over multiple frames. In: Proceedings of European Conference on Computer Vision, Stockholm, Suède, pp. 316–327, May 1994

20. Grewe, L., Kak, A.C.: Interactive learning of a multiple-attribute hash table classifier for fast object recognition. Comput. Vis. Image Underst. **61**(3), 387–416 (1995)

21. Rowley, H.A., Baluja, S., Kanade, T.: Neural network-based face detection. IEEE Trans. Pattern Anal. Mach. Intell. **20**(1), 23–38 (1998)
22. Viola, P., Jones, M.J., Snow, D.: Detecting pedestrians using patterns of motion and appearance. Int. J. Comput. Vis. **63**(2), 153–161 (2005)
23. Papageorgiou, C.P., Oren, M., Poggio, T.: A general framework for object detection. In: Sixth International Conference on Computer Vision 1998, pp. 555–562. IEEE, January 1998
24. Wang, S., Miao, Z.: Anomaly detection in crowd scene. In: IEEE 10th International Conference On Signal Processing, pp. 1220–1223. IEEE, October 2010
25. UMN: Unusual crowd activity dataset of university of minnesota, Minneapolis, MN, USA (2006). http://mha.cs.umn.edu/movies/crowd-activity-all.avi
26. PETS: Multisensor sequences containing different crowd activities, Vellore, India (2009). http://www.cvg.rdg.ac.uk/pets2009/a.html
27. Blunsden, S.J., Fisher, R.B.: The BEHAVE video dataset: ground truthed video for multi-person behavior classification. Ann. BMVA **4**, 1–12 (2010). http://groups.inf.ed.ac.uk/vision/BEHAVEDATA/INTERACTIONS/
28. Mehran, R., Oyama, A., Shah, M.: Abnormal crowd behavior detection using social force model. In: Proceedings of IEEE Conference on Computer Vision and Pattern Recognition (CVPR), Miami, FL, USA, pp. 935–942, June 2009

Model-Based Applications

Enabling Agile Web Development Through In-Browser Code Generation and Evaluation

Alejandro Cortiñas[1]([⊠]), Carlo Bernaschina[2], Miguel R. Luaces[1],
and Piero Fraternali[2]

[1] Databases Laboratory, Universidade da Coruña, A Coruña, Spain
{alejandro.cortinas,luaces}@udc.es
[2] DEIB, Politecnico di Milano, Milan, Italy
{carlo.bernaschina,piero.fraternali}@polimi.it

Abstract. Rapid evolution and flexibility are the key of modern web application development. Rapid Prototyping approaches try to facilitate evolution by reducing the time between the elicitation of a new requirement and the evaluation of a prototype by both developers and customers. Software generation, with disciplines such as Software Product Lines Engineering or Model Driven Engineering, favours the required flexibility for the development process. Nevertheless, each small change in the design of an application requires a full redeployment of complex environments in order to allow customers to test and evaluate the new configuration. In this work we present an approach that improves the development process reducing the complexity of deploying evaluation prototypes and enabling an agile development cycle. The approach can be applied using software generation and it is based on in-browser generation and evaluation. We also describe two real world tools that have integrated the proposed approach in their development cycle.

Keywords: Software Product Lines · Model Driven Engineering · Agile software development · Rapid prototyping

1 Introduction

Reducing time-to-market is a major concern in all software engineering disciplines. Software development methodologies have dealt with these problems using rapid development techniques such as agile development and continuous deployment, and automatic code generation techniques such as Model-Driven Engineering (MDE) and Software Product Line Engineering (SPLE). However, in order to allow the final user to review the software, all these techniques require

The work of the authors from UDC has been funded by MINECO (PGE & FEDER) [TIN2016-78011-C4-1-R, TIN2016-77158-C4-3-R, TIN2013-46238-C4-3-R, TIN2013-46801-C4-3-R]; CDTI and MINECO [Ref. IDI-20141259, Ref. ITC-20151305, Ref. ITC-20151247]; Xunta de Galicia (FEDER) [Ref. ED431G/01]; predoctoral research stay grant Inditex-UDC.

© Springer International Publishing AG 2017
Y. Ouhammou et al. (Eds.): MEDI 2017, LNCS 10563, pp. 311–323, 2017.
DOI: 10.1007/978-3-319-66854-3_24

that the software artefacts are deployed to a production environment. This task is often time and resource-consuming and hinders real-time interaction between the final user and the analyst in charge of eliciting requirements. To avoid this problem, rapid prototyping techniques have been proposed. However, prototypes are not the final products and it is often required a large effort to build them.

In order to further reduce time-to-market, we propose a new approach that integrates software-generation techniques with rapid development techniques to reduce drastically the deployment time of web applications. Furthermore, considering that web applications are the most popular kind of software products developed right now, and taking into account that they run on web browsers, it is possible to use the actual software product as the prototype during the development stages for the final user to review.

In order to evaluate the approach, we present two different implementations of our approach as use cases. The first use case is an academic example that uses for MDE as the software generation technique. The second use case is an industrial example of a tool developed by Enxenio[1] using SPLE.

This work is organized as follows: Sect. 2 summarizes the concepts involved in our approach; Sect. 3 explains the approach itself; Sect. 4 presents two use cases of applying it; Sect. 5 draws conclusions and future work.

2   Related Work

Developing software following a classic approach is a slow and costly process. When a client orders a new product, an analyst has to understand what the client wants and, more importantly, what the client needs. From the ideas the analyst captures, the set of requirements for the product is forged and, eventually, the set of features that will comply with them. Then, the analysis and design of the new software is finished and the development team starts implementing the required features. Once the product is implemented, tested and deployed, the client can finally see the product he or she asked for. At this point, the client always requires changes, even with the best of the analysis. Therefore, a refinement stage is required, so a new analysis is made and the changes implemented. This goes on until the client is finally satisfied, an even then, the process starts again for every new feature that the product must support.

With a naked eye, the process does not seem very efficient, and several methodologies have appeared to decrease the costs in time and effort. Some of the new methodologies focus on the implementation and testing stages [3,15,21], whereas others try to improve the general workflow and the interaction between the analyst and other stakeholders. Examples of the former are SPLE and MDE, two fields based on the generation and reusing of software artefacts; an example of the latter is Rapid Development, a field which aims at avoiding overly complicated solutions.

---

[1] http://www.enxenio.es.

2.1 Rapid Development

In past years many approaches have been proposed to reduce the time required to bring a product to market. They are specially useful with large and medium size projects, which require a complex and long development cycle before having a product that can be evaluated by customers and users.

Agile Software Development. [1] is an incremental and iterative approach which aims at increasing productivity and adherence to requirements, while keeping the process as lightweight as possible. As an example, workflows such as SCRUM [21] simplify the introduction of new functionalities by organizing the work in small tasks and iterative sprints which reduce the time required to develop, integrate and test them.

Continuous Deployment. [10] is an approach which aims at immediately deploying software to customers as soon as new code is developed. It has great advantages like: new business opportunities, reduced risk for each release, and preventing the development of wasted software. It has been successfully implemented by many companies like Facebook, Microsoft, and IBM.

2.2 Software Product Line Engineering

Traditionally, the development of every software product goes through a series of steps: elicitation of requirements, design, implementation, testing and maintenance. Following this approach, if a software development company has to build a family of products, all the stages mentioned must be done for each one of them, even when the products share functionalities or are focused in the same specific market. The downside of this approach is that it requires high development and maintenance costs in order to produce high quality products, while the *time-to-market* for each product is long since development starts from scratch.

In other classic manufacturing industries, such as the automotive or the textile, the way the products are built evolved from a manual manufacturing process to industrial processes that use proper machinery. Software Product Lines Engineering is a discipline that aims at applying the same kind of evolution to the way software is built, i.e., applying mass-production, mass-customization and reuse strategies to software development. A Software Product Line (SPL) is a family of software products sharing features developed from a common set of reusable core assets that can be combined and configured in different ways for different products [11]. A SPL separates the development of these core, reusable assets (i.e., the *platform*), and the development of the actual applications (i.e., the *products*). The family of products is modelled as a set of *features*, which are end-user visible aspects or characteristics of a software system [12]. Features can be mandatory or optional, and each product is built from a selection of features made by an *analyst*. The main advantages of SPL are the reduced costs and the improved quality of the products, and the drastic reduction of the time-to-market for new products compared to the traditional approaches [20]. All these advantages are simply derived from the fact that the software assets are shared between all the products, so they are implemented once but used and tested in every product.

There are several types of SPL regarding the way the products are generated [4]. In some cases, the product is not expected to be modified after the generation, or even it is automatically deployed. In other cases, the product is generated as independent source code that can be extended or refined by a development team, and that has to be manually deployed afterwards. In the latter cases, the cost in time and effort from the generation of the source code to the deployment may be high.

2.3   Model Driven Development

Model Driven Development (MDD) is the branch of software engineering that advocates the use of *models*, i.e., abstract representations of a system, and of *model transformations* as key ingredients of software development [15]. With MDD, developers use a general purpose (e.g. UML [2]) or domain specific (e.g., IFML [18]) modelling language to portray the essential aspects of a system, under one or more perspectives, and use (or build) suitable chains of *transformations* to progressively refine the models into executable code.

Agile Model Driven Development has been advocated as a promising approach [3], which has not yet fully expressed its potential [17]. Its idea is to organize the MDD process in ways that take advantage of the agile development principles:

1. Enabling an incremental and iterative development cycle by using tool chains able to test and validate even incomplete models [13].
2. Applying a Test-Driven Development, a distinctive feature of extreme programming [5], to MDD [22].
3. Merging agile workflows such as SCRUM [21] with MDD in novel methodologies, to achieve system-level agile processes [23].

3   Our Approach

SPLE, MDD or similar methodologies for the semi-automatic generation of software tackle intrinsic repetitive structures in the development of software products, either full software components like the ones assembled within a SPL, or actual generation of code from high level descriptions and model-to-model/code transformations like in MDD. These approaches are particularly suited to the iterative evolution of the project, by means of small improvements which can be easily tested and validated. However, the nature of web applications makes the evaluation of these new features complex, due to the fact that a new full deployment is necessary after each change.

Continuous deployment is particularly suited to bring these new functionalities to a set of evaluators, but it is not suitable for an integration in the development cycle itself due to its complexity. The main problematic in trying to integrate an evaluation of the final product within SPLE or MDE is related to the full code generation intrinsic in these approaches. Changes to the final product cannot be applied directly to the deployed application, but instead the high level description needs to be updated and a full code generation triggered.

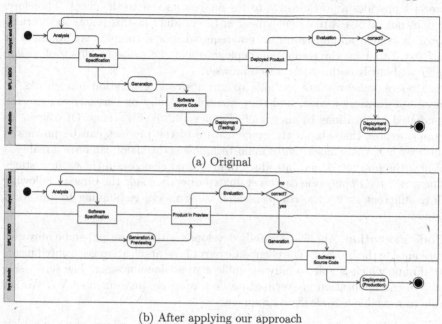

(a) Original

(b) After applying our approach

Fig. 1. Activity diagram of the development process

We show in Fig. 1a a simplified workflow with processes and stakeholders involved in the development of a web application with automatic or semi-automatic generation of software. We can see how the analyst, with input from the client, elaborates the *Software Specification*; then the generation of the product, which can be based on SPLE, MDD or any other methodology, begins. The generated software has to be deployed for evaluation by a different actor, the system administrator. At this point, the analyst and the client can, together, evaluate the product and determine whether the product is the one required by the client or some changes are required. If the product is finished, then the system administrator can deploy the final version into production environment and the process ends. If the product is not complete, then the process starts again and the system administrator is involved, again, to make a redeployment in the testing environment. There are some cases when the analyst is the one that deploys the product for evaluation. In these cases, even when there is not an extra actor involved, this deployment still needs a complex environment and it is time consuming.

We propose an approach to simplify and improve the workflow for the development of web applications through automatic generation techniques by removing the necessity of an actual deployment during the development process. Only when the analyst decides that a project is correct, the full-source is generated and deployed.

The workflow, when our approach is applied, is shown in Fig. 1b. It is analogous to the previous one but, in this case, the same tool that generates the product provides a preview of it to the analyst and/or to the client. Therefore, it does not involve a real deployment of the product at this point, so the third actor, a system administrator, is not required, nor a complex environment or any extra tool for the evaluation deployment of the project. This tool we are talking about is nothing but a web browser.

Modern web browsers are able to execute code generation frameworks by means of Javascript code, and they are able to fully or partially execute the generated applications by means of *iFrames* and *WebWorkers*. Of course, we cannot expect that absolutely every feature of the product can be previewed this way but, using mocks and similar techniques, the client can have a real idea of how the product is and introduce the required changes on the earliest stage. The generated application can be evaluated directly inside the browser following three different strategies, complemented using mocks responding to any XHR request.

Code Execution. Applications fully developed with Javascript can be fully executed inside the browser. The client-side part of the application is executed inside an iFrame which is able to fully resemble a standalone browser. The server-side part of the application is executed inside a properly instrumented WebWorker able to resemble a NodeJS environment.

Full Emulation. Applications developed with different technologies can exploit the full code generation intrinsic to SPLE and MDD to trigger a different version of the transformation. This way, it can generate a functionally equivalent version of the application in Javascript which can be tested using the previous strategy.

Partial Emulation. Applications developed with a mixture of Javascript and other technologies can use a mixed strategy; this is, the non Javascript parts can be replaced by a functionally equivalent version and then the product is executed within an iFrame.

All the three strategies can be used to evaluate the final application without the need of complex server side deployed infrastructures, increasing productivity and reducing tools configuration complexity.

We have tried our approach within two different tools, one based in SPLE and the other one in MDD, but our approach can be applied to any other software generation technique as long as the engine is built with Javascript, which is the programming language that can be run on a web-browser[2].

---

[2] In any other case our approach is still conceptually valid but the generation must occur in the server side and after it, the source code must be loaded within the web client.

4   Implementations

In this section we present two academic (see Sect. 4.1) and industrial (see Sect. 4.2) tools which apply the proposed approach to real world scenarios.

4.1   IFMLEdit

IFMLEdit.org[3] is an online environment for the specification of IFML models, the investigation of their properties by means of a mapping to Place Chart Nets [14], and the generation of code for web and mobile architecture.

IFML (Interaction Flow Modeling Language [18]) is an OMG standard that supports the platform-independent description of graphical user interfaces (UIs) for devices such as desktop computers, laptops, mobile phones, and tablets. IFML focuses on the structure and behaviour of the application as perceived by the end user, and references the data and business logic aspects insofar they influence the users experience, i.e., the domain objects that provide content displayed in the interface and the actions triggered from the interface.

IFML allows developers to specify the following aspects of an interactive application:

- **The view structure and content:** the general organization of the interface is expressed in terms of *ViewElements*, along with their containment relationships, visibility, and activation. Two classes of ViewElements exist: *ViewContainers*, i.e., elements for representing the nested structure of the interface, and *ViewComponents*, i.e., elements for content display and data entry. *ViewComponents* that display content have a *ContentBinding*, which expresses the link to the data source.
- **The events:** the occurrences that affect the state of the user interface, which can be produced by the users interaction, the application, or an external system.
- **The event transitions:** the consequences of an event on the user interface, which can be the change of the *ViewContainer*, the update of the content on display, the triggering of an action, or a mix of these effects. *Actions* are represented as black boxes.
- **The parameter binding:** the input-output dependencies between *ViewElements* and *Actions*.

The tool [9], which is developed using ALMOsT.js [6], supports the following workflow: (1) the developer edits the IFML model of the application in the online editor, possibly providing hints for the generation of the fast prototype (e.g., sample data); (2) he (optionally) maps the model into a PCN and simulates the network to understand the dynamics of the application in response to events; (3) he generates the code of a fast prototype, for the web or for a cross-platform mobile language, executes and validates the prototype; (4) he turns the validated prototype into a real app, by customizing look&feel and replacing mock-up data access and operational APIs calls with real ones.

---

[3] http://www.ifmledit.org.

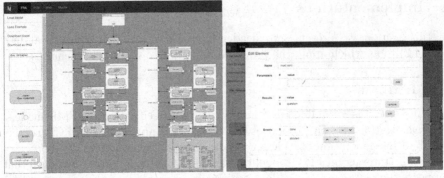

(a) Model editor   (b) Element property editors

Fig. 2. IFML editing

IFML Model Editing. Figure 2a shows how the integrated IFML editor allows the developer to compose and edit the model by means of drag&drop from the palette on the left side.

Data-Bindings. Once the structure of the application is modelled, the developer can use the property editor (Fig. 2b) to specify how *ViewComponents* connect between them and to the data sources.

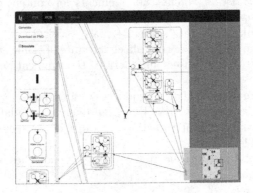

Fig. 3. Model semantics simulation

Model Semantics and Simulation. The developer can generate a formal description of the application by running the model-to-model transformation from IFML to PCNs. The application behaviour is rendered visually by means of tokens moving in the net, displaying the control flow in the interface and the change of status of *ViewElements*. Figure 3 illustrates the PCN model generated from the IFML diagram of Fig. 2a; the PCN simulation helps the developer identify inconsistencies in the specified application, such as unreachable states and race conditions.

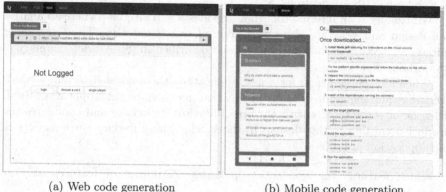

(a) Web code generation   (b) Mobile code generation

Fig. 4. Code generation

Code Generation. The developer can generate a fully functional prototype for both the web and mobile architecture, launching a model-to-code transformation. Figure 4a shows the generated web prototype, run on top of the web server emulated inside the browser. Figure 4b shows the generated mobile prototype, run within the mobile emulator inside the browser. In-browser emulation allows the developer to test the current web or mobile release of the prototype without installing any web server and also in absence of the Internet connection. The *Browser-Server emulator* is a pure Javascript component able to emulate a web browser, a Node.js server and the whole request response cycle that connects the two. It is used to support online and offline work seamlessly. The *Mobile emulator* is a Javascript component able to emulate a mobile cross-platform environment (now Cordova); it supports the instantaneous execution of the generated cross-platform mobile code.

Prototype Download. The previous steps can be reiterated to evaluate different application structures (e.g., single vs multiple pages) and interaction approaches (e.g., update on object selection vs explicit update events). The generated prototype can be downloaded and refined to produce the final application. Each IFML Action and ViewComponent data query is encoded as a web service, which can be replaced by an external implementation.

4.2   GISBuilder

Enxenio[4] is a Spanish SME (small and medium enterprise) with expertise in GIS. Enxenio has collaborated with the Database Laboratory at the University

---

[4] http://www.enxenio.es.

of A Coruña many times in the past, and several works, such as [7, 16, 19], are the result of this collaboration. For some time now, Enxenio and the Database Laboratory have been working on the design of a SPL for the automatic generation of web-based GIS applications [8].

GISBuilder is an internal tool that provides a web interface where an analyst can design and generate the source-code of web-based GIS. The GISBuilder initial architecture is shown in Fig. 5a and described in [8]. A brief summary of its workflow follows.

When a client comes in for a new application, the analyst determines which are the requirements of the new application and designs the application itself. Then he or she interacts with the **specification interface** and configures the product according to this design. In the specification interface three aspects of the application are set:

- Which features the application provides. Examples of features are *csv importer* or *user management*.
- The data model for the application: entities, properties and relationships. From this data model, the analyst can define lists, forms or map viewers, and link these elements with menu entries.
- Several aspects of the graphical user interface, such as the menu configuration, the static pages or the UI layout.

Once the configuration or specification of the product is done, the **derivation engine** is invoked. This engine takes the product specification and assembles/generates the source code of the final products, taking the required components from the **component repository**. Since the derivation engine is based on scaffolding, the different components are nothing but annotated source code files, or templates. Furthermore, the product specification is also stored in the **project repository** so it can be reloaded and edited in the future if required.

The output provided by GISBUilder is a ZIP file with the source code of the product that has to be manually deployed within a web server with some previously installed software (such as Java, Tomcat, Node.js, npm, PostgreSQL with PostGIS, etc.). Even if it has been deployed previously, it has to be fully redeployed again. This process is slow and it usually requires more than one person, since the analyst is not in charge of preproduction deployments. In the case a client is providing feedback to the analyst, this redeployment causes the interaction with him to be slow and absolutely not in real-time.

We wanted to facilitate the interaction between the client and the analyst of the company by allowing the client to propose and evaluate changes to the product in real-time while it is being configured. To achieve this, we have applied the approach presented in this paper and we have enhanced GISBuilder to generate and show a preview of the designed products at runtime, directly on the browser, without the need of any server-side structure.

In order to get this, we have changed the way GISBuilder is designed, as we can see in Fig. 5b. The main changes are:

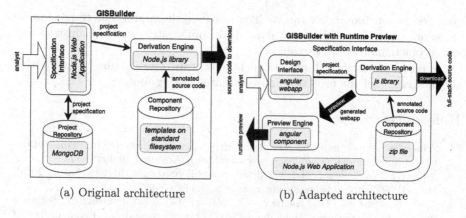

(a) Original architecture   (b) Adapted architecture

Fig. 5. Architecture changes in GISBuilder

(1) We have implemented a new version of the **derivation engine** that is able to run entirely on the web browser.

(2) The **derivation engine** is integrated within the **specification interface**, as well as the **component repository**, provided as a ZIP file.

(3) Our preview component intercepts XHR request of the previewing application and returns mocks responses to each specific REST petition.

(4) GISBuilder produces full-stack web applications with Spring in the server side and Angular in the client side. In the adapted version, GISBuilder creates two different versions of the products, depending on whether the analyst wants to preview them or to download the full-stack version.

This way, after a reconfiguration of the product, the analyst can simply run its preview and show the client its aspect. Of course, the previewing component does not run every feature of the SPL, but it can still show enough to provide the customer a realistic view of the application. When the client is satisfied with the preview, the actual full-stack version of the product can be generated and deployed, just as before.

5   Conclusions and Future Work

Reducing the time required to introduce a new functionality is a key requirement of modern software development. Approaches like Software Product Lines Engineering and Model Driven Engineering exploit recurrent structures through high-level descriptions that are refined into final product via full code generation.

In web-based development tools, the ability to generate the code and to execute or emulate the final application in the browser enables iterative development cycles based on the evaluation of the final product after small changes without the need of complex infrastructures or development environments. We have proposed in this paper an approach that can be used to modify software development methodologies to enable agile web development through in-browser

322   A. Cortiñas et al.

code generation and evaluation. We have also used the approach in two real world tools: an academic tool that was developed from scratch, and an industrial tool whose functionalities were extended.

In future works we will propose a standard framework aiming at facilitating the integration of the proposed approach into existing tools.

References

1. Principles behind the Agile Manifesto. http://agilemanifesto.org/principles.html
2. UML unified modeling language. www.uml.org/. Accessed 10 Jan 2017
3. Ambler, S.W.: Agile model driven development is good enough. IEEE Softw. **20**(5), 71–73 (2003). http://www.springer.com/us/book/9783642375200
4. Apel, S., Batory, D., Kästner, C., Saake, G.: Feature-Oriented Software Product Lines. Springer, Heidelberg (2013). http://www.springer.com/us/book/9783642375200
5. Beck, K.: Extreme Programming Explained: Embrace Change. Addison-Wesley Longman Publishing Co., Inc., Boston (2000)
6. Bernaschina, C.: ALMOsT.js: an agile model to model and model to text transformation framework. In: Cabot, J., De Virgilio, R., Torlone, R. (eds.) ICWE 2017. LNCS, vol. 10360, pp. 79–97. Springer, Cham (2017). doi:10.1007/978-3-319-60131-1_5
7. Brisaboa, N.R., Cotelo-Lema, J.A., Fariña, A., Luaces, M.R., Parama, J.R., Viqueira, J.R.R.: Collecting and publishing large multiscale geographic datasets. Softw. Pract. Exp. **37**(12), 1319–1348 (2007). http://onlinelibrary.wiley.com/doi/10.1002/spe.807/abstract
8. Brisaboa, N.R., Cortiñas, A., Luaces, M.R., Pedreira, O.: GISBuilder: a framework for the semi-automatic generation of web-based geographic information systems. In: Proceedings of the 20th Pacific Asia Conference on Information Systems (PACIS 2016) (2016)
9. Carlo, B., Sara, C., Piero, F.: IFMLEdit.org: a web tool for model based rapid prototyping of web and mobile applications. In: Proceedings of the International Conference on Mobile Software Engineering and Systems, MOBILESoft 2017 (2017, accepted)
10. Claps, G.G., Svensson, R.B., Aurum, A.: On the journey to continuous deployment: technical and social challenges along the way. Inf. Softw. Technol. **57**, 21–31 (2015). http://www.sciencedirect.com/science/article/pii/S0950584914001694
11. Clements, P., Northrop, L.: Software Product Lines: Practices and Patterns. Addison-Wesley, Boston (2002). https://books.google.es/books/about/Software_Product_Lines.html?id=tHGFQgAACAAJ&pgis=1
12. Kang, K.C., Cohen, S.G., Hess, J.A., Novak, W.E., Peterson, A.S.: Feature-oriented domain analysis (FODA) feasibility study. Distribution 17(November), 161 (1990). http://www.sei.cmu.edu/reports/90tr021.pdf
13. Kirby Jr., J.: Model-driven agile development of reactive multi-agent systems. In: Proceedings of the 30th Annual International Computer Software and Applications Conference, COMPSAC 2006, vol. 02, pp. 297–302. IEEE Computer Society, Washington, DC (2006). http://dx.doi.org/10.1109/COMPSAC.2006.144
14. Kishinevsky, M., Cortadella, J., Kondratyev, A., Lavagno, L., Taubin, A., Yakovlev, A.: Coupling asynchrony and interrupts: place chart nets. In: Azéma, P., Balbo, G. (eds.) ICATPN 1997. LNCS, vol. 1248, pp. 328–347. Springer, Heidelberg (1997). doi:10.1007/3-540-63139-9_44

15. Kleppe, A., Warmer, J., Bast, W.: MDA Explained - The Model Driven Architecture: Practice and Promise. Addison Wesley Object Technology Series. Addison-Wesley, Boston (2003). http://www.informit.com/store/mda-explained-the-model-driven-architecture-practice-9780321194428

16. Luaces, M.R., Pérez, D.T., Fonte, J.I.L., Cerdeira-Pena, A.: An urban planning web viewer based on AJAX. In: Vossen, G., Long, D.D.E., Yu, J.X. (eds.) WISE 2009. LNCS, vol. 5802, pp. 443–453. Springer, Heidelberg (2009). doi:10.1007/978-3-642-04409-0_43

17. Matinnejad, R.: Agile model driven development: an intelligent compromise. In: Proceedings of the 2011 Ninth International Conference on Software Engineering Research, Management and Applications, SERA 2011, pp. 197–202. IEEE Computer Society, Washington, DC (2011). doi:10.1109/SERA.2011.17

18. OMG: Interaction flow modeling language (IFML), version 1.0. (2015). http://www.omg.org/spec/IFML/1.0/

19. Places, Á.S., Brisaboa, N.R., Fariña, A., Luaces, M.R., Paramá, J.R., Penabad, M.R.: The Galician virtual library. Online Inf. Rev. 31(3), 333–352 (2007). http://www.emeraldinsight.com/doi/full/10.1108/14684520710764104

20. Pohl, K., Böckle, G., Linden, F.V.D.: Software Product Line Engineering: Foundations, Principles and Techniques, vol. 49. Springer, Heidelberg (2005). doi:10.1007/3-540-28901-1

21. Schwaber, K., Beedle, M.: Agile Software Development with Scrum. Prentice Hall, Upper Saddle River (2002)

22. Stahl, T., Voelter, M., Czarnecki, K.: Model-Driven Software Development: Technology, Engineering, Management (2006)

23. Zhang, Y., Patel, S.: Agile model-driven development in practice. IEEE Softw. 28(2), 84–91 (2011). doi:10.1109/MS.2010.85

DAGGTAX: A Taxonomy of Data Aggregation Processes

Simin Cai[✉], Barbara Gallina, Dag Nyström, and Cristina Seceleanu

School of Innovation, Design and Engineering, Mälardalen University,
Västerås, Sweden
{simin.cai,barbara.gallina,dag.nystrom,cristina.seceleanu}@mdh.se

Abstract. Data aggregation processes are essential constituents for data management in modern computer systems, such as decision support systems and Internet of Things (IoT) systems. Due to the heterogeneity and real-time constraints in such systems, designing appropriate data aggregation processes often demands considerable effort. A study on the characteristics of data aggregation processes is then desirable, as it provides a comprehensive view of such processes, potentially facilitating their design, as well as the development of tool support to aid designers. In this paper, we propose a taxonomy called DAGGTAX, which is a feature diagram that models the common and variable characteristics of data aggregation processes, with a special focus on the real-time aspect. The taxonomy can serve as the foundation of a design tool, which we also introduce, enabling designers to build an aggregation process by selecting and composing desired features, and to reason about the feasibility of the design. We apply DAGGTAX on industrial case studies, showing that DAGGTAX not only strengthens the understanding, but also facilitates the model-driven design of data aggregation processes.

Keywords: Data aggregation taxonomy · Real-time data management · Feature model

1 Introduction

In modern information systems, data aggregation has long been adopted for data processing and management in order to discover unusual patterns and infer information [12], to save storage space [14], or to reduce bandwidth and energy costs [10]. Amid the era of cloud computing and Internet of Things (IoT), the application of data aggregation is becoming increasingly common and important, when enormous amounts of data are continuously collected from ubiquitous devices and services, and further analyzed. As an example, a surveillance application monitors a home by aggregating data from a number of sensors and cameras. The aggregated surveillance data of individual homes can then be aggregated again in the cloud to analyze the security of the area. In this example, data aggregation serves as a pillar of the application's workflow, and directly impacts the quality of the software system.

© Springer International Publishing AG 2017
Y. Ouhammou et al. (Eds.): MEDI 2017, LNCS 10563, pp. 324–339, 2017.
DOI: 10.1007/978-3-319-66854-3_25

Within such systems, different aggregations may have various requirements to be satisfied by the design. For instance, while one aggregation receives data passively from a data source, another aggregation must actively collect data from a database which is shared concurrently by other processes. This heterogeneity increases the difficulty in designing a suitable solution with multiple aggregations. In addition, many applications such as automotive systems [11], avionic systems [4] and industrial automation [16] have timing constraints on both the data and the aggregation processes themselves. The validity of data depends on the time when they are collected and accessed, and the correctness of a process depends on whether it completes on time. These real-time constraints also add to the complexity of data aggregation design.

In this paper we focus on the design support for data aggregation processes (or DAP for short), which are defined as the processes of producing synthesized forms from multiple data items [24]. We consider a DAP as a sequence of three ordered activities that allow raw data to be transformed into aggregated data via an aggregate function. First, a DAP starts with preparing the raw data needed for the aggregation from the data source into the aggregation unit called the aggregator. Next, an aggregate function is applied by the aggregator on the raw data, and produces the aggregated data. Finally, the aggregated data may be further handled by the aggregator, for example, to be saved into storage or provided to other processes. The main constituents of these activities are the raw data, the aggregate function and the aggregated data.

The main contribution of this paper is a high-level taxonomy of data aggregation processes, called DAGGTAX, presented as a feature diagram [15]. The aim of our taxonomy is to ease the design of aggregation processes, by providing a comprehensive view on the features and cross-cutting constraints, by a systematic representation. The intuition is that, to design a DAP, we must understand the desired features of its main constituents, as well as those of the DAP itself. Such features, ranging from functional features (such as data sharing) to extra-functional features (such as timeliness), are varying depending on different applications. One aspect of the understanding is to distinguish the mandatory features from the optional ones, so that the application designer is able to sort out the design choices. Another aspect is to comprehend the implications of the features, and to reason about the (possible) impact on one another. Conflicts may arise among features, in that the existence of one feature may prohibit another one. In this case, trade-offs should be taken into consideration at design time, so that infeasible designs can be ruled out at an early stage. The proposed taxonomy can serve as a basis for such automated reasoning. To evaluate the usefulness of DAGGTAX, we have developed a DAGGTAX-based tool called DAPComposer, which enables constructing DAP by selecting the desired features, and have applied it on two industrial case studies. The evaluations demonstrate that DAGGTAX raises the awareness of design issues in DAP, and helps to reason about possible trade-offs between different design solutions.

The remainder of the paper is organized as follows. In Sect. 5 we discuss the existing taxonomies of data aggregation. In Sect. 2 we provide background information. Section 3 presents our proposed taxonomy, followed by the tool and the case studies in Sect. 4. In Sect. 6 we conclude the paper and outline possible future works.

2   Background

In this section, we first recall the concepts of timeliness and temporal data consistency in real-time systems, after which we introduce feature models and feature diagrams that are used to present our taxonomy.

2.1   Timeliness and Temporal Data Consistency

In a real-time system, the correctness of a computation depends on both the logical correctness of the results, and the time at which the computation completes [5]. The property of completing the computation by a given deadline is referred to as *timeliness*. A real-time task can be classified as *hard*, *firm* or *soft* real-time, depending on the consequence of a deadline miss [5]. If a hard real-time task misses its deadline, the consequence will be catastrophic, e.g., loss of life or significant amounts of money. Therefore the timeliness of hard real-time tasks must always be guaranteed. For a firm real-time task, such as a task detecting vacant parking places, missing deadlines will render the results useless. For a soft real-time task, missing deadlines will reduce the value of the results. Such an example is the signal processing task of a video meeting application, whose quality of service will degrade if the task misses its deadline.

Depending on the regularity of activation, real-time tasks can be classified as *periodic*, *sporadic* or *aperiodic* [5]. A periodic task is activated at a constant rate. The interval between two activations of a periodic task, called its *period*, remains unchanged. A sporadic task is activated with a *MINimum inter-arrival Time (MINT)*, that is, the minimum interval between two consecutive activations. During the design of a real-time system, a sporadic task is often modeled as a periodic task with a period equal to the MINT. Similarly, *MAXimum inter-arrival Time (MAXT)* specifies the maximum interval between two consecutive activations. An aperiodic task is activated with an unpredictable interval between two consecutive activations. A task triggered by an external event with unknown occurrence pattern can be seen as aperiodic.

Real-time applications often monitor the state of the environment, and react to changes accordingly and timely. The environment state is represented as data in the system, which must be updated according to the actual environment state. The coherency between the value of the data in the system and its corresponding environment state is referred to as *temporal data consistency*, which includes two aspects, the *absolute temporal validity* and *relative temporal validity* [26]. A data instance is absolute valid, if the timespan between the time of sampling its corresponding real-world value, and the current time, is less than a specified *absolute validity interval*. A data instance derived from a set of data instances (base data) is absolute valid if all participating base data are absolute valid.

A derived data instance is relative valid, if the base data are sampled within a specified interval, called *relative validity interval.*

Data instances that are not temporally consistent may lead to different consequences. Different levels of strictness with respect to temporal consistency thus exist, which are *hard, firm* and *soft* real-time, in a decreasing order of strictness. Using outdated hard real-time data could cause disastrous consequences, and therefore this should not appear. Firm real-time data are useless if they are outdated, whereas outdated soft real-time data can still be used, but will yield degraded usefulness.

2.2   Feature Model and Feature Diagram

The notion of *feature* was first introduced by Kang et al. in the Feature-Oriented Domain Analysis (FODA) method [15], in order to capture both the common characteristics of a family of systems as well as the differences between individual systems. Kang et al. define a feature as a prominent or distinctive system characteristic visible to end-users. Czarnecki and Ulrich extend the definition of a feature to be any functional or extra-functional characteristic at the requirement, architecture, component, or any other level [8]. This definition allows us to model the characteristics of data aggregation processes as features. A *feature model* is a hierarchically organized set of features, representing all possible characteristics of a family of software products. A particular product can be formed by a combination of features, often obtained via a configuration process, selected from the feature model of its family.

A feature model is usually represented as a *feature diagram* [15], which is often depicted as a multilevel tree, whose nodes represent features and edges represent decomposition of features. In a feature diagram, a node with a solid dot represents a common feature (as shown in Fig. 1a), which is mandatory in every configuration. A node with a circle represents an optional feature (Fig. 1b), which may be selected by a particular configuration. Several nodes associated with a spanning curve represent a group of alternative features (Fig. 1c), from which one feature must be selected by a particular configuration. The cardinality [m..n] ($n \geq m \geq 0$) annotated with a node in Fig. 1d denotes how many instances of the feature, including the entire sub-tree, can be considered as children of the feature's parent in a concrete configuration. If $m \geq 1$, a configuration must include at least one instance of the feature, e.g., a feature with [1..1] is then a mandatory feature. If $m = 0$, the feature is optional for a configuration.

A valid configuration is a combination of features that meets all specified constraints, which can be dependencies among features within the same model, or dependencies among different models. An example of such a constraint is that the selection of one feature requires the selection of another feature. Researchers in the software product line community have developed a number of tools, providing extensive support for feature modeling and the verification of constraints. For instance, in FeatureIDE [27], software designers can create feature diagrams using a rich graphic interface. Designers can specify constraints across features

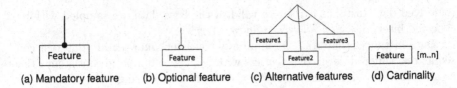

Fig. 1. Notations of a feature diagram

as well as models, to ensure that only valid configurations are generated from the feature diagram.

3   Our Proposed Taxonomy

In this section we propose a taxonomy of data aggregation processes, called DAG-GTAX, as an ordered arrangement of common and variable features revealed by the survey in our referred report [6]. The taxonomy for these common and variable characteristics not only leads to a clear understanding of the aggregation process, but also lays a solid foundation for an eventual tool support for analyzing the impact of different features on the design. In this paper, we also present an initial version of such tool.

We choose feature diagrams as the presentation of our taxonomy, mainly due to two reasons. First, features may be used to model both functional and extra-functional characteristics of systems. This allows us to capture cross-cutting aspects that have impact on multiple software modules related to different concerns. Second, the notation of feature diagrams is simple to construct, powerful to capture the common and variable characteristics of different data aggregation processes, and intuitive to provide an organizational view of the processes. The taxonomy is shown in Fig. 2.

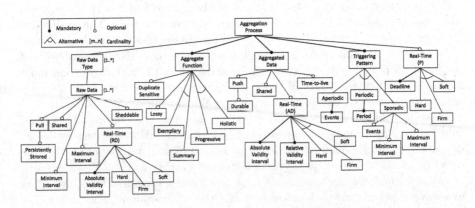

Fig. 2. The taxonomy of data aggregation processes

In the following subsections, these features are discussed in details with concrete examples. More precisely, the discussion is organized in order to reflect the logical separation of features. We explain Fig. 2 from the top-level features under "Aggregation Process", including "Raw Data Type", "Aggregate Function" and "Aggregated Data", which are the main constituents of an aggregation process. Features that characterize the entire DAP are also top-level features, including the "Triggering Pattern" of the process, and "Real-Time (P)", which refers to the timeliness of the entire process. Sub-features of the top-level features are explained in a depth-first way.

3.1 Raw Data

One of the mandatory features of real-time data aggregation is the raw data involved in the process. Raw data are the data provided by the DAP data sources. One DAP may involve one or more types of raw data. The multiplicity is reflected by the cardinality [1..*] next to the feature "**Raw Data Type**" in Fig. 2. Each raw data type may have a set of **raw data**. For instance, a surveillance system has two types of raw data ("sensor data" and "camera data"), while for the sensor data type there are several individual sensors with the same characteristics. Each raw data may have a set of properties, which are interpreted as its sub-features and constitute a sub-tree. These sub-features are: Pull, Shared, Sheddable, and Real-Time.

Pull. "Pull" is a data acquisition scheme for collecting raw data. Using this scheme, the aggregator actively acquires data from the data source, as illustrated in Fig. 3a. For instance, a traditional DBMS adopts the pull scheme, in which raw data are acquired from disks using SQL queries and aggregated in the main memory. "Pull" is considered to be an optional feature of raw data, since not every DAP pulls data actively from data source. If raw data have the "pull" feature, pulling raw data actively from the data source is a necessary part of the aggregation process, including the selection of data as well as the shipment of data from the data source. If the raw data do not have the "pull" feature, they are pushed into the aggregator (Fig. 3b). In this case, in our view the action of pushing data is the responsibility of another process outside of the DAP. From the DAP's perspective, the raw data are already prepared for aggregation.

An optional sub-feature of "Pull" is "**Persistently Stored**", since raw data to be pulled from data source may be stored persistently in a non-volatile storage, such as a disk-based relational DBMS. The retrieval of persistent raw data involves locating the data in the storage and the necessary I/O.

Shared. Raw data of a DAP may be read or updated by other processes at the same time when they are read for aggregation [14]. The same raw data may be aggregated by several DAP, or accessed by processes that do not perform aggregations. We use the optional "shared" feature to represent the characteristic that the raw data involved in the aggregation may be shared by other processes in the system.

Fig. 3. Raw data acquisition schemes

Sheddable. We classify the raw data as "sheddable", which is an optional feature, used in cases when data can be skipped for the aggregation. For instance, in TAG [18], the inputs from sensors will be ignored by the aggregation process if the data arrive too late. In a stream processing system, new arrivals may be discarded when the system is overloaded [1]. For raw data without the sheddable feature, every instance of the raw data is crucial and has to be computed for aggregation.

Real-Time (RD). The raw data involved in some of the surveyed DAP have real-time constraints. Each data instance is associated with an arrival time, and is only valid if the elapsed time from its arrival time is less than its **absolute validity interval**. "Real-time" is therefore considered an optional feature of raw data, and "absolute validity interval" is a mandatory sub-feature of the "real-time" feature. We name the real-time feature of raw data as "Real-Time (RD)" in our taxonomy, for differentiating from the real-time features of the aggregated data ("Real-Time (AD)" in Sect. 3.3) and the process ("Real-Time (P)" in Sect. 3.5).

Raw data with real-time constraints are classified as "**hard**", "**firm**" or "**soft**" real-time, depending on the strictness with respect to temporal consistency. They are represented as alternative sub-features of the real-time feature. As we have explained in Sect. 2, hard real-time data (such as sensor data from a field device [16]) and firm real-time data (such as surveillance data [13]) must be guaranteed up-to-date, while outdated soft real-time data are still of some value and thus can be used (e.g., the derived data from a neighboring node in VigilNet [13]).

***MINT** and **MAXT**.* Raw data may arrive continuously with a MINimum inter-arrival Time (MINT), of which a fixed arrival time is a special case. For instance, in the surveillance system VigilNet [13], a magnetometer sensor monitors the environment and pushes the latest data to the aggregator at a frequency of 32 Hz, implying a MINT of 32.15 ms. Similarly a raw data may have a MAXimum inter-arrival Time (MAXT). We consider "MINT" and "MAXT" optional features of the raw data.

3.2   Aggregate Function

An aggregation process must have an aggregate function to compute the aggregated result from raw data. An aggregate function exhibits a set of characteristics, which have been studied by existing taxonomies [10,12,18], and are represented as features in DAGGTAX.

Duplicate Sensitive. "Duplicate sensitivity" has been introduced as a dimension by Madden et al. [18] and Fasolo et al. [10]. An aggregate function is duplicate sensitive, if an incorrect aggregated result is produced due to a duplicated raw data. For example, COUNT, which counts the number of raw data instances, is duplicate sensitive, since a duplicated instance will lead to a result one bigger than it should be. MIN, which returns the minimum value of a set of instances, is not duplicate sensitive because its result is not affected by a duplicated instance. "Duplicate sensitive" is considered as an optional feature of the aggregate function.

Exemplary or Summary. According to Madden et al. [18], an aggregate function is either "exemplary" or "summary", which are alternative features in our taxonomy. An exemplary aggregate function returns one or several representative values of the selected raw data, for instance, MIN, which returns the minimum as a representative value of a set of values. A summary aggregate function computes a result based on all selected raw data, for instance, COUNT, which computes the cardinality of a set of values.

Lossy. An aggregate function is "lossy", if the raw data cannot be reconstructed from the aggregated data alone [10]. For example, SUM, which computes the summation of a set of raw data instances, is a lossy function, as one cannot reproduce the raw data instances from the aggregated summation value without any additional information. On the contrary, a function that concatenates raw data instances with a known delimiter is not lossy, since the raw data can be reconstructed by splitting the concatenation. Therefore, we introduce "lossy" as an optional feature of aggregate functions.

Holistic or Progressive. Depending on whether the computation of aggregation can be decomposed into sub-aggregations, an aggregate function can be classified as either "progressive" or "holistic". The computation of a progressive aggregate function can be decomposed into the computation of sub-aggregates. In order to compute the AVERAGE of ten data instances, for example, one can compute the AVERAGE values of the first five instances and the second five instances respectively, and then compute the AVERAGE of the whole set using these two values. The computation of a holistic aggregate function cannot be decomposed into sub-aggregations. An example of holistic aggregate function is MEDIAN, which finds the middle value from a sequence of sorted values. The correct MEDIAN value cannot be composed by, for example, the MEDIAN of the first half of the sequence together with the MEDIAN of the second half.

3.3   Aggregated Data

An aggregation process must produce one aggregated result, denoted as mandatory feature "Aggregate Data" in the feature diagram. Aggregated data may have a set of features, which are explained as follows.

Push. In some survey DAP examples, sending aggregated data to another unit of the system is an activity of the aggregator immediately after the computation of aggregation. This is considered as an active step of the aggregation process, and is represented by the feature "push". For example, in the group layer aggregation of VigilNet [13], each node sends the aggregated data to its leading node actively. An aggregation process without the "push" feature leaves the aggregate results in the main memory, and it is other processes' responsibility to fetch the results.

The aggregated data may be "pushed" into permanent storage [3,16]. The stored aggregated data may be required to be durable, which means that the aggregated data must survive potential system failures. Therefore, "**durable**" is considered as an optional sub-feature of the "push" feature.

Shared. Similar to raw data, the aggregated data has an optional "shared" feature too, to represent the characteristic of some of the surveyed DAP that the aggregated data may be shared by other concurrent processes in the system. For instance, the aggregated results of one process may serve as the raw data inputs of another aggregation process, creating a hierarchy of aggregation [1,13]. The results of aggregation may also be accessed by a non-aggregation process, such as a control process [11].

Time-to-Live. The "time-to-live" feature regulates how long the aggregated data should be preserved in the aggregator. For instance, Aurora system [1] can be configured to guarantee that the aggregated data are available for other processes, such as an archiving process or another aggregate process, for a certain period of time. After this period, these data can be discarded or overwritten. We use the optional feature "time-to-live" to represent this characteristic.

Real-Time (AD). The aggregated data may be real-time, if the validity of the data instance depends on whether its temporal consistency constraints are met. Therefore the "real-time" feature, which is named "Real-Time (AD)", is an optional feature of aggregated data in our taxonomy. The temporal consistency constraints on real-time aggregated data include two aspects, the absolute validity and relative validity, as explained in Sect. 2. "**Absolute validity interval**" and "**relative validity interval**" are two mandatory sub-features of the "Real-Time (AD)" feature.

Similar to raw data, the real-time feature of aggregated data has "**hard**", "**firm**" and "**soft**" as alternative sub-features. If the aggregated data are required to be hard real-time, they have to be ensured temporally consistent in order to avoid catastrophic consequences [3]. Compared with hard real-time data, firm real-time aggregated data are useless if they are not temporally consistent [13], while soft real-time aggregated data can still be used with less value (e.g., the aggregation in the remote server [16]).

3.4   Triggering Pattern

"Triggering pattern" refers to how the DAP is activated, which is a mandatory feature. We consider three types of triggering patterns for the activation of DAP, represented by the alternative sub-features "**periodic**", "**sporadic**" and "**aperiodic**".

A periodic DAP is invoked according to a time schedule with a specified "**Period**". A sporadic DAP could be triggered by an external "**event**", or according to a time schedule, possibly with a "**MINT**" or "**MAXT**". An aperiodic DAP is activated by an external "event" without a constant period, MINT or MAXT. The event can be an aggregate command (e.g. an explicit query [19]) or a state change in the system [3].

3.5   Real-Time (P)

Real-time applications, such as automotive systems [11] and industrial monitoring systems [16], require the data aggregation process to complete its work by a specified deadline. The process timeliness, named "**Real-Time (P)**", is considered as an optional feature of the DAP, and "**deadline**" is its mandatory sub-feature.

Aggregation processes may have different types of timeliness constraints, depending on the consequences of missing their deadlines. For a **soft** real-time DAP, a deadline miss will lead to a less valuable aggregated result [9]. For a **firm** real-time DAP [16], the aggregated result becomes useless if the deadline is missed. If a **hard** real-time DAP misses its deadline, the aggregated result is not only useless, but hazardous [4]. "Hard", "firm" and "soft" are alternative sub-features of the timeliness feature.

We must emphasize the difference between timeliness ("Real-Time (P)") and real-time features of data ("Real-Time (RD)" and "Real-Time (AD)"), although both of them appear to be classified into hard, firm and soft real-time. Timeliness is a feature of the aggregation process, with respect to meeting its deadline. It specifies when the process must produce the aggregated data and release the system resources for other processes. As for real-time features of data, the validity intervals specify when the data become outdated, while the level of strictness with respect to temporal consistency decides whether outdated data could be used.

4   Case Studies

In this section, we evaluate the usefulness of DAGGTAX in aiding the design of data aggregation via two industrial projects together with the engineers from Ericsson, in Sects. 4.1 and 4.2, respectively. Prior to the case studies we have implemented a tool called DAPComposer (Data Aggregation Process Composer) in Javascript. The tool provides a graphical interface for designers to create DAP, by simply enabling/disabling features from DAGGTAX. Although to date only primitive constraints intrinsic to the feature model are checked by DAPComposer, we plan to mature the tool with more sophisticated analysis capabilities, such as timing analysis, in the next version.

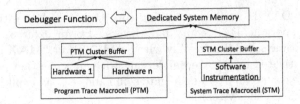

Fig. 4. General architecture of the Hardware Assisted Trace system

4.1   Case Study I: The Hardware Assisted Trace (HAT) Framework

In our first case study we apply DAGGTAX to analyze the design of the Hardware Assisted Trace (HAT) [28] framework. HAT, as shown in Fig. 4, is a framework for debugging functional errors in an embedded system. In this framework, a debugger function runs in the same system as the debugged program, and collects both hardware and software run-time traces continuously. Together with the engineers we have analyzed the aggregation processes in their current design. At a lower level, a Program Trace Macrocell (PTM) aggregation process aggregates traces from hardware. These aggregated PTM traces, together with software instrumentation traces from the System Trace Macrocell (STM), are then aggregated by a higher level ApplicationTrace aggregation process, to create an informative trace for the debugged application.

We have analyzed the features of the PTM aggregation process and the ApplicationTrace aggregation process in HAT based on our taxonomy. The diagram of the PTM aggregation process created using DAPComposer is presented in Fig. 5. Triggered by computing events, this process pulls raw data from the local buffer of the hardware, and aggregates them using an encoding function to form an aggregated trace into the PTM cluster buffer. The raw data are considered sheddable, since they are generated frequently, and each aggregation pulls only the data in the local buffer at the time of the triggering event. The aggregated PTM and STM traces then serve as part of the raw data of the ApplicationTrace aggregation process, which is shown in Fig. 6. The dashed arrows represent the data flow between DAP. The ApplicationTrace process is triggered sporadically with a minimum inter-arrival time, and aggregates its raw data using an analytical function. The raw data of the ApplicationTrace should not be sheddable so that all aggregated traces are captured.

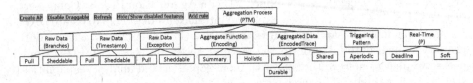

Fig. 5. The aggregation process in the PTM

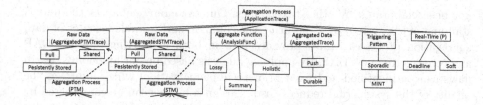

Fig. 6. The aggregation processes in the investigated HAT system

Problem Identified in the HAT Design. With the diagrams showing the features of the aggregation processes, the engineers could immediately identify a problem in the PTM buffer management. The problem is that the data in the buffer may be overwritten before they are aggregated. It arises due to the lack of a holistic consideration on the PTM aggregation process and the ApplicationTrace aggregation process at design time. Triggered by aperiodic external events, the PTM process could produce a large number of traces within a short period and fill up the PTM buffer. The ApplicationTrace process, on the other hand, is triggered with a minimum inter-arrival time, and consumes the PTM traces as unsheddable raw data. When the inter-arrival time of the PTM triggering events is shorter than the MINT of the ApplicationTrace process, the PTM traces in the buffer may be overwritten before they could be aggregated by the ApplicationTrace process. This problem has been observed on Ericsson's implemented system, and awaits a solution. However, if the taxonomy would have been applied on the system design, this problem could have been identified before it was propagated to implementation. We have provided two solutions to solve the identified problem. Due to lack of space, the details of this case study is included in the technical report [6].

4.2 Case Study II: A Cloud Monitoring System for Enhanced Auto-Scaling

In our second case study we apply DAGGTAX to design a cloud-monitoring system that enables auto scaling based on both virtual-machine-level and application-level performance measurements, by extending the open-source OpenStack framework, which collects measurements only from the virtual-machine level. DAGGTAX is applied to both the existing framework, as well as the new design. Based on the feature diagrams, we analyze the pros and cons of different feature combinations, and decide the design solution. Some features and DAP of the existing framework are identified as reusable, and reused in the solution. We refer the details of this case study to the paper [7].

4.3 Summary

The engineers in the evaluation acknowledge that our taxonomy bridges the gap between the properties of data and the properties of the process, which has not been elaborated by other taxonomies. Our taxonomy enhances the understanding of the system by structuring the common and variable features of data aggregation processes, which provides help in both identifying reusable DAP and constructing new DAP. By applying analysis based on our taxonomy, design flaws can be identified and fixed prior to implementation, which improves the quality of the system and reduces costs. Design solutions can be constructed by composing reusable features, and reasoned about based on the taxonomy, which contributes to a reduced design space. Due to these benefits, the engineers see great value in a more mature version of DAPComposer for data aggregation applications, based on our taxonomy.

5   Related Work

Many researchers have promoted the understanding of data aggregation on various aspects. Among them, considerable effort has been dedicated to the study of aggregate functions. Mesiar et al. [22], Marichal [21], and Rudas et al. [24] have studied the mathematical properties of aggregate functions, such as continuity and stability, and discussed these properties of common aggregate functions in detail. A procedure for the construction of an appropriate aggregate function is also proposed by Rudas et al. [24]. In order to design a software system that computes aggregation efficiently, Gray et al. [12] have classified aggregate functions into distributive, algebraic and holistic, depending on the amount of intermediate states required for partial aggregates. Later, in order to study the influence of aggregate functions on the performance of sensor data aggregation, Madden et al. [18] have extended Gray's taxonomy, and classified aggregate functions according to their state requirements, tolerance of loss, duplicate sensitivity, and monotonicity. Fasolo et al. [10] classify aggregate functions with respect to four dimensions, which are lossy aggregation, duplicate sensitivity, resilience to losses/failures and correlation awareness. Our taxonomy builds on such work that focuses on the aggregate functions mainly, and provide a comprehensive view of the entire aggregation processes instead. Lenz and Shoshani [17] have classified aggregation into "stock", "flow" and "value-per-unit", based on whether the raw data has a cumulative semantics over a period. Their classification is used to analyze summarizability, that is, whether the aggregation is semantically suitable for the particular data. Our taxonomy is orthogonal to their classification as we address the temporal data consistency and timeliness of aggregation, while assuming the aggregation is summarizable.

A large proportion of existing work has its focus on in-network data aggregation, which is commonly used in sensor networks. In-network aggregation is the process of processing and aggregating data at intermediate nodes when data are transmitted from sensor nodes to sinks through the network [10]. Besides a classification of aggregate functions that we have discussed in the previous paragraph, Fasolo et al. [10] classify the existing routing protocols according to the aggregation method, resilience to link failures, overhead to setup/maintain aggregation structure, scalability, resilience to node mobility, energy saving method and timing strategy. The aggregation protocols are also classified by Solis et al. [25], Makhloufi et al. [20], and Rajagopalan [23], with respect to different classification criteria. In contrast to the aforementioned work that focuses mainly on aggregation protocols, Alzaid et al. [2] have proposed a taxonomy of secure aggregation schemes that classifies them into different models. All the existing related work differ from our taxonomy in that they provide taxonomies from a different perspective, such as network topology for instance. Instead, our work strives to understand the features and their implications of DAP and its constituents in design.

6 Conclusions and Future Work

In this paper, we have investigated the characteristics of data aggregation processes in a variety of applications, and provided a taxonomy of the DAP called DAGGTAX, with a particular focus on the real-time properties. DAGGTAX is presented as a feature diagram, in which the common and variable characteristics are modeled as features. The taxonomy provides a comprehensive view of data aggregation processes for the designers, and allows the design of a DAP to be achieved via the selection of desired features and the combination of the selected features via the DAPComposer tool. The usefulness of the taxonomy has been demonstrated on two industrial case studies. Flaws can be identified at design time, and solutions can be proposed at design level, by applying the taxonomy to the analysis.

The description of DAGGTAX as a feature diagram allows our taxonomy to be extended with characteristics for specific domains. New features can be added to the feature diagram. For instance, in telecommunication domain, DAP could be triggered with known distributions. Such distributions could be added as new optional subfeatures under the triggering pattern feature. In such a case, potential conflicts with existing features need to be analyzed by the domain experts.

Our taxonomy can be viewed as a framework for analyzing the dependencies between features and between DAP. Our future work aims to integrate more advanced analysis techniques, such as model checking and schedulability analysis, to detect conflicting features and provide guidance for trade-offs. These techniques can be integrated into DAPComposer. We also plan to extend the DAPComposer so that users can specify their constraints and validate the design through the tool automatically. Last but not least, due to the semantics of feature diagrams in boolean logic, we plan to analyze the consistency of DAP requirements and constraints automatically, by involving SAT solving techniques and tools.

Acknowledgment. This work is funded by the Knowledge Foundation of Sweden (KK-stiftelsen) within the DAGGERS project. We acknowledge Alf Larsson, Andreas Ermedahl and Carlo Vitucci from Ericsson Research for their help in the case studies.

References

1. Abadi, D.J., Carney, D., Çetintemel, U., Cherniack, M., Convey, C., Lee, S., Stone-braker, M., Tatbul, N., Zdonik, S.: Aurora: a new model and architecture for data stream management. VLDB J. **12**(2), 120–139 (2003)
2. Alzaid, H., Foo, E., Nieto, J.M.G., Park, D.: A taxonomy of secure data aggregation in wireless sensor networks. IJCNDS **8**(1–2), 101–148 (2012)
3. Baulier, J., Blott, S., Korth, H.F., Silberschatz, A.: A database system for real-time event aggregation in telecommunication. In: Proceedings of the 24rd VLDB, pp. 680–684 (1998)
4. Bür, K., Omiyi, P., Yang, Y.: Wireless sensor and actuator networks: enabling the nervous system of the active aircraft. IEEE Commun. Mag. **48**(7), 118–125 (2010)
5. Buttazzo, G.C.: Hard Real-Time Computing Systems: Predictable Scheduling Algorithms and Applications, vol. 24. Springer Science & Business Media, Berlin (2011)
6. Cai, S., Gallina, B., Nyström, D., Seceleanu, C.: DAGGTAX: a taxonomy of data aggregation processes. Technical report (2016). http://www.es.mdh.se/publications/4628-
7. Cai, S., Gallina, B., Nyström, D., Seceleanu, C.: Design of cloud monitoring systems via DAGGTAX: a case study. In: Proceedings of the 8th ANT, May 2017
8. Czarnecki, K., Ulrich, E.: Generative Programming: Methods, Tools, and Applications. Addison-Wesley, Boston (2000)
9. Defude, B., Delot, T., Ilarri, S., Zechinelli, J.L., Cenerario, N.: Data aggregation in VANETS: the VESPA approach. In: Proceedings of the 5th MobiQuitous, pp. 13:1–13:6 (2008)
10. Fasolo, E., Rossi, M., Widmer, J., Zorzi, M.: In-network aggregation techniques for wireless sensor networks: a survey. IEEE Wirel. Commun. **14**(2), 70–87 (2007)
11. Goud, G., Sharma, N., Ramamritham, K., Malewar, S.: Efficient real-time support for automotive applications: a case study. In: Proceedings of the 12th RTCSA, pp. 335–341 (2006)
12. Gray, J., Chaudhuri, S., Bosworth, A., Layman, A., Reichart, D., Venkatrao, M., Pellow, F., Pirahesh, H.: Data cube: a relational aggregation operator generalizing group-by, cross-tab, and sub-totals. Data Min. Knowl. Disc. **1**(1), 29–53 (1997)
13. He, T., Gu, L., Luo, L., Yan, T., Stankovic, J., Son, S.: An overview of data aggregation architecture for real-time tracking with sensor networks. In: Proceedings of the 20th IPDPS, p. 8 (2006)
14. Iftikhar, N.: Integration, aggregation and exchange of farming device data: a high level perspective. In: Proceedings of the 2nd ICADIWT, pp. 14–19 (2009)
15. Kang, K., Cohen, S., Hess, J., Novak, W., Peterson, A.: Feature-oriented domain analysis (FODA) feasibility study. Technical report CMU/SEI-90-TR-021, Software Engineering Institute, Carnegie Mellon University, Pittsburgh, PA (1990). http://resources.sei.cmu.edu/library/asset-view.cfm?AssetID=11231
16. Lee, A.N., Lastra, J.L.M.: Data aggregation at field device level for industrial ambient monitoring using web services. In: Proceedings of the 9th INDIN, pp. 491–496. IEEE (2011)
17. Lenz, H.J., Shoshani, A.: Summarizability in OLAP and statistical data bases. In: Proceedings of the 9th SSDM, pp. 132–143 (1997)
18. Madden, S., Franklin, M.J., Hellerstein, J.M., Hong, W.: TAG: a tiny aggregation service for ad-hoc sensor networks. ACM SIGOPS Oper. Syst. Rev. **36**(SI), 131–146 (2002)

19. Madden, S.R., Franklin, M.J., Hellerstein, J.M., Hong, W.: TinyDB: an acquisitional query processing system for sensor networks. ACM Trans. Database Syst. **30**(1), 122–173 (2005)
20. Makhloufi, R., Doyen, G., Bonnet, G., Gaïti, D.: A survey and performance evaluation of decentralized aggregation schemes for autonomic management. Int. J. Netw. Manag. **24**(6), 469–498 (2014)
21. Marichal, J.L.: Aggregation functions for decision making. In: ISTE, pp. 673–721 (2010)
22. Mesiar, R., Kolesárová, A., Calvo, T., Komorníková, M.: A review of aggregation functions. In: Bustince, H., Herrera, F., Montero, J. (eds.) Fuzzy Sets and Their Extensions: Representation, Aggregation and Models. Studies in Fuzziness and Soft Computing, vol. 220, pp. 121–144. Springer, Heidelberg (2008). doi:10.1007/978-3-540-73723-0_7
23. Rajagopalan, R., Varshney, P.: Data-aggregation techniques in sensor networks: a survey. IEEE Commun. Surv. Tutor. **8**(4), 48–63 (2006)
24. Rudas, I.J., Pap, E., Fodor, J.: Information aggregation in intelligent systems: an application oriented approach. Knowl.-Based Syst. **38**, 3–13 (2013)
25. Solis, I., Obraczka, K.: In-network aggregation trade-offs for data collection in wireless sensor networks. Int. J. Sens. Netw. **1**(3–4), 200–212 (2006)
26. Song, X., Liu, J.: How well can data temporal consistency be maintained? In: Proceedings of the 1992 CACSD, pp. 275–284 (1992)
27. Thüm, T., Kästner, C., Benduhn, F., Meinicke, J., Saake, G., Leich, T.: FeatureIDE: an extensible framework for feature-oriented software development. Sci. Comput. Program. **79**, 70–85 (2014)
28. Vitucci, C., Larsson, A.: Hat, hardware assisted trace: performance oriented trace & debug system. In: Proceedings of 26th ICSSEA (2015)

Automating the Evolution of Data Models for Space Missions. A Model-Based Approach

Lynda Ait Oubelli[1,2]([envelope]), Yamine Ait Ameur[2], Judicaël Bedouet[1],
Benoit Chausserie-Lapree[3], and Beatrice Larzul[3]

[1] ONERA - The French Aerospace Lab, Toulouse, France
{Lynda.Ait-Oubelli,Judicael.Bedouet}@onera.fr
[2] University of Toulouse, INP, IRIT - Research Institute of Computer Science,
Toulouse, France
yamine@enseeiht.fr
[3] CNES - The French Space Agency, Toulouse, France
{Benoit.Chausserie-Lapree,Beatrice.Larzul}@cnes.fr

Abstract. In space industry, model-driven engineering (MDE) is a key
technique to model data exchanges with satellites. During the preparation of a space mission, the associated data models are often revised
and need to be compared from one version to another. Thus, due to the
undeniably growth of changes, it becomes difficult to track them. New
methods and techniques to understand and represent the differences,
as well as commonalities, between different model's revisions are highly
required. Recent research works address the evolution process between
the two layers (M2/M1) of the MDE architecture. In this research work,
we have explored the use of the layers (M1/M0) of the same architecture
in order to define a set of atomic operators and their composition that
encapsulate both data model evolution and data migration. The use of
these operators improves the quality of data migration, by ensuring full
conservation of the information carried by the data.

Keywords: Model driven engineering (MDE) · Data model comparison · Data model evolution · Data migration · Composite evolution
operators · Semantic transformation patterns

1 Introduction

Context

Space agencies in Europe like CNES, the French space agency, have been involved
in data modelling and in the standardization of data modelling techniques for
more than 20 years. They have defined some Consultative Committee for Space
Data Systems (CCSDS) recommendations. These recommendations are related
to syntactic and semantic data description techniques, long term data preservation, data producer and archive interface. Furthermore, CNES, jointly with the
European Space Agency (ESA), have also developed tools to support the recommended approaches and to support data engineering for various space projects.

© Springer International Publishing AG 2017
Y. Ouhammou et al. (Eds.): MEDI 2017, LNCS 10563, pp. 340–354, 2017.
DOI: 10.1007/978-3-319-66854-3_26

One of these tools is the BEST [1] workbench that came beyond EAST, the Enhanced Ada SubseT. It allows a non-ambiguous description of data formats including syntactic and semantic information. This tool is used in the frame of space projects by scientists and engineers. It allows them to easily describe their data formats and make them evolve, to quickly produce test data conform to the format specification, to access and interpret data without having to write specific code. The formal description of space-related data is crucial and should be taken into account from the early stages of the mission when:

- the space system (one or more satellites, a ground control center, a mission center, etc.) is designed;
- the satellite, once launched, starts to send telemetries and the ground segment starts to send commands;
- a large amount of data is produced, processed, transformed and sent to end-users during the life of the satellite;

All different stakeholders have to understand the data, to be able to interpret it and to make use of it. Any misunderstanding might cause important delays in mission planning. Arguably, a complete and non-ambiguous definition of any kind of data produced is a key factor for meeting the deadlines of the project. This formal definition can be used to generate different pieces of code that will be used in the frame of the project (eg. on-board software, simulation software, etc.). Code generation is highly valuable for a project, since some parts of the application can be updated in a fast and efficient way with a minimum development cost [2]. However, data generated (Data V1) with a particular release of the application (DataModel V1) are not necessarily compatible with another release (DataModel V2). Thus, starting the creation or the generation of data that conforms to (DataModel V2) from scratch is a tedious operation.

Motivations

Research into how complex industrial data models evolve from one version to another and how their data migrate still stands as one of the most scientific challenges to be addressed. This is due to the disability of existing solutions to face with the huge complexity of changes in terms of type and number. Interpreting comparison results of two small data models may be an easy thing. Meanwhile, interpreting comparison results of two huge data models is still a hard task.

Objectives

In this research study, we intend to tackle the following objectives:

- being able to recognize many differences as a unique composite operator;
- ensuring evolution schema by finding structural and descriptive changes;
- full data migration without any loss of information.

To achieve these objectives, we decide to investigate and improve several methods to compare data models (M1 level) governed by structured data-oriented meta-models (M2 level) as shown in Fig. 1. Then, we propose to transform the obtained differences to evolution operators working at data model level (M1) as well as

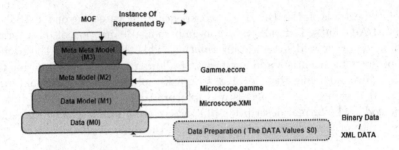

Fig. 1. Four-layer architecture of MDE

data level (M0). At the data model level, an evolution operator defines a data
model transformation capturing a common evolution [3]. At the data level, it
defines a model transformation capturing the corresponding migration.

Depending on the final usability goals of data and depending on the modeller's skills, the same concept may be modeled in different ways. For example,
to define the structure of data with BEST, only *"composition"* relationship can
be used (e.g. in the XIF meta-model[1]) whereas *"inheritance"* relationship may
be preferred (e.g. in the XTCE meta-model[2]). Such a difference in the way of
modeling induces a huge number of syntactic differences between a XIF data
model and a XTCE data model, even if they represent the same concept.

Understanding the semantic differences that may exist between the two data
models is difficult because these real differences are hidden by a large number
of syntactic differences. Once we can recognize these differences as a unique
composite operator, we can clearly identify other syntactic differences. This
is an extreme example of data model transformation but we often meet such
cases while studying how data models evolve. Indeed, modellers often need to
reconstruct their model to meet new end-users needs. But, they do not want
to completely break the ancient model or make it obsolete. Even if ascendant
compatibility is not kept, they try to preserve information contained in old data.

The remainder of this research paper is organized as follows. The next section
summarizes the previous related work for the different approaches being used
for meta-model evolution and model co-evolution. The theoretical description
of the proposed approach to formalize space data model evolution and data
migration using semantic composite operators is presented in Sect. 3. A case
study is discussed in Sect. 4 followed with conclusions and future work.

---

[1] The underlying language used to formally define data is XML formatted according to a CNES standard named XIF. XIF is a join implementation of two CCSDS
standards: CCSDS 644.0-B-3 Data Description Language EAST Specification and
CCSDS 647.1-B-1 Data Entity Dictionary Specification Language.

[2] When exchanging satellite database including telemetry and telecommand definitions with satellite manufacturers or other space partners, we may use another
CCSDS standard: 660.0-B-1 XML Telemetric and Command Exchange (XTCE).

2   Related Work

Many researchers studied the discipline of evolution, which was defined by [4] as «*All programming activity that is intended to generate a new software version from an earlier operational version*». This section summarises the different existing approaches for model-based comparison, evolution and migration. Capturing and formalizing evolution stages for composite systems is a challenging task, due to the nature and characteristics of such systems. Furthermore, the rapid changes, the density and the type of differences, which change according to the evolution of end-user's requirements, are the reasons of proposition of a variety of algorithms, methods and evolution laws by scientific community.

2.1   Model Comparison

The history of comparing algorithms is composed of three stages. At the beginning, we compared character to character. For instance, *diff* programs [5], are used to solve the longest common subsequence problem (LCS). They are based on finding the lines that do not change between files. Then, we leveled up by focusing on the attributes and nodes of a structured document. A number of advanced algorithms are being available to capture differences for XML such as XDiff [6] or Aladin [7]. However, even if they give logical results, they lack the ability to recognise a huge number of complex changes in a reasonable time. Finally, we are interested in the meaning of these nodes and attributes by comparing a class node with a class node, an attribute node with an attribute node, for instance, with the assistance of the well accepted EMF framework [8].

2.2   Evolution Operators

The process of capturing and constructing evolution operators have been investigated by [3]. Authors of this paper have worked on the definition of 61 reusable evolution operators (30 are atomic and 31 are composite) with the aim of treating the coupled-evolution of meta-models (M2) and models (M1). The authors have provided a catalog based on EMOF meta-modeling formalism in which they have outlined a set of migration rules specified at a model level. However, even if they tackled the generation of evolution operators, the authors did not discuss the detection mechanism of these operators. This was treated later in [9], where the authors proposed a detection engine of complex changes. They have addressed the two challenges of variability and overlap between evolution operators. A research prototype named COPE [10] was extended into a transformation tool tailored for the migration of models in response to meta-model co-evolution named Edapt [11]. Furthermore, authors in [12] introduced the Silift, generic tool environment able to lift incomprehensible low level differences derived from EMF Compare into representations of user-level edit operations.

2.3 Data Migration

Nowadays, the majority of research teams [9–12] have tackled the phenomenon based on the M2/M1 architecture layers of MDE, where the authors presented a semi-automatic process to co-evolve model-to-model transformations upon meta-model evolution. Authors in [13] introduced a comparison study between various model migration tools such as AML, COPE, Ecore2Ecore and Epsilon Flock. Indeed, each one of them has a set of criteria, that will support users to select the most appropriate tool according to their needs.

3 Proposed Approach

To ease the migration process of data in a critical domain, where each data value vulnerability is so height, a solid protocol for controlling the evolution of data models is required. Therefore, deriving and capturing the set of changes might even be largely different from one version to another.

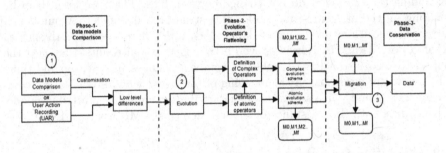

Fig. 2. The pipeline architecture of model-based approach for data migration

In this paper, we propose a novel model-based approach for automating the evolution of data models. An overview of the proposed approach is illustrated in Fig. 2, where three different successive processes (data models comparison, evolution operator's flattening and data migration) should be able to reuse the results of each other. We introduce a pipeline protocol in order to guarantee the conservation of data values during the migration.

It is worth noting that the proposed scenario based on three processes can be applied to other domains, where the main goal of the migration process is data preservation. However, in other cases, where the main purpose is functionalities conservation processing, many other approaches that tackled the comparison, evolution and co-evolution processes are available. They act separately at M2/M1 level in different ways with different tools.

3.1   Phase 1. Data Models Comparison

As shown in Fig. 3, the comparison process is the first step in our approach. It requires two data models (M1 level) that conform to the same meta-model (M2 level). After customizing EMF Compare's matching, differencing and filtering engines, the comparison results will be a syntactic delta which contains equals i.e. commonalities as well as differences *(ResourceAttachementChange, Attribute Change, ReferenceChange and FeatureMapChange)*. These are based on four atomic operators: *Add, Delete, Change and Move*. Lot of efforts are being made by [14] to improve the algorithms of EMF Compare in order to help the developers to customize the engines according to their requirements. But the framework provides low level comparison results that are not always logic or difficult to understand by human as mentioned in [12].

Another alternative to get the differences between the old and the new data models would be to record end-user's actions on the editor (UAR) using action observers. These methods immediately produce a complete evolution schema.

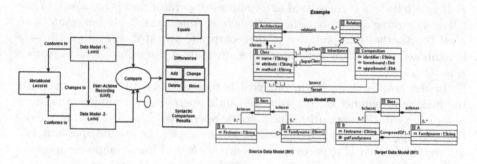

Fig. 3. Overview of the input/output for the comparison process.

3.2   Phase 2. Evolution Operators Flattening

The kinds of differences delivered by the previous phase are at a low level. They are not easy to interpret. Thus, we transform the differences to a set of atomic operators. These operators are independent of the previous phase, defined according to the treated metal-model and help to move to upper level. Most of the time, each difference is represented by one atomic operator. Each cascading difference is represented by the most priority operator. For example: *Add Attribute A to Class C* and *Add Class C to Model M* can be considered as one atomic operator: *Add Class C to Model M*. Indeed, adding a new class implies the addition of all its properties. Furthermore, sometimes we can find differences that cause the same change. For instance, in the case of eOpposite references in Ecore meta-model, modifying one of the two references will automatically update the other side of the opposition. Both changes will be detected as two differences and can be seen as one atomic operator.

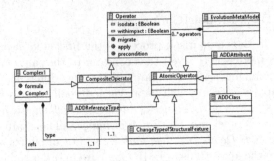

Fig. 4. Evolution atomic and composite operator's meta-model

Once atomic operators are found, we instantiate composite operators (see Fig. 4) as compositions of atomic ones, in order to rise from syntactic differencing delta to semantic one. In practice, we can find implicitly one or many composite operators derived from a composition of many atomic operators. For example, *Pull up attribute A* is considered as a composite operator that is composed of the following atomic operators: *Delete attribute A from class C, Add attribute A to class C'*. Another interpretation of this composite operator is: *Pull up attribute* is composed of the atomic operator *Move attribute A from Class C to its mother class C'*.

In the proposed approach, our goal is to build an evolution schema with the maximum number of composite semantic operators and minimum number of atomic syntactic operators. Each atomic operator is specified by a precondition an apply and a migrate operation. For example, the atomic operator *Add attribute A to class C* requires the existence of *class C*. Each composite operator is characterized by four properties: *a formula, a precondition, an apply and a migrate*:

– a formula is a sequence of atomic operators that define a composite operator. Identical formulas do not necessarily lead to a composite operator or to the same composite operator, depending on the precondition.
– a precondition responsible for managing the dependency between atomic operators in term of existence, order and priority. For example: *Add Literal L* requires the precondition *Exist Enumeration E*, which checks the existence of the enumeration E in the old data model or the existence of the operator *Add Enumeration E*.
– an apply is used to make evolve the old data model. Apply calls are used to check if the new data model is equivalent to the final evolved old data model.
– a migrate is a property where each composite evolution operator encapsulates its own migration behavior in order to ensure data conservation.

Moreover, to avoid conflicts, we suggest to integrate the end-user to resolve ambiguity during the building of composite operators, as shown in Fig. 5(a). He/she can modify the found evolution schema and apply a checking operation on his/her evolution schema; after calling the different *apply*, the final evolved data

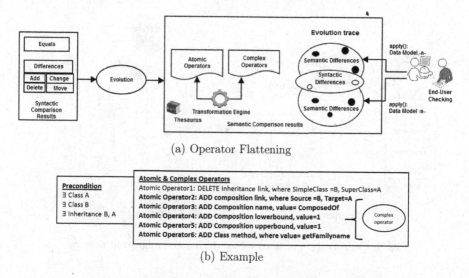

(a) Operator Flattening

(b) Example

Fig. 5. The passage from syntactic comparison delta to semantic one

model M must be identical to the original new data model. If some differences are found between these two data models, the evolution schema based on atomic and composite operators is wrong and needs to be corrected by the end-user.

3.3 Phase 3. Data Conservation

In our study, we classify the operators into two categories: safe operators without impact and operators with impact. The impact is considered at the M0 level. For example, the operator *Add Attribute* may need or not a migration of existing and corresponding object instances.

Furthermore, inspired by information theory concepts defined by [15], where the author distinguish between data representing cost side of the system, and information representing the value side, we propose a sub-classification of the operators with impact into two other sub-categories: operators where migration is data-conservative and operators where it is not. Figure 6(a) illustrates the concept by an evolution example of a UML composition relationship to an aggregation UML relationship. In this case we change the data structure but we do not lose any information and we do not need to create additional pieces of information as shown in (Fig. 7).

The last phase of our approach is the migration process as shown in (Fig. 6(b)). We migrate the existing instance attributes in data from the source M0 to the target M0'. We define M0 as instances of the model M1 and S0 as physical data, which represent the M0 instances into different formats.

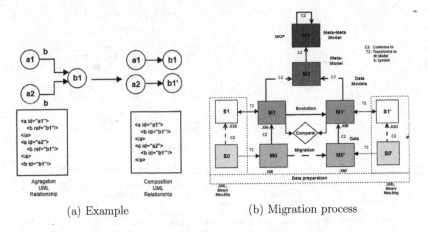

(a) Example   (b) Migration process

Fig. 6. Conservation of data values during the migration process

Fig. 7. Example of data values conservation during data models reconstruction

4   Case Study from the MICROSCOPE Project

In this section, we will see how the previous approach is applied to a particular revision of a data model used in the MICROSCOPE project [16]. This project studies the universality of free fall in space thanks to two differential accelerometers supplied by the French National Aerospace Research Center, ONERA, and embedded in a microsatellite from the CNES. While CNES models the telecommands (TC) and the telemeasures (TM), ONERA models the processing of telemeasures. In both cases, there is an intensive use of model-driven engineering to handle the complexity of such project thanks to two respective in-house metamodels Best [1] and GAMME [2]. In the following, we detail the comparison, evolution and migration strategies that could be used to co-evolve parameters used during the telemeasures processing, following the pipeline architecture.

This case study interests in the way of combining two telemeasures: class *Signaux* with two attributes *signal1* and *signal2*. Both attributes were typed by an enumeration called *Signal*, identifying the different telemeasures. Then, it was decided that it is possible to combine other signals than a telemeasure. As shown in Fig. 8 the modeller decided to reconstruct the data model by replacing the two attributes by two composition relationships towards a new class, called *DataAbstract*. The original attributes *signal1* and *signal2* are factorized in a class

DonneesSession, inheriting from *DataAbstract* and owning a *signal* attribute of type*Signal*. In this way, end-users can combine two telemeasures, a telemeasure with another signal or two signals. As a result:

- a new abstract class named *DataAbstract* is added;
- new two classes named *DonneesSession*, *AutresDonnees* inheriting from *DataAbstract* are added;
- a new attribute named *signal* of type *Signal* is added to the class *DonneesSession*;
- a new attribute named *signalExt* of type *String* is added to the class *AutresDonnees*;
- the types of *signal1* and *signal2* are changed from *Signal* to *DataAbstract*.

4.1 Comparison Process

After using the default engines of EMF Compare 3.0.1, we find many false-negatives (i.e. undetected correspondences) and false-positives (i.e. unexpected correspondences) in the matching results. 247 differences are obtained. However, when moving to release 3.2.0 of EMFCompare, we get better matching results. Moreover, after customizing the matching engine policy (based on id), we get only 17 differences. The idea is to find a unique name to identify each element in the model (for example, the unique name of an attribute is its name concatenated to the name of the container class). EMFCompare considers the two compared versions as two graphs. At the beginning, it makes a matching between ancestors. Each matching is composed of zero or many sub-matches. In other words, EMFCompare uses a top-down matching approach. Next, a differencing engine is employed to obtain all the differences using all the matched elements. Then, we decide to keep some interesting differences: when a data model element is updated or when an added data model element has an impact on data. Therefore, we neglect hidden changes given by cascading EMF *diffs*. Finally, we get 7 differences.

4.2 Evolution Process

In fact, the seven differences provided by EMF Compare (Table 1) are satisfying in term of correctness and precision. However, it is not easy to exploit them. Thus, we decide to transform these low level differences to atomic operators (Table 2) by applying a java transformation template on EMFCompare differencing engine and by running an evolution operator's defined at the meta-model level.

In the end, we obtain three *ADD Classes* as atomic operators and two composite operators *ChangeTypeofStructuralFeature*, that concern type changes of the attributes *signal1* and *signal2* from *Signal* to *Data Abstract*. In this case, our evolution schema is hybrid, i.e. it is a mixture of atomic and composite operators.

Table 1. Syntactic comparison results between two data models obtained by EMF compare customization.

EMFCompare diff	Kind	Matching
ReferenceChangeSpec	CHANGE gType	(GStructuralFeature: signal1 in GClass: Signaux) matched to (GStructuralFeature: signal1 in GClass: Signaux)
AttributeChangeSpec	CHANGE type	(GMetaModel_Element_property: null in GAttribute: Signal1) matched to (GMetaModel_Element_property: Composition in GReference: Signal1)
ReferenceChangeSpec	CHANGE gType	(GStructuralFeature: signal2 in GClass: Signaux) matched to (GStructuralFeature: signal2 in GClass: Signaux)
AttributeChangeSpec	CHANGE type	(GMetaModel_Element_property: null in GAttribute: Signal2) matched to (GMetaModel_Element_property: Composition in GReference: Signal2)
ReferenceChangeSpec	ADD gContents	(GClass: null in GModel: Lap1nDataModel) matched to (GClass: DataAbstract in GModel: Lap1nDataModel)
ReferenceChangeSpec	ADD gContents	(GClass: null in GModel: Lap1nDataModel) matched to (GClass: DonneesSession in GModel: Lap1nDataModel)
ReferenceChangeSpec	ADD gContents	(GClass: null in GModel: Lap1nDataModel) matched to (GClass: AutreDonnees in GModel: Lap1nDataModel)

In the evolution meta-model (Fig. 8) we define four atomic operators *ADD-Class, ADDAttribute, ChangeTypeofStructuralFeature and ADDReferenceType*. Each composite operator is a transformation pattern composed of a set of atomic operators. For example, Complex1 as shown in Table 3 is composed of two atomic operators: *ChangeTypeofStructuralFeature* and *ADDReferenceType*. The sequence of both operators is the formula. As shown in Fig. 8, a precondition checks the dependency between atomic and composite operators where:

- F' respresents the new gStructuralFeature in the gClass DonneesSession: *signal*;
- *new((f.gType).allFeatures)* represents the new gType of the two new gStructuralFeature signal1 and signal2: *Data Abstract*;
- $F'.gType$ represents the gType of the gattribute signal: *Signal*;

Table 2. From differences to atomic operators.

Atomic Operator	GModelElement	Value
ADDgContents	GClass	DataAbstract
ADDgContents	GClass	DonneesSession
ADDgContents	GClass	AutreDonnees
ADDReferenceType	type	Composition
ChangeTypeofStructuralFeature	GAttribute	DataAbstract
ADDReferenceType	type	Composition
ChangeTypeofStructuralFeature	GAttribute	DataAbstract

– *old(F).gType* represents the old gType of the two old gStructuralFeature signal1 and signal2: *Signal*.

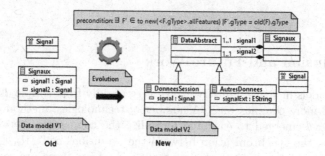

Fig. 8. Evolution from the old to new data model

We use this precondition to check our evolution schema with five operators. In the end, if the precondition is true, a full data conservation is immediately achieved. By calling the apply() of each operator, we can compare the transformed old (the final old data model) with the new version used during the comparison process. In our case the results are positive, i.e. the proposed evolution schema based on evolution operators is correct.

Table 3. Evolution schema based on atomic and composite operators

Atomic Operator	GModelElement	Value
ADDgContents	GClass	DataAbstract
ADDgContents	GClass	DonneesSession
ADDgContents	GClass	AutreDonnees

Composite Operator	GModelElement	Value
Complex1	ADDReferenceType	Composition
	ChangeTypeofStructuralFeature	DataAbstract
Complex2	ADDReferenceType	Composition
	ChangeTypeofStructuralFeature	DataAbstract

4.3 Migration Process

In our case, migration concerns composite operators only. We need to migrate the values of the gattributes as shown in Fig. 9. Initially, we have *signaux* an instance of the *gclass Signaux*. In the end, we arrive to three instances, one is instantiated from the *gclass Signaux* and the two others are instantiated from the *gclass DonneesSession*.

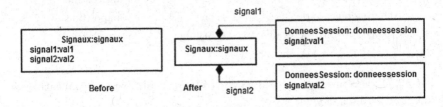

Fig. 9. Data conservation during the migration process

5 Conclusion and Future Work

The data models in space industry evolve very rapidly from simple data models to more and more complex ones. A number of technologies, methodologies and platforms have emerged to ease and formalize the comparison between different revisions, the synchronization between the evolutions of UML, EMF meta-models (M2) and the co-evolution of models. In fact, there are many model evolution and migration tools and each one has its own characteristics. But it is still difficult for end-users to extract the correct evolution. Moreover, most of these tools do not interest in the evolution of data models (M1) and co-evolution of data model instances (M0).

Thus, in this research study, we propose a protocol at M1/M0 level to automate the migration process of our data based on the comparison and on the evolution of their data models. Because reconstruction of composite operators based on the atomic ones provide a rich source of evolution strategy, an approach is being investigated to formalize comparison, evolution and migration processes using a model-based setting. This can be a major milestone for data model evolution with data values conservation as a primary priority during the migration.

Several other research directions to pursue our work can be investigated. First, we are interested in extending our approach to handle during the evolution process semantic meaning of elements by the integration of end-user via a graphical user interface (GUI) and a definition of a thesaurus, that concerns space data models. The thesaurus contains words that belong to the same lexical field. During the comparison process, it is used to check weather the meaning of data model elements is kept or not, in case we have syntactic changes. Furthermore, we want to validate our approach on more complex data models in term of number and type of changes. We also want to tackle the conservation of APIs. Instead of working on a complex formula to recognize an evolutionary operator, we could look at whether the data API is conserved.

Acknowledgments. Authors would like to express their gratitude to all members of the TCS team: Patrice Carle, Romain Kervarc, Rémi Lafage, Antoine Ferlin and Rémi Plantade from ONERA. This paper relies on their excellent comments and their constructive suggestions.

References

1. National Center for Space Studies (CNES) and The European Space Agency (ESA).: Best (2016). http://goo.gl/3awkpg
2. Bedouet, J., Huynh, N., Kervarc, R.: GAMME, a meta-model to unify data needs in simulation modeling (WIP). In: Proceedings of the Symposium on Theory of Modeling and Simulation-DEVS Integrative M and S Symposium, p. 14. Society for Computer Simulation International (2013)
3. Herrmannsdoerfer, M., Vermolen, S.D., Wachsmuth, G.: An extensive catalog of operators for the coupled evolution of metamodels and models. In: Malloy, B., Staab, S., van den Brand, M. (eds.) SLE 2010. LNCS, vol. 6563, pp. 163–182. Springer, Heidelberg (2011). doi:10.1007/978-3-642-19440-5_10
4. Lehman, M.M.: Software evolution. In: Marciniak, J.L. (ed.) Encyclopedia of Software Engineering. Wiley, Hoboken (1994)
5. Hunt, J.W., MacIlroy, M.D.: An Algorithm for Differential File Comparison. Bell Laboratories, New York (1976)
6. Wang, Y., DeWitt, D.J., Cai, J.Y.: X-Diff: an effective change detection algorithm for XML documents. In: Proceedings of the 19th International Conference on Data Engineering, pp. 519–530. IEEE (2003)
7. National Center for Space Studies (CNES): Aladin. https://logicels.cnes.fr/content/best
8. Toulmé, A.: Intaloi Inc. Presentation of EMF compare utility. In: Eclipse Modeling Symposium, pp. 1–8 (2006)
9. Khelladi, D.E., Hebig, R., Bendraou, R., Robin, J., Gervais, M.P.: Detecting complex changes and refactorings during (Meta) model evolution. Inf. Syst. **62**, 220–241 (2016)
10. Herrmannsdoerfer, M., Benz, S., Juergens, E.: COPE - automating coupled evolution of metamodels and models. In: Drossopoulou, S. (ed.) ECOOP 2009. LNCS, vol. 5653, pp. 52–76. Springer, Heidelberg (2009). doi:10.1007/978-3-642-03013-0_4
11. Vissers, Y., Mengerink, J.G.M., Schiffelers, R.R.H., Serebrenik, A., Reniers, M.A.: Maintenance of specification models in industry using Edapt. In: 2016 Forum on Specification and Design Languages (FDL), pp. 1–6. IEEE (2016)
12. Kehrer, T., Kelter, U., Ohrndorf, M., Sollbach, T.: Understanding model evolution through semantically lifting model differences with SiLift. In: 2012 28th IEEE International Conference on Software Maintenance (ICSM), pp. 638–641. IEEE (2012)

13. Rose, L.M., Herrmannsdoerfer, M., Williams, J.R., Kolovos, D.S., Garcés, K., Paige, R.F., Polack, F.A.C.: A comparison of model migration tools. In: Petriu, D.C., Rouquette, N., Haugen, Ø. (eds.) MODELS 2010 Part I. LNCS, vol. 6394, pp. 61–75. Springer, Heidelberg (2010). doi:10.1007/978-3-642-16145-2_5
14. Brun, C., Pierantonio, A.: Model differences in the eclipse modeling framework. UPGRADE Eur. J. Inform. Prof. **9**(2), 29–34 (2008)
15. McDonough, A.M.: Information Economics and Management Systems. McGraw-Hill Book Co., New York (1963). p. 11
16. Baghi, Q., Métris, G., Bergé, J., Christophe, B., Touboul, P., Rodrigues, M.: Gaussian regression and power spectral density estimation with missing data: the MICROSCOPE space mission as a case study. Phys. Rev. D **93**(12), 122007 (2016)

Ontology-Based Applications

Towards an Emergent Semantic of Web Resources Using Collaborative Tagging

Sara Qassimi[✉], El Hassan Abdelwahed, Meriem Hafidi, and Rachid Lamrani

Faculty of Sciences Semlalia Marrakech FSSM,
Cadi Ayyad University, Marrakesh, Morocco
{sara.qassimi,meriem.hafidi,rachid.lamrani}@ced.uca.ma,
abdelwahed@uca.ac.ma

Abstract. Within powerful social web interactions, we have witnessed an explosive growth of shared documents on the web. Indeed, the social web has been scaled up with massive shared web resources annotated by ordinary folks. The collection of folks' tags creates a folksonomy. This collaborative tagging system enables an open exploration of each user's tags describing web resources. Despite its simplicity of organizing web resources, it rises up ambiguous and inconsistent tags that semantically weaken the description of web resources' content. To achieve an enriched and structured map of knowledge, it is essential to optimally retrieve organized web resources through pertinently describing them with relevant descriptors "metadata". This article represents a combined semantic enrichment strategy using collaborative tagging guided by ontology towards pertinently describe web resources. In fact, relevant measures of performances attest the efficiency of our proposal that explores relevant folksonomy's tags to extract web resources' content main keywords and retrieve matching terms from a defined lightweight ontology. The alignment of social labeling with the ontology's formalism will implicitly build an emergent semantic of enriched web resources that will establish new challenges to improve context-aware recommender systems of web resources.

Keywords: Folksonomy · Semantic web · Ontology · Web resource · Context · Recommender system

1 Introduction

A huge amount of web resources is regularly created and stored on the web. This extended set of shared web contents has called the attention to the importance of extracting only relevant information from these data sources. Back in time, the identification of the main topics of documents has been done by professional indexers or domain's experts in traditional libraries. These main extracted topics or terms, experts' summarizes, reduce the dimensionality of a document's text content to its most important features. The need of a thematic overview has wide-spread in all areas and institutions. Instead of hiring professional indexers, owners of extensive collections lean on search technologies that enable an

© Springer International Publishing AG 2017
Y. Ouhammou et al. (Eds.): MEDI 2017, LNCS 10563, pp. 357–371, 2017.
DOI: 10.1007/978-3-319-66854-3_27

efficient organization and management of their massive documents. Throughout this technological century, the need for automatic and semi-automatic processes of expressing the main documents' topics has expanded as well as for advanced automatic grouping of related documents. The process of extracting main text summarizations involves deploying text mining techniques such as tools of natural language processing. However, recent semantic web researchers believe that the collaborative tagging is more reliable knowledge sources than free texts [1].

Within the current social web, users have been empowered and encouraged to bring their own topical keywords "tags" describing web resources "multimedia documents". Attributed tags, ordinary users' summarizes, are social web words derived from a commonly used vocabulary. A collection of tags creates a folksonomy. The folksonomy defines the three-dimensional relationship "user - web resource - tag". Tags hold the users' view of the web resource's topic, classify its type also denote its characteristics. Regardless of its overwhelming and diverse descriptive tags, folksonomy lacks semantic and suffers from inconsistent tags. However, social labeling brings up ambiguous tags by neutralizing the context. For instance, in a context-free environment, two unrelated web resources might be misconceived because of their attributed same tags holding different meanings. Like, abbreviations having multiple meaning "'Ca' means calcium and cancer", or terms having various meanings "plethora means a large amount of something. But in medicine, it expresses an excess of a bodily fluid, particularly blood".

The most fundamental challenge is to combine semantic enrichment strategies in order to gain an accurate and deep intuitive understanding of web resources by gathering their relevant metadata. The identification of a set of terms from an existing ontology matching a web resource's descriptive and the extraction of its text content's main keywords will provide the basis of the recommendations of tags. This paper focuses on exploring collaborative tagging to develop a combined strategy of extracting relevant web resources' descriptors "metadata" towards an emergent semantic.

The rest of the paper is organized as follows: Sect. 2 presents the motivating application scenario and the positioning of the purpose of this paper within the overall research challenges. The related work is reviewed in Sect. 3. The proposed approach of combining semantic enrichment strategies to extract pertinent metadata describing the content of a web resource is depicted in Sect. 4. The evaluation and discussion on the results are described in Sect. 5. Finally, the conclusion with future direction is drawn in Sect. 6.

2   Motivating Scenario and Research Challenges

To motivate our research studies, we have initiated contextual scenarios of applications domain "health care, education, tourism" (Level III) where our proposal (level I) will take place to enhance recommender systems "RSs" of web resources (Level II) (see Fig. 1). The RSs recommend items to a user based on its profile, preferences and contextual parameters by referencing information related to similar users and content-based resources. The context-awareness of RSs is determinate by the circumstances coming from the spatial, temporal and other defined contextual environmental parameters arising from the application domain and users' data sources. A health care scenario is chosen to be covered in this article. Within the current citizen life of the north-African developing country, we are witnessing changes in health care areas. The dynamism of a hospital is gained by the quality of services delivered by its doctors, specialists, medical technicians and nurses. Our perception of the future is shaped by revolutionizing the way current hospitals work. We are putting the advantage of technology into perspective to efficiently rebuild hospitals' strategies. The centralization of each patient's health data annotated with relevant metadata will enable authorized health care professionals and doctors to get a full oriented-patient decision-making by comparing similar patients' health cases. For instance, based on the pertinent emergent semantic (Level I), the context-aware RS will detect fitting similarities between the archived documents, then generate meaningful recommendations for a diabetic patient's case to prevent complications in diabetes mellitus. The RS solution will serve health care professionals by pertinently matching their search queries and the expected results in the context of medical documents' retrieval. Health care leaders are aware of the importance of sharing and spreading knowledge thought social interactions by tagging medical web resources. The involvement of humans' perception, cognition and ability to summarize (abstract summary) will advance the RSs' learning strategy of extracting web resources' descriptive emerging from users' interactions within a contextual and collaborative environment. The foundation of strengthening the intended context-aware recommender system of a particular domain (e.g. health care) is done based on the two following main steps.

The first step (Level I) focuses on defining the strongest way to pertinently describe web resources and explicitly construct semantic links bridging web resources' metadata in order to reach out the principals of the web of data. The aim is to explore the three-dimensional connection between users-tags-web resources by aligning folksonomy with ontology (enriching a lightweight ontology with folksonomy's tags and guiding this enrichment by the ontology's formalism [2]). Furthermore, inner the collaborative tagging system, a new approach (see Fig. 2) of pertinently describing web resources must be attendant by filtering generated tags guided with extracted matching terms from a domain ontology and content-based main keywords. This basic essential stride will be discussed in this paper.

The second step sets our future research studies challenges (Level II). Its main goal is to achieve an optimized context-aware recommender system founded on the formalism of the semantic web emerging from the shared web resources within communities' interactions. Beyond exploring combinations of several approaches to calculate the filtration of items based on content and collaborative profiles' methods. Our vision goes further than proving the validation of previous researches works in recommender systems' methods, but rather explores the minimization

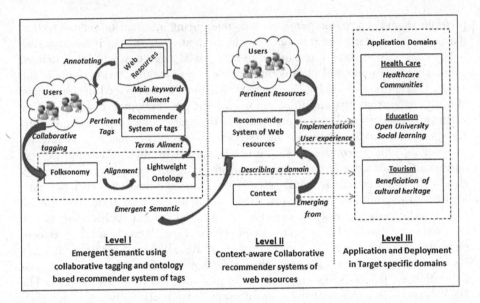

Fig. 1. General architecture of the research studies

of the empirical risk of recommending when the number of items rises by taking on account the emerging context from the defined application domain.

This paper mainly focuses on the first step of the proposed architecture, called "Emergent semantic using collaborative tagging and ontology based recommender system of tags" (see Fig. 1, Level I). The components of this architecture will be spotlighted in details alongside this paper (see Fig. 2).

3   Related Work

The act of indexing documents is the process of annotating them with different main shortcuts descriptors "metadata" that vary radically depending on whether the topics originate from a controlled vocabulary (terms), text contents (keywords) or a collaborative tagging system (tags) [3].

An expert has an advanced and a high level of knowledge about a particular domain [4]. The main keywords assigned by authors, or by professional indexers construct a controlled vocabulary (ontology, classifications and thesauri) representing a strong knowledge representation by expressing semantic relations [5]. The expert-based tagging method is called term assignment or subject indexing method that uses a controlled vocabulary. This method has been addressed in two ways. One way, the application of manually generated or automatically induced rules to classify a document's properties into categories (terms) extracted from a vocabulary. Another way, the generation of a document's candidates terms by mapping them onto vocabulary's terms. Then, based on statistical methods, the evaluation of the document's candidates terms is performed by attributing weights to analyze their ranking. The main disadvantages of both manual and automatic classification rules lead to an unsuccessful recovery of all documents' terms. These techniques are vulnerable to errors by assigning unpopular terms for users. Mapping documents phrases to vocabulary's terms is advantageous over classification-based methods. This comes due to the tremendous cost of manual work, which is both time-consuming and expensive.

Each web resource usually holds a rich text content. Data mining algorithms can do the extraction of information from the resource so as to retrieve its relevant keywords. The advantage of using content-based tagging is the working automatic processes independent of human involvement. The content-based tagging strategy relies on keyphrases or keywords extraction methods that derive keywords from the text content. The online RESTFul APIs "semantic annotators" (that identify meaningful sequences of words "spots" in an unstructured text and link them to a pertinent Wikipedia page), they are shown to be unable to outperform keyword extractors [6]. The automatic keyword extraction "extractive summary" is classified into four categories, namely, simple statistical approach, linguistics approach, machine learning approach, and hybrid approaches [7]. The keywords extraction method is improved by the machine learning model that combines several features. It begins with two competing methods: GenEx [8] "Genitor and Extractor" a hybrid genetic algorithm followed by KEA [9] "Keyphrase Extraction Algorithm" that generates and filters candidates based on their weights of features. More attention has been given to KEA for its open availability and simplicity of usage. The keywords extraction methods have achieved impressive results, but require training data. The unsupervised extraction techniques use heuristic filtering to compensate the lack of training data by using complex analysis like shallow parsing (deep analytics) or statistical-based methods based on an independent domain like KP-Miner [10]. The dominant disadvantage of content-based tagging method (keyword extraction from the original text descriptive) is the limitation consistency of the resulting keywords based only on author's words of a document. Even if they offer certain flexibility without a controlled vocabulary, but they lack semantic (e.g. synonymous words are not clustered together).

The social tagging has the advantage of producing a large scale of tags' collections. The main goal of collaborative tagging is to generate tags matching the human understanding of the web resource "abstractive summary". As keywords extraction methods, tagging suffers from inconsistency: polysemous and synonymous words [2]. One way to address inconsistency problem is to use an automatic tags' suggestions [3]. Most tags' recommendations techniques use the same strategy by finding similar resources that have been already tagged, then rank the extracted collection of tags. This strategy is restricted on suggesting only pre-existing tags. Similar approaches have been adherent by combining multi-features "tag frequency, co-occurrence and document similarity" [11]. Almost none of researchers of tagging's field have explored term assignment and keyword extraction strategies to support failures of tagging methods. The keywords extraction methods lack from the availability of a huge collection of tagged documents that rapidly evolves on collaborative environments. Moreover, multiple tags' sets are created by multi-authors (folks) instead of keywords' sets emerging from just one author's descriptive.

Table 1. Collecting descriptive metadata's approaches

Approaches	Advantages	Disadvantages	Methods
Experts	Expert-high-level tags;	Costly process;	Term assignment
	Semantic web;	Difficult scalability;	
	Coverage of the main topic	Uncommon language;	
		Time spending;	
Content-based	Automated process;	Noise;	Keyword extraction
	Not involving human;	Computationally intensive;	
	Avoid cold start	Limited notion;	
		Lack of semantic;	
Social tagging	Large scalability;	Polysemy and synonymy;	Social tagging
	Social indexing;	Lack of semantic;	
	Wisdom of the crowds;	Cold start problem;	
	Common folks words;	Ill-formed words;	
	Diversity	Uncleaned tags	

Inside out this analysis, the three major types of assigning descriptive metadata's approaches "expert's term assignment, content-based keyword extraction and social tagging" have a common objective of identifying the main topics of a web resource. But, they address it with slightly different methodologies (see Table 1). The current hybrid approaches employ the use of background knowledge in the form of a hierarchical ontology [12,13] to improve the performance of text mining tasks. However, maintaining a specific domain's ontology within the rapid growth of shared web resources on the web is expensive in term of time spending and expenses of charging indexers to enrich the ontology. Moreover, the semantic web researchers are no longer coping with extracting knowledge from texts [14] but rather they have centered their debates on emergent social involvement. Compared to the mentioned approaches, we propose a combined methodology (detailed in Sect. 4) of semantically enrich the description of web resources that explores collaborative tagging (integrating human cognition) by bridging between the discussed collecting descriptive metadata's approaches and filling each others gap within a collaborative environment of social labeling.

4 Proposed Approach: A Combined Semantic Enrichment

The proposed approach describes a combined semantic enrichment strategy of describing a web resource's content by retrieving relevant tags from the folksonomy and extracting main keywords not only from the text content, but also with a reference to a controlled vocabulary's matching terms. Within a collaborative tagging environment, the curation of the collection of tags could be assessed by recommending tags (e.g. web resources' main keywords) to users in order to address the cold start problem and set a contextual orientation of tags' generation. Extracting keywords from web resource's text content could be inconsistent. For instance, two authors might be publishing similar documents described with different main keywords. In order to introduce semantics to describe and relate web resources, it is relevant to use a controlled vocabulary "lightweight ontology" by identifying its set of terms that matches the descriptive of a given web resource. The steps of the proposed methodology are as follows.

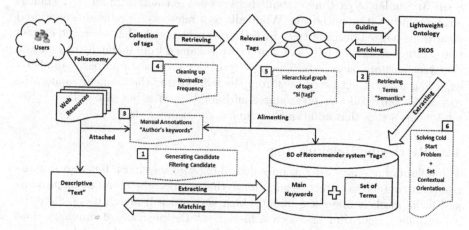

Fig. 2. Combined semantic enrichment strategy

4.1   Content-Based Main Keywords and Extracted Terms

The main keywords' extraction captures the best accurate expressions representing the main topic of a document. Extracting main keywords not only from the web resource's text content, but also identifying a matching set of terms from a lightweight ontology SKOS [15].

Step 1: The act of extracting main keywords consists of two stages. The first stage of the main keywords' extraction involves generating candidates keywords by using stop words (as boundaries) and tokenizing text into sentences then extracting candidates (one or more words). Those extracted candidates are reduced to their roots by applying a stemmer (e.g. Lovins stemmer [16]). The second stage is about filtering candidates that involves generating features for each candidate. Each feature is normalized to lie between 0 and 1. The used features capture: The frequency of each candidate (TFxIDF score that combines the word's frequency with the inverse document's frequency to pick out relevant frequent keyword); the occurrence (a candidate appears at least more than two times); The type of a candidate (noun phrase, not exceed trigrams); The positioning of the candidate in the text content (beginning and end).

Step 2: The extraction of the set of terms matching the text content of a web resource relies on the semantic relatedness feature (calculated by matching each candidate to a descriptive of a concept existing in the lightweight ontology, then compares the relatedness of a given candidate to all other candidates "the more a candidate is related to others, the more is significant"). For each extracted content-based main keyword of a web resource and each retrieved matching term from a lightweight ontology, is assigned to a computed classification probability "score".

Step 3: Similar to existing systems for keyword extraction Maui [17]. Maui is KEA's reincarnation with using Wikipedia as a reference. It relies on supervised algorithms bagged decision trees by training their models that learn the extraction strategy from manually annotated corpus gained from manually chosen web resources authors' keywords. The novelty of our proposed approach stands on exploring relevant extracted tags from the folksonomy: the manually annotated corpus not only contains prerequisite authors' keywords but also adds relevant folksonomy's tags that additionally aliment the training data.

4.2 Retrieving Relevant Tags

The folksonomy's tags are not only describing web resources, but also summarize their content "abstractive summary" that express the users' understanding and make implicit inferences about which keyword will match users' interests. No standard algorithm has been achieved yet the abstractive summary done by humans [7]. Thus, relevant tags reflect users' opinions and provide membership and sense-making that attract readers and invite them to bring their own opinion too. Besides, web resources' authors' keywords are often not sufficiently expressive for ordinary users. However, not all generated tags are meaningful because most of them are uncleaned (personal and misspelled tags).

Step 4: Establishing a blacklist of forbidden words and using a spell checker (e.g. Google spell checker) will eliminate personal tags, correct misspellings, and tokenize multi-word tags (e.g., "BreastCancer" and "Breast-Cancer"). The folksonomy suffers from noises due to the uncontrolled nature of tagging that introduces synonymy and polysemy of tags. Through, applying a stemmer will reduce words' variation to their stems (e.g.,"Infectious" and "Infection" are reduced to their root word "Infect"). The consistency of each tag is computed by finding it in a dictionary (e.g.: Wikipedia), or it has to be used by at least two distinct users depending on the size of the community. Within a community of users U, a user u_i annotates a web resource r with a tag t_i. Each tag t_i is related to its degree of frequency $d°(t_i)$ (1) calculated by two features: (2) Frequency of the tag t_i annotating the resource r "$F_t(t_i)$"; (3) Frequency of users who use the tag t_i to annotate the resource r "$F_u(t_i)$". The relevant tags are those with a higher degree of frequency. We set integers i, j, n $\in$ N* and n is a finite number.

$$d°(t_i) = F_t(t_i) \times F_u(t_i) \tag{1}$$

$$F_t(t_i) = \frac{Number\ of\ t_i\ annotating\ the\ resource\ r}{\sum_{j=1}^{n} t_j\ annotating\ the\ resource\ r} \tag{2}$$

$$F_u(t_i) = \frac{Number\ of\ users\ who\ use\ t_i\ to\ annotate\ the\ resource\ r}{Number\ of\ users\ who\ annotate\ the\ resource\ r} \tag{3}$$

Step 5: Each tag t_i has its inclusion score $S_i(t_i)$ (4) that identifies its taxonomic relationships (broader, narrower) among other tags. The purpose of building a hierarchical graph of tags is to highlight the differences of specification amongst a collection of tags holding the same meaning (synonymous tags). The hierarchy of tags is built based on the inclusion score of each tag t_i by using the inclusion index [2]. For instance, "Inclusion (t_1, t_2) > Inclusion (t_2, t_1)" scales how general a tag t_1 is compared to another tag t_2 (tag t_1 is broader than tag t_2).

$$S_i(t_i) = \sum_{j=1}^{n} Inclusion(t_i, t_j) = \sum_{j=1}^{n} \frac{NRA(t_i, t_j)}{NRA(t_j)} \tag{4}$$

Where, $NRA(t_i, t_j)$ is the total Number of web Resources Annotated with both t_i and t_j. And $NRA(t_j)$ is the total Number of web Resources Annotated with t_j, for $i \neq j$.

Within a contextual environment, the enrichment of the concepts of the lightweight ontology is done due to mapping relevant tags to the matching concept's attributes guided by the ontology's formalism defined by the Simple Knowledge Organization System SKOS [2].

Step 6: Significant variations across tag usages to describe a web resource are induced because of the lack of guidelines. Recommendations of tags enhance users' tagging performances and skills. They stabilize the folksonomy and solve the cold start problem also set contextual orientation. Moreover, existing assigned web resource's tags will influence users choices of assigning new descriptive tags [18]. However, little attention is given to new web resources, the suggestion of tags could be done only if the resource has been tagged earlier. Consequently, it will be pertinent to aliment the database of the recommender system of tags with extracted main keywords, associated with matching terms retrieved from the lightweight ontology. This RS of tags' database is permanently enriched with relevant resulted tags describing a web resource to achieve pertinent suggestions of tags related to a given web resource's content.

5   Evaluation and Results

To evaluate the performance of the proposed approach (see Fig. 2) of combining methods to semantically enrich web resources' descriptive, we choose the Medical Subject Heading (MeSH) as the controlled vocabulary "lightweight ontology". Managed by the U.S National Library of Medicine, MeSH terms describe biomedical research items [19]. We collected 550 random biomedical articles "web resources" annotated with their authors' keywords and associated tags from the "folksonomy" CiteULike [20]. We set 2 articles for testing and 548 for training.

In order to extract 8 main keywords from the two biomedical testing articles, namely Article A [21] and Article B [22] containing 7,672 words and 8,009 words respectively, we surveyed some keyword extraction tools by comparing their performances with measures of Precision P (the percentage of correct keywords among those extracted), Recall R (the percentage of correctly extracted keywords among all correct ones) and F-Measure F (combination of both). We tested the python implementation of the Rapid Automatic Keyword Extraction RAKE [23] against the Multi-purpose automatic topic indexing Maui [17]. We trained Maui by using two ensemble machine learning classifiers to rank candidates: Maui based on the bagging decision trees classifier (Maui Bag); And based on the boosting classifier called AdaBoostM1 using classification trees as single classifiers (Maui Boost). The highest measures' values for precision, recall, and F-measure are highlighted in bold. The manual annotations of "authors' keywords with relevant tags" brings high results achieved with Maui by using the bagging classifier (Table 2). But in the cold start, training the boosting classifier (AbaBoostM1) only on "authors' keywords" shows better performances. The accuracy is improved by training Maui on manually chosen relevant tags added to authors' keywords, which builds a model that learns the keyword extraction strategy based on bagging decision trees classifier. Whereas, RAKE shows its limited accuracy due to the lack of normalization of candidates that throws away valid ones.

Table 2. Comparing performances of keyword extracting tools (Main keywords)

Manual annotations	RAKE			Maui bag			Maui boost		
	P	R	F	P	R	F	P	R	F
Authors' keywords	6.25	10.0	7.69	12.5	16.67	14.29	12.5	20	15.38
Tags	-	-	-	81.25	8.22	14.92	37.5	3.93	7.12
Authors' keywords + Tags	6.25	0.34	0.64	75	6.68	12.26	56.25	5.14	9.42
Authors' keywords + Relevant tags	6.25	2.17	3.22	**81.25**	**35.25**	**49.17**	50	22.98	31.49

The lightweight ontology used is a SKOS version of the MeSH thesaurus, provided by the Vrije Universiteit Amsterdam [24]. The highest results are shown again with the fourth category "Authors' keywords + Relevant Tags" by using Maui (Table 3). The term assignment model is built by matching each keyword candidate against the ontology's MeSH terms. It extracts 10 MeSH terms from each of the testing biomedical articles. The evaluation proves the relevancy of exploring relevant folksonomy's tags to aliment the manual annotation corpus. By gathering two types of manually assigned keywords "authors' keywords and relevant tags", we notice a better performance of both: extracting MeSH terms and content-based main keywords.

Table 3. Comparing performances of keyword extracting tools (MeSH terms)

Manual annotations	Maui bag			Maui boost		
	P	R	F	P	R	F
Authors' keywords	10	16.67	12.5	10	18.33	12.94
Tags	35	4.9	8.95	25	2.97	5.31
Authors' keywords + Tags	40	5.32	9.4	10	1.2	2.14
Authors' keywords + Relevant tags	**45**	**26.55**	**33.4**	10	5.75	7.3

We consider that each web resource is represented by a vector of a set of attributes (5). The vector's attributes are represented by the couple metadata and its computed score. A web resource's metadata represents relevant tags, extracted content-based main keywords, and assigned terms retrieved from the predefined lightweight ontology. We delineate the definition of a web resource's description:

$$Description\ Web\ Resource = \{(metadata, score)\} \qquad (5)$$

Description Article $A = \{(cancer, 0.936),$ (breast, 1.409), (breast cancer, 0.488), (risk factors, 0.437), (sequence Analysis DNA, 0.199), (signature, 0.0003), (microarray, 0.0003), (human, 0.0003), (breast neoplasms, 0.870), (neoplasms, 0.854), (computational Biology, 0.544), (systems biology, 0.496), (gene expression, 0.309), (classification, 0.293), (network, 0.344), (gene expression profiles, 1.105), (lighting, 0.20)$\}$.

Description Article $B = \{(cancer, 1.004),$ (breast, 1.342), (breast cancer, 0.565), (signature, 0.804), microarray, 0.421), (prognosis, 0.351), (human, 0.012), (gene expression, 0.818), (oncogenes, 0.304), neoplasms, 0.288), (carcinogens, 0.304), (breast neoplasms, 0.860), (survival, 0.345), (hospitals urban, 0.274), (survival analysis, 0.391), (prognostic gene, 0.325), (menopause, 0.287), (classification, 0.003)$\}$.

The semantic similarity between the two vectors describing the two articles is related to the analytics of the score of their similar metadata. The measure of similarity between the two vectors is computed by applying cosine similarity of Salton [25]. The more the cosine similarity measure value is small comparing the similarity of two vectors, the more the descriptive of these two vectors brings up consistent meaning (i.e., avoid mistakenly grouping two distinct web resources into a cluster). The comparison (see Fig. 3) of the two vectors describing the corresponding web resources "Article A, Article B" is based on their descriptive metadata using either their text content's main keywords, or extracted Mesh terms deriving from the ontology, or on both of them added to relevant tags. We notice that the relevant value of cosine similarity measure "0.8547211" is obtained based on web resources' vectors described with the three types of

Vectors describing The Two articles (based on Main Keywords)

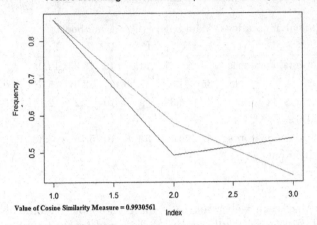

Value of Cosine Similarity Measure = 0.9930561

Vectors describing The Two articles (based on Extracted MeSH Terms)

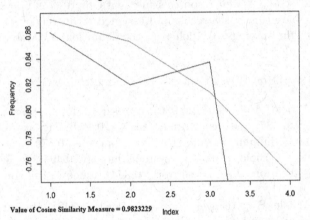

Value of Cosine Similarity Measure = 0.9823229

Vectors describing The Two articles (based on Relevant Tags + Main Keywords + Extracted MeSH Terms)

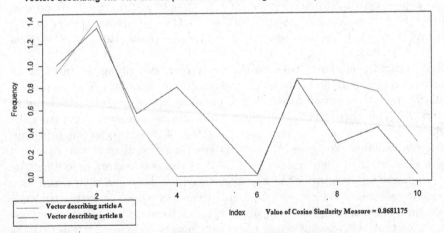

Vector describing article A
Vector describing article B

Value of Cosine Similarity Measure = 0.8681175

Fig. 3. Comparing similarity of the two vectors

metadata "main keywords, relevant tags, and extracted MeSH terms". These results demonstrate the effectiveness of our proposal of the combined semantic · enrichment strategy towards pertinently describing a web resource's content.

6   Conclusion and Future Works

An expansion of web resources has been raised by the oncoming of the collaborative social web's era. This extended set of shared web resources has called the attention to the importance of extracting only their relevant descriptive information. Indeed, to achieve an optimal organization of the growing shared web resources, it is essential to pertinently retrieve their relevant semantic descriptors. This paper has introduced a combined semantic enrichment strategy to pertinently describe web resources by overcoming folksonomy's weaknesses. Moreover, setting a recommender system of tags not only alimented with a web resource's previous relevant tags, but also with its text content's extracted main keywords added to matching ontology's terms will solve the cold start problem of tagging and guide generation of new tags (raise up the human understanding and invite users to annotate more). The methodology of the semantic enrichment of a web resource's descriptive explores the collaborative tagging to develop a combined strategy for extracting relevant web resources' descriptors "metadata". The experimental evaluation of the effectiveness of our work has been attested with relevant results of measures of performances. Future perspectives will focus on expanding the collaborative community to validate the scalability of the approach. As well as, integrating gamification techniques to benefit from users' potential (e.g. curating folksonomy's tags). A future implementation is planned to describe the threat of the validation process. In future works, a full exploration of the context arising from adapted collaboration scenarios (application domains) will set up new challenges to improve context-aware recommender systems of web resources based on a strong emergent semantic. An enhanced context-aware recommender system based on emergent semantic of web resources and contextual awareness extended within open communities application projects (health care, social learning, tourism) will feed users needs and increase their interests by promoting their interactions of sharing and annotating web resources.

References

1. Lau Raymond, Y.K., Leon Zhao, J., Wenping, Z., Yi, C., Ngai Eric, W.T.: Learning context-sensitive domain ontologies from folksonomies: a cognitively motivated method. INFORMS J. Comput. **27**(3), 561–578 (2015). doi:10.1287/ijoc.2015.0644
2. Qassimi, S., Abdelwahed, E.H., Hafidi, M., Lamrani, R.: Enrichment of ontology by exploiting collaborative tagging systems: a contextual semantic approach. In: Third International Conference on Systems of Collaboration (SysCo), IEEE Conference Publications, pp. 1–6 (2016)

3. Klašnja-Milićević, A., Vesin, B., Ivanović, M., Budimac, Z., Jain, L.C.: Folksonomy and tag-based recommender systems in e-learning environments. E-Learning Systems. ISRL, vol. 112, pp. 77–112. Springer, Cham (2017). doi:10.1007/978-3-319-41163-7_7

4. Marinho, L.B., Nanopoulos, A., Schmidt-Thieme, L., Jschke, R., Hotho, A., Stumme, G.: Social tagging recommender systems. In: Ricci, F., Rokach, L., Shapira, B., Kantor, P. (eds.) Recommender Systems Handbook, pp. 615–644. Springer, Berlin (2011). doi:10.1007/978-0-387-85820-3_19

5. Špiraneca, S., Ivanjko, T.: Experts vs. novices tagging behavior: an exploratory analysis. Procedia - Soc. Behav. Sci. **73**, 456–459 (2013)

6. Jean-Louis, L., Zouaq, A., Gagnon, M., Ensan, F.: An assessment of online semantic annotators for the keyword extraction task. In: Pham, D.-N., Park, S.-B. (eds.) PRICAI 2014. LNCS (LNAI), vol. 8862, pp. 548–560. Springer, Cham (2014). doi:10.1007/978-3-319-13560-1_44

7. Thomas, J.R., Bharti, S.K., Babu, K.S.: Automatic keyword extraction for text summarization in e-newspapers. In: Proceedings of the International Conference on Informatics and Analytics, pp. 86–93. ACM (2016)

8. Turney, P.D.: Learning to extract keyphrases from text. Technical report ERB-1057, National Research Council Canada, Institute for Information Technology (1999)

9. Witten, I.H., Paynter, G.W., Frank, E., Gutwin, C., Nevill-Manning, C.G.: KEA: practical automatic keyphrase extraction. In: Proceedings of ACM Conference on Digital Libraries, Berkeley, CA, US, pp. 254–255. ACM Press, New York (1999)

10. El-Beltagy, S.R., Rafea, A.: KP-miner: a keyphrase extraction system for English and Arabic documents. Inf. Syst. **34**(1), 132–144 (2009)

11. Budura, A., Michel, S., Cudre-Mauroux, P., Aberer, K.: To tag or not to tag - harvesting adjacent metadata in large-scale tagging systems. In: Proceedings International ACM SIGIR Conference on Research and Development in Information Retrieval, Singapore, pp. 733–734. ACM Press, New York (2008)

12. Hassan, M.M., Karray, F., Kamel, M.S.: Automatic document topic identification using Wikipedia hierarchical ontology. In: Proceedings of the Eleventh IEEE International Conference on Information Science, Signal Processing and their Applications, pp. 237–242 (2012)

13. Allahyari, M., Kochut, K.: Semantic tagging using topic models exploiting Wikipedia category network. In: Proceedings of the 10th International Conference on Semantic Computing (2016)

14. Fang, Q., Xu, C., Jitao, S., Shamim Hossain, M., Ghoneim, A.: Folksonomy-based visual ontology construction and its applications. IEEE Trans. Multimedia **18**(4), 702–713 (2016)

15. SKOS Simple Knowledge Organization System. https://www.w3.org/TR/skos-reference/

16. Lovins, J.B.: Development of a stemming algorithm. Mech. Trans. Comput. Linguist. **11**(1–2), 11–31 (1968)

17. Maui - Multi-purpose automatic topic indexing. http://www.medelyan.com/software

18. Fu, W.-T., Kannampallil, T., Kang, R., He, J.: Semantic imitation in social tagging. ACM Trans. Comput.-Hum. Interact. **17**(3), 1–37 (2010)

19. US National Library of Medicine National Institutes of Health: Medical Subject Headings (MeSH). https://www.nlm.nih.gov/mesh

20. CiteULike. http://www.citeulike.org/

21. Chuang, H.-Y., Lee, E., Liu, Y.-T., Lee, D., Ideker, T.: Network-based classification of breast cancer metastasis (2007). doi:10.1038/msb4100180
22. Naderi, A., Teschendorff, A.E., Barbosa-Morais, N.L., Pinder, S.E., Green, A.R., Powe, D.G., Robertson, J.F.R., Aparicio, S., Ellis, I.O., Brenton, J.D., Caldas, C.: A gene-expression signature to predict survival in breast cancer across independent data sets (2007). doi:10.1038/sj.onc.1209920
23. RAKE Homepage. https://hackage.haskell.org/package/rake
24. Vrije Universiteit Amsterdam, MeSH terms Homepage. http://libguides.vu.nl/PMroadmap/MeSH
25. Salton, G., McGill, M.J.: Introduction to Modern Information Retrieval. Mcgraw Hill Computer Science Series (1983)

Ontology to Profile User Models
with Disabilities

Brunil Dalila Romero-Mariño[1(✉)], Vanesa Espín[2],
María José Rodríguez-Fórtiz[2], María Visitación Hurtado-Torres[2],
Luis Ramos[3], and Hisham M. Haddad[4]

[1] Simón Bolivar University, Sartenejas, Venezuela
bromero@usb.ve
[2] University of Granada, Granada, Spain
{vespin,mjfortiz,mhurtado}@ugr.es
[3] National Open University, Maracay, Venezuela
lramos@una.edu.ve
[4] Kennesaw State University, Kennesaw, GA, USA
hhaddad@kennesaw.edu

Abstract. Accessibility enhances software applications by promoting e-inclusion through tools that allow the profiling of users with disabilities. Our research aims to develop an ontology that involves the Accessibility domain. This paper describes the design and implementation of the proposed ontology. We apply the NeOn methodology, by reusing and reengineering the AEGIS/ACCESSIBLE ontology, in order to allow making recommendations based on the profile and capabilities of user models with disabilities. This enables the proposed ontology to provide suitable support assistance according to each user action, especially when users interact with any software application. Moreover, it allows identification of activity limitations for each user profile in day-to-day life, among others. Furthermore, the Accessibility ontology is designed to support inference processes, and to provide adequate answers to several Competency Questions (CQs).

Keywords: Accessibility · AEGIS/ACCESSIBLE ontology · E-inclusion · User profile

1 Introduction

The World Health Organization report on disability [1] states that "Disability is part of the human condition. Almost everyone will be temporarily or permanently impaired at some point in life, and those who survive to old age will experience increasing difficulties in functioning". In the same document, the report states that "in the years ahead, disability will be an even greater concern because its prevalence is on the rise". On the other hand, MADHIE (Measuring Health and Disability in Europe: Supporting Policy Development) Consortium [2] considers Disability as the umbrella term for impairments, activity limitations and participation restrictions, referring to the negative aspects of interactions between an individual (with a health condition) and the individual's contextual factors (environmental and personal factors).

© Springer International Publishing AG 2017
Y. Ouhammou et al. (Eds.): MEDI 2017, LNCS 10563, pp. 372–385, 2017.
DOI: 10.1007/978-3-319-66854-3_28

Current society is characterized by involving Information and Communication Technologies (ICT) in daily tasks. For people with disabilities, their access to ICT should be guaranteed and recognized as a human right [3]. In this sense, Accessibility is considered a key factor to encourage digital inclusion in society. Stephanidis et al. [4] point out that accessibility implies global requirement for access to information by individuals with different abilities, requirements and preferences, in a variety of contexts of use.

The characterization of the user profile is essential to know the users' needs, capabilities and limitations, in order to offer the user the best customization of ICT. This obviously has an effect on user satisfaction, given the quality of the user's interactions with ICT. After reviewing the user profile models and standards, we found that according to Madrid et al. [5], the semantic modeling in the domain of Accessibility and e-inclusion has been addressed in several projects.

Based on these projects, we have defined an ontology of accessibility to profile users when they interact with software applications, taking into account their capabilities and limitations, and characteristics of the support assistance to use the applications. This ontology is a module that will be used by a Recommender System for Customer Relationships Manager Systems (CRMs). It will suggest software adaptations and assistance to support customers with disabilities. In addition, the Recommender System will use another ontology module to model CRMs. In this paper we only focus on the design and implementation processes of the ontology of the accessibility module.

The paper is organized as follows: Sect. 2 describes related work, Sect. 3 describes how the proposed ontology module was developed, and Sect. 4 presents the conclusion and future work.

2 Related Work

An ontology is an explicit specification of a conceptualization [6] and it can be understood as a description of the concepts and relationships in a specific domain [7]. Ontology engineering enables the representation of knowledge and the identification of context and dependency information more easily than using data modelling or database-centric structures [8]. Ontologies are widely used in different disciplines. Using ontologies in the health domain is an active research field because ontology based systems can be used to improve the management of complex health systems [9]. In this domain, ontological user profiles allow accurate and homogeneous representations of the user in terms of features such as needs and preferences. Furthermore, the use of ontologies enhances sharing and reusing a profile among different systems and provides the opportunity to reason together with the rest of the components of these systems. Previous studies have defined or reused ontologies to represent users in health-care environments such as: monitoring users in ambient assisted living [10], providing healthy food recommendations [11] or storing standard health records for interoperability in medical systems [12]. A more related example is ADOLENA (Abilities and Disabilities OntoLogy for ENhancing Accessibility) [13], which is an ontology to represent user profiles with regards to abilities and disabilities for ontology-based data access for web portals. It is based on ICDH-2 [14], a previous version of ICF (International Classification of Diseases) [15], from the World Health Organization (WHO) framework. However, ICDH-2 ontology does not characterize low level operations to be carried out by users when they interact and need assistance.

One of the best known ontologies for modelling accessibility is the AEGIS/ ACCESSIBLE ontology (version 5.1) [16], based on two previous projects, AEGIS and ACCESSIBLE.

The AEGIS project places users and their needs at the center of all ICT developments. Korn et al. [17]. It is "based on a holistic User-Center Design (UCD), AEGIS identifies user needs and interaction models for several user groups and develops open source-based generalized accessibility support into mainstream ICT devices and applications, such as desktop, rich web applications, and Java-based mobile devices".

The AEGIS ontology is the result of the AEGIS Project [18]. It provides support for the formal and unambiguous definition of Accessibility domains, and for possible semantic interactions between them. Its architecture consists of three categories of aspects [19]: (1) Personal aspects: characteristics of users with disabilities, functional limitations and impairments. (2) Technical aspects: technical characteristics of I/O devices, general and functional characteristics of web, desktop and mobile applications, and other assistive technology that should be taken into account when describing an audience with disabilities and developing software applications. (3) Natural aspects: user actions and logical interactions while using applications.

The ACCESSIBLE project [16] aims to research and develop an Open Source Assessment Simulation and accreditation environment, for collating and merging different methodological tools, checking coherence with the W3C/WAI ARIA and other standardization works in order to enable organizations or individuals (developers, designers, etc.) to obtain software products of higher accessibility and quality, with appropriate measures, technologies and tools that improve their accessibility. The project resulted in its own ontology, named ACCESSIBLE [20]. The ACCESSIBLE ontology consists of three dimensions: Generic Ontology, Domain-Specific Ontologies, and Rules Ontology.

The previous available versions of the AEGIS ontology and the ACCESSIBLE ontology became one integrated ontology, called AEGIS/ACCESSIBLE ontology (ver. 5.1), which uses a more recent version of ICF. This ontology is part of an ambitious project to develop a complete ontological framework for assessing new multi-domain applications in terms of accessibility. It consists of a subsumption relation hierarchy; each class has its respective Domain and Range, and there are no Defined Classes.

The process followed to create our ontology starts from the reuse of AEGIS/ ACCESIBLE. In order to do this, a methodology has to be adopted. In several cases, an ontology is created from other previous ones following a process of reengineering, this is the case of the Ontology Reengineering process [21]. Its four levels of abstraction are (from bottom to top): implementation level, epistemological level (or conceptualization), linguistic level (or specification) and scope level.

At the implementation level, the ontology description focuses on implementation characteristics and is represented in an ontology language understandable by computers and usable by automatic reasoners. At the epistemological level, the ontology characteristics such as structure and components are described. At the linguistic level, the requirement characteristics for an ontology are described in detail. The scope level describes the general scope for an ontology. Software developers and ontology practitioners should decide at which level they want to carry out the ontology reengineering process.

The methodologies for building ontologies include the ontology requirements specification activity, which is located at the scope level. In this activity the Ontology Requirements Specifications Document (ORSD) is used and the following aspects are identified: the purpose of the ontology to be developed, the intended uses and users of the ontology to be developed, and the set of ontology requirements that the ontology should satisfy after being formally implemented.

Most of the existing methodologies suggest the identification of competency questions (CQs), as the technique for establishing the ontology requirements [22]. Gómez-Pérez et al. [23] defined CQs as questions written in Natural Language to help specify the ontology requirements.

The ontology reengineering process [24] consists of the following three main activities: ontology reverse engineering, ontology restructuring, and ontology forward engineering.

3 Proposed Ontology

This section describes the accessibility ontology requirements and how the ontology was developed taking into account the methodology that was followed to design and implement it. The proposed design can be viewed in the OWL file of our proposed ontology, which is available at https://goo.gl/MkfT2O.

3.1 Ontology Requirements

To better understand the proposed ontology requirements, it is important to briefly define the main concepts involved. They are: User, Impairment, Disability, Support Assistance, Capability, User Action and Activity Limitation.

- User describes "personas" with disabilities and capabilities. The term "personas" is used instead of "people" from the AEGIS previous version to indicate hypothetical archetypes of users [25].
- Impairments are problems in body function or structure, temporary or permanent; progressive, regressive or static; intermittent or continuous [15]. There are five impairments such as Vision, Upper Limb, Cognitive, Hearing, and Communication.
- Functional Limitation, according to the World Health Organization (WHO) [15], any health problem that prevents a person from completing a range of tasks, whether simple or complex.
- Disability describes subtypes of impairments. Disability can be temporary or permanent, and it can be partial or total. Each Disability has a group of associated Functional Limitations, which contains the ICF classification [15].
- SupportAssistance presents standard or assistive devices, or adaptive strategy to help users with impairments to interact with any software applications.

- Capability refers to the user's capabilities regardless of the user's disabilities, with respect to the use of support assistance.
- UserActions are dependent on physical and cognitive abilities.
- ActivityLimitations are defined by WHO [15] as difficulties that an individual may have in executing everyday life tasks.

User models can be considered as explicit representations of the properties of an individual user and can be used to reason about the needs, preferences or future behavior of that user [5]. The proposed ontology has several subgroups of users (profiles) according to combinations of impairments.

A user profile is a set of user characteristics (personal attributes, disabilities and capabilities), represented as variables. The accessibility ontology needs to describe situations dependent on the user profiles with disabilities, when users interact with software applications.

The proposed ontology is designed to model the following information and relationships:

- One user has personal attributes such as name, age, etc.
- One user can have one or more disabilities.
- One impairment includes several disabilities, then one disability belongs to one impairment.
- One disability is associated with a functional limitation, then a functional limitation is part of one or more disabilities.
- One user can also have capabilities.
- There are user actions to interact with a software application.
- If a user action can be executed regardless of disability, it is suited for that disability.
- One disability needs one or more support assistance and then one support assistance is intended for a disability.
- Some support assistance contributes to execution of a user action.
- Some user actions are assisted by support assistance because of a disability.
- The use of support assistance requires that a user has specific capabilities.
- There are difficulties that an individual may have in executing everyday life tasks, this is called activity limitation.
- One disability affects activity limitations.
- An activity limitation is due to one or more disabilities.

The ontology should help us answer the following competency questions:

CQ1: What impairment or combination of impairments (profile) does a user have?
CQ2: Which support assistance could be recommended to a user who has a specific profile and capabilities?
CQ3: Which user actions could a user execute without support assistance according to the user's profile?
CQ4: Which activity limitations exist according to the user's profile?

Some of the previous requirements are represented in the AEGIS/ACCESSIBLE ontology, but others are not.

The reused ontology was designed taking into account the accessibility assessment of products and services that cover the domains of web applications, mobile-web applications, web services and Description Languages. On the contrary, we are interested in generalizing the accessibility independent of the platform. The proposed ontology is based on this ontology, eliminating some aspects and adding other new ones.

3.2   Methodology: Ontology Reengineering Process

Scenario 4 of NeOn methodology is followed to define the proposed ontology, which is identified by Aguado de Cea et al. [26] as "Building ontology networks by reusing and reengineering ontologies or ontology modules". We reused and reengineered the AEGIS/ACCESSIBLE ontology because it is the most complete ontological implementation we found that deals with the accessibility and e-inclusion domains. In previous research [27], we presented an extended background that highlighted other relevant ontologies in this domain. The scenario corresponds to the ontology reengineering process. Below, we provide more details about the three main activities performed.

Although the NeOn project has its own ontology engineering environment named NeOn toolkit, we selected the Protégé version 5.0 [28] because it is open source and is supported by academic, government and corporate users. OWL (Ontology Web Language) is also used to allow our ontology to be reused by other ontologies.

Ontology Reverse Engineering. According to Gómez-Pérez et al. [23], the objective of reverse engineering is to define the ontology conceptual model from its source code. The architecture of the AEGIS/ACCESIBLE ontology [20] (adjusted to OWL file) is shown in Fig. 1.

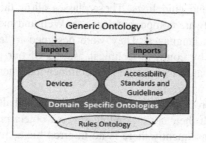

Fig. 1. AEGIS/ACCESSIBLE ontology architecture.

After examining its implementation code, organized in 17 OWL files, we found the following aspects to highlight, with their corresponding classes:

1. Generic ontology: User (28 instances), Impairment (5 instances), Disability (38 instances), FunctionalLimitation (125 instances) and Capability (1 instance).
2. Devices: class Device in file GenericOntology.owl is used to import Devices. Device instances are separated in 8 OWL files. The files are grouped by application,

such as AlternativeKeyboardsOrSwitches.owl (7 instances), Braille.owl (3 instances), ListeningDevices.owl (3 instances), ScanningSoftware.owl (3 instances), ScreenMagnifiers.owl (6 instances), ScreenReader.owl (5 instances), SpeechDevices.owl (2 instances), and TextBrowsers.owl (3 instances).

3. Accessibility standard and guidelines: the file GenericOntology.owl includes various classes such as Standard (4 instances); OutputResult (698 instances), Application (which imports instances from CORE.owl (6 instances), CSS.owl (17 instances), HTML.owl (13 instances)), and WaiAria (which imports instances from WAIARIA.owl (138 instances)). The classes Checkpoint, Guideline, and Technique are imported from the files Descriptionlanguage.owl, MWBP.owl, WCAG2.owl, and Webservice1.owl.

Ontology Restructuring. Its goal is to get a new conceptual model obtained from the previous activity. It was carried out in two phases, analysis and synthesis. The following is a more detailed explanation about each of these phases.

Analysis Phase. We determined the classes that must be eliminated as they do not contribute - are not related - to our proposed ontology module and those classes that are part of our proposed ontology. The relationships between classes (object properties) will also be reviewed to address the requirements.

We get all classes from the Generic ontology module. User class is related only to Disability. We propose to add a new relationship between the User and Capability classes. Impairment is only related to Disability and vice versa. FunctionalLimitation is also related to Disability and vice versa. Capability has only one object property.

Regarding the Device class, there are 30 instances that are grouped by type of use with its respective data property assertions and that are only related to class Disability. Its instances are assistive technology devices.

We propose to eliminate all classes related to the Accessibility standard and associated checkpoints and guidelines. These classes allow the analysis and accessibility verification of software components such as Web and mobile applications, web services and description languages. They were designed to tackle technical aspects from specific domains, by contrast, technical aspects of our proposed ontology are focused on support assistance that should be recommended when users with disabilities interact with a software application.

Finally, there is no property restriction for each class, and all object properties have Domain and Range with their corresponding inverse object properties. There are no Defined Classes and consequently there is no inferred hierarchy.

Synthesis Phase. For the class Device, we decided to change the class name to "SupportAssistance" to include software adaptive strategies, not only hardware solutions.

The class UserAction does not exist in the AEGIS/ACCESSIBLE ontology, it is part of the AEGIS first version. We use this class to represent the different ways the user interacts with an application, the interactions could be performed depending on the capabilities or disabilities of the user and the assistance given to support them. This class is related to the SupportAssistance, and Disability classes to improve support recommendation depending on the capabilities and disabilities of the user regarding the action to be carried out.

The class Capability is used to identify capabilities that users must have to obtain the correct support assistance, in case they need it when executing a user action. The users, regardless of their disabilities, can have specific capabilities or skills. This information helps us to offer users the correct support. Therefore, we propose to relate the class Capability to the class SupportAssistance.

Property restriction is refined, the Domain and Range of each object property was corrected in order to guarantee the correct result of inferences in ontology. In view of the fact that OWL reasoning is based on Open World Assumption (OWA), which assumes incomplete information by default, it is important to explicitly limit relationships between concepts (logical axioms), restrictions, and Domain/Range.

Ontology Forward Reengineering. The aim of forward engineering is to implement a new ontology based on a new conceptual model [24]. After examining the AEGIS/ACCESSIBLE ontology in Protégé 5.0 and verifying the reasoners function, we did not find results inferred in the class hierarchy. Therefore, to create our proposed ontology, the level of abstraction required for this activity is at the scope level.

To make our proposed ontology easier to understand and help avoid some common modeling mistakes, we considered the set of conventions for the ontology elements in the context of the NeOn project [29]. The new classes, instances and object property names were adjusted with regards to delimiters and capitalization, and prefix conventions.

The architecture comparison between reused ontology and accessibility ontology is shown in Table 1. The first column lists class names; the second and third columns describe the number of instances and object properties from the AEGIS/ACCESSIBLE ontology and Accessibility ontology, respectively. The proposed ontology consists of the following three aspects: Personal Aspects consists of User, Impairment, Disabilitity, FunctionalLimitation, Capability and Activity Limitation; a Technical Aspect called SupportAssistance; and a Natural Aspect called UserAction.

To understand the accessibility ontology architecture, a short description and reengineering details for each class is presented. To finalize this section, and due to space limitation, we show only one CQ and a specific example to demonstrate how the ontology satisfies our requirement and can answer that question. The proposed ontology can answer all CQs proposed (see OWL file).

Classes' Description and Reengineering Details. The classes Impairment, Disability, FunctionalLimitation, and User were imported with their instances from the AEGIS/ACCESSIBLE ontology.

The class Disability instances were grouped by the type of Impairment through Defined Classes. We used numbers to identify each impairment as follows: 1. Vision Impairment, 2. UpperLimb Impairment, 3. Cognitive Impairment, 4. Hearing Impairment, and 5. Communication Impairment. The naming system to identify each combination of impairments (profile) to which a user belongs, consists of all impairment identifiers in numerical order.

The class SupportAssistance was created instead of Device, and the 8 OWL files were imported as Subclasses of SupportAssistance. New subclasses were added:

Table 1. Architecture comparison between reused ontologies and accessibility ontology.

Class name	Aegis/Accessible ontology	Accessibility ontology
User	28 User_has_Disability User_has_Capability User_linksTo_Device User_linksTo_FunctionalLimitation	28 hasDisability hasCapability
Impairment	5 Impairment_linksTo_Device Impairment_linksTo_User Impairment_has_Disability Impairment_linksTo_FunctionalLimitation	5 includes
Disability	38 Disability_linksTo_Capability Disability_belongsTo_Impairment Disability_belongsTo_User Disability_has_FunctionalLimitation Disability_has_Device	38 needs belongsTo associatedWith affects
Functional limitation	125 FunctionalLimitation_linksTo_Device FunctionalLimitation_linksTo_Impairment FunctionalLimitation_linksTo_User FunctionalLimitation_linksTo_Capability FunctionalLimitation_belongsTo_Disability	125 isPartOf
Capability	1 Capability_belongsTo_User Capability_has_Device Capability_linksTo_FunctionalLimitation Capability_linksTo_Disability Capability_linksTo_Impairment	27 relatedTo
Activities limitation	Does not exist	15 dueTo
Support assistance	30[a] Device_linksTo_Impairment Device_belongsTo_Capability Device_linksTo_User Device_belongsTo_Disability Device_linksTo_FunctionalLimitation	53 intendedFor contributesTo requires
User action	Does not exist	15 suitedFor assistedBy
	28 Object Properties	15 Object properties

[a]It is called Device and is divided in separate OWL files according to type.

"Adaptive_Strategy" (technical recommendations to assist people with disabilities when they interact with software – 5 new instances); "Video_Calling" (2 new instances); "Head-tracking_Technology" (2 new instances); "Eye-tracking_System" (2 new instances); "Mouse_Gesture" (2 new instances); "Gesture_recognition" (5 new instances) and "Pointing_Device" (3 new instances).

The class Capability was created and its instances are based on a list of 27 new capabilities, they are skills that users could develop in spite of their disabilities.

The class User Actions instances were taken from the AEGIS previous version [30] such as: point, read, write, gesture, click, tap, and swipe. Other new user actions [15, 31] were added such as: listen, speak, drag & drop, press, rotate, choose, slide, and pinch-stretch.

The class ActivityLimitations is included to determine how users are performing their everyday life tasks.

Figure 2 shows the classes of the accessibility ontology and how they are related through specific object properties.

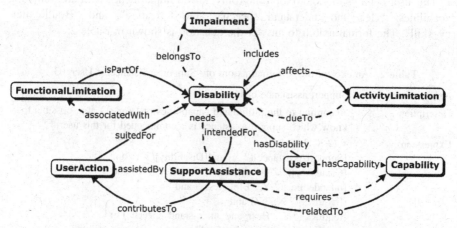

Fig. 2. Classes and objects properties of accessibility ontology.

Competency Questions. The Ontology Requirements Specifications Document (ORSD) proposed in the NeOn methodology allows us to determine why the ontology module is being built. This document includes a Group of Competency Questions (CQs). The Accessibility ontology CQs are:

CQ1: What impairment or combination of impairments (profile) does a user have?
CQ2: Which support assistance could be recommended to a user who has a specific profile and capabilities?
CQ3: Which user actions could a user execute without support assistance according to the user's profile?
CQ4: Which activity limitations exist according to the user's profile?

Considering these CQs, we created Defined Classes for the following Classes: User, SupportAssistance, UserAction and ActivityLimitation. They are formal axioms used to formulate and answer each CQ. Then we selected CQ2 to illustrate how the Defined

Class of SupportAssistance works, and we focused on User_03. The property assertion of this individual is shown in Fig. 3.

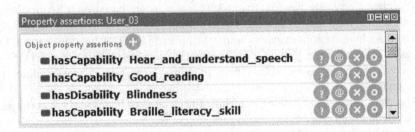

Fig. 3. Property assertion of User_03.

This user belongs to 1.0.0.0.0 profile (only Vision impairment), with the following capabilities: "Hear_and_understand speech", "Good_reading", and "Braille_literacy_skill". The formal axiom to answer the question is shown in Table 2.

Table 2. An excerpt of the formal axiom of "Support assistance of User_03".

Axiom name	Support assistance of User_03
Description	According to the profile and capabilities of User_03, it is possible to know which support assistance is recommended for this user
Expression	$\forall$ (? X, ? Y, ? Z) [SupportAssistance](? X) and[Disability](? Y) and [Capability](? Z) → ([intendedFor](? X, ? Y) and [intendedFor](? Y, "Blindness") and ([requires](? X, ? Z) and [requires](? Z, "Hear_and_understand_speech") or [requires](? Z, "Good_reading")or [requires](? Z, "Braille_literacy_skill"))
Concepts	Support assistance, disability, capability
Ad hoc binary relations	intendedFor, requires
Variables	?X, ?Y, ?Z

After running the reasoner Hermit 1.3.8.413, you can see the results in the Defined Class called "03User.SupportAssistance".

The results inferred for User_03, grouping by subclasses of Support Assistance are: Braille (Alva_584_Satelite_Pro, and Alva_BC640), Screen reader (Apple_VoiceOver, Fire_Vox, Mobile_Speak, Nuance_TALKS, and Spoken_Web) and Text browser (ELinks, Lynx, and WebbIE).

4   Conclusion and Future Work

In order to deal with the problem of how to profile users with disabilities when they interact with software applications and how to offer them an accessible and customized attention, we decided to create a modular ontology that involves the Accessibility domain and the CRM applications domain. This paper focuses on the design and implementation of an Accessibility Ontology to profile user models taking into account his/her disabilities and capabilities.

To create the proposed ontology module, we reused and reengineered the AEGIS/ACCESSIBLE ontology because it is the most complete ontological implementation we found that deals with the Accessibility and e-inclusion domains. This case corresponds to scenario 4 in the NeOn methodology framework, called "Building ontology networks by reusing and reengineering ontologies or ontology modules". In the implementation process we used Protégé version 5.0 and the reasoner HermiT version 1.3.8.413.

The proposed ontology consists of Personal Aspects (User, Impairment, Disability, Functional Limitation, Capability and Activity Limitation), Technical Aspect (Support Assistance) and a Natural Aspect (User Action). One example was chosen to show how the Defined Classes work and consequently the ability of our proposed ontology to infer.

Future work will focus on the development of the CRM applications ontology, considering ontology modularization implications. The final integration will be presented and discussed in future research papers. Our ultimate goal is to create and evaluate the modular ontology in order to offer a tool that allows the profiling of customers with disabilities to enhance CRM applications. The developed modular ontology will be part of a Recommender System that shows how to support customers with disabilities and identifies adaptations that could be made in CRM applications.

Acknowledgement. This work was conducted using the Protégé resource, which is supported by grant GM10331601 from the National Institute of General Medical Sciences of the United States National Institutes of Health [21].

References

1. World Health Organization – WHO: World Report on Disability, OMS, Ginebra, Suiza (2011)
2. Leonardi, M., Bickenbach, J., Ustun, T.B., Kostanjsek, N., Chatterji, S., MHADIE Consortium: The definition of disability: what is in a name? Lancet **368**(9543), 1219–1221 (2006)
3. United Nations (UN): Convention on the Rights of Persons with Disabilities (A/RES/61/106). United Nations, New York (2016)
4. Stephanidis, C., Akoumianakis, D., Sfyrakis, M., Paramythis, A.: Universal accessibility in HCI: process-oriented design guidelines and tool requirements. In: Proceedings of the 4th ERCIM Workshop on User Interfaces for all. Stockholm, Sweden (1998)

5. Madrid, J., Peinado, I., Koutkias, V.: Cloud4all Project Website. D101.1. Cloud4all Priority Applications and User. http://www.cloud4all.info/wp-content/uploads/2014/09/D101.1.-Priority-applications-and-User-Profile-Ontology.pdf

6. Gruber, T.: A translation approach to portable ontology specifications. Knowl. Acquis. 5(2), 199–220 (1993)

7. Osterwalder, A.: The Business Model Ontology. A Proposition in a Design Science Approach. University of Lausanne, Switzerland (2004)

8. Spyns, P., Meersman, R., Jarrar, M.: Data modelling versus ontology engineering. ACM SIGMod Rec. 31(4), 12–17 (2002)

9. Valls, A., Gibert, K., Sánchez, D., Batet, M.: Using ontologies for structuring organizational knowledge in home care assistance. Int. J. Med. Inf. 79(5), 370–387 (2010)

10. Skillen, K.L., Chen, L., Nugent, C.D., Donnelly, M.P., Solheim, I.: A user profile ontology based approach for assisting people with dementia in mobile environments. In: 2012 Annual International Conference of the IEEE Engineering in Medicine and Biology Society (EMBC), pp. 6390–6393 (2012)

11. Espín, V., Hurtado, M.V., Noguera, M.: Nutrition for elder care: a nutritional semantic recommender system for the elderly. Expert Syst. 33(2), 201–210 (2016)

12. Orgun, B., Vu, J.: HL7 ontology and mobile agents for interoperability in heterogeneous medical information systems. Comput. Biol. Med. 36(7), 817–836 (2006)

13. Keet, C.M., Alberts, R., Gerber, A., Chimamiwa, G.: Enhancing web portals with ontology-based data access: the case study of south Africa's accessibility portal for people with disabilities. In: Proceeding of the Fifth International Workshop OWL: Experiences and Directions (OWLED), Karlsruhe, Germany (2008)

14. World Health Organization - WHO: International Classification of Functioning, Disability and Health IDH-2. WHO Press, Geneva, (2001). https://unstats.un.org/unsd/disability/pdfs/ac.81-b4.pdf

15. World Health Organization - WHO: Towards a Common Language for Functioning, Disability and Health (ICF). WHO Press, Geneva (2002). http://www.who.int/classifications/icf/icfbeginnersguide.pdf?ua=1

16. Tzovaras, D., Votis, K., Kaklanis, N., Oikonomou, T., Kastori, M., Lopes, R., Michael-Loupis, C., RIngler, M., Papadopoulou, M., Partarakis, N., Korn, P.: ACCESSIBLE EC Project. D 3.3a – ACCESSIBLE System Architecture Specification (Beta). CERTH/ITI (2009). http://www.accessible-eu.org/documents/ACCESSIBLE_D3.3a.pdf

17. Korn, P., Bekiaris, E., Gemou, M.: Towards open access accessibility everywhere: the AEGIS concept. In: Stephanidis, C. (ed.) UAHCI 2009. LNCS, vol. 5614, pp. 535–543. Springer, Heidelberg (2009). doi:10.1007/978-3-642-02707-9_60

18. AEGIS: Open Accessibility Everywhere: Groundwork, Infrastructure, Standards. AEGIS Ontology (2012). http://www.aegis-project.eu/index.php?option=com_content&view=article&id=107&Itemid=65

19. Kontotasiou, D., Drosou, A., Darlagiannis, V., Giatsoglou, M., Kastori, G., Giakoumis, D., Tsakiris, A., Jerry, D., Tsakou, G., Jon, A., Jan, R., Patrick, W., Peter, K., Kostas, K.: AEGIS Outcomes. Public Deliverables. Common AEGIS Context Awareness Ontologies, Security, Privacy, QoS and Interoperability Guidelines (2011). http://www.aegis-project.eu/images/docs/AEGIS_D1.2.2_final.pdf

20. Votis, K.: ACCESSIBLE & AEGIS ontologies. In: European Thematic Network on Assistive Information Technology (ETNA) - Workshop, Copenhagen (2011)

21. Byrne, E.: A conceptual foundation for software re-engineering. In: Proceedings of the International Conference on Software Maintenance and Reengineering, Orlando, Florida (1992)

22. Suárez-Figueroa, M., Gómez-Pérez, A., Villazón-Terrazas, B.: How to write and use the ontology requirements specification document. In: Proceedings of the Confederated International Conferences, CoopIS, DOA, IS, and ODBASE 2009 On the Move to Meaningful Internet Systems: Part II, OTM 2009, Vilamoura, Portugal (2009)
23. Gómez-Pérez, A., Suárez-Figueroa, M., Villazón, B.: NeOn methodology for building ontology networks: ontology specification. NeOn Integrated Project EU-IST-027595 (2008)
24. Gómez-Pérez, A., Fernández-López, M., Corcho, O.: Ontological Engineering: with examples from the areas of Knowledge Management, e-Commerce and the Semantic Web. Springer, London (2004). doi:10.1007/b97353
25. AEGIS: Open Accessibility Everywhere: Groundwork, Infrastructure, Standards. AEGIS Outcomes – Personas. AEGIS is an Integrated Project (IP) within the ICT programme of FP7 (2012). http://www.aegis-project.eu/index.php?Itemid=53&id=63&option=com_content&view=article
26. Aguado de Cea, G., Buil, C., Caracciolo, C., Dzbor, M., Gómez-Pérez, A., Herrrero, G., Lewen, H., Montiel-Ponsoda, E., Presutti, V.: NeOn Project – Deliverables - D5.3.1 NeOn Development Process and Ontology Life Cycle (2007). http://www.neon-project.org/deliverables/WP5/NeOn_2007_D5.3.1.pdf
27. Romero, B., Rodríguez, M.J., Hurtado, M.V., Haddad, H.M.: An ontological approach to profile customers with disabilities in e-business. In: 13th International Conference WWW/Internet 2014, Porto (2014)
28. Stanford Center for Biomedical Informatics Research – BMIR: Protégé. Standford University (2015). http://protege.stanford.edu/about.php
29. Haase, P., Rudolph, S., Wang, Y., Brockmans, S., Palma, R., Euzenat, J., d'Aquin, M.: NeOn Project – Deliverables - D1.1.1. Networked Ontology Model (2006). http://neon-project.org/deliverables/WP1/NeOn_2006_D1.1.1.pdf
30. Strobbe, C., Vystrcil, J., Mik, Z.: AEGIS Outcomes. Public Deliverables - D1.3.1 Accessible user interaction models and profiles per User Group (2010). http://www.aegis-project.eu/images/docs/ApprovedDeliverablesForWebsite/AEGIS_D1.3.1_final.pdf
31. Microsoft: Touch: Tap, swipe, and beyond. Microsoft (2015). https://www.microsoft.com/

Ontology-Based User Profile Modelling to Facilitate Inclusion of Visual Impairment People

María Isabel Torres-Carazo[✉], María José Rodríguez-Fórtiz,
Vanesa Espin-Martin, and María Visitación Hurtado

ETSIIT, Dpto. Lenguajes y Sistemas Informáticos,
University of Granada, Granada, Spain
misabeltorres@gmail.com,
{mjfortiz, vespin, mhurtado}@ugr.es

Abstract. People with special needs can have difficulties accessing and using mobile applications if they are not adapted or designed for them. A key feature in accessing and using successful mobile applications is to build user profiles that accurately represent the user's characteristics and disabilities. The main goal of this research is to present a new classification of the user's disabilities that implicitly build ontology-based user profiles that can be used by a recommender system. This classification includes some other characteristics such as personal details to perform a complete user profile. A complete user profile could provide better accessibility to new technologies for users with any impairment, leading to greater inclusion.

Keywords: Ontology · User profile · Disabilities · Inclusion · Apps · Visual impairment

1 Introduction

New technologies are becoming more present every day in our daily life because they have characteristics that allow us to access information, to be entertained, to communicate or to help in the daily life of users with functional difficulties.

Mobile devices include some applications (apps) that facilitate and support different kinds of tasks, communications or interactions with other users. Sometimes, information provided by these apps is shown in the wrong way because it is unstructured, is presented only in a graphic and visual way without alternative text description or descriptive audio, so people that have any visual disability cannot have access to their content. To provide software and hardware accessibility it is necessary to consider the profile of users, the physical context or the technology being used.

Apps are stored in repositories such as Google Play or App Store [1, 2] from where they can be downloaded and installed in mobile devices to increase or provide new functionality. Searching and finding a specific app in a repository could be more difficult than users imagine: searches, exhaustive listings, wrong categorization, wrong classifications (we can find that some apps are classified as educational but in fact they

© Springer International Publishing AG 2017
Y. Ouhammou et al. (Eds.): MEDI 2017, LNCS 10563, pp. 386–394, 2017.
DOI: 10.1007/978-3-319-66854-3_29

could also be considered as games or serious games [3] that help to develop some ability), difficult access to information about the app, descriptions in foreign languages, apps without an indication of what kind of users they are intended for, or without specifying their purpose. Moreover, accessibility is not managed yet.

Our research is focused on people with visual disability and their problems when they use mobile devices and apps installed on them. To consider the best way to obtain the right app when they make a search, we have designed a system called m-RECACC, the complete system architecture of which is explained in [4]. It recommends the best apps according to the user's needs taking into account some characteristics such as the user's context, his mobile device and accessibility features.

The remainder of the paper is organized as follows. Section 2 presents some related work about user profiles. Section 3 explains the methodology to create an ontology for the user profile. Section 4 summarizes the conclusions and ongoing research.

2 Related Work

According to the World Health Organization (WHO), about 15% of the world population may have some form of disability throughout his life. Due to the process of world globalisation, there is a need for a clear idea about definition and classification of disabilities using a common language. That is the reason why WHO approved the ICF, Disability and Health [5], that tries to approximate, simplify and unify terminology and problems related to disabilities. This document is complementary to the ICD and related health problems [6] created previously by WHO.

Some organizations (Red Cross [7], Spanish Laws [8, 9] and Educational Spanish Field [10]) have established a different classification of disabilities. Following their analysis, we have made a new proposal of classification to unify all the terms in four groups: Physical Disability, Cognitive Disability, Communication Disability and Sensory Disability that includes Auditory and Visual Disability. This classification should be taken into consideration for the modelling of a user profile with disability.

Several projects have developed some interfaces and ontologies with that objective and some of them have been reviewed.

- AEGIS Ontology [11]: links the characteristics of users with disabilities, functional limitations and impairments (personal aspects) among other topics.
- Rat Genome Database Disease Ontology [12]: models the Sensory Organ Diseases associated with the five human senses.
- GUMO [13]: models user profiles. It considers four dimensions of users: Basic, Context, Sensors and Domain.
- DAML [14]: provides other generic ontologies which only model personal details with some basic data or friendships.

The AEGIS ontology categorizes the user's disabilities, functional limitations and impairments as a list of interesting terms as individuals that represent the knowledge related to the disabilities domain. As the items are not created as classes, disabilities cannot be classified according to type and degree to maintain a relation with the proposed classification (Physical, Cognitive, Communication and Sensory disabilities).

At the same time it does not allow new knowledge to be obtained by reasoning. This ontology does not offer a user profile with personal details.

The GUMO ontology has some interesting data for building a user profile such as contact information like email or address, demographics such as birthday or gender, mood such as sadness or excited or abilities such as the ability to drive, but it must be extended to represent preferences and requirements about disabilities because they are not available or obtained from other dimensions.

The RGD Disease Ontology (RGD-DO) has terms related to disabilities and diseases of humans but it is made from an exhaustive medical view point.

None of the previous ontologies offer a complete user profile according to our proposal: user's personal details, disabilities (classification, degree and diseases) and method and results from the evaluation of the user's disabilities.

The option to merge the mentioned ontologies by modifying their organisation, changing individuals by classes and solving incompatibilities is harder than making a new ontology. These are the reasons why we have made a new ontology but based on all of them, organized and extended according to our requirements. The next section shows the creation process of this new ontology to model the user profile.

3   Semantic Modelling of the User Profile

This paper is focused on the development of the set of ontologies that models the necessary information for the m-RECACC system [4].

To model all the information related to a user of apps with some special needs, we have analysed the relevant domains. The two main ontologies to develop are (1) User profile and (2) Apps characteristics. However they are not enough to perform all the involved data in the m-RECACC system. The user's context is also another important component, due to the necessity to individualize any recommendation according to the user's needs in his current environment. The context was divided in some parts in order to facilitate the reusability of the ontologies. The result was a set of four new ontologies: (3) Context with data extracted from the ambient environment, date-time and location; (4) Mobile Devices which collects information about its features such as type of device (watch, tablet or telephone), size of screen, camera and so on; (5) Accessibility Features that model features provided by mobile devices. It also models some other accessibility characteristics that are desirable or are available for apps and for users with disabilities according to the recommended accessibility guidelines from WCAG 2.0 [15] and MWBP [16]; And finally (6) Languages that was created as a way to avoid duplicating necessary information (app language and the user's languages).

Six ontologies have been created and after that, a process of merging will be carried on to create a unique ontology to form the knowledge base of the m-RECACC system. Protégé [17] has been the tool used to build all the mentioned ontologies because it allows the modelling of ontologies in OWL, and the reasoning and deduction of new semantic information. The next steps focus on the user profile ontology, and how to build it in Protégé.

3.1 Creating the Ontology

The Noy and McGuiness [18] method has been followed with a top-down approach and it is composed of the following 6 steps that guide the users through the development of the ontologies. Operations performed in each step of this method will be detailed.

Step 1. Determine the Domain and Scope of the Ontology. The scope of the ontology is: Context, Apps and User Profile. In this way we are covering the main scopes that define the profile of a user of an app especially aimed at people with a visual disability or that may be used by them because their designs are inclusive.

For this paper, only the domain of the user profile will be developed.

1. *User's Personal Details.* Personal characteristics in the user profile are useful for categorizing or classifying individuals or even for detecting special needs that require accessible apps.

   The characteristics chosen coincide with the data that repositories of apps offer. For example, the age classification is key because one of the ways in which repositories classify apps is using the recommended age.

   New kinds of data can be added such as personal details in order to complete the knowledge about a user, increasing the user profile and improving the recommendations based on it.

2. *Disabilities.* As we have explained in Sect. 2, the term disability has a wide range of definitions depending on the scope we reference. We have proposed a new classification based on the collected properties related to disabilities and the division of the visual function according to WHO and ICD-10.

   In order not to extend this paper too much, we have focused our study on people with visual impairment and blindness. That is the reason why the visual sensory disability is developed and the rest of the disabilities are described to a lesser extent.

   Depending on the degree of the disease [5] we could consider that people could have a limitation or a disability, so here there are two new terms to take into account in this classification: the name and the degree of the disease.

3. *Evaluation of the User's Disability.* The information obtained from the user's evaluation could help to deduce other characteristics about the user's disabilities and to situate them in the previous classification of disabilities.

   Professional opticians use a set of tests to evaluate visual disability by mean of parameters that define the level of vision. These data are transformed into a value according to laws [19] that indicate, in a generic way, a percentage of disability that is recognized by government to get access to social and health grants.

Step 2. Consider Reusing Existing Ontologies. The developed ontology is based on the AEGIS, RGD-DO and GUMO ontologies. We have taken a part of the user personal details from GUMO and some of the disability characteristics from AEGIS and RGO-DO. Besides, other characteristics have been added to complete the domain information of the user's profile.

Step 3. Enumerate Important Terms in the Ontology. The most relevant terms in the user's profile ontology are: Disabilities, User's Personal Details and User's Disability Evaluation.

Step 4. Define the Classes and the Class Hierarchy. We have refined the previous terms by using a top-down approach, obtaining a new class hierarchy that shows the necessary information. With all the previous information, a new schema can be built by joining all of them in a unique user profile. This schema is shown in Fig. 1.

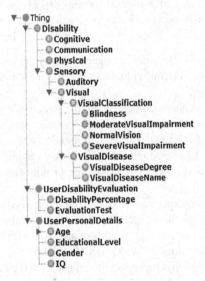

Fig. 1. User profile in Protégé

Step 5. Define the Properties of Classes-Slots. In this step we define the object properties and the data type properties. The necessary object properties and data type properties have been created in order to make the relationships between objects and data.

Step 6. Create Instances. In this step, some instances have been created. To populate the Disability Class and its subclasses with real and concrete values, we have used the ICF and ICD-10. To test the ontology we have created several users with some different characteristics to validate the correct functioning (Fig. 2).

3.2 Completing the Ontology

To complete the process of the ontology creation, we have added three new steps in order to check the consistency and the necessity of adding some items that allow the provided information to be enriched.

Step 1. Create Rules. We have added some rules with SWRL (Semantic Web Rules Language) [20] to enrich the information that the ontology provides because some

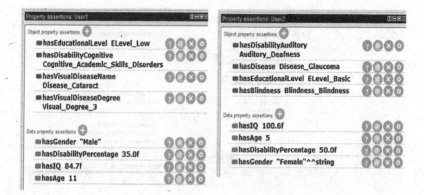

Fig. 2. Two examples of user profiles

information cannot be represented in another way. As we mentioned in Sect. 3, we have added some rules to classify users according to their ages and other rules to indicate how a different degree in the user's visual disease influences the degree of visual injury. This information is shown in Fig. 3.

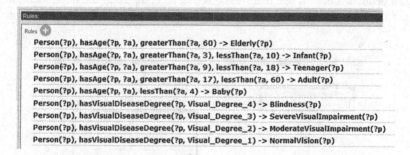

Fig. 3. Rules to classify by age and by degree of disease

Step 2. Test Anomalies and Inconsistences with the Reasoner. To test anomalies in the ontology, we have used the Pellet reasoner [21]. It allows us to use and reason with the created rules. To test the consistency of the ontology, we have introduced some non-valid data illustrating it with two examples (Fig. 4).

Example 1: we have changed the percentage of disability of User 1, introducing a string value but it should be a float number. The result is a data inconsistency error.

Example 2: we have tested that any class of the classification of visual disabilities cannot be disjoint with any auditory disability. To make this test, Auditory Disability has been marked in its properties as Disjoint With Blindness. The result is an error and the reason is that any person can have more than one kind of disability. This reason can be extended to the rest of the disabilities. This example is shown in Fig. 4.

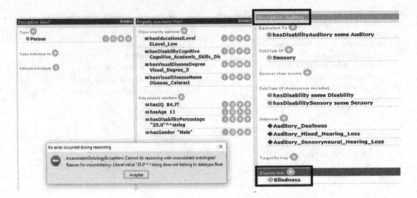

Fig. 4. Test of consistency. Examples 1 and 2

Step 3. Deduced Information. If an incomplete user profile is provided, the system can deduce some important information. In the next example, User 3 only knows about his own disease (cataracts) and its degree (degree 3). The system indicates that if one user has a disease with degree 3, he is classified as a person with a severe visual impairment. Therefore the system classifies this user with a visual sensory disability, and also deduces from his age that he is a teenager, completing the information in the user profile. The marked information in Fig. 5 is deduced by the system's reasoner.

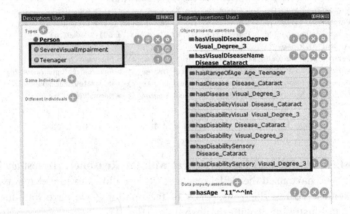

Fig. 5. Deduced information

4   Conclusions and Future Work

People with visual impairment have difficulties in managing mobile devices and their apps, and also in searching in app repositories. We have established a new classification of disabilities that is used as a part of a user profile. We have also included personal details and the evaluation of the user's disabilities to make a complete user profile. We have used ontologies to model the information of the user profile by using a structured method. The ontology allows us to obtain a complete user profile on the basis of partial information and reasoning. Having a personalized user profile can facilitate the inclusion of people with disabilities because of the possibility of making personalized recommendations of apps as in the m-RECACC system.

For future work, the modelling of the five other ontologies is being developed as well the building of the recommender system.

References

1. Google Play. https://play.google.com/store. Accessed 8 May 2017
2. App Store. https://itunes.apple.com. Accessed 8 May 2017
3. Torres-Carazo, M.I., Rodríguez-Fórtiz, M.J., Hurtado, M.V.: Analysis and review of apps and serious games on mobile devices intended for people with visual impairment. In: IEEE 6th International Conference on Serious Games and Applications for Health (SeGAH), Orlando, FL, USA, 11–13 May 2016
4. Torres-Carazo, M.I., Rodríguez-Fórtiz, M.J., Hurtado, M.V., Samos, J., Espín, V.: Architecture of a mobile app recommender system for people with special needs. In: Hervás, R., Lee, S., Nugent, C., Bravo, J. (eds.) UCAmI 2014. LNCS, vol. 8867, pp. 288–291. Springer, Cham (2014). doi:10.1007/978-3-319-13102-3_47
5. World Health Assembly: International Classification of Functioning, Disability and Health, May 2001
6. World Health Organization: International Statistical Classification of Diseases and related health problems, 10th revision (2011)
7. Red Cross: http://www.redcross.org. Accessed 8 May 2017
8. RD Legislativo 1/2013, de 29 de noviembre, por el que se aprueba el Texto Refundido de la Ley General de derechos de las personas con discapacidad y de su inclusión social. Spain
9. Ley 26/2001, de 1 de agosto de Adaptación normativa a la Convención Internacional sobre los Derechos de las Personas con Discapacidad. Spain
10. Instrucción del 22/06/2015, de la D.G. de Participación y Equidad, por la que se establece el protocolo de detección, identificación del alumnado con NEAE y organización de la respuesta educativa. Spain
11. AEGIS Project. http://www.aegis-project.eu/. Accessed 8 May 2017
12. Shimoyama, M., De Pons, J., Hayman, G.T., Laulederkind, S.J., et al.: The rat genome database 2015: genomic, phenotypic and environmental variations and disease. Nucleic Acids Res. **43**(Database issue), D743–D750 (2015). PMID: 25355511
13. Basit, K.A., Matskin, M.: GUMO inspired ontology to support user experience based Citywide Mobile Learning. In: IEEE, International Conference on User Science and Engineering (i-USEr), pp. 195–200 (2011)
14. DAML Ontology example. http://www.cs.umd.edu/projects/plus/DAML/onts/personal1.0. DAML. Accessed 8 May 2017
15. WCAG 2.0: Web Content Accessibility Guidelines 2.0. http://www.w3.org/TR/WCAG20
16. MWBP: Mobile Web Best Practices. http://www.w3.org/TR/mobile-bp
17. Protégé. http://protege.stanford.edu. Accessed 8 May 2017
18. Noy, N., McGuinness, D.: Ontology development 101: a guide to creating your first ontology. Stanford Knowledge Systems Laboratory Technical report KSL-01–05 and Stanford Medical Informatics Technical report SMI-2001-0880 (2001)

19. Wecker Scale: WHO Study Group on the Prevention of Blindness. N 518, Geneva, 6–10 November 1973
20. Horrocks, I., Patel-Schneider, P.F., Boley, H., Tabet, S., et al.: SWRL: a semantic web rule language combining OWL and RuleML. W3C Member submission (2004)
21. Irin, E., Parsia, B., Grau, B.C., Kalyanpur, A., Katz, Y.: Pellet: a practical owl-dl reasoner. Web Seman.: Sci. Serv. Agents World Wide Web **5**, 51–53 (2007)

Author Index

Printed in the United States
By Bookmasters

Printed in the United States
By Bookmasters